Political Parties and Democracy

Endorsements for *Political Parties and Democracy*
(See back cover for additional endorsements)

"To learn about the state of party politics across the world, consult Kay Lawson's sweeping five-volume publication, *Political Parties and Democracy*, a monumental, up-to-date survey of party systems in 45 countries. The set of books should be acquired by all research libraries and should sit on the shelves of all scholars doing comparative research on political parties. It provides a combination of breadth and depth, of comparative and particular analysis. While the strength of this multi-volume set lies in its rich and convenient trove of information about party politics in regions and countries, it also makes important conceptual contributions upon which party scholars may draw."

Kenneth Janda
Professor of Political Science, Northwestern University

"Editing an excellent five-volume set of studies on parties in 46 systematically chosen countries seems an impossible mission. Yet, Kay Lawson attests to the contrary. Teachers on democratic polities, students of comparative politics, and researchers on political parties can find in these volumes a treasure of recent data, analysis, and comprehension. Country chapters address a similar set of questions, and not fewer than 54 country authors answer them with a wise combination of local expertise and sensibility to more general issues of democratic theory. Lawson has been extremely successful in putting forward a common framework—examining the relationship between parties and democracy—that is able to integrate the study of regions as different as the Americas, Europe, Russia, Asia, Africa, Oceania, and the Arab world. At the end, the five volumes restate once again the utmost relevance of parties within an amazing diversity of political contexts, processes, and institutions. If sometimes there are occasions in which a book is a must for its decisive contribution to our knowledge on political parties, this is certainly one of them."

José Ramón Montero
Departamento de Ciencia Política y Relaciones Internacionales
Facultad de Derecho Universidad Autónoma de Madrid

"A pathbreaking collection of top-quality writings on party politics by leading scholars around the world, *Political Parties and Democracy* opens a genuinely new frontier of knowledge, expanding the scope of analysis to the entire globe, combining theory with history, and raising a series of new research questions."

Byung-Kook Kim
Professor, Department of Political Science, Korea University

"This monumental work consists of five volumes with 46 chapters each devoted to the parties of a different nation. Many of the party systems included in the volumes are studied here for the first time in a systematic way with unprecedented levels of knowledge and competence by authors who are native to the respective countries. The chapters are not limited to summary descriptions of the systems they study, but present extremely interesting and original insights. This is crucial for the usefulness and scientific relevance of the chapters dedicated to the more established American, European and, in general, Western democracies' party systems, whose authors manage to present novel views of extensively researched subject areas. Saying that with this work Kay Lawson has set new standards for editorship in the field of political science would be an obvious understatement. *Political Parties and Democracy* is the result of an impressive project that will greatly benefit the scientific community. I am sure that the five volumes it has produced will become fundamental references for the field of political party studies and will take a very prominent place in every party expert's library."

Luciano Bardi
Professor of Political Science, University of Pisa

"This welcome and remarkable collection of original essays covers assessments of political parties in an unusually broad range of countries. Taking into account the critical importance of parties for the operation of democracy, juxtaposed with their weaknesses both as democratic organizations and as agents of state democracy, results in clear and honest assessments of the state of parties today. Bickerton on Canada and Dwyre on the U.S. represent this well-reasoned approach with the confidence that comes from a thorough understanding of their own country's situation."

Mildred A. Schwartz
Professor Emerita at University of Illinois and Visiting Scholar,
New York University

"These volumes provide a valuable in-depth and up-to-date analysis of the state of political parties across five continents, written by country experts, and will be an important source for scholars interested in the comparative study of political parties."

Lars Svåsand
Professor of Comparative Politics, University of Bergen, Norway

"Kay Lawson's *Political Parties and Democracy* is a tremendous success in giving readers the most recent information and insights about political parties around the globe. The set includes not only excellent contributions on the party systems that exemplify strong democratic regimes like the United States and the United Kingdom, but careful insights on volatile party systems in newer democracies such as Poland, and on systems still transitioning to democratic rule in places as diverse as Kenya and Morocco. The universal challenges to parties as linkage mechanisms in the early 20th century are everywhere apparent."

Robin Kolodny
Associate Professor of Political Science, Temple University

Political Parties and Democracy

Five Volumes
Kay Lawson, General Editor

Volume I: The Americas
Kay Lawson and Jorge Lanzaro, Volume Editors

Volume II: Europe
Kay Lawson, Volume Editor

Volume III: Post-Soviet and Asian Political Parties
Baogang He, Anatoly Kulik, and Kay Lawson,
Volume Editors

Volume IV: Africa and Oceania
Luc Sindjoun, Marian Simms, and Kay Lawson,
Volume Editors

Volume V: The Arab World
Saad Eddin Ibrahim and Kay Lawson, Volume Editors

Political Parties in Context
Kay Lawson, Series Editor

Political Parties and Democracy

General Editor, Kay Lawson

Volume II: Europe

KAY LAWSON
VOLUME EDITOR

Political Parties in Context
Kay Lawson, Series Editor

 PRAEGER

AN IMPRINT OF ABC-CLIO, LLC
Santa Barbara, California • Denver, Colorado • Oxford, England

Library of Congress Cataloging-in-Publication Data

Political parties and democracy / Kay Lawson, set editor.
    p. cm.—(Political parties in context series)
  Includes bibliographical references and index.
  ISBN 978-0-275-98706-0 (hard copy : alk. paper)—ISBN 978-0-313-08349-5 (ebook)—ISBN 978-0-313-38314-4 (vol. 1 hard copy)—ISBN 978-0-313-38315-1 (vol. 1 ebook)—ISBN 978-0-313-38316-8 (vol. 2 hard copy)—ISBN 978-0-313-38317-5 (vol. 2 ebook)—ISBN 978-0-313-38060-0 (vol. 3 hard copy)—ISBN 978-0-313-38061-7 (vol. 3 ebook)—ISBN 978-0-313-35302-4 (vol. 4 hard copy)—ISBN 978-0-313-35303-1 (vol. 4 ebook)—ISBN 978-0-275-97082-6 (vol. 5 hard copy)—ISBN 978-0-313-08295-5 (vol. 5 ebook) 1. Political parties. 2. Democracy. I. Lawson, Kay.
  JF2051.P5678 2010
  324.2—dc22   2009047965

ISBN: 978-0-275-98706-0 (set)
EISBN: 978-0-313-08349-5 (set)

14 13 12 11 10   1 2 3 4 5

This book is also available on the World Wide Web as an eBook.
Visit www.abc-clio.com for details.

Praeger
An Imprint of ABC-CLIO, LLC

ABC-CLIO, LLC
130 Cremona Drive, P.O. Box 1911
Santa Barbara, California 93116-1911

This book is printed on acid-free paper ∞

Manufactured in the United States of America

Contents

Political Parties and Democracy: Three Stages of Power

Kay Lawson

Political Parties and Democracy consists of five volumes with 46 chapters, each devoted to the parties of a different nation. The first volume is dedicated to the Americas: Canada and the United States for North America, and Argentina, Bolivia, Brazil, Chile, Mexico, Peru, and Uruguay for Central and South America. Volume II is on European parties: Denmark, France, Germany, Italy, Norway, Spain, and the United Kingdom in the West, and the Czech Republic, Hungary, and Poland in the East. Volume III begins with four chapters on the parties of the post-Soviet nations of Georgia, Moldova, Russia, and Ukraine and continues with the parties of five Asian nations: China, India, Japan, Malaysia, and South Korea. Parties in Africa and Oceania are the subject of Volume IV: Cameroon, Kenya, Namibia, Nigeria, and South Africa, followed by Australia, Fiji, New Zealand, Samoa, and the Solomon Islands. Finally, Volume V is devoted first and foremost to the Arab world, beginning with the parties of Algeria, Egypt, Lebanon, Mauritania, and Morocco and continuing with the parties of two neighboring states in which Arab politics play an important role: Israel and Turkey. All authors are themselves indigenous to the nation they write about. Indigenous[1] co-editors, whose essays introduce each section, have helped recruit the authors and guide the development of their chapters; final editing has been my responsibility as general editor, and the final volume concludes with my Conclusion to the Set.

The purpose of each chapter is to examine the relationship between political parties and democracy, providing the necessary historical, socio-economic, and institutional context as well as the details of contemporary political tensions between the two. To understand this relationship requires a serious effort to understand as well the basic nature of the state. That nature shapes the work of the parties. Whatever mission they give themselves, it is control of the state that they seek. Without that power, programs are mere words on paper or in cyberspace.

Parties are expected to provide the key building blocks of democracy by forming a strong link between citizens and the state. It is a challenge fledging parties commonly accept, because promising to establish a government in keeping with the will of the people is the best way to achieve adequate support and wrest power away from nondemocratic leadership. Even today's most democratic and established parties trace their roots to that primeval calculation and the struggle it entails. Many of the parties studied here are still trapped in that early stage.

Some of the parties formed to wage the battle for democracy have accepted defeat, at least for now, and live on only in puppet-like roles that permit them to share the perquisites but not the substance of power. Others have only recently formed organizations strong enough to have led the way forward from dictatorship and are still working out the new relationship. They came to power waving the banners of democracy, but they are not necessarily bound—or able—to obey its precepts once in power. In some cases, the move to democratic governance has been short-lived and military, religious, or ethnic autocracy has retaken control.

Still other parties, such as the ones scholars in the West have studied hardest and longest, have thrived for many years as more or less genuine agencies of democracy, but are now gradually but perceptibly moving forward to a third stage of power. Serious links to the populace no longer seem to be necessary, as the central organization becomes expert at using the tools of political marketing and the victorious party leaders adopt policies that satisfy their most powerful supporters. Moving steadily away from participatory linkage, parties tend to maintain a degree of responsive linkage, but the answer to the question of to whom they are responsive is not necessarily a reassuringly democratic one.

In short, the development of political parties over the past century is the story of three stages in the pursuit of power: liberation, democratization, and dedemocratization. In every volume of *Political Parties and Democracy* the reader will find parties at all three stages. Sometimes the story of liberation will be part of the recent history that must be understood; in other chapters the unfinished quest for freedom is the only story that can yet be told. Sometimes the tale of post-liberation democratization is very much "a work in progress" (and perhaps a dubious one). Sometimes dedemocratization takes the form of accepting failure under impossible circumstances after the first joys of liberation have been tasted, and sometimes it is a more deliberate effort to escape the bounds of what still hungry leaders consider a too successful democratization. Understanding parties—and their relationship with democracy—means understanding the stage of power their leadership has reached.

Is democracy always dependent on parties, or are there other agencies capable of forcing governments to act on behalf of the entire demos? Perhaps mass movements working via the Internet can be used to hasten liberation, fine tune democratization, and even to forestall dedemocratization. Possibly in the future such movements will not only help the parties take control of the state, but then tame them to live in comfortable league with democracy, offering party leaders sufficient rewards for staying in power democratically and followers better designed instruments for reasonable but effective participation.

However, party democracy, cybertized, is still no more than an interesting dream, and one that goes well beyond the purview of these studies. What one can find in *Political Parties and Democracy* is the actual state of the play of the game.

Introduction to *Political Parties and Democracy: Europe*

Kay Lawson

In preparing the four other volumes of *Political Parties and Democracy*, I have worked with indigenous coeditors who have been extremely helpful. In this volume, however, I have worked alone to find and edit the chapters. As a possibly honorary European who has lived half-time in France for the past 22 years, who taught political parties for eight spring semesters at the Sorbonne, and who has often compared European parties to those in the United States, I thus slightly bend the rule of indigeneity and seek to do honor and justice to the 10 excellent chapters that follow.

The focus of this, the second volume of five in *Political Parties and Democracy*, is on the relationship between parties and democracy in 10 nations, with chapters on each in the following order: France, Germany, Italy, Spain, the United Kingdom, Denmark, Norway, Poland, Hungary, and the Czech Republic. As in all the other volumes, all authors are indigenous to the nations they write about. They have stayed "on message" throughout, yet at the same time provided the context we need to understand what is going on and where present conditions came from. They have told the truth, with no embellishment other than, sometimes, at the end, the interesting expression of their own evaluation of what they find that truth to be. Not all their compatriots—or readers—will agree with all of them, but all will acknowledge that where there may be arguments, those presented here have been well documented and well defended. Because they speak so very well for themselves, here I offer only brief comments on each.

France. The purpose of *Political Parties and Democracy* is to seek the unvarnished truth, so where better to begin in this volume than with the always self-critical French? Nicolas Sauger does not disappoint. French parties change constantly, he tells us in "Political Parties and Democracy in France: An Ambiguous Relationship," and this reflects the general weakness of party organizations in France. Their problems go back to the ascension of strongly antiparty General Charles de Gaulle to power in 1958 and the party-weakening constitution he made sure was put in place. De Gaulle blamed parties for poor decision making and general instability, and the Fifth Republic was built on the idea of getting rid of the *regime des parties* once and for all. French democracy has more or less survived and the parties have also survived, as agencies for winning and organizing power, but the relationship between them is not a happy one: "French parties have contributed neither to the establishment of representative democracy nor to supporting it in its most difficult periods."

Germany. Having multiple parties does not always mean a multiparty system (as opposed to a two-party system). According to Juergen Falter in "The Development of a Multiparty System in Germany: A Threat to Democratic Stability?," the recent development of quite a large number of smaller parties, several of which are powerful enough to swing elections left or right according to coalition calculations, leaves German voters unable to predict where their votes may lead at a time when popular dissatisfaction, both with life chances and with the performance of governments, has led to startlingly high new levels of abstention, distrust, and disinterest. Paradoxically, the existence of a "system-stabilizing fundamental consensus" regarding many questions "allows party political conflicts to become mere political posturing," a situation that does not improve the confidence of observant citizens. The role of parties in maintaining German democracy is consequently considerably weaker now than in the past.

Italy. In "The Three Ages of Party Politics in Postwar Italy," Piero Ignazi traces the role of historical context and popular opinion in shaping the role of Italian parties as agencies of democracy in three distinct periods since World War II. The post-war golden age, when all parties including the still powerful Communist Party played by and large within the rules of the system, was succeeded in the 1960s by an iron age, "when the governing parties dramatically accelerated the colonization of the state" and thereby "produced a backlash in terms of declining legitimacy." In the succeeding "rust age," stronger parties did not

mean a stronger democracy and certainly did not improve public opinion vis-à-vis the parties. Although corruption and stalemate finally produced the collapse of the old party system altogether in the mid-1990s,
the new system, betraying the hopes of an electorate willing to believe
in change, soon reproduced and even heightened the ills it was supposed to have ended. Here, too, the author concludes on a strong note
of dismay: "Parties are no longer an asset for democratic institutions. . . .
Instead they seem to have become a liability."

Spain. No contemporary western European party system began with a
stronger determination to reestablish democracy than Spain's in 1978, as
Luis Ramiro and Laura Morales make clear in "Spanish Parties and Democracy: Weak Party–Society Linkage and Intense Party–State Symbiosis." Parties were "the core players in the formulation of the new
institutional architecture in Spain" and continue to play a critical role in
Spanish democracy. Nonetheless, they worry that Spanish parties are
losing credibility as agencies of democracy. They have, they say, "gradually placed themselves in a position where they are more solidly linked
to state than to society." While the governing functions of parties in a democracy are carried out well, they have not been able to develop strong
partisan identities with the electorate. Election turnout remains high but
is declining slightly, membership organizations are weak, and citizen
participation in the parties is very low. As "electoral-professional organizations that are strongly dependent on state subsidies," the parties do little to promote political participation beyond the vote.

United Kingdom. Although in "New Questions for Parties and Democracy in the United Kingdom: Participation, Choice, and Control" Paul
Webb finds ample evidence that British voters are annoyed by signs of
"cronyism" in their parties, and that the parties are in general less ready to
offer participatory linkage than formerly, his overall evaluation is not
severe. Unpersuaded by "participationist visionaries" of the importance
of parties in building community or civic orientations, he dismisses the
whole Rousseauian notion of "community" as "unrealistic utopianism in
a large, pluralistic, and modern industrial society." Rather more serious
for him is the widespread *perception* that parties fail to offer meaningful
choices to the voters, and that they can be seen as too closely linked to the
state. Webb finds this perception perhaps simplistic but also problematic
and urges more care "in matters of party funding, electoral reform, and
the process of making public appointments." Yet he doubts whether either
this kind of reform or others to create more opportunities for participation
will have much impact on public opinion. Thus it is, and thus it shall
remain. Perhaps unfortunate, but not too serious, according to Webb.

Denmark. A crisp brisk wind blows into the volume when we turn to
Denmark, where the traditional western European commitment to
party democracy in all its forms appears to be still alive and well. Of
course small size and national homogeneity may make it easier, but

nowhere in the world are the links between parties and the maintenance of democracy likely to be found stronger than in Scandinavia.
There are, however, certain flaws. In "The Massive Stability of the
Danish Multiparty System: A Pyrrhic Victory?" Christian Elemelund-
Præstekær, Jørgen Elklit, and Ulrik Kjaer suggest that the very stability
of the Danish political system, including the party system, may at present be tending to stifle necessary change, reminding us that "change
and short-term instability can be a good thing for democracy." New
parties representing new values have had little success in securing a
place in the system, and policies continue to be passed by a slim majority of the old guard. In Denmark as elsewhere, "electoral change is not
automatically translated into party system change."

Norway. Elin Haugsgjerd Allern is similarly unsure that Norwegian
parties are performing as well as heretofore as agencies of democracy.
In "Parties as Vehicles of Democracy in Norway: Still Working after All
These Years?," she carefully examines their performance in all the
domains normally assigned to them as partners in democracy. She
finds the democratic chain of command from voter to government
through parties still very strong, and praises the level of competitiveness maintained, but notes that the parties no longer provide the same
opportunities for the participatory and deliberative aspects of democracy, that declining membership makes them less able to reflect new
issues and conflict dimensions, and that once in office they find their
ability to govern nationally challenged by new international constraints,
local autonomy, and increased party fragmentation.

Part III of this volume examines *Eastern Europe*. The slight but apparent
decline in the capacity of parties in Western Europe to fill absolutely all the
democratic functions commonly assigned to them no doubt appears to be a
minor concern to scholars examining the evolution of parties in Eastern
Europe. The progress in democratization made in the two decades since the
breakaway from the Soviet Union is impressive in all three nations examined here, including the building of ever more stable party systems; nevertheless, serious problems remain and new ones are evolving.

Poland. For Hieronim Kubiak, in "Political Parties and Democracy:
The Polish Case," the problem is how to create parties that can credibly
address the anger of those who have sustained great socioeconomic
losses during the period of system transformation. Parties that ignore
this suffering—or that make promises they cannot possibly keep in the
near future—stimulate the growth of abstention and general withdrawal from public life and a dangerous retreat into "primitive nationalism, xenophobia, and demonstrative religiosity." For Kubiak, context
is overwhelmingly important: Polish parties must find a way to address
the nation's poverty and "the exclusion of millions." He believes this
can be done only via greatly improved participation, acceptance of the
rules of the game, and renewed trust in social contracts.

Hungary. In "The Relationship between Parties and Democracy in Hungary," Attila Ágh insists on the exceptionalism of the Hungarian parties. Like parties in the other new democracies, they are organizationally weak, have small memberships, and have recently developed a greater readiness to make demagogic appeals to the voters, but they are exceptional in their very low electoral volatility and in the great stability of the party system. It is, however, a form of stability that does not enhance their role as democratizing agents, nor as efficient makers of policy. Based more on cultural than on socioeconomic cleavages, they are much more politically and ideologically oriented than policy oriented. The divide between Left and Right, pro-EU and Eurosceptic, is very wide, and a change of government from one side to the other means old-fashioned purges of enemies from public administration offices and redistribution of the spoils of power. Here too the Left is weakened by its failure to achieve social consolidation, and the Right relies ever more heavily on national and social populism. The party system is, says Agh, "still very far from . . . democratization."

Czech Republic. In the final chapter in this volume, "The Czech Party System and Democracy: A Quest for Stability and Functionality," Miroslav Novak concludes with a reminder: "No party system is perfect, so our demands must be suitably modest." Nonetheless, he is not pleased. For this author, creating functioning governments is the sine qua non of party democracy—other attributes follow distantly in importance. Although the Czech party system no longer faces excessive fragmentation or volatility, the parties are, says Novak, very much in need of "greater stability, efficiency, and smoother relationships among themselves." In the Czech Republic the ideological distance between the relevant parties may be diminishing, but it is still so great that it slows democratization and thus makes it difficult to form governments capable of action. He concludes with strong recommendations for changes in Czech electoral law to increase the parliamentary weight of the two major system parties and thereby the functionality of the shifting governments, but doubts such changes will take place. One could argue with this author that you do not need strong parties to have strong functioning governments, but that misses his point—he agrees governments should be formed democratically, but insists they be able to do the job. It is hard to argue with that.

Working from inside, the authors of these chapters on 10 European party systems are clearly sensitive to what aspects of our topic actually matter the most in their countries today and give their remarks as much contextual depth as one could hope for. Here we find party systems at all three stages of party power seeking, discussed in the Set Introduction for *Political Parties and Democracy.* The Eastern European chapters, although presented last, show party leaders at the earliest stage, struggling to organize themselves successfully during and immediately after national liberation, when socioeconomic conditions, domestic and international, make it next to impossible to meet the hopes of those who expect more from democracy than fine speeches and congratulations. The two Scandinavian chapters present parties maintaining a close and supportive relationship with the tenets and practice of democracy despite minor drawbacks. The other west European party systems, although discussed first, are in fact the farthest along the path to de-democratization.

Of course the 10 chapters offer more than these broader truths and more than brief summarizing comments can provide. Like Gobelin tapestry artists, the authors present complex stories within a carefully woven fabric of explanation and detail. We invite our readers to examine more closely what they have to say.

PART I

Western Europe

CHAPTER 1

Political Parties and Democracy in France: An Ambiguous Relationship

Nicolas Sauger

INTRODUCTION

Democratic life initially developed without parties in France. Clubs, factions, and cliques prospered during the early episodes of the Revolution of 1789 and the Second Republic (1848). These early forms of political activism largely ignored organizations and participated only marginally in structuring electoral choice.[1] Political parties first emerged in the French Parliament in the early Third Republic, in 1875. The first permanent and centralized parties appeared on the left of the political spectrum, with the formation in 1901 of the Radical and Radical Socialist Republican Party. The Socialist Party closely followed under the label of the French section of the Workers' International (SFIO) in 1905. The right had more difficulties giving birth to fully developed parties.[2] Parties have nonetheless prospered since the end of World War I.

French parties have frequently changed their labels, organizations, and strategies.[3] This propensity to change reflects the general weakness of party organizations in France in terms of resources and legitimacy,[4] especially when compared to their European counterparts. Thus, the prominent feature of French political parties over the past century has been change. Since the beginning of the 21st century, two parties have largely dominated national politics: the Socialist Party (PS) and the right-wing UMP (Union for the Presidential Majority). The incumbent party—the UMP—was launched only in 2002; the main party in opposition, the PS, dates back to 1971. Only two parties have survived over the long run. The Radicals have managed to keep their label intact, though they are actually absorbed within the UMP. The French Communist Party (PCF) has persisted on the left, 90 years after its creation in 1920, despite a long electoral agony since the late 1970s. In the presidential election of 1969, the PCF received 21.27 percent of the votes, but in 2007 its candidate received only 1.93 percent.

Major reshuffles of the party system have taken place after each major crisis: the two world wars, decolonization, and civil war in Algeria in the 1950s. Most parties voted to give *pleins pouvoirs* to Maréchal Pétain, the collaborationist leader of Vichy France, in 1940. The Algerian civil war at the end of the 1950s demonstrated how incapable the parties were to deal with major events effectively. The solution to this crisis came from outside the political system, through the providential figure of General Charles de Gaulle, who was able to take power and guide the nation to a change of the regime itself with the foundation of the Fifth Republic in 1958. This solution did not emerge from democratic means; in 1958 de Gaulle was brought in to counteract the explicit threat of the army to overthrow the government. To a large extent, the ascension of de Gaulle is the result of a coup d'état, although the semblance of a democratic process was followed in his investiture.

French parties have thus contributed neither to the establishment of representative democracy in France nor to support of it in its most difficult periods. The contribution of parties to the maintenance of French democracy can thus be expected to be limited. This chapter begins by assessing the role of French parties with regard to democracy in the contemporary—and far more pacified—period. It then presents the context in which parties have developed and describes how the contempt of de Gaulle for political parties has left a durable imprint. The three following sections detail the main dimensions of analysis of the relations between parties and democracy: the dimensions of contestability, decidability, and availability. These sections largely build on theoretical frameworks proposed by Stefano Bartolini in his perspective emphasizing party system dynamics.[5]

THE FIFTH REPUBLIC: AN AMBIGUOUS RELATIONSHIP WITH POLITICAL PARTIES

The Fifth Republic was built on the idea of eliminating the *régime des partis* embodied by the Fourth Republic. Parties were accused by de Gaulle of being the root of two related evils: the absence of decision and the general instability of the system. Up to a certain extent, de Gaulle failed in his project. Even if the National Assembly was dispossessed of most of its prerogatives, parties have nonetheless flourished with an unexpected vigor. Furthermore, the configuration of the party system into a bipolar structure of competition has in fact been one of the most important reasons for the stability and efficiency of the political system as a whole. The initial ambition of de Gaulle has, however, left traces. Parties have remained weak organizations, and instability within the framework of bipolarization has characterized the whole period. This section develops these two aspects of the relations between parties and the Fifth Republic.

The Institutional Structure of the Fifth Republic

The early Fifth Republic hesitated between two readings of the constitution. According to the first, the president was to be a consensual arbiter above the parties. This "presidential reading" responded to the perceived excesses of partisan power and competition under the parliamentary Fourth Republic. The second interpretation—a partisan reading—adhered to the traditional view of the importance of parties in modern democracies.

In 1962, a major revision of the constitution introduced the direct election of the president, forming thus the model of a semipresidential regime.[6] This change intensified the politicization of the presidency. Henceforth, partisan competition would be structured around the presidential figure.

However, two different inspirations were at work in the early evolution of the constitutional text of the Fifth Republic. On the one hand, de Gaulle's vision positioned the president as the cornerstone of the whole regime. The Gaullist imprint can thus be found in the 1962 revision, which introduced the direct election of the head of state. On the other hand, Michel Debré, who drafted the constitution and served as the first prime minister, had a far more traditional parliamentary model in mind. The "rationalization" of the relationships between government and parliament was his grand oeuvre.[7] Both visions lean toward more efficiency and stability in the system of decision making. To some extent, these two visions have complemented each other in achieving these goals.

However, the institutional system also contains certain contradictions. The balance of power between the president and the prime minister is not always clear-cut. Competition and challenges within the executive have been recurrent features of the political life of the Fifth Republic. But this competition is not enshrined in a context of checks and balances. Powers overlap—largely because the president has gone beyond what is formally allowed him by the constitution—and the instances of conflict resolution are not symmetric. The president can dissolve the National Assembly or force the government to resign. Once elected, the president is "untouchable." But the president needs government action for most decisions, with the exception of his few though important personal powers.

Periods of cohabitation—the situation in which different parties control the presidency and the legislature—have shed considerable light on the power relations between the president and prime minister. It has revealed the ways in which the Fifth Republic is a constitutional system, permitting two quite different kinds of regimes.[8] When the president is supported by a majority in Parliament, the regime is clearly marked by the domination of the president, even if its parliamentary majority is weak or internally split. This happened, for instance, at the end of the 1970s when Valéry Giscard d'Estaing was supported by a party that would have been only the junior partner of the governing coalition in a parliamentary regime, and again during the minority government of Michel Rocard, from 1988 to 1991. In periods of cohabitation, the president is brought back to a more limited role, with the prime minister taking over the effective political leadership from the president.

These two interpretations of the Fifth Republic are in fact in constant tension.[9] General elections may, of course, tip the balance in favor of either of those two logics. Yet, this will not make the opposing logic disappear—at least until recently. Rather, the two logics coexist in permanent tension, achieving only a fragile and temporary equilibrium.

The presidential logic of the Fifth Republic is largely embodied by de Gaulle's vision. In this vision, the president has fundamentally three roles: he incarnates the nation, he is the supreme judge both in conflicts among institutions and on key decisions in defense and foreign affairs, and, finally, he is in charge of the state of the nation under exceptional circumstances thanks to a quite liberal provision of exceptional powers in the constitution. As such, the president is presented as a consensual figure. He is "above the parties," to use the words of de Gaulle. Every president since 1958 has presented himself in his first speech as the "President of all the French people." None of them has ever kept any party responsibility or even formal membership in any organization after taking charge. In keeping with these practices, the constitution does not provide any means to question the political responsibility of the president,[10] and the office of the president does not benefit from important administrative services, which are essentially located in ministerial departments.

De Gaulle was able to sustain this role through his own personal legitimacy and through the repeated popular support gained in early referendums about the regime. A full 82.6% of the voters approved the new constitution on September 28, 1958. To comfort the positions of his successors, de Gaulle pushed for the direct election of the president. He furthermore wanted this election to be a two-round election, so that the future president would secure the support of an absolute majority of the population, or, at least, of the voters. He succeeded in imposing direct election in a controversial move in 1962. Paradoxically, this also condemned the ideal of a consensual president. This could be seen immediately, when de Gaulle did not manage to get elected in the first round of the 1965 election. Although he eventually won, the second round of the presidential election brought about the bipolarization of the party system and thus the resurgence of political parties. Hence, even if no formal constitutional role is allotted to parties beyond the rather vague Article 4 of the constitution ("political parties and groups shall contribute to the exercise of suffrage"), their role has remained central with regard to both legislative and presidential elections. Presidential candidates have been partisan candidates, at least since de Gaulle left the political arena.

Under the partisan logic of the Fifth Republic, the president is like a super prime minister, albeit protected against any form of censure, designated by universal suffrage, and effectively governing the country. In this vision, the presidential race does not rest on individuals as heavily as in other democracies but is rather policy or ideologically orientated.

These two readings of the Fifth Republic complement each other. Each of these logics has structured or affected all dimensions of the political system. For example, legislative elections are largely influenced by the results of presidential elections, and the first round of presidential elections is always influenced by legislative concerns. The multiplication of second-order candidates with no chance of winning the presidency has illustrated this point since the 1970s. Of the 16 candidates in 2002 or the 12 in 2007 elections, 3 at best could reasonably hope to make it to the second round. For all the others, their purpose was to signal specific policy preferences to the "major" candidates through their relative capacity of electoral nuisance.

The regular intervention of the president in policy-making decisions strengthens the salience of policy issues in presidential elections. This of course reduces the president's ability to act as a suprapartisan arbiter. Moreover, given his limited resources, the president depends on the support of a legislative majority and the large resources located in the hands of the prime minister and government. This process has often been analysed in terms of "presidentialization."[11] Yet, this is quite contrary to the original presidential logic. Presidentialization rather appears to be the consequence of the rise of the partisan logic, federating parties in favor or against the incumbent or future president, at the expense of the president-as-arbiter.

The different logics of the Fifth Republic, presidential and partisan, are thus inextricably linked. It is the tension between the two logics that structures the political life and history of the Fifth Republic. All in all, the partisan logic appears to have become increasingly dominant. Recent changes in the institutional architecture may finally resolve the tension between the presidential and the partisan logic in favor of the latter.

The Dynamics of the Party System

The principal dynamic of the French party system under the Fifth Republic has been that of bipolarization. Bipolarization has been a stable but not unchallenged pattern of party competition throughout the whole period. If defined in Sartori's terms,[12] bipolarization is a type of limited pluralism (the number of parties is superior to two but does not exceed five), organized into two stable coalitions (or two blocs), with polarized party positions but a centripetal direction of competition. More precisely, France has been characterized by the so-called bipolar quadrille. By the end of the 1970s, four parties of approximately equal strength—the Communist Party, the Socialist Party, the centrist Union for French Democracy (UDF), and the Gaullist Rally for the Republic (RPR)—monopolized over 90 percent of the vote in their respective Left and Right blocs.[13] It took 20 years to produce this end state, concluding in fact only in 1978 with the formation of the UDF from different center—right parties. But this lasted only a few years. As early as the beginning of the 1980s, two decisive evolutions appear clearly: the domination of one party within each block, forming a quasi two-party system,[14] and the surge of "antiestablishment" parties,[15] namely the Greens and the far-right Front National.

Within this context of bipolarization, the chief characteristic of the French party system is instability. Even if periods of evolution can be delineated, the very institutional context of the Fifth Republic provides mixed incentives that largely explain the apparently erratic changes around bipolarization. It is true that party change and party system change should not be confused,[16] but the vulnerability of French parties to external and internal pressures have regularly led to changes in the structures of competition among parties. The emergence of the Greens and the extreme right Front National in the 1980s, the quasi-disappearance of the Communist Party, and the dramatic changes of strategies of centrist forces between independence and alliance with the right are obvious examples of such transformations. Despite evidence of change, the general picture remains quite confusing at first sight. To take the words of Stefano Bartolini, "the French party system presents inconsistent and mixed characteristics."[17] The picture is all the more complicated by the very changing nature of electoral competition from one election to another. There is no linear evolution over the period of the Fifth Republic. Sometimes resembling more a stochastic process than a clearly identifiable dynamics, the transformation of the French party system has undergone both incremental change and complete turnarounds. The 2002 elections best exemplify this ambivalence, with the first round of the presidential election representing the conclusion of a period of 20 years of fragmentation of the party system while the legislative elections, held only a few weeks later, led to the imposition of a quasi two-party system.

Beyond persistent instability, four phases of the party system can be distinguished.[18] The initial phase, from 1958 to 1962, has been that of consolidation of the system. Fragmentation had been dramatically reduced, and the system of alliances had begun to emerge. From 1962 to 1974, Gaullist domination prevailed. After 1974, the ideal type of a bipolar quadrille was achieved, until 1984, when the period of concentration ended to open a new era of fragmentation of the party system. Yet this fragmentation went along with a relative depolarization of the system, the rise of the National Front compensating only partially for the fall of the Communist Party. Fragmentation led to the surprising 2002 presidential election. When the expected frontrunner, incumbent Lionel Jospin, did not even make it to the runoff, as his putative supporters chose various protest parties in the first round of voting. This eventually forced a dynamic of concentration around the two main parties and led to a partial repolarization of the system visible in the outcomes of the legislative elections that took place only a few weeks later. These successive cycles of fragmentation and concentration on the one hand and polarization and depolarization on the other can be considered as the consequences of the dynamic of the system itself (the consequence of the fragmentation of 2002 is thus concentration) but also of the institutional system of the Fifth Republic. Presidentialization of the regime and the electoral system can particularly be considered as key to understanding these constant evolutions.[19] The assumption is that the institutional system does in fact provide two kinds of contrary incentives: incentives for concentration around two main parties or coherent blocks but, at the same time, incentives for the entry of new challengers. The Fifth Republic has thus had an ambiguous relationship with political parties. Many political parties have considered the new regime undemocratic, especially because of the concentration of power in the hands of the president. Built against parties, the Fifth Republic has, however, finally made it possible for parties to flourish with unexpected vigor. Furthermore, the change in behaviors and the strategy that the new institutions impose on parties have led to the development of a model of party organizations closer to the "responsible party" model.

Moving from this general picture of the relations between parties and democracy under the Fifth Republic, the rest of this chapter elaborates on the issue of the extent to which parties contribute or are detrimental to democratic developments in the contemporary period. To this end, we build on the distinctions of three main dimensions of analysis: to what extent parties have improved or hindered contestability, decidability, and availability of electoral competition. These three dimensions are drawn from various theoretical works on the relations between parties, competition, and democracy, and each is defined and developed in the three following sections.[20]

CONTESTABILITY

The contestability of electoral competition generally refers to the existence of opportunities to contest incumbents through legal and institutionalized means. As such, it entails the possibility of entering the electoral competition and the "fairness" of this competition. In other words, democratic electoral competition presupposes a certain degree of openness or possibilities of entry in the competition and the vulnerability of incumbents.

Political competition in France presents an important degree of contestability, as in any regime that can be considered democratic. Conditions for entering the political race are easily met for most elections. In fact, beyond weak conditions of nationality and age, there are no other restrictions except for the presidential contest. Since 1976, any candidate for that office must be endorsed by at least 500 office holders.[21] There are in fact around 45,000 officials whose signatures can count as proof of support, among which three-quarters are mayors of small or rural towns. This requirement was introduced after the progressive fragmentation of the first round of the presidential elections: There were 6 candidates in 1965, 7 in 1969, 12 in 1974, 10 in 1981, 9 each in 1988 and 1995, 16 in 2002, and 12 in 2007. This does not mean that the initial requirement was no longer efficient in the 2000s; in 2007, more than 50 launched their own campaign to enter the presidential race but did not secure sufficient support to qualify.

The second condition of contestability, the vulnerability of incumbents, is also largely fulfilled. From 1981 to 2007, every election has led to a defeat of the incumbent government. This systematic alternation in power succeeded a long period of domination of the Gaullist party from the beginning of the Fifth Republic. In 2007, the right managed to maintain its incumbent status, but the landslide defeat of the UMP during the municipal elections of 2008 has largely proven that holding government office still does not represent a definite advantage in electoral competition.

Although the contestability of French elections is not endangered, several attempts to limit competition have been made over recent years. Battles over electoral rules have been the locus of strategic manipulation and debates. At the local level, competition is also limited by forms of dominance.

Strategic Manipulations of Electoral Rules

Among Western democracies, France has one of the longest records of electoral system change, just behind Italy.[22] The main reform, under the Fifth Republic, has been the introduction of the direct election of the president, as noted above. This has largely contributed to the definition of the regime. The electoral system of the legislative elections has also been changed twice, before and after 1986. The traditional two-round electoral system was first replaced by a system of proportional representation (although the magnitude, that is the average number of seats by constituency, was rather low, with an average of about five) and then brought back into place after the 1986 elections. The first move was made by François Mitterrand, the first left-wing president ever elected under the Fifth Republic, in a context of undisputable turmoil for his camp. In 1985, when the transition to proportional representation was implemented, there was no doubt the left would lose the forthcoming elections. Two motives were at the basis of this change. First, Mitterrand wanted to soften the extent of this defeat because representation in the new system would clearly be less disproportional than under the two-round majoritarian system. Second, Mitterrand also imagined that this move represented an opportunity to alter fundamentally the working of the party system. The mid-1980s witnessed the emergence of the far-right National Front (FN) and its leader Jean-Marie Le Pen. With a two round system, the FN had little chance to gain a large representation in the National Assembly. A change in the electoral system would, however, make this possible. From 1986 to 1988, the National Front actually had a parliamentary group within the National Assembly, for the first and last time in its history. Mitterrand had the idea that the presence of the FN might lead to a minority government for the right in 1986. This would of course represent a serious handicap for the right and exacerbate dissent within it: The question of whether it was appropriate to make an alliance with the far right was the basis of heated debate within the right at the time and remained so until 1999. As it turned out, the victory of the moderate right was sufficient to keep it from having to bring the National Front into the government. But the question was raised, and this did heighten conflict within the right. The motives guiding the change show clearly that bringing new actors into the political arena is not always a guarantee of more democracy.

These reforms of the electoral system are the most massive attempts at strategic manipulation of electoral competition by parties. Yet, more systematic efforts in this direction can be found. In fact, since the late 1970s, successive reforms have tried to implement changes in the party system in two directions: the fragmentation of the party system into myriad small parties and, at the same time, the construction of the dominance of two parties, one on the right and one on the left.

Three reforms have in particular been viewed as playing an important role.[23] First, conditions to move from the first to the second round of the legislative elections have been reinforced over time. In 1958, 5 percent of the ballots were sufficient to be included in the second round if no candidate won an absolute majority in the first round. In 1966, the threshold was moved to 10 percent of the registered voters. In 1976, it was raised to 12.5 percent of the registered voters. This hardening of thresholds had clear consequences. Whereas there were up to five candidates in the second round of legislative elections in 1958, by the 1970s the contest at this stage had become strictly bipolar, with only two contenders, except for the legislative elections of 1997 when the National Front managed to have candidates in more than 100 constituencies and thus provoked a significant number of "triangular confrontations" (i.e., competition among three candidates, one from the left, one from the right, and one from the far right).

Second, new elections have been introduced, with the election of deputies to the European Parliament since 1979 and regional elections since 1986. These two new elections have been organized with a proportional representation system, not a majoritarian system. This has provided clear opportunities for new parties to enter the game of French politics, and the National Front, the Greens, and the euroskeptic parties have all built their early success in such a context.

The third major innovation in French institutions has been the introduction of a system of public funding for political parties and electoral campaigns since 1988,[24] substituting for the ban of corporate donations. The system of public subsidies has been designed so that both major and fringe parties benefit from it. These two reforms have contributed significantly to the fragmentation of the party system in the 1980s and 1990s and to the discrepancy between electoral results and institutional representation.

The Issue of Dominance

As Graham White has pointed out, party dominance can be defined at least at three levels, from the very local one (that of the district or constituency especially for electoral systems with low district magnitude) to the regional and national levels.[25] These different levels seem in fact quite disconnected. A nationally dominant party can rely on only weak bases at the local level, and a country whose districts are all dominated by a single party may have a pattern of political competition at the national level if the local dominant parties are different. In the case of France, we may note the transition from the nationally dominant Gaullist party in the 1960s to the dominance of local candidates since the 1990s. De Gaulle and his party largely embodied the "spirit of the French 1960s." Their dominance, at least until 1968, is indisputable. The fact that de Gaulle was not elected in the first round of the first direct presidential election, in 1965, was seen as both a surprise and an affront to him, yet his victory was certain. This is precisely the definition of domination.

To some extent, the foundation of the UMP in 2002 can be considered the beginning of the return to an era of domination by one political party. This new right-wing party, created by merging the former RPR with part of the UDF,[26] had gained control of most of the different institutions of the Fifth Republic. President Jacques Chirac, around whom the UMP was created, was elected in 2002 with more than 80 percent of the votes (in the second round of the presidential election). The following legislative elections gave a majority to the UMP in the National Assembly (the UMP garnering 365 of 577 seats).[27] A majority of members of the Constitutional Council were nominated by UMP members,[28] and a majority of local governments (regions, departments, and cities) were controlled by UMP representatives.[29]

Moreover, for the first time under the Fifth Republic, a single party had a majority in the Senate as well as the other branches.[30] Such parliamentary and executive dominance of a single party had never been achieved before. The congruence of the majorities among the executive (presidential majority), the National Assembly, and the Senate is thus an exceptional feature. Of course, the fact that French bicameralism is not symmetrical lessened the importance of the congruence between the National Assembly and the Senate, since it did not have a great impact on policy making (and none at all on government stability). Nonetheless, the Senate has veto powers in some legislative areas and some significant amendment powers,[31] and the president of the Senate has a right to nominate one-third of the Constitutional Council. Lack of congruence between the National Assembly and the Senate did in fact cause political troubles in other regimes, especially for presidents de Gaulle and Mitterrand.

Is the UMP therefore now a dominant party at the national level? Not entirely. Even after the election of UMP candidate Nicolas Sarkozy in 2007 and despite the preceding presidential victories of Chirac in 1995 and 2002, the electoral base of the UMP remains weak and uncertain. It cannot be truly considered a dominant party. Its electoral basis remains too weak, and its strength depends too heavily on the fragmentation of the Socialist Left.

Meanwhile, individual candidates have sometimes considerably consolidated their own personal position at the local level, regardless of their party. Depending on the type of indicator, from one-quarter to one-third of legislative seats can currently be considered safe seats in France.[32] Contestability is probably even lower in the local office or in the Senate. An important explanation for this feature is the particular habit of *cumul des mandats* (i.e., the right and practice of holding different offices at the same time). In the 2000s, about 91 percent of French legislators held at least one other elected position.[33] The practice of *cumul* has clear electoral advantages as well as democratic disadvantages. It decreases the accountability to voters since the candidate is less dependent on each mandate to manage his or her political career. It above all increases the likelihood of being (re-)elected since notability has a significant positive impact on voters,[34] and incumbency is furthermore associated with more resources for campaigning.[35] We may add that the significant democratization of the process of candidate selection in major French parties,[36] with the generalization of membership consultation before nominations, has thus far had no effect on this pattern.

Despite the repeated alternations in power since the early 1980s, contestability in French electoral competition has weakened over the past few decades. On the one hand, two parties—the UMP and the PS—have largely consolidated their domination over the whole political spectrum, creating a situation of quasi two-party competition.[37] On the other hand, the considerable dispersion of the political offer, which is largely due to changes in the electoral system, has made it harder to challenge the domination of the two main parties because this dispersion raises insuperable problems of coordination. Extreme fragmentation poses a clear impediment to the decidability of electoral competition.

DECIDABILITY

Decidability refers to the extent to which the outcome of electoral competition is foreseeable or, more precisely, to what extent structures of political competition make it possible to know what the likely consequences of individual decisions are. The mandate vision of democratic representation is typically linked to a type of competition we call decidable. Decidability is the possibility of making an assessment of the risks of moral hazard and adverse selection, as identified in delegation theory.[38] Three key areas of political competition can be considered as central for the decidability of elections: the fragmentation of the party system, the cohesion of parliamentary groups, and the politics of coalition making.

The Fragmentation of the Party System and Its Effects

Fragmentation of a party system can be interpreted in different ways with regard to democracy. Fragmentation is a positive sign of contestability of a system (see previous section) and increases the likelihood of availability of the electoral offer (see the next section). Fragmentation is, however, not a net contributor to a more democratic system. An increase in fragmentation of a system may complicate the identification of actual alternatives. It may produce unexpected electoral outcomes. If fragmentation is linked with instability of the system, it may hinder the overall accountability of governments. The French party system appears particularly vulnerable to these biases, notably in the 2002 presidential election.

Counting the number of parties is a task far more complicated than imagined at first sight, especially in France. Legal definitions of parties would for instance lead us to acknowledge the existence of about 200 organizations registered as parties,[39] among which only 20 were represented by candidates in the official campaign for the 2007 legislative elections. More classical definitions of parties, in terms of type of organization, goal, and activity, are not any easier to apply in the French case. The UDF is the most obvious example of the difficulties that can be encountered.[40] This party was created in 1978 as an "umbrella organization," representing the grouping of three then-existent parties. Because its leader, the incumbent president Giscard d'Estaing, lost the 1981 presidential election against François Mitterrand, the process of consolidation of the new party was frozen at its early stage.[41] It was then impossible to say whether the UDF or its component parts were the actual parties. More generally, the Fifth Republic has been characterized since the 1970s, on the one hand, by fairly stable electoral coalitions on the left (among communists, socialists, and left-radicals), and on the right (between different center-right parties and the different Gaullist parties), and, on the other hand by sometimes highly factionalized parties.[42] This simply means that one party can sometimes run more than one candidate for one office and sometimes not run any on its own separate ticket. In 1988, for instance, the UDF ran in only half the legislative constituencies, because it filed common candidates with the RPR for this election, but was then represented in two different parliamentary groups in the National Assembly. Some of its representatives chose to have their own group, which regularly supported the minority government of the Socialist Michel Rocard. These features are not particularly favorable to the decidability of electoral competition.

Keeping this in mind, the number of French parties can be computed according to a number of indexes proposed by the comparative literature on the question, among which the most widely used is the effective number of parties, as described by Lakso and Taagepera.[43]

Figure 1.1 proposes a systematic application of this index for France, computing this index at four different levels to take into account the limitations mentioned before: the effective number of presidential candidates from 1958 to 2007, the effective number of parties from data about first round votes for the legislative elections, the effective number of parliamentary parties from data about parties represented in the French National Assembly, and finally the average of the effective number of candidates by electoral constituency. What appears clearly on this figure is the important variation of the fragmentation of the French party system over indicators and over time. Electoral results and accompanying values of the indexes are reported in the appendix to this chapter.

Figure 1.1. Party System Fragmentation in France.

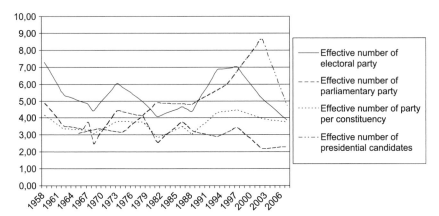

Source: National electoral results; indexes computed according to the effective number of parties' formula.

Differences and variations of indicators of fragmentation of the party system are huge. In 2002, for instance, the effective number of parliamentary parties was just above two, the effective number of candidates by constituency about four, the effective number of electoral parties was five, while the effective number of presidential candidates was higher than eight. More generally, the number of parties at the national level is higher than the average number of candidates by constituency and higher than the number of parliamentary parties. The former difference reflects the importance of electoral pacts. Parties frequently form alliances to present common candidacies for the first round of legislative elections, sharing the distribution of these candidacies at the national level, a practice motivated by extremely disproportional nature of the electoral system in France.

The differences between presidential and legislative elections are not systematic. From 1965 to 2002, the effective number of presidential candidates jumped from three to eight. This underlines a clear discrepancy with the number of parliamentary parties, which followed a steady decline through the same period. Meanwhile, the number of electoral parties for the legislative elections is more stable, with a high variability from one election to the other at the national level but a certain permanence in constituencies. The trend seems to end in 2007. The series of presidential and then legislative elections in that year witnessed a clear convergence of the different indicators around an average number of 3.5 parties.

These different results can be interpreted as proof of the strength of bipolarization of the French party system throughout the Fifth

Republic. The differences between the effective number of electoral parties and the average number of effective candidates by constituency shows the importance of electoral alliances in the first round, at least until 2002. The difference between fragmentation in the first round of legislative elections and the composition of the National Assembly highlights the determinant character of alliances for the second round. No party outside a system of alliance has ever managed to win sufficient seats in the second round to secure a parliamentary group since the 1960s.

What is however less clear from these results is the passage of a system with three partly confused sets of alliances (left, center, and right), until the 1960s, to a system with only two sets of alliances (left and right) from the 1970s. The presidential contest is in this context an exception. The growing number of candidates from 1965 to 2002 can be explained by three factors. First, the institutional regime clearly underwent a tendency toward presidentialization.[44] This presidentialization of the working of the institutions has progressively led to the presidentialization of the parties and their strategies and hence of the electoral competition. Whereas the communists agreed to have a common candidate (François Mitterrand) with the socialists in 1965 and 1974, French parties have all progressively accepted the overriding importance of the role of the president and come to consider the presidential election as the most important stake.

To a large extent, the inability of the PC (because of its political position) and the UDF (because of its organization) to present credible presidential candidates is a central explanation for their current failure. This presidentialization has in turn led to the impossibility of forging alliances for the first round of the presidential election.

Second, the logic of the two-round electoral system leaves room for two possible equilibriums.[45] On the one hand, if a candidate is close enough to the threshold of the absolute majority in the first round, the only strategic incentives for voters is to choose whether they want a second round to take place. On the other hand, if no candidate is in this situation, there is room for at least three candidates, since the real issue is the competition for the second and third places to determine which of these two candidates will make it for the second round.

Third, the conjunction of the dynamics of presidentialization and the multiplication of proportional electoral systems for regional and European elections (plus the 1986 legislative elections) have led to the "proportionalization" of the first round of the presidential election.[46] Because the presidential election is the only election with a coherent offer over the entire territory and a high turnout rate, the results of its first round have been thought of as the opportunity to observe the real balance of powers among parties. It has been widely used in this perspective in negotiations among parties to form coalitions for the legislative elections. This proportional interpretation of the first round has also led voters to send messages to candidates and then seek to influence parties' positions over issues by an "inverted strategic vote."[47] This explains why so many socialist voters in 2002 preferred to cast a vote for candidates of the extreme left despite their preference for the socialist candidate.

The 2002 presidential election in France was seen as a contest between an incumbent president of the center right, Jacques Chirac, and an outgoing prime minister of the center left, Lionel Jospin, coming after a period of cohabitation between left and right that marked the end of the final seven-year presidential term. Both candidates were expected to make it through the first round, and then to fight it out in the second round, in what has been depicted as a "predicted pre-selection."[48] Indeed, many of the published opinion polls in the run up to the presidential elections concentrated mainly on what the result of this anticipated second round contest would be.[49] The first-round election results were a shock. The 2002 presidential election produced what many regarded as a very surprising result: the defeat of the incumbent socialist prime minister, Lionel Jospin, in the first round of the presidential election. This resulted in a run-off election two weeks later between the incumbent president, the center right Jacques Chirac, and an established far-right challenger, Jean-Marie Le Pen. Chirac went on to a victory of unprecedented magnitude, with his vote share leaping from under 20 percent in the first round to over 80 percent in the second, apparently gaining second-round votes from left-wing voters who found themselves without a candidate to support and faced with a choice between abstaining or voting for what for them was the lesser of two evils.

Raymond Kuhn suggests that this happened because Jospin for some reason failed to observe the "iron law" of the two-round system and "alienated sections of the traditional Socialist vote without attracting sufficient support from elsewhere."[50] However, 2002 was not an accident, even if many voters claimed they regretted their choice in the first round. It was, to a certain extent, a logical consequence of three electoral trends that had been clearly observable since the beginning of the 1980s: the fragmentation of the candidacies and of the votes in the first rounds of elections, the steady decline of turnout, and the rise of protest votes in a context characterized by a so-called crisis of representation.[51]

The Cohesion of Parties

A second traditional obstacle to the decidability of electoral competition in France has been the problem of the cohesion of parties. Traditionally, characterizations of French parliamentary behavior have stressed the lack of partisan discipline among deputies. Proposing an overview of cohesion in the French Parliament from the Third to the Fourth Republic, Williams offers a skeptical view of the progress of party cohesion over the period: "The party group brought some much needed discipline into the individualist disorder of the old Chamber. But members' allegiance to them was never exclusive and rarely complete [so that groups] could not cure the congenital individualism of the French politician."[52] This judgment is largely confirmed by the literature of the early Fifth Republic. In a comparative survey of party cohesion, Ozbudun claimed that "among European nations party cohesion is in general least developed in France."[53]

Lack of cohesion among French parties has largely contributed to the instability of the French party system. In only 12 years (1946–1958), the Fourth Republic experienced 21 governments. However, cohesion is not only a key feature for governmental stability but also a necessity for voters to anticipate the consequences of their vote (all the more in that it is well known from the work of Marquis de Condorcet and Kenneth Arrow that the multiplication of actors and issues inevitably lead to random choice and suboptimal decisions).[54]

From basic statistics such as the Rice Index,[55] it appears that the first legislature of the Fifth Republic did not represent any improvement in terms of party cohesion. On the contrary, average cohesion fell to 80, with center parties (Radicals, Christian Democrats of the Popular Republican Movement [MRP], and Independent Republicans) experiencing deep internal divisions with Rice Indices between 61 and 73. Yet, after 1962, the overall impression is one of generally high party unity.[56] Since 1967, no group fell below 90 except the Christian Democrats. The average index indicator ranges between 92 (1962–1967) and 97 (1967–1968). The contemporary period is no different. From 1988 to 2007, the average index of cohesion is about 98,[57] with low variance across parliamentary groups. Center parties, however, still appear slightly less cohesive than their counterparts (average index 95). Yet, dissents are generally limited to a few legislators on each vote and are more common on a few symbolic votes over a legislature.[58] Cohesion and discipline have thus increased from the Third to the Fifth Republic, with 1962 representing the crucial turning point. Yet, during this period, the most dramatic change in parliamentary voting has been the emergence of a clear cleavage between government and opposition. To illustrate this idea, I propose two simple figures: during the Fourth Republic (1951–1956), the likelihood that two parties that voted the same way in a roll-call will vote again the same way the following roll-call was 62%. Between 2002 and 2007, this likelihood increased to 88%. This change is crucial. Contemporary parliamentary democracies are indeed characterized by cohesion across parties. In Europe, cohesion across parties of a same bloc is even significantly higher than the level of cohesion among members of the same party in the U.S. Congress.[59]

The Fifth Republic is indeed characterized by better decidability of electoral competition if compared to past experience, but this is owing in large part to the new politics of coalition making.

The Politics of Coalition Making

As already pointed out, the question of cohesion concerns not only individual parties but also coalitions of parties, upon which the electoral system has had a significant impact. Coalitions are here understood in a broad sense, designating actual cooperation among different parties. Cohesion, in this sense, increased dramatically during the Fifth Republic, achieving a state where the cleavage between opposition and government is almost perfect. However, the main point is that these coalitions have become durable, with two camps—the left and the right—alternating in power since the beginning of the Fifth Republic. This situation has been described as bipolarization, a condition that came into effect in the 1960s in the National Assembly. It was achieved through the progressive alignment of the moderate and center parties on the Gaullist right; a smaller fringe was made up of the left Radicals. From the 1970s to the 1990s, bipolarization remained almost perfect in Parliament. Its main challenges remained outside Parliament, due to the high disproportionality of the electoral system. The sudden rise of the National Front in the 1980s led to the formation of an extreme right parliamentary group only from 1986 to 1988, remaining largely isolated by a strategy of *cordon sanitaire.*

The minority government of Michel Rocard, from 1988 to 1991, did provoke transgressions of the left—right cleavage through the formation of a centrist group, regularly supporting bills of the government without participating in it. However, this group was short lived, and the following legislature returned to a more traditional pattern of opposition. The UDF and recently the Democratic Movement (MoDem) have tried to reinvigorate this centrist tradition since 2005. However, each attempt to cross established lines has led to deep internal divisions, with the parliamentary group splitting into two roughly equal parts. In 2007, most of the UDF deputies refused to follow their former leader François Bayrou in forming the new MoDem to escape from an explicit centrist strategy. They finally grouped together to create the New Center, gathering mainly incumbent UDF deputies, coming back to a close alliance with the dominant UMP. The contemporary challenge to bipolarization is in fact now a clear move toward bipartisanism in Parliament, with the UMP and PS representing now more than 90% of the Chamber.

The second characteristic of coalition making in France has been the presence of preelectoral coalitions. If we consider the frequency of elections with a preelection coalition, the difference between France and other systems is striking. Sona Golder finds that the percentage of elections with a preelectoral coalition present is 27% in majoritarian systems and 46% in proportional systems.[60] But from the beginning of the Fifth Republic, preelectoral alliances have been absent only once: in the first election of 1958. Moreover, these alliances are used strategically by parties to maximize their own chances of election.[61] To this extent, preelectoral coalitions have largely compensated for the fragmentation of the electoral system. Furthermore, preelectoral coalitions constrain government formation. With few exceptions, who is to be in power is clearly identifiable for the electorate, given the known chances of victory of each camp.

In short, there is a fundamental tension throughout the Fifth Republic between tendencies toward simplifications of political competition organized around cohesive parties clustered in stable coalitions and fragmentation.

AVAILABILITY

The third dimension of analysis of relations between French parties and democracy is availability. This term refers generally to what is called the responsiveness of political parties to demands of the electorate. The basic question is thus whether people feel well represented by political parties. In France, the short answer is obviously no. On a scale from 0 to 10 with 0 representing no trust in political parties and 10 complete trust of political parties, only 10.4 percent of French people give a ranking higher than 5 according to data from the European social survey (third wave).[62] Thirty-five percent have almost no trust (rank inferior to 3). Of course this is not uniquely French. In this matter France is an average European country, shown as well on other indictors of attitudes toward parties such as party identification, still relatively high (52.5 percent of French people feel closer to one party than to any other).

The issue of availability is analyzed in accordance with two related questions: To what extent is there effective policy competition in France (are there centrifugal or centripetal tendencies in the party system) and to what extent have new issues that are salient for a significant number of people been incorporated within institutionalized cleavages?

Bipolarization refers not only to the logics of coalition but also to specific positions of political parties in the policy space. The left—right divide has been the most enduring cleavage in French politics. It subsumes many policy issues but is clearly focused on economic and social questions. Party positions on this dimension have already been described; this section systematizes that information. The most important point is that cleavages have changed over this dimension, especially because of the existence or nonexistence of center parties in terms of functional role (capacity to form alliances on both left and right) and not only position. More recently, a new cleavage has appeared on this dimension since the National Front has been opposed by the strategy of *cordon sanitaire* (i.e., excluding all possibility of alliance, with any party).

Figure 1.2 depicts the evolution of the positions of individual parties according to data from the manifestos group.[63] From a method based on counting the emphasis put on different issues, it is possible to infer the underlying left—right dimension in France.[64] This graph does not reveal any important surprises in terms of the position of individual parties. What is worth notice, however, is the clear depolarization of the system from the 1980s. Mainstream parties have clearly converged toward the center of the left—right dimension. However, polarization of the system itself has experienced only a limited depolarization over the period, since the National Front, in particular, has occupied a polar position at the extreme right.

The left—right dimension has been seen as a unique dimension of the French policy space, but since the 1990s, a second dimension of political conflict has been described.[65] It forms part of a broader change that Ronald Inglehart calls postmodernization[66] and is anchored in attitudes and values about authority or libertarianism. Gérard Grunberg and Etienne Schweissguth have shown that Europe is part of this second dimension of the French political space, which ranges from universalism to antiuniversalism.[67] Contrary to this thesis, other authors have demonstrated the stability of the French political space.[68] Building on

Figure 1.2. Party Positions under the Fifth Republic.

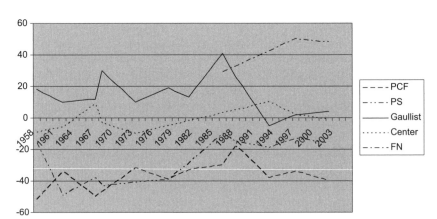

Source: Ian Budge et al., *Mapping Policy Preferences* (Oxford: Oxford University Press, 2001).

the example of the role of the European issue, Céline Belot and Bruno Cautrès claim that despite the fact that Europe remains "invisible," it contributes to a redefinition of the whole meaning of political cleavages in France, transforming them rather than substituting new ones.[69] With what are finally quite similar conclusions, Jocelyn Evans shows that the limited impact of Europe on French electoral competition is explained because views about Europe simply replicate traditional delineations in social structures and mass ideological views.[70] In other words, the European issue is interpreted from the traditional frames of national politics.

This issue of the dimensionality of the French political space can in fact be discussed from three points of view. First, from an historical point of view, more than one dimension of conflict has been present during the Fifth Republic. During its first decade, the issues of institutions and decolonization were central, with the former dividing those accepting from those opposing the new constitution and particularly the role it grants to the president. Throughout the life of the Fifth Republic, Europe has been another divisive issue, cross-cutting the left—right cleavage since positions about Europe are in quadratic relation with this first dimension.[71] Second, perspectives on parties and on electorates should be distinguished. This dimension of political conflict is more important for electorates than for parties per se. One reason for that is that even if the National Front as a party can be easily located at the extreme right of the political spectrum, its electorate is spread all over it. Third, the salience of a second dimension of political conflict has increased over the past two decades. Figure 1.3 represents positions of the candidates of the contemporary period using these two dimensions.

Figure 1.3 is drawn from automatic content analysis of party programs, and, more precisely in this case, of presidential programs according to the Wordscores technique.[72] Building on a first application of this technique for the 2002 elections,[73] this graph compares the positions of the five main candidates in 2002 and 2007 according to an approximation of the two formerly described dimensions of conflict. The important results of this figure are twofold: on the one hand, candidates' positions are lined up on an underlying dimension, reinforcing the idea of the redefinition of the left—right dimension by new issues; on the other hand, there is a clear trend in 2007 toward repolarization of party positions. The socialist and the right-wing candidates follow a clearly centrifugal path, getting closer to extreme left or extreme right. This in fact might explain the new interest in the presidential contest in 2007.

CONCLUSION

Analyzing relations between parties and democracy in France has inevitably led to pessimistic conclusions in the early 2000s.[74] The 2002

Figure 1.3. Main Presidential Candidates' Positions Using Wordscores Technique, 2002–2007.

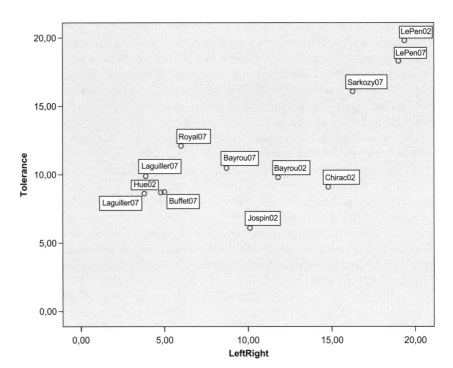

presidential election has particularly been considered an illustration of the crisis of the French political system: turnout fell to an unprecedented low level and the party system was so fragmented it allowed Le Pen to move to the second round. Yet despite these facts, the two major parties, the PS and the UMP, were capable of monopolizing 90 percent of the parliamentary representation, even though their two leaders gathered no more than one-third of the electorate in the first round of the presidential election. France was a "disconnected democracy."[75]

To some extent, the 2007 presidential election marked a "rupture." The 2007 election could have resembled that of 2002. President Chirac and the government led by Dominique de Villepin were highly unpopular. In 2005, the referendum on the European Constitutional Treaty (ECT) failed. Despite the official support of all the major parties (although the PS was highly split on the subject), a large majority voted no on the ECT.[76] In June 2006, only 16 percent of respondents declared themselves satisfied with President Chirac and 17 percent with Dominique de Villepin. In December 2006, two-thirds of the French voters said they did not trust either right or left to govern the country. Yet everything seemed to get back to "normal politics" with even remarkably high levels of participation in the first round of the presidential election.[77] As in 1981, political parties prospered, with significant increases in membership figures and leaders with a real electoral appeal—Ségolène Royal for the PS and Nicolas Sarkozy for the UMP.[78] The PS even managed to orchestrate a positive vision of its presidential candidate selection process with actual competition despite its internal divisions. As in 1981, this bright period may, however, be short lived. The executive has rapidly become unpopular, whereas the Socialist Party seems to be unable to build a new leadership. As described in this chapter, French parties fundamentally work toward protecting their position in a rather unfavorable environment. Contestability is more and more limited, with the even more dominant monopoly of the UMP and the PS on all instances of political representation. Decidability and availability are thus limited by the long-term exclusion from powers of main forms of contestation. To some extent, France is thus an interesting illustration of "cartelization,"[79] with limited party accountability and responsiveness. Yet, this is not the fault of the parties alone. The main issue identifying the relationship between political parties and democracy in France today is the gap between voters' expectations and what parties can actually do.

APPENDIX: ELECTORAL RESULTS OF PRESIDENTIAL AND LEGISLATIVE ELECTIONS

Table 1.1 Presidential Elections Results

	1965	1969	1974	1981	1988	1995	2002	2007
Radical Left (%)	—	1.06	2.70[1]	3.41[1]	2.37[1]	5.30	10.44[1]	7.07[1]
PCF (%)	—	21.17	—	15.35	8.86[1]	8.64	3.37	1.93
PS (%)	31.72[2]	5.01	43.25[2]	25.85[2]	34.11[2]	23.3[2]	16.18	25.87[2]
Other Left (%)	1.71	3.61	0.69	2.21	—	—	7.65[1]	—
Greens (%)	—	—	1.32	3.88	3.78	3.32	7.13[1]	1.57
UDF/Centre (%)	15.57	22.31[2]	32.60[2]	28.32[2]	16.54	—	11.94[1]	18.57
Gaullist (%)	44.65[2]	44.47[2]	18.28[1]	20.99[1]	19.96[2]	39.42[1,2]	19.88[2]	31.18[2]
Extreme Right (%)	6.35[1]	1.27	1.16[1]	—	14.38	20.02[1]	19.20[1,2]	12.67[1]
Effective number of candidates	3.09	3.35	3.13	4.88	4.77	5.97	8.63	4.70

Notes: PCF, French Communist Party; PS, Socialist Party; UDF, Union for French Democracy. Blank cell indicates not applicable.
[1]More than one candidate.
[2]Second round candidate.
Source: French Ministry for Interior and Assemblée Nationale.

Table 1.2 Legislative Elections Results

	1958	1962	1967	1968	1973	1978	1981	1986[1]	1988	1993	1997	2002	2007
Radical Left (%)	1.2	2.0	2.2	4.0	3.2	3.3	1.2	1.5	0.4	1.7%	2.6%	2.74%	3.44%
PCF (%)	18.9	21.9	22.5	20.0	21.4	20.6	16.1[2]	9.7	11.2	9.1%	9.9%[2]	4.91%	4.62%
PS (%)	15.5	12.4	18.9	16.9	21.2	26.3	38.3[2]	32.8	37.6[2]	20.2%	27.9%[2]	26.67%	27.67%
Other Left (%)	5.8	5.0											
Greens (%)						2.0	1.1	1.2	0.4	11%	6.9%[2]	4.44%	3.25%
Centre (%)	15.0	10.4	22.9[2]	20.5[2]	27.8[2]								7.76%
UDF—	20.0[2]	13.8[2]				23.9[2]	42.9	44.6[2]	40.5	44.1[2]	36.2%	5.52%	45.52%[2]
Moderates (%)	20.6[2]	33.7[2]	33.0[2]	38.0[2]	24.6[2]	22.8[2]							
Gaullist/UMP (%)	2.6	0.8	0.6	0.1	0.5	0.8	0.3	9.9	9.9	12.9%	15.3%	38.35%[2]	
Extreme Right (%)	7.29	5.38	4.79	4.42	6.04	4.96	4.08	4.64	4.39	6.84	7.01	12.2%	4.7%
Effective number of parties	7.29	5.38	4.79	4.42	6.04	4.96	4.08	4.64	4.39	6.84	7.01	5.15	3.87
Effective number of parliamentary parties	4.85	3.51	3.71	2.49	4.42	4.08	2.54	3.76	3.23	2.87	3.42	2.16	2.29
Effective number of parties per constituency	4.14	3.35	3.27	3.06	3.78	3.75	2.82	3.48	3.02	4.3	4.45	3.93	3.74
Index of balance	0.811	0.558	0.618	0.540	0.720	0.963	0.610	0.501	0.652	0.508	0.631	0.595	0.439

Notes: PCF, French Communist Party; PS, Socialist Party; UDF, Union for French Democracy. Blank cell indicates not applicable.

[1] Election with proportional electoral system.

[2] Part of the new government coalition.

Source: Data computed from electoral results of French Ministry for Interior and Assemblée Nationale.

CHAPTER 2

The Development of a Multiparty System in Germany: A Threat to Democratic Stability?

Juergen Falter

INTRODUCTION

At the beginning of the German Federal Republic (Bundesrepublik Deutschland), there was a multiparty system that in many ways resembled the party system of the Weimar Republic much more than that of the later fully established Federal Republic. Today we live in a Germany that, though not yet a multiparty system again, is at least a multiple party system that is fundamentally different from the structures that formed the politics of the Federal Republic between the end of the 1950s and the beginning of the 1980s. In this chapter I trace the postwar development of the German party system, identifying four distinct phases: 1945–1961, 1961–1983, 1983–1990, and 1990 to the present. I then discuss the nature and causes of the decline in voter support for the parties and conclude with a consideration of the likely prospects for the future relationship between German parties and democracy.

THE FOUNDING YEARS: 1945–1961

After World War II, which ended with the total defeat of the Third Reich and its unconditional surrender, political parties were initially licensed by the four Allies. At first only four parties were licensed, namely, from left to right, the KPD (Kommunistische Partei Deutschlands, Communist Party of Germany), the SPD (Sozialdemokratische Partei Deutschlands, Social Democratic Party of Germany), and the two

"Union" parties, the CDU (Christlich-Demokratische Union, Christian Democratic Union) outside of Bavaria and the CSU (Christlich-Soziale Union, Christian Social Union) in Bavaria. The foundation or reestablishment of the parties took place from the bottom up, from the local to the regional (i.e., state level and from there to the level of the occupied zones). Some parties were reestablished as linear continuations of Weimar parties, as in the case of the SPD and the KPD. Some were new parties that had not existed in this form before 1933, such as the CDU and the FDP (Freie Demokratische Partei, Free Democratic Party). The Union parties represented a continuation of the Catholic-dominated Center Party (Zentrum) of the Weimar Republic and the Bavarian People's Party (BVP, Bayerische Volkspartei) in Bavaria, although now the interdenominational element clearly prevailed as was reflected in their new names. Nonetheless, the Union parties also gathered politicians and former voters of the more conservative groupings into their ranks. The FDP, which was also founded at that time but would not operate at the national level under this name until 1951, was a coalition movement seeking to unite the rival liberal currents that had coexisted during the empire (Kaiserreich) and the Weimar Republic into a single party. To this day, the FDP displays a left-liberal orientation as well as a strong economically and nationally oriented wing.

The parties that were reestablished or were newly created in 1945–1946 represented, to a large extent, the old cleavage structure of the Weimar Republic and the empire: the KPD and SPD represented the workers and union side of the workers versus owners cleavage, while the CDU and CSU represented the denominational or religious side of the laicism versus religion/denomination cleavage. In the case of the initially quite successful regional Bayernpartei (Bavaria Party), the center versus periphery cleavage reappeared for a short time.

At the first local and state elections, the four so-called licensed parties were successful practically nationwide. In addition, due to the different licensing practices of the allies, other regional parties appeared such as the "Deutsche Partei" (DP, German Party) in Lower Saxony (Niedersachsen), the Zentrum in Nordrhein-Westfalen (North Rhine-Westphalia), the Wirtschaftliche Aufbauvereinigung (Economic Reconstruction Coalition), which was successful in Bavaria for a short time, and many other regional or local groups, which, however, soon disappeared from the political landscape.

The first elections to the Bundestag (German parliament) in 1949 could be characterized as the last Weimar election as well as the first Federal Republic election based on the results (11 parties were represented in the first Bundestag). The Union parties and the SPD were about equal; the bourgeois coalition that was eventually formed by the Union parties, the FDP and the DP, ruled with the smallest majority possible.

However, a discussion soon erupted about which party was, in the eyes of the electorate, the successor to the NSDAP (Nationalsozialistische Deutsche Arbeiterpartei, National Socialist German Worker's Party), which, after all, in the last somewhat free elections in March 1933 received almost 44% of the votes (with over 17 million votes). Moreover, at the end of the Third Reich in 1944–1945, there were approximately 8 million NSDAP members. The question of the relationship between political parties and democracy in Germany was thus closely linked to the question of the fortunes of the ex-NSDAP members and the related question of how to block the reemergence of extremist parties. These questions were never far below the surface in the early years of the postwar political system.

In fact, we know from ecological election analyses using aggregate data that the NSDAP voters very often turned back to where they once came from prior to the landslide electoral success of the NSDAP after 1930. In light of the heterogeneous composition of the NSDAP electorate in party political terms, this meant that all parties, with the probable exception of the KDP, profited from former NSDAP voters after the war.[1]

Although the election to the Bundestag in 1949 was still characterized by serious party fragmentation, which inevitably brought back memories of the Weimar Republic and the associated fear of incapacity to govern the newly founded republic, the so-called *deutsches Wahlwunder* (German election wonder) began as early as 1953. The beginning of the 1960s then introduced a period of almost two and a half decades of political stability. Between 1961 and 1983, there were only three parties (four if the CSU is considered to be an independent party) represented in the German parliament: the Union parties, the SPD, and the FDP. This concentration process was facilitated by several developments: the 5% threshold for legislative seats was extended to apply to elections at the national level, after being applied in 1949 only within the states, the KPD fell into decline due to the increased East—West conflict and the division of Germany; and finally the Federal Constitutional Court (Bundesverfassungsgericht) outlawed an extreme right party, the Socialist Reich Party (SRP, Sozialistische Reichspartei), which had achieved relatively large election successes, particularly in northern Germany.

Another important contribution to the concentration of the German party system is certainly the concept of the so-called defensive democracy (*wehrhafte Demokratie*), which was introduced in 1949 in the German constitution, and the practice of the Federal Constitutional Court in enforcing this concept. As an answer to the threat of the Weimar democracy from extremist forces, especially from the right, the creators of the German constitution, through several complementary provisions, gave the administration and courts the instruments with which they could prevent such developments. These included the right of the Federal Constitutional Court (and, in the case of regional parties, the State Constitutional Courts) to pronounce a party illegal. In addition, it is possible to prohibit and disband organizations that are not parties, on account of extremist tendencies.

Finally, among the instruments of defensive democracy anchored in the constitution are the ability of the Federal Constitutional Court to revoke the citizenship of individual persons for a limited or unlimited period of time, and the right of resistance of the individual, as a last resort, to fight for the survival of the Federal Republic of Germany and the upkeep of the constitution. In the first few years of the young Federal Republic, the Federal Constitutional Court, in compliance with the request of the federal government, returned two verdicts against extreme political parties: the aforementioned SRP verdict in 1952, which was of great importance for further jurisdiction and political practice, and the KPD verdict in 1956 that banned the Communist Party of Germany, which was already in the throes of downfall, as unconstitutional. Both verdicts had a disciplinary effect on political practice and on the new foundation of extreme right or left fringes of the political spectrum, which is not to be underestimated. To this day, parties strive to make their programs constitutionally compliant, and the instruments of defensive democracy (particularly the ability to ban parties) has, in spite of the high hurdles that the legislation and the Federal Constitutional Court have set themselves, an overall tempering effect on the form and content of the political agitation of extremist parties and thus a salutary effect on the capacity of the party system to build and maintain German democracy.

By banning the two parties, in particular the SRP, the extreme wings of the party system were, to some extent, clipped. At the second German Bundestag elections in 1953, only seven parties managed to win seats. Five parties that had been represented in the Bundestag between 1949 and 1953 failed to pass the newly introduced federal 5% hurdle of the election law; a new additional party, the League of Expellees and Those Deprived of Rights (the BHE, Bund der Heimatvertriebenen und Entrechteten), a party representing the interests of refugees and expellees, managed for the first time to get into the Bundestag, and two other parties (Deutsche Partei and Zentrum) won seats in the Bundestag only by invoking the so-called basic mandate clause. This clause is designed to aid smaller parties and provides an alternative rule to the 5% hurdle of the Federal Election Law. As first promulgated in 1953, it allowed any party winning a single direct mandate to be seated in the Bundestag and to have its share of overall party votes count in determining the number of seats it would have based on the number of actual votes it won nationwide. In 1957, this basic mandate clause was tightened, and now it is only after winning three direct mandates that a party may have taken into account the percentage of votes it achieved overall when determining the mandate distribution (provided that with those votes its score still falls under 5% of the valid votes).

In 1957, the process of concentration was continued in the third elections to the Bundestag. Now there were only five parties represented in the Bundestag, and of these the Deutsche Partei, which had been particularly successful in Northern Germany, only managed to get into parliament by the so-called piggyback method; it won six direct mandates but only because the CDU abstained from nominating direct candidates in a range of constituencies in which the DP candidate had a good chance of winning. Incidentally, in this third Bundestag election, the Union parties achieved for the first and last time not only the absolute majority of mandates but also, with 50.2%, the absolute majority of the valid votes submitted.

In 1961, the concentration process took a final step and for the next 23 years only three groups were represented in the Bundestag, namely the SPD, the FDP, and the CDU/CSU, which was made up of two parties but which had formed an alliance as a parliamentary group since the first Bundestag convened. The causes for this concentration process, which is described as the German election wonder, are manifold. On the one hand, it was the aforementioned legal regulations, in particular the extension of the 5% hurdle and the tightening of the basic mandate rule, which contributed to the concentration, and on the other hand, it was owing to the exercise of the defensive democracy instrument, especially through the prohibitive effect of the two party bans in 1952 and 1956. There were also external reasons such as the Cold War, the foundation and existence of the German Democratic Republic (GDR), and the permanent threat to West Berlin from the Soviet Union and the GDR, reflected in the Berlin ultimatums in the 1950s. The tabooing of right-wing extremism based on recent Germany history must also be included, as well as the legitimizing effects of the extremely positive economic development that lasted until the mid-1960s (the so-called economic miracle).

Another cause of this concentration process was the integration policy followed by the two main parties. The CDU was particularly successful in integrating and finally swallowing the smaller bourgeois parties, while the SPD integrated former KPD voters. Finally, another causal element that should be specified is the initially economic and then increasingly social integration of the 14 million expellees and refugees, which altogether accounted for a quarter of the population living in West Germany at the time, perhaps the greatest of all political, economic, and social achievements of the young Federal Republic.

A QUARTER CENTURY OF A THREE-PARTY SYSTEM: 1961–1983

The phase of the three-party system lasted almost two and a half decades and was characterized by very high voter participation; by the

fact that both large parties, SPD and Union, together regularly aggregated over 90% of all valid votes; and by relatively stable long-term
party commitments. During this period, almost three-quarters of the
Germans entitled to vote showed a long-term stable party commitment
in terms of party identification. This led to an enormous stability in the
party system, at least in terms of seats won by proportional representation. Alternative forces on the left and right wings of the party spectrum
had little or no chance at this time. In the Bundestag elections in 1969 the
right-wing extreme party NPD (Nationaldemokratische Partei Deutschlands, National Democratic Party of Germany) came close to gaining
seats with 4.3% of the votes, but still failed the 5% hurdle of the election
law, after which its rapid downfall commenced and lasted until long after the reunification. During the 1960s, in the course of the détente policy, the reestablished, but badly named KPD on the left side of the
political spectrum, which was now known as DKP (Deutsche Kommunistische Partei, German Communist Party), had no chance whatsoever.

Thus three parliamentary parties formed the governments of
Germany among themselves for almost a quarter of a century. Which
coalition formed the government almost always depended on the FDP,
which was in a position to tip the scales and could therefore form
either a Christian—liberal or a social—liberal coalition with one of the
large parties. The party leaders, in fact the whole political class, with
the exception of the representatives of the extreme right- and left-wing
parties, were unmistakably democratically oriented. There was widespread consensus regarding the basic rules of the political system. All
the parties represented in the Bundestag felt unswervingly bound to
the German constitution, regardless of differences in interpretation.

There was also considerable consensus in regard to basic political
decisions, particularly after the reorientation of the SPD around a new
program created in 1959 (the Godesberg program). Both the integration
into the west and the decision for a social market economy as well as
membership in NATO and membership in the European Economic
Community (EEC) were now undisputed. There were, however, differences regarding the policies to be followed toward East Germany
(Ostpolitik), policies, which had already experienced a slight modification during the 1966–1969 grand coalition and then underwent a fundamental change under Willy Brandt as chancellor with Walter Scheel
from the FDP as foreign minister in the social—liberal coalition. However, the fundamental goal of reunification of both German states was
never abandoned in the process. The differences instead concerned different opinions regarding the correct, effective way to get there.

In this phase, and far beyond it, the country was sociopolitically oriented to the ideal of the social market economy in which the welfare-
state element was emphasized. This led to the dictum of Ralf

Dahrendorf and others that the Federal Republic had been led for a long time by two social democratic parties, the SPD and the Union. Even the FDP, which was more strongly socially than economically liberal at that time, went along most of the time with the policy of the continual expansion of the welfare state.

During this period the antidemocratic powers gathered, if they were not already organized in an extremist wing party, into the so-called nonparliamentary opposition and the student movement. However, the majority of both the nonparliamentary opposition and the student movement, which were only partly identical, were by no means antidemocratically oriented, but strongly criticized the liberal direction of the state. This was particularly true for a range of leaders of the student movement who were normally not die-hard liberal democrats in terms of the representational democracy of the German constitution but rather envisioned another form of democracy in the form of Rousseau's theory of identity of the ruler and the people.

However, the student movement, which profoundly shook the self-image of the country with its activism, its radical democratic demands, and fundamental criticism of the Bonn all-party consensus, lasted only three semesters at the most. Thereafter it began to separate into many small political groups, among them several Maoist groups and groups that idolized the Albanian dictator Enver Hoxha or the North Korean dictator Kim Il Sung, and which wished to overthrow the Federal Republic. Despite a certain publicity that these groups received, they played no significant role in political life. In elections, if they competed at all, they received the minimal support of sometimes just several hundred or several thousand votes.

However, although the student movement was a matter of a relatively limited group of activists and followers that was probably no more than a few thousand, it left behind lasting traces, both sociopolitical and temperamental, and a little later also party political. Many of the activists of the Maoist and other splinter groups were to be found later in the established parties, and especially in the newly founded Green Party (Die Grünen). Today some of them are at the center of political power in Berlin, among them politicians like Ulla Schmidt from the SPD, Jürgen Trittin, and Rainer Bütikofer of the Greens, but also previous economic leaders like Rainer-Olaf Henkel.

FOUR PARTIES, TWO POLITICAL CAMPS: 1983–1990

The second phase of the clear three-power system lasted until 1983 at the federal level. It passed into a new phase with the end of the social-liberal coalition and the takeover of the chancellorship by Helmut Kohl, who replaced Helmut Schmidt after a constructive vote of no confidence[2] in 1982, and who was confirmed in office in 1983 by new elections. These new elections brought a new party into Parliament, the Greens. It was the first party to get into Parliament under its own steam since the tightening of the barriers in the Federal Election Law. It was not foreseeable in 1983 that this new phase, which was now characterized by a four-party or two-camp system, would only be an interim phase.

At the time, many observers, including a majority of professional psephologists, gave the Greens only a slight chance of survival. The party was characterized as a protest movement that, like a flash in the pan, would soon extinguish. Only a few observers at that time foresaw that the entry of the Greens would cause the locus of political power to shift in the medium and long-term. Originally the Greens represented a coalition of various new and old social movements. They united radical and moderate ecologists, pacifists, women's liberationists, representatives of lesbian and gay emancipation, and antinuclear activists as well as members of former Maoist and communist groups. The image of the Greens was correspondingly colorful. The bond holding this multicolored group together was the demand for a fundamental change in values and their role as the inheritors of the nonparliamentary opposition and the student movement.

At first, the Greens presented themselves in many respects as an antiparty, thoroughly critical of the existing political system. Idealists and radical system opponents, Marxists, ecosocialists, and various other would-be system changers united in this party, which had many of the characteristics of a movement. After various moldings, party resignations, and expulsions, it evolved into the current Green Party, which is made up at heart of idealistically disposed, well-educated high earners, and has long been a support for democracy and civil rights. In the 1980s, the Greens still considered themselves to be a decidedly left-wing, system-changing party, and to this day the party's self-image is characterized by a greater closeness to the SPD and if necessary to the new party "the Left" (Die Linke) rather than to the CDU/CSU and the FDP. It is indisputable that today's leading Green politicians and at least to the same extent the individual party members and Green voters think of themselves as defenders of civil and constitutional rights, as advocates of an expansion to democratic participation rights at all levels.[3] The reasons for the success and the long-term establishment of the Greens can be seen first in the fundamental change in values that were kicked off or at least accelerated by the so-called nonparliamentary opposition and the student movement, and furthermore in the arrival of new topics not sufficiently covered by the established parties. These were partially based on the report of the Club of Rome in the early 1970s and focused on ecological topics, in which the fear of forest decline (so-called Waldsterben) in particular, and today of the effects of climate change, play a large role. Also important are the psychological medium- and long-term effects of the Chernobyl catastrophe and the general fear of war in the late 1970s and early 1980s, which was very widespread in the Federal Republic of Germany and reintensified by the NATO Double-Track decision.[4]

It could be asked why parties such as the Greens (i.e., ecological movements) were almost exclusively successful at the political level in the "Germanic" countries. A plausible answer to this question could be the evidence of a stronger romantic closeness to nature in these countries, a certain idealistic absoluteness that is foreign to the moderation of American or more generally speaking Anglo-Saxon pragmatism. But it should also be noted that as a whole the Greens seem to be more successful in federally organized states than in centrally organized states, especially when such states work subject to the majority vote. The role of the increase in education and the accompanying change in values, as postmaterial values replace materialistic values, should not be overlooked. However, despite its important impact on the German party system, the emergence of the Greens should not be seen as a new cleavage in the classical Lipset-Rokkan sense.[5] The party is not the domain of a clearly differentiated secondary group nor does it represent group-specific interests. It is a reflection of a partial value shift in German society, i.e. the emergence of postmaterial values especially within the well-educated younger age cohorts. The party was somewhat successful in implementing ecological and alternative lifestyle policies between 1998 and 2005. Since then it has not only dropped out of federal government but also out of most state governments.

AFTER REUNIFICATION: REINSTATEMENT OF A MULTIPLE PARTY SYSTEM—1990 TO THE PRESENT

The reunification of the two German states in 1990 (legally and economically this was an accession of the new states to the old Federal Republic) led to a further differentiation in the party system. The Greens united, first in the form of an election alliance, later by a merger with the East German Alliance 90 (Bündnis 90),[6] in which mainly former civil rights representatives had teamed up. More important than this eastern expansion of the Greens, which progressed simultaneously with the eastern expansion of practically all of the West German parties, was the addition of a new power, the successor party to the SED (Sozialistische Einheitspartei Deutschlands, Socialist Unity Party of Germany), which appeared under different names and finally for years was known as the PDS (Partei des Demokratischen Sozialismus, Party of Democratic Socialism).

The election alliance of the Greens with the Alliance 90 proved to be a lifesaver for the Greens at the elections to the Bundestag in 1990, because at this election, which is not incorrectly referred to as the so-called reunification election, they would not have gotten over the 5% hurdle on their own. The Greens would have possibly remained what many observers prophesized in the early years after their foundation, namely a transitory event, a fashionable party that would soon disappear from the political ring. The PDS, which in the first few years after the reunification was always referred to, not without reason, as the successor party to the SED, would also not have made it into the Bundestag at the first reunified German election in 1990 if were not for the help of the Federal Constitutional Court in Karlsruhe, because in reunified Germany it did not have enough votes to get over the 5% hurdle of the Federal Election Law. The Federal Constitutional Court decided, at that time and only for this election, to divide reunified Germany into two election areas, a west election area consisting of the old federal states and an east election area that encompassed the new federal states, in order to create equal opportunities between the established West German parties and the new East German parties. The Alliance 90 and the PDS managed during this first reunified German election to the Bundestag to get over the 5% hurdle only in the new federal states. The Greens remained under the 5% barrier, not only overall, but also in the traditional election areas of the old Federal Republic because the party had reacted very ambivalently to the reunification; they had no answer to the reunification process that was taking place at top speed, and it had become very obvious that many of their protagonists, just like many left-wing intellectuals in the Federal Republic, took a negative view of the reunification.

In the new federal states the PDS managed easily to overcome the 5% hurdle. It established itself there as the second or third strongest party across the board. In polls, after the merger with the West German WASG (Arbeit und soziale Gerechtigkeit—Die Wahlalternative, Labour and Social Justice—the Electoral Alternative), it even represented the strongest political power east of the Elbe. Its recipe for success consisted of a program mixture that contained democratic socialism as a long-term goal but also had social political demands that followed the old Swedish welfare state, along with its character as a protest party.

The PDS was led and supported by old SED cadres from the second and third ranks of the party and in a few cases by old German leftists. Although it gained its power as a representative of the new federal states, it was unsuccessful until 2005 in the old federal states. Before the Bundestag elections in 2005, the PDS joined forces, first in the form of an alliance, later as a merger, with the WASG, which was founded in the last years of the Schröder-Fischer government. It thereby established itself as a pan-German left-wing party. The WASG was founded by social democratically oriented union members and social democrats who were dissatisfied with the economic and social policies of the

Gerhard Schröder government. The criticism was sparked by the so-called Hartz IV laws and the Agenda 2010, a program to modernize the welfare state by forming social policy under the rubric of support and demand. This attempt to integrate performance requirement elements into social policy was found by many, namely left-wing social democrats, to not be social democratic and to be unjust. With the alliance and later merger with the WASG the PDS was able for the first time to get a foothold across the board, even in the west of the Federal Republic. The merger was accompanied by a renaming of both parties to a newly founded party Die Linke (the Left) headed, along with representatives of the PDS, by the former SPD chairman Oskar Lafontaine in a double function as one of two party chairmen and as one of two faction chairmen in the German Bundestag.

With the establishment of a pan-German left-wing party, the last step has been taken for the time being in the development of the German party system into a five-party system. This step led from the clarity of a two camp system, which had existed since the 1980s, to a new, much more confusing, multiparty system without clear coalition perspectives, with the SPD caught between a conservative middle and a left-wing competitor party, which as long as it was in the opposition could always purport to be more social democratic and more for a welfare state than is possible for the SPD, which is involved in governmental responsibility. As long as the Left party is not accepted as a coalition partner at a federal level, in the near future there will probably be either a three-party coalition government led by the Union parties or the SPD or the continuation of a grand coalition of the CDU/CSU and the SPD.

It can already be seen today that sometime after 2009, presumably at the latest by 2013, the political quarantine of the Left will end, a development that is already becoming apparent at the state level where coalitions between the SPD and the PDS and joint efforts to elect a social democratic minister president (Ministerpräsident) are taking place.

It is still unclear whether the Left party represents a passing phenomenon or whether it will manage to establish itself in the long run. After the merger of PDS and WASG, there was an overlay of two cleavages that are more or less represented by the Left party, namely, the still existing and only very gradually attenuating east—west cleavage, which is politically represented by the PDS, and the revitalization that has come with the removal of the borders of the national state through Europeanization and globalization of an old—new cleavage between the once again increasing lower class and the rest of the population, between the relative have nots and haves, between the unemployed and those threatened with unemployment and the employed. These cleavages are represented by both the PDS section and the WASG section of the Left party, especially the latter. The social and political tensions resulting from these cleavages will remain in effect in Germany at least in the medium term. The cleavage between losers and winners will probably become more virulent because of the effects of the Agenda 2010 policy and the Hartz IV laws as well as of European-ization and globalization, which will probably intensify the differences between the poorly educated, those threatened with unemployment, or those already unemployed and the employed in the next few years. This development could be further enhanced by the ongoing global economic and financial crisis.

These sociopolitical processes are supported by the consequences of demographic change, the after effects of which are considered by large parts of the population to be unjust. Thus, the increase to 67 (from orig-inally 65) in the legal age for retirement by the large coalition is rejected by almost four-fifths of the population. The majority of voters react with outrage or at least quiet resignation to a further anticipated consequence of the demographic change, namely, the looming gradual decrease in the legal pension. In the meantime, more than two-thirds of the population believe that things are not being done justly in German society. The Left party has been taking political advantage of this increasing feeling of injustice in the past few years, whereas the speak-ers of the Left, the SPD chairman Oskar Lafontaine, and the former PDS chairman and current cofaction chairman Gregor Gysi are also ex-traordinarily talented agitators against the felt injustice.

This does not amount to the end of the differentiation in the German party system. Considering the existing voter potential, a further expan-sion of the party spectrum at the federal level toward the right is imag-inable and possible. Three extreme right-wing parties have been active in the 1990s and the first years of the new century: the Republicans (REP, Republikaner), the DVU (Deutsche Volksunion, German People's Union), and the NPD (Nationaldemokratische Partei Deutschlands, National Democratic Party of Germany). The REP, formed from a split-off from the CSU, quickly developed into a leading power of the extreme right wing at the beginning of the 1990s, but hardly plays a role today, as opposed to the DVU, which is currently (2009) repre-sented in two state parliaments, and the NPD, which is also repre-sented in two state parliaments with double-digit results. The party program and propaganda of the NPD in particular are clearly outside the democratic consensus. It has also been proven in several studies that the majority of the followers of these three right-wing groups are either convinced extremists or tending strongly in that direction.[7] There clearly exists a voter potential open to right-wing conservative and extreme right-wing positions, which, depending on the chosen cutting point, could be up to 15%.[8] In addition, the taboos based on the bur-dens of German history, which still influence political discourse and thoughts, become weaker as time goes by. Those whose circumstances are precarious owing to lower levels of education are particularly likely to be susceptible to extreme right-wing slogans. The voters of the Republicans, DVU, and especially the NPD relate more to the social and educational political composition of the lower class than all other parties.

The voters of extreme right-wing parties are characterized by an overlapping of ideology and protest. The probability of success of these parties increases in the case of deeper long-term economic crises and reasonably popular front men. In this respect the development of the German party system is by no means inevitably finished. With each year farther from World War II and the decline of the GDR, the probability grows that the "normality" that exists in other Western and Southern European countries will arrive in Germany.

VOTER SUPPORT AND PARTICIPATION IN PARTY POLITICS: CAUSES OF DECLINE

The present development of the German party system is accompanied by declining voter participation, an age-specific varying decrease of interest in politics, a change in information behavior, especially among the younger generation, and an increasing distrust of the parties and their representatives. The last is often subsumed in the term political disenchantment, which is not a well-chosen expression inasmuch as disenchantment with politics is hardly verifiable, but there is certainly a growing criticism, even a renunciation of established party politics and their representatives.

Political interest is sinking in different ways depending on age. While among the older age group, over 50, hardly any change can be determined in self-confessed political interest, the decrease of interest among the under 40 age group and especially among those under 30 is highly visible. Apart from peaks during specific critical times and at the climax of elections, politics play a subordinate role in the scale of values of the Germans, as well as all other inhabitants of Western and Northern Europe. Nonetheless, the gap between the generations regarding levels of self-declared political interest is striking. Fewer than 30% of the 18- to 30-year-olds describe themselves as being politically interested or very interested; among the older age groups, particularly the 60- to 70-year-olds, it is significantly more than 50%. This in spite of the increase in education, which in the meantime has led to almost 40% with a high school diploma or university entrance qualification, while with the 60-year-olds it is less than 20%.[9]

The decrease in political interest over the generations can be connected to a change in information behavior. Daily and weekly newspapers and the information programs of public television and public radio stations are hardly used by the generation under 30. There is a great difference in the television habits of the generations. The first and second German television networks (Erstes and Zweites Deutsches Fernsehen) and the Dritte Programme (third channels; regional channels of public television), with their comparatively high percentage of political programs, are watched by an audience that on average is over 50, but are scarcely watched by anyone under 30 years old. The younger and middle generations, especially the youngest viewers and listeners, rely almost entirely on private stations, which on average have very little political coverage. Entertainment has a higher subjective value than information, and news without the human touch is barely followed.

There is also an age-specific decrease in election participation. There was always an overrepresentation of the youngest age groups among the nonvoters, but the gap has never been as large as it is now. By far the largest participation in elections is found among the 60- to 70-year-olds, even if factors such as sickness, social isolation, and infirmity are controlled for the generation 70 and older. For the past three decades the Federal Republic has recorded at all election levels a substantial, in parts even dramatic, decrease in election participation. Although the citizens of the old Federal Republic participated very differently in elections, where the deciding factor seemed to be the respective esteem given to Parliament to be elected, in the meantime the gap has grown far more than in the 1970s and 1980s. Although voter participation at Bundestag elections is still at the international average level, strictly speaking even in the upper average level, it has fallen so low at local elections and especially European elections, but even at state elections, that the question of possible deficits in legitimacy are being questioned. Thus, voter participation at the European parliament election in 1994 was still at 60%, by 2004 (i.e., within only 10 years) it sank to 43% nationwide. In the old federal states the decline in voter participation at the European elections is even more dramatic. In 1979, 65.7%, almost two-thirds of the electoral register, took part in that year's election; in 2004, 45%, less than half of the electoral register, participated. That is a decrease of over 20%.[10]

A similarly large decrease in participation can be observed in local elections across the board in all federal states. Between 1984 and 2004, the average election participation at local elections in Baden-Württemberg decreased from 62.5% to 53.1%,[11] in Berlin from 85.3% in 1981 to only 55.8% in 2006.[12] The decrease was similar in Hesse, from 76.3% in 1981 to only 45.8% in 2006.[13] Moreover, the decrease is not limited to the old federal states. Strong losses can also be observed in the new federal states for the very much shorter period from 1990. In Saxony, for example, the participation in the county council elections between 1994 and 2004 plummeted from 73.6% to 48.2%. In Saxony-Anhalt the voter participation at the county council elections in 2007 was only 36.4%. Only a third participated at all in this type of election. Thus, within 13 years the voter participation in county council elections in Saxony-Anhalt dropped by half.

The same trend, if at a slightly higher level, can be seen in state elections. In Baden-Württemberg, voter participation decreased by 20% since 1988. In 2006, only every second person on the electoral register took part in the election of the Baden-Württemberg state parliament; in 1972 it was at least still 80%.[14] The same development occurred in Bavaria, Bremen, Hamburg, Hesse, and other states. On average, the participation in the last state parliament election in each of the old federal states was less than two-thirds of the electoral register, in 1966–1969 in the new federal states less than 60%. In contrast, in the mid-1970s, there was 80% participation in the state parliament elections in the old federal states.[15]

However, even in Bundestag elections a very strong decrease in voter participation can be noted at times. This is not reflected so strongly nationwide because in the comparative year 1990, the year of the reunification, voter participation was already unusually low at 77.8%. Compared to 1998, the loss in 2005 was around 5% nationwide. Since the 1970s the decline in voter participation in the old federal states has been on average 10% to15%.[16]

What lies behind this nationwide loss in election participation across all voter types? Does it represent nothing more than a tendency to normalization, as some observers assumed after the low participation in the first reunified election to the Bundestag in 1990, or is it a sign of increasing political disenchantment?

To attempt to answer these questions we can begin by noting that the loss in voter participation is not an isolated event. It has also been accompanied by a gradual but persistent shrinkage of the parties' memberships. Since 1990 the SPD has lost a third of its members, and in 2008 it was displaced by the CDU as the party with the greatest number of members in the Federal Republic. However, the CDU has not gone against the trend and become larger but rather simply has lost members more slowly than the SPD, so that the falling member curves met in mid-2008. Also the CDU has lost 200,000 members since the reunification. With the exception of the Greens and the special case of the Left party, this trend is valid for all parties. Only the CSU has managed to remain relatively constant compared to the reunification year. The membership loss was the highest in the PDS. Even if 1991 is used as the initial position, and not the exceptional year 1990, the PDS has lost two-thirds of its members during its existence, with a simultaneously rapid increase in the average age of the members. In the year of its merger with the WASG, it was, as far as members are concerned, by far the oldest party in the Federal Republic after the Greys (Die Grauen). In 1990, there were approximately 2.4 million party members in total in the Federal Republic. In 2005, there were only 1.5 million, a decrease of 900,000 in only 15 years. Seen relatively, that is a loss of almost 40%.[17]

It looks even worse in the youth organizations of some parties. The Jusos, the youth organization of the SPD, has lost almost four-fifths of its original members between 1975 and today. Also in the Young Christian Democrats (Junge Union), the youth organization of the CDU/CSU, the member loss was over 50% compared to the 1980s.[18]

During the same period, there was a downward trend in the number of people with long-term fixed associations with a party. What is meant here is emotional bonding, the feeling that one is more closely associated with a party through a certain level of identification with its goals and its personalities. In a poll in 1980 in the old federal states, four out of five on the electoral register indicated a party identification; in 2005 it was only two out of three, which represents a loss of 13%.[19] Additionally, citizens are increasingly prepared to change parties from election to election. If recall (i.e., the question of voting behavior in the previous election of the same type) is used as an indicator, party switchers have about doubled to 22% in the old federal states. In the new federal states, the number of the self-declared floating voters is about 25% to 32%.[20] Since self-disclosure in recall polls tends not to capture all floating voters, this must actually be an underestimation of their real number; panel interviews (polling the same people at two consecutive elections) raise the figure by 10%. It is probable that about a third of the voters in the old federal states change parties from one election to another; in the new federal states the likely figure is between 40% and 50%.[21]

The increase in floating voting behavior is accompanied by an increasing number of undecided who state in general polls that they do not yet know how they will vote. Their number increased between 1994 and 2005 from less than 7% to almost 24%. It is becoming more difficult to forecast elections, as the last-minute swing phenomenon is increasing and leads to more surprising results than before. In light of the decreased participation, the success or failure of the mobilization efforts of the parties play a more important role than at earlier elections.

It can be argued that these tendencies simply reflect the growing "normalization" of German politics connected to a general development process that can be seen in all Western industrial states and effective in areas other than politics, namely the process of individualization (i.e., the turning away of many people from collective forms of organization and a concomitant turning toward stronger private, sporadic, and individual-structured participation and association forms). It is not only membership in parties that has decreased in the observed period, but also membership in other important large organizations, such as trade unions and organized religion. The unions in the Federal Republic have lost about 40% of their members since 1991. In 15 years they went from almost 12 million to only 6.6 million members in 2006. The negative trend is a continual process; a short-term increase occurred in 2001 only. As a result of this development, the rate of unionization in Germany for blue- and white-collar workers has declined from 38.4% in 1991 to only 23.3% in 2002.[22]

The declining trend in members of both Christian denominations, the Catholics and the Protestants, is less dramatic but is also clear. The share of both Christian denominations in the population was reduced nationwide from 72.3% in 1990 to 62.6% in 2004. An explanation for this cannot be the increase in the Islamic population, since this grew only slightly from 3.2% to 3.9% in the same period. For the first time in 2005, polls in the Federal Republic showed slightly more Roman Catholics than Protestant church members. However, these figures represent the nominal membership, that is to say the number or share of church taxpayers, not the actual believers. But the development of commitment to the church followed a similar trend, as demonstrated by other indicators such as the frequency of church visits. In both the Protestant and Catholic churches, the number of regular church-goers, weekly in the Catholic churches, at least once a month in the Protestant churches, also decreased significantly.

These tendencies are important not only as other examples of lowered participation in large organizations, but also because the unions and the churches, especially the Catholic Church, have played an important role in structuring the German party system. The unions, closely associated with the SPD, provided a natural recruiting base for the SPD and served at the same time as transmission belts bringing social democratic beliefs into the factories. For decades both Christian denominations, especially the Catholic Church, formed the roots of the CDU and CSU. Even today union associated workers and employees vote well above the average for the SPD, and church-associated Catholics vote with much higher probability than the average voter for the CDU and CSU.

As these organizations shrink, so then does voter support for both large parties. In addition, both parties have lost important recruiting bases for new members. The decline in these supportive structures dramatically changes the traditional working-class environment and the Catholic rural and small town environment and not only contributes to the decline in the parties' own membership but also means that they are also losing the behavior-controlling, institutionally secured mechanisms of support and assurance that are only possible with large memberships and strong affiliations. Instead, we see a growth of profound political alienation. Satisfaction with democracy has greatly decreased, both in the old and in the new federal states. In the old federal states from about 70% in 1991 to less than 60% in 2005, in the new federal states during the same time period from 46 to less than 35%.[23]

The individualization reflected in the decrease of union and church affiliation helps explain these developments, but there are other factors. First, it is increasingly obvious that not only in the German political system but in almost all Western political systems, political parties play a thankless role. Party competition has an integral, theoretically absolutely intended element of conflict, which is intensified in elections. But at the same time there is a need for compromise in western election systems and party systems, at least in consensus democracies, leading to a need to build coalitions. Otherwise it would not be possible to form a government that could rule efficiently. The result is political sparring in elections featuring the proposal of maximum demands with minimum chances of success. This is built into the political system and can only be changed if fundamental institutional changes are made, for example, in the election system.

This structural deficit is compounded by the fact, that in light of the presently established five-party system in the Federal Republic, with the now 50-year-old system of proportional representation, the voter no longer knows which coalition his or her vote will put into office. It then follows that the parties cannot be measured by what they promised before the election, since at that time all parties present themselves as able to rule alone. Moreover, since they do not often know who their coalition partner will be, they also do not know what compromises they will need to make. As a result, it is only in exceptional cases that they can keep the election promises made during the election campaign. Only in the case of an absolute majority is it possible to take the party at its word. Through this structural defect in our election system, with which, in extreme cases, completely different coalitions are voted into office than voters had reason to expect when voting, disenchantment with politicians and parties is undoubtedly strengthened. Only fundamental institutional changes, for example, the introduction of stronger, majority-forming elements into the German voting system, could change this mechanism.

This problem is reinforced by the modern method of media-compatible election campaigning. Modern election campaigns are more and more centered on the candidate and programmatically diffuse; the parties make populist promises and thereby produce unavoidable voter disappointment. This dilemma could only be avoided if it were clear from the beginning which government the voter is choosing with his or her vote. In the meantime, an ever growing number of citizens do not trust either large party to solve the really important problems of the country. The share of those who believe in the competency of large parties to find solutions is smaller than ever before. Part of the dissatisfaction with democracy and the disappointment with its concrete performances certainly results from this fundamental conflict in the political system.

However, this fundamental conflict has existed for a long time, and it cannot explain why the trend in the past two decades has so greatly accelerated. In my opinion, the reasons for this acceleration are found in such fatal keywords as Europeanization and globalization and the development of an ever more borderless world. Through national policies, finance capital and large companies are no longer taxable to the same extent as before and, therefore, are largely free of party politically motivated actions. This is true for banks, insurance companies, heavy industry, all of the communication branches, and more and more for mid-sized industry as well. Politics now lacks the instruments of control; national state instruments are more and more insufficient, and transnational and supranational instruments have not yet been adequately developed.

As long as the national parties operate under the pretense that all is the same as in the good old times when everything seemed possible, as long as they present themselves to the voter as all-powerful, while at the same time having continually less power to influence, the disappointment of the citizen is preprogrammed. Disillusionment and resignation are the unavoidable results, the doubt of the competency of all parties to find solutions grows, and with it the beginning of a diffuse systemwide criticism.

There is an additional consideration for the Federal Republic. The system-stabilizing fundamental consensus of German society and German politics regarding many questions is in itself reassuring and allows party political conflicts to become mere political posturing, more and more transparent to the citizen. The period of directional decisions seems to be over, at least at the national level. Important decisions were made in the 1950s and 1960s regarding the social market economy, attachment to the West and German rearmament, NATO membership, and other factors. The great decisions in the 1970s to the 1990s concerned European Union (EU) integration, the reunification, and giving up the national currency for the euro. Almost all parties, apart from the extreme left wing, have long accepted the associated changes of direction, although some only after long adjustment and persuasion processes. However, this led to the fact that fundamental conflicts were hardly argued, at least not by the parties in the middle. Arguments about the right solutions for collectively shared goals are not exciting, and this also helps explain the decrease in election participation and party member numbers.

CONCLUSION: PROSPECTS FOR THE FUTURE

What is next for parties and democracy in Germany? If current trends continue, it is obvious that at some point in time the threshold to delegitimization will be crossed, a point difficult to specify in advance. But can this tendency be changed?

German rates of election participation, especially at the local and state levels, are very low compared to many other European nations.

Would the election participation increase if the voter knew which coalition or which government his or her vote would choose? Perhaps our party system, with six national parties represented in the Bundestag, cannot operate under the auspices of proportional representation. Yet international experience tells us differently. Majority election systems do not, on average, have more voter participation than proportional representation systems, but rather quite the opposite, even if there are other determining reasons for the low participation rates. In the case of proportional representation, there is uncertainty as to what parties will do with the vote given and with whom they will form a coalition, but in majoritarian elections votes that are given to the losing party in a constituency, save for the winning party, count for nothing.

As disenchantment with parties and politics grows, and there are disquieting signs of a kind of creeping away from the idea of democracy, another possibility may be considered. That is to give the citizen more co-decisive rights. According to many interviewees, not a small portion of the dissatisfaction with the parties and their representatives comes from the feeling of being excluded from the political decision process. Many would like to make decisions themselves. This has been possible at the local level in at least some German states for many years, particularly Bavaria and Baden-Württemberg. Here the disenchantment with political parties and politics is lower than in other states. In comparison, a possibility for participation at the national level hardly exists at all. The German constitution set forth only one specific point where the citizen can directly decide, namely, when it concerns an area change.[24] There is potential for expansion and improvement here, in the view of a majority of Germans. A look at other political systems teaches us that there are a wide range of possibilities from legislative initiatives, to petitions for referenda, to public opinion polls, to referenda. However, the highest form of citizen participation, the referendum at national level, comes up against a very serious constitutional obstacle in Germany, which is often gladly overlooked or played down by supporters of an expansion of direct democracy. In the constitution of the Federal Republic of Germany there is a so-called eternal clause, a clause that forbids forever and irreversibly a change in the constitution regarding certain points. Among those points is the fundamental participation of the states in the legislation process. This participation is currently provided via the Bundesrat (German Federal Assembly), the parliamentary representative of the state governments at the federal level. Referenda would be at least made difficult and complicated by the participation right of the states guaranteed by the eternal clause. However, all possible forms of expansion of participation are conceivable at the next lower level. This is potentially a path that could be taken to counter the creeping legitimacy crisis of the political system and enhance the future relationship between parties and democracy in the Federal Republic of Germany.

CHAPTER 3

The Three Ages of Party Politics in Postwar Italy

Piero Ignazi

INTRODUCTION

Parties are essential to democracy. Without parties (in the plural), no political system could be defined as a democracy. Yet parties have long been seen in many countries as a liability rather than a resource. This is because parties have not been at ease in performing two—among other—particular functions: channeling the volitions of the mass public (or, at least, of their voters) to the officials, and channeling the party members' opinions to the party leadership. A democratic political system requires parties to be responsive and accountable to the mass public, since the decision makers are chosen by and through parties, and the policies are defined by partisan policy makers. But their responsiveness and accountability follow yet another route, the party's internal structure. Thus, parties themselves are required to be democratic in order to guarantee the full democratization of the system. The two above-mentioned functions have different degrees of acceptance: while the first systemic function is universally ascertained and accepted, the second has an opaque and uncertain recognition. In fact, parties may not be fully democratic in their internal mechanics, yet operate in a democratic setting. This disjunction between a party's internal dynamic and the feature of the (democratic) system in which parties operate is at the heart of the clumsy legitimacy of parties in many countries.

This chapter will follow this double track. On one side, I will analyze parties' relationship with the system, in other words, investigate the role Italian parties played in establishing and enforcing democracy as well as how they may have harmed the democratic system through their discourse or their activity. On the other side, I will investigate whether Italian parties adopted a democratic (i.e., open, accountable, and responsive) internal system, thereby respecting the democratic principles supposedly guiding the state.

THE GOLDEN AGE: THE AFTER-WAR STRENGTH AND FULL LEGITIMACY OF PARTIES

The establishment of a multiparty democracy in Italy after the collapse of the fascist regime at the end of World War II did not follow the same path as in the other European countries that had suffered the same authoritarian rule in the 1930s and 1940s. What was unique about the Italian way was the dominant role—and according to some the monopolist role—played by political parties in the establishment of democracy.[1]

When King Vittorio Emanuele III arrested the head of the fascist regime, Benito Mussolini, on July 25, 1943, after the Gran Consiglio del Fascismo (a sort of executive committee of the fascist regime) had passed a vote of no confidence to Mussolini himself, the regime collapsed, and a certain degree of liberalization was introduced. Six weeks later, on September 8, 1943, when the armistice with the Allied forces was signed, the state itself collapsed. The ambiguity of the armistice message broadcast to the population, the absence of any order whatsoever in the army and its inability to decide whether to join the Allies and combat the German troops or remain neutral, and the escape of the king, the government, and the civil and military headquarters from Rome to the south left the country in complete disarray. In that dramatic phase, when no authority was apparently on duty, the antifascist parties emerged from their clandestine life and took political power back into their own hands by forming a National Liberation Committee (Comitato Nazionale di Liberazione), by supporting the first nonfascist government since 1922, and then (April 1944) by entering directly into the government.

This was just the beginning of the involvement of political parties in the direct rule of the country. From the autumn of 1943 until the end of the war (April 25, 1945), antifascist militias fought against the newly established fascist regime in the north of Italy, backed by Germany. This development brought even more involvement of, and legitimization to, political parties. The antifascist militias were in fact composed, to a large extent, by groups aligned along partisan lines: The communists and socialists, together in the Garibaldi "brigades," were by far the most numerous followed by the liberal-radicals and the Catholics. That part of the Italian army that had remained loyal to the crown also participated in the military activities, fighting beside the Allied forces in their conquest of the peninsula. However, the bulk of the fight was conducted by the antifascist partisan militias in the area occupied by the fascist and German troops in the center-north of Italy for almost two years until the very end of the war. The partisans' guerrilla warfare had much more impact than the Italian army's low-profile cooperation with the Allied troops, since the partisan operations were conducted amid the population with high risks and causalities. The parties themselves used those activities as a propaganda tool to vindicate their primary role.[2]

Italian democracy was thus established thanks to the participation of political parties at two levels: at the grassroots level with the military actions of the partisans' militias, which cost thousands of causalities, and at the central level with direct participation in the governments of the liberated part of Italy between the armistice and the end of the war.

This path is completely different from the one followed by Germany or France. In Germany political parties had been destroyed by the brutal Nazi rule and there was no clandestine activity even in the last months of war. As a consequence, parties were "re-created" by the Allied powers and were subject to their approval and monitoring: no autonomous role was given to them in the immediate aftermath of the war. In France parties did play a role in the fight against the German occupation, but their authority and prestige were counteracted and downsized by the charismatic figure of General Charles de Gaulle, who imposed his seal on the country's liberation.

Only in Italy was the liberation to a large extent due to the contribution of parties, or, to put it in a different way, were parties able to create a strong narrative on their major role. At the same time, no other domestic actor could compete with them by providing an alternative narrative. Moreover, parties were accepted as legitimate partners by the Allies (by the Americans more than by the British) during the war, and thus there was no invasive surveillance by them over party activities after the war. The contrast with the German case could not be more vivid.

The party primacy in the Italian system thus had a solid basis: It was founded on the parties' crucial role in establishing the new system. Their legitimacy as pillars of the new democratic system was widely accepted. Only minor fringes expressed an antipolitical and partisan feeling in the first postwar years. This sentiment was voiced by a magazine and later by a political movement (L'Uomo Qualunque—The Common Man), which reframed the Italian traditional populist, antiestablishment, and antipolitical sentiment, addressing it to the "parties of the North" that wanted to impose a hyperpoliticization of common life. This message was directed to that part of the population that had not experienced the 1943–1945 civil war. Since the civil war was basically fought in the center-north of the country, the southern constituency, plus Rome, had remained extraneous to the experience and insensitive to the epic of the liberation war. Therefore, the parties that had led the partisans' militia were not perceived in the south in the same way as in the north. The antipolitics feeling emerged in support for the L'Uomo Qualunque list in the first election of the Constituent Assembly on June 2, 1946. This movement was not even an official party, but individuals grouped around the magazine of its flamboyant editor (Guglielmo Giannini) and collected 5.3% of the votes, almost all in the southern constituencies. However, two years later, in 1948, in the first election for Parliament, this movement lost all its votes and disappeared shortly afterward. But the dissatisfaction and suspicion vis-à-vis parties continued and came to the surface again.

In the early 1950s, these sentiments manifested themselves in a different way.[3] Now they were voiced by two antisystem parties rather than by a populist anti-politics one such as the L'Uomo Qualunque. These two antisystem parties were the neo-fascist Movimento Sociale Italiano (Italian Social Movement [MSI]) and the monarchist Partito Democratico di Unità Monarchica (Democratic Party of Monarchic Unity [PDIUM]). (See appendix for list of parties discussed in this chapter.) Both were already present in the first parliamentary elections of 1948, but they scored much better results in the following decade, especially in local elections. The appeal fostered by both parties, while similar on certain topics such as nostalgia for the "old times," respectively, the fascist regime and the monarchical past, differed in tune and style. The neo-fascists rejected the democratic political system because of their ideological commitment to fascism; the monarchists did not refuse the democratic system as such, but advocated the return to a monarchical form of state and bitterly contested the result of the referendum on this issue held in June 2, 1946, where the republican form of government won a slim majority over the monarchist model.

Moreover, the antisystem profile of these two parties was expressed in different forms. The MSI was much more militant and did not rule out the use of direct and even violent actions. The monarchists stayed low profile and relied more on notables' consent and clientelistic practices (the most famous of which was the Neapolitan wealthy shipowner Achille Lauro, who distributed to his supposed voters only one shoe before the election and the other after the ballot). The monarchists' approach was in tune with the regional concentration of the party constituency in the south of the country where this political style still survived.

Both antisystem parties focused their antagonism to the democratic system especially on the (antifascist and republican) political parties, since they were directly responsible for the establishment of the new political system. Different from the apolitical distrust of parties represented by L'Uomo Qualunque, MSI and PDIUM contested the role of political parties not because of their inefficiency, corruption, selfishness, oligarchical structure, or other perceived faults, but because of their mere existence, given their primary role in re-creating (republican) democracy. Their opposition to all the other political parties was, in a way, "ontological."

However, the neo-fascist and monarchist polemic did not profit them for long. After an increase in votes and membership in the early-1950s, they lost attractiveness. By the 1950s, the party system had in fact consolidated itself.[4]

The party system that emerged after the war kept its basic features almost unaltered until its collapse in 1994. It was structured in an extreme multiparty format—at least seven relevant parties—with very minor changes in the late 1970s, and in a polarized type since it displayed a high ideological distance and a divisive and adversarial style of party competition. That party system collapsed abruptly in 1994 (see below), leaving room for new parties and different dynamics. The change was so dramatic (volatility was even greater than it had been between the Fourth and Fifth French Republics) that the two phases are treated separately in this analysis.

The axis of the pre-1994 party system was the Democrazia Cristiana (Christian Democracy [DC]), a Catholic party whose votes ranged from 35% to 40% until the 1980s, and that kept the premiership until 1981 and entered all governments until 1993. The DC claimed to have more than one million members during that time, plus a large network of Catholic associations directly or indirectly sponsored by the Catholic Church. The second party was the Partito Comunista Italiano (Italian Communist Party [PCI]), whose votes ranged from 25% to 30%; it never entered any governments after the breakdown of the all-parties antifascist coalition in May 1947, but it was by far the most strongly organized party with around 1.5 million members and a large and penetrating network of flanking organizations. Third was the Partito Socialista Italiano (Italian Socialist Party [PSI]), which never gained more than 15% of the vote and became a member of a government coalition only after 1964. Quite often less than 5% of the votes were for the three so-called minor secular parties: Partito Socialista Democratico Italiano (Italian Social-Democratic Party [PSDI]), Partito Repubblicano Italiano (Italian Republican Party [PRI]), and Partito Liberale Italiano (Italian Liberal Party [PLI]). Despite their small size, their location in the political space—and the ability of their high-profile leaderships—made them indispensable partners of almost all the governing coalitions, albeit with a sort of rotation among them. Marginalized and excluded from any government coalition were the MSI and the monarchists, whose votes hardly surpassed the 5% threshold (except for the 1972 election where the MSI scored 8.7%).[5]

In the era of the first party system (1945–1994), parties played different roles in relation to the reinforcement, or weakening, of the democratic rule. In the first years, from the collapse of fascism to the early 1950s, parties benefited from general acceptance, as already noted. Together they collected millions of members, mobilized even more people directly or indirectly through their web of flanking organizations had local branches everywhere, promoted a continuous flow of initiatives (not only strictly political, but also formative, cultural, leisure, social, etc.), and had intense internal participation. In that phase, Italian politics was very pervasive and intense, thanks to the activities of political parties. Even those antisystem parties (MSI and to a lesser extent PDIUM, but not the PCI) that contested the legitimacy of the party system had nonetheless adopted the same organization model of the other parties: the mass party model.

As early as the 1950s, all Italian parties (with some reluctance by the most bourgeois ones such as the liberals and the monarchists) had adopted the mass party model. This party model needs some conditions to work effectively: the openness of the parties to the population, membership incentives to participate, and a bottom-up democratic internal decision-making process. In other words the mass party model presupposes a democratic external environment (that is, a democratic political system) as well as a democratic internal environment (that is, a democratic party organization).

In a phase of collective enthusiasm, such as during the (re)establishment of freedom and democracy after a period of authoritarian rule, this kind of party model is more likely to prosper compared to other models. People are eager to involve themselves because they have discovered the "pleasure" of freedom and, by consequence, they require various loci where their participatory drive can be expressed. In postwar Italy, such conditions for mass party success were there. But that phase never lasts long and is bound to vanish sooner or later. The recent examples of the democratization in the Mediterranean countries in the mid- to late 1970s and in the central-eastern European countries in the 1990 demonstrate how rapidly the euphoria for regime change vanishes, giving way to the *desencanto*. Political parties are the first to suffer the blow, becoming the target of antipolitics and antiestablishment feelings.

In postwar Italy the decline of confidence in, and support for, political parties took time to formulate. The delay was due to the legitimacy political parties had gained in the aftermath of the 1943 armistice when they supplanted an evaporated state authority and led the liberation war against Nazi fascism. The party role in that historical passage was particularly important because it enabled parties to face the contestation occasioned by extreme right antisystem parties as well as by deeply rooted attitudes of mistrust and wariness vis-à-vis the political institutions that parties actually embodied at the time. On the other hand, the wave of politicization in the 1940s and 1950s, exemplified by the strengthening of political parties adopting the mass party format, might also be attributed to the fascist heritage: The mass mobilization induced by the Fascist Party to accomplish its totalitarian project of full control of the society, had brought—or forced—into politics large sectors of the population never before politicized.[6] This encounter with politics via the (sole) party might have counteracted the traditional sense of "extraneousness" vis-à-vis politics held by a large part of the population.

Whether totalitarian socialization to politics in the prewar two decades, or collective enthusiasm for the recasting of freedom, or the positive role played by political parties for the country's liberation from Nazi fascism was the most important factor, but all these cooperated in producing participative and working parties. In sum, until the end of the 1950s Italian parties enjoyed a favorable wind. They were strong and legitimate. It was a golden age for them.

The democratic system profited from parties' strength and legitimacy. Since parties provide the primary linkage between civil society and the state, their good health reinforces democratic institutions. Even antisystem parties of the right such as the MSI and the PDIUM, and of the left, such as the PCI, did not harm democracy so much. What these parties offered was a coherent antisystem proposal, antithetical to the republican-liberal-capitalist system. All three presented radically alternative worldviews and institutional settings. Although these political attitudes and proposals were dangerous for the democratic system, these parties—particularly, the communists—nevertheless performed the function of "negative integration" for millions of people. The PCI, in particular, brought into the political sphere what Stein Rokkan[7] described as "inarticulated masses" and socialized its members to democratic rules. Paradoxically, the antisystem parties themselves played an important role in stabilizing Italian democracy, not through their open, vocal antisystem rhetoric, but rather through their mass mobilization that could not break the legal democratic set of rules and was rather forced to follow (with some exceptions) the institutional, thus democratic, channels. Finally, the internal party life was inevitably osmotic to the external context. For example, both PCI and MSI paid homage to the democratic bottom-up procedure for the delegates' selection for their party congresses and for the election of party officials. Although the PCI adopted democratic centralism and the MSI a mild version of the *Führerprinzip*, they both had to relax somewhat their organizational philosophy and acquaint themselves with the one man-one vote rule and the principle of delegation.

THE IRON AGE: THE PARTIES' HOLD ON THE SYSTEM AND THE DEVELOPMENT OF PARTOCRACY

The golden age of parties declined in the late 1950s. Two intertwined factors operated to enfeeble their position in public opinion. The first concerns the societal changes affecting all European societies: the decline of ideology and the loosening of class and religious identities due to economic development and secularization; the second concerns the parties' penetration in the public administration and state-controlled economy (which in Italy was, by far, larger than in any other capitalist country). The expansion of the role of the state in the economic and financial sector and the diffusion of electronic media created new opportunities for the (governing) parties to colonize multiple sectors of society, far beyond the simple handover of the agencies of public administration. This party penetration into so many societal spheres came to be labeled as partitocrazia (partocracy), which literally means "party power" but actually meant "party autocracy." Together with this phenomenon, cases of sleaze and corruption by party officials became more common and better known. Clientelistic, unfair, and dishonest behavior by partisan officials reached the highest level among the industrialized countries (with a partial exception of Japan).[8] Few, scattered, and unsystematic data are available until the 1980s, but journalistic accounts and judiciary investigations depict an uncontroversial picture of widely diffused party colonization over the public administration and the public sector of the economy accompanied by a high level of dishonest and corrupt practices. This pattern of behavior concerned the governing parties only—and thus communists and neo-fascist parties were untouched—but it nevertheless projected a negative image on all political parties. The combination of parties increasing power and declining legitimacy affected citizens' involvement and militants' mobilization. Even if the electoral turnout did not decline significantly and the parties still exhibited high levels of membership, the parties' internal participation declined. The catch-all party model supplanted the mass party model in almost all Italian parties.[9] Only the two bilateral oppositions, PCI and MSI, mainly because of their rigid exclusion from the governmental area and partly because of their ongoing recourse to ideological discourse, slowed down the passage to "catchallism."

This general tendency, as Otto Kirchheimer lamented at the time, depressed party legitimacy in general, and, in particular, weakened Italy's democracy. Since Italian democracy, as stated earlier, was indebted to political parties for its establishment, the legitimacy crisis of parties impacted democracy itself.

Dissatisfaction erupted in the late 1960s. Student and blue-collar social movements in 1968–1969 constituted the most visible and vocal reactions to the party stalemate. They addressed their protest against the (capitalist-bourgeois) "system" as such, but they also targeted, albeit for very different reasons and with very different impact, the communist and the neo-fascist oppositions, notwithstanding they were the least responsible for the party colonization of the society. The reason these opposition parties (and much more the large PCI rather than the small MSI) were touched lies in their internal structural and attitudinal characteristics, similar to all the other (governing) parties. More precisely, it concerned their lack of openness to the civil society and their disdain of effective internal democratic procedures. All parties were charged with being bureaucratic, closed, authoritarian, and insensitive to the demands of the people—and especially of the youth—and thus "antidemocratic." Even if the social movements of that period were imbued with neo-Marxist revolutionary rhetoric, the "direct participation"—la prise de parole, to use a slogan of the French 1968 student revolt—was at the top of the movement's goals.

All these charges, which concerned the PCI for its democratic centralism principle and the MSI for its caesarism (a mild version of the Führerprinzip), invaded the DC, too, although with a different set of motives. The DC was under attack from the Catholic movements mobilized by the demand for renovation brought by the Council Vatican II (1962–1965). The DC was accused of having lost spirituality and its sense of mission for human emancipation, devoting instead itself to the mere seeking of power. As a consequence, the Catholic movements declared it was impossible to continue direct involvement in party activities. This fissure deprived the DC of the more devout and militant component and the detachment of the most religious activists depressed the party's standing in terms of moral reliability even more.

The social movements of the "cycle of protest" in 1968–1969 complained about a democratic deficit in the political system in general and inside political parties, too, irrespective of their presence in government. This criticism, which continued far beyond the movement's peak of mobilization and spread out in other, even elite, sectors of the society, did not produce any reaction by the parties. The parties did not change their internal life or their relationship with the civil society. There was much talk about the malaise of the society, youth unrest, and so on, on one side, and the inability of the parties to respond to the new environment, on the other side, but no relevant internal party reform was enforced nor was any change in the party-civil society relationship introduced.[10]

Little changed until a scandal erupted in the early 1970s, related to oil-trade briberies with (many) partisan complicities, which gave the parties the opportunity to introduce, in 1974, the state financing of parties. All parties, with the exception of the tiny PLI, voted in favor of the bill with the motivation that, since the parties would finally be provided with enough money, corruption and illegal financing would no longer be "necessary." This assumption proved to be dramatically false, as the Clean Hands operation would show later in the early 1990s. But even before that shakeup, the public had an opportunity to express its disapproval. A referendum was called in 1978 to cancel the bill on parties' state financing by a very minor political party, one devoid of parliamentary representation, the libertarian Partito Radicale (Radical Party [PR]), and produced an astonishing result. Although the cancellation was supported by parties and groups well below 5% of votes in previous elections (plus the MSI split on the side to take), it received 43% of the popular vote. The distance between voters and established parties thus emerged in all its amplitude.

A third, much sterner attack on parties, beyond the 1968–1969 social movements and the 1978 referendum, was put forward by terrorist groups throughout the 1970s. During that decade, not by chance labeled the iron years for the high level of political violence, parties were criticized by public opinion for their inefficiency and inability to tackle that challenge. Although criticism was raised in the late 1960s by the social movements and by large sectors of public opinion in the intellectual sphere and in the mass public, mainly concerning parties' honesty, accountability, and openness, the criticism raised during the iron years concerned their ability to respond, particularly to the growing number of terrorist attacks: bombing by radical right terrorist groups and killings and kidnappings by radical left terrorist groups. Parties were forced to demonstrate that they were still a bastion of democracy. Similar to the aftermath of World War II, they were given the opportunity to impose themselves at the center of the political system, escape the charge of irrelevance, and, at the same time, reject the temptation of an authoritarian response to terrorism. Finally, after the 55-day-long kidnapping and subsequent killing of the prominent DC leader Aldo Moro by the Red brigades, all parties, but especially the DC, the pillar of the system—not by chance often called the "party-state" in that period-reacted with vigor and identified their survival with the survival of democracy. Thanks to this equation and to a more efficacious counteracting of terrorism (which by 1982 was totally dismantled), parties were able to put aside the public's queries on their transparency, honesty, and fair internal working and gained a bonus of legitimacy for several more years.

Paradoxically, Italy's "lead years" reinforced the parties' standing in public opinion because they resisted and won without endangering the democratic system. The antiterrorist laws did not harm the rule of law, and social and political radical dissent was not demonized or restricted. In sum, parties were still perceived as bastions of democracy. To a certain extent, they regained a positive role for the "stability" of the system, if not for its working and its efficiency.

THE RUST AGE: THE ERUPTION OF HIDDEN IMPATIENCE AND THE COLLAPSE OF THE PARTY SYSTEM

In the 1980s parties fully recovered their primary role. Neither social movements that had largely vanished during the previous decade nor other social and political actors, all virtually inexistent or largely irrelevant, challenged the party dominance. Nor had any sizable change in the party system emerged to justify the recasting of the old order. The format of the party system had remained anchored with the same parties presented in the first 1948 Parliament, still well entrenched in the present Parliament and exhibiting more or less the same relative dimension (but for a decline of the DC), now flanked by very small newcomers—the two postmaterialist parties, Radicals and Greens—which never met the 5% threshold for representation in Parliament. The dynamic of the party system, on the other hand, had displayed signs of deradicalization of the political conflict, even as polarization remained quite high.[11] The distance between the rightmost and the leftmost parties had remained somewhat stable, the largest among European countries.[12]

However, this stability negatively affected political parties. The persisting absence of a government alternative, given the resilience of anti-system parties (even if the PCI was less and less perceived in this way) at the two poles, favored ever more uninhibited behavior regarding the extraction of financial resources by the governing parties (DC, PSI, PSDI, PRI, PLI). Between 1979 and 1987, 60 billion liras, that is 75% of the total of state funding for parties, were illegally allocated to those parties.[13] By the turn of the century the amount the governing parties received illegally was estimated at 10 times (!) the official budget for party funding.[14] The sclerosis of a party system, immutable for decades, and its generalized clientelistic and corrupt practices distanced citizens from parties. In 1986 almost 80% had negative attitudes toward political parties, politicians, and politics in general.[15] Moreover, the percentage of the public who were "much" or "somewhat" interested in politics halved between 1985 and 1990, plummeting to 17%; and in 1990, 36% of the people declared themselves to be "little" interested in politics and 47% "not at all"; 83% considered politics an extraneous and alien world, and 79% rated parties "not interested in the opinion of people like me."[16] Finally, the percentage of those who were not attached to any party rose from 25% in 1980 to 35% in 1990.[17] The persistent high level of membership and party identification (53% declared that they would continue to vote for the same party "irrespective of the errors it might have committed")[18] plus the parties' hold on various sectors of the economy projected a more apparent than real image of strength. Underneath, a creeping sentiment of distrust was growing. The window of opportunity for expressing this sentiment came at the beginning of the 1990s. The magistrates' investigation into the political briberies and corruption in Milan—known as Clean Hands—then spread all over the country and unveiled to the public the enormous dimension of the phenomenon, creating a general uproar. Actually, everybody knew about it, but it had never been demonstrated so clearly and, above all, never conceded openly by prominent national politicians. That investigation, which started in February 1992 with the first wave of arrests, provoked the downfall of all five governing parties, leaving untouched the former antisystem oppositions, the communists and neo-fascists.

Among all the speculations advanced as the reasons for the sudden, catastrophic collapse of the governing parties, one stands out: those parties had lost legitimacy. The indulgence that public opinion and mass media had offered to the governing parties in spite of their lamentable behavior could not hold any longer because the premises of the party system dynamic had changed: the collapse of the Berlin Wall and the consequent profound transformation the PCI undertook (adopting the name of Partito Democratico della Sinistra [Democratic Party of the Left or PDS] in 1991) had implicitly lifted the ban on that party. The dam against the "communist danger," which had justified for so long any and all acts of corruption by the governing parties, no longer worked.

Thus, the general sentiment of distrust toward parties already circulating in the electorate at large for a long time "exploded" when given the opportunity of the Clean Hands investigation. When the magistrates, given extensive media coverage, revealed with abundance of evidence the dimension of illegal financing and corruption and the responsibility of the top party leaders, four of five governing parties practically disappeared.

Only the DC, transforming itself into the Partito Popolare Italiano (Italian Popular Party [PPI]), somewhat resisted, even if in 1994 it lost more than half of the votes it received in 1992, and its organization was radically downsized. The crisis that flooded the governing parties in 1994 also demonstrated how the internal life of those parties had become more and more inconsistent with a democratic system. All internal control mechanisms had been bypassed, the voice of concerned members went unheard, and the leadership's accountability and responsiveness had become nonexistent. These considerations reintroduce the question of the democracy within parties.

As already stated, Italian parties of what is sometimes called the "first republic" (that is, until 1994) had progressively adopted a homogeneous model of organization following, first, the mass party model, and then, with a different pace, the catch-all model. Criticism for the bureaucratic, close, unaccountable features of traditional parties had emerged since the 1960s and increased in the 1970s, favored by the societal mood of unrest and contestation, but the parties did not react to these criticism and challenges. Not even the rise of libertarian postmaterialist parties organized along the principles of what Thomas Poguntke has called *basis-demokratie* induced parties to change their internal arrangements.[19] However, some innovations had been introduced by the three main parties (DC, PCI, and PSI), although for quite different reasons and with quite different outcomes.

The DC has always been a highly factionalized party. Internal democracy was "forced," and actually implemented, by the struggle among factions. Internal participation was stimulated by each faction in order to get positions in the internal competition and thus gain offices, resources, and so forth. Democratic procedures were invoked by the minority factions so as not be wiped out by the dominant coalition and thus excluded from the spoils system. The steady encroachment of the party into the state-controlled economy and in the public administration and the consequent hemorrhage of its most religious components after the 1960s left room for a ruthless internal struggle, with the distribution of resources (the selective and material incentives) at stake. Factions were compensated with positions in the party internal structure, which could ensure an adequate level of extraction of resources. Internal democracy was conceived not in terms of leadership accountability and responsiveness but rather in terms of fair access to resources. In the 1980s, the DC introduced some changes in order to open the party. For example, it created a national body of high-profile Catholics willing to support the party but not to become full members. This assembly produced many interesting papers and proposals, but very few (if any) were taken into consideration and actually implemented by the party leadership. Other internal reforms of that period were intended to strengthen the linkage between the national leadership and the local (regional) party officials. But these latter reforms were sabotaged by the faction's rival to the party secretary, claiming to fear that local leaders would no longer be responsive to the party's rank-and-file membership but only to the national leadership. This claim was, of course, perfectly democratic, but the real goal was not to lose the bargaining power in the allocation of internal and external resources at the local level. Further attempts to centralize decision making in the hands of the party leader failed, again because of the fear of an excessive concentration of power that might marginalize the other factions and thus their access to the spoils of power.[20]

The PSI also had a long tradition of ruthless factionalism. However, in the late 1970s the new party leader, Bettino Craxi, was more successful than his DC counterpart. The party introduced many reforms along the line of centralization of power: a concentration of the decision making in the national executive through the transformation of the central committee into a very large and powerless structure, the direct election of the secretary in Congress, and the secretary's direct control over the activities of the different departments of the party. All these reforms were intended to reduce factionalism and increase efficiency and leadership control. By the 1980s the mission was accomplished thanks in part to the resources the party leadership had acquired by adopting an aggressive attitude toward the DC in the managing of the spoils system. The PSI party leader now had a never before seen concentration of

power in his hands and went totally uncontested in the remaining period of his office.

The PCI followed a different route. The organizational principles of
the democratic centralism prohibited any organized faction inside the
party. Dissent could be expressed (if one really wanted to) inside the
party organs, but no external transmission of such dissenting opinion
was allowed. Once the party adopted a position, everybody was
obliged to follow it. The question of the PCI democratic standard was
often raised by the other parties as a polemic tool; but inside the PCI
itself, not only because of the democratic centralism principle but also
for the intensity of the political identification and commitment, very
few raised the issue until the party faced its first (albeit small indeed)
electoral backlash in 1987. After that moment, the demand for a relaxa-
tion of the practice of democratic centralism (already slightly relaxed at
the 1983 congress) mounted from within. The post-1989 congresses
(1990 and 1991), which decided the party's overall transformation,
finally introduced democratic rules.[21]

ITALIAN PARTIES AND DEMOCRACY SINCE 1994: NEW PARTIES, (SOME) OLD HABITS

After the 1994 shakeup, new or deeply renewed parties composed
the party system of the "second republic." Beyond the heirs of traditional parties, such as the PDs (ex-PCI), the PPI and CCD (both stemming from DC), and the AN (ex-MSI), two new parties gained the stage:
the Lega Nord, operating since the late 1980s as a fringe regionalist movement but expanding to medium-sized dimension nationally and becoming dominant regionally in the 1990s, and, above all, Forza Italia, the
party founded by the media tycoon Silvio Berlusconi at the beginning of
1994, on the eve of the general elections of that year. These parties, for
quite different reasons and with different aims, introduced many innovations in their organizations. In addition, their relationship with democratic institutions (in terms of system support) proved quite different
compared to the parties rooted in the pre-1994 party system (former communists, Christian Democrats, and neo-fascists) (Table 3.1).

As for the party's internal changes, the general trend of the post-1994
Italian parties could be summarized as: (1) higher centralization and
verticalization of internal power, (2) less relevance for the membership
and local units, (3) growing relevance of the elected officers, and (4)
skyrocketing personalization.

Higher Centralization and Verticalization of Internal Powers

Centralization of internal power means the reduction of functions
and prerogatives by the collective bodies in favor of the executive ones,

Table 3.1 Elections to the Camera dei Deputati (Chamber of Deputies), 1994 and 1992

	1994[1]			1992		
	Votes	*Votes (%)*	*Seats*	*Votes*	*Votes (%)*	*Seats*
Segni Pact/Patto Segni	1,795,270	4.6	13	—	—	—
Democratic Alliance/Alleanza Democratica (AD)	452,396	1.2	18	—	—	—
Go Italy/Forza Italia	8,119,287	21.0	134	—	—	—
National Alliance/Alleanza Nazionale (AN)	5,202,698	13.5	109	2,103,692	5.4	34
North League/Lega Nord	3,327,026	8.4	117	3,394,917	8.7	55
Pannella List-Reformers/Lista Pannella-Riformatori	1,355,73	3.5	6	485,339	1.2	7
Popular Party/Partito Popolare (PPI)	4,268,940	11.1	33	11,627,657	29.7	206
Party of the Democratic Left/Partito Democratico della Sinistra (PDS)	7,855,610	20.4	109	6,315,815	16.1	107
Communist Refoundation/Rifondazione Comunista (RC)	2,334,029	6.0	39	2,202,574	5.6	35
Greens/Verdi	1,042,496	2.7	11	1,092,783	2.8	16
Socialist Party/Partito Socialista Italiano (PSI)	841,739	2.2	14	5,336,358	13.6	92
The Network/La Rete	718,403	1.9	6	728,661	1.9	12
Republican Party/Partito Repubblicano Italiano (PRI)	—	—	—	1,721,658	4.4	27
Social-Democratic Party/Partito Socialdemocratico Italiano (PSDI)	—	—	—	1,063,048	2.7	16
Liberal Party/Partito Liberale Italiano (PLI)	—	—	—	1,119,492	2.9	17
Others	—	3.5	5	—	5.3	6

[1] In 1994 a new electoral system was introduced. Three-fourths of the seats were allotted with a plurality system (first past the post) and one-quarter of the seats with a PR with clause of representation of 4% of the votes nationally. This is why some parties—such as the Lega Nord, for example—increased their seats even if their share of votes had remained the same.

and verticalization means the concentration of the decision-making power in the national leadership and executive organs to the detriment of the lower strata of the party. In approximately the past 15 years, the collective bodies, intermediate organs between the congress and the executive, such as the central committees, lost relevance, either through formal reduction of functions or, more commonly, through the inflation of the number of their members. Having become unmanageable and plethoric assemblies, the collective bodies have been marginalized. Similarly, the balance in the center-periphery relationship is now skewed toward the center. The executive organs and the leadership itself increased control over the composition and function of the lower strata. The inflated number of ex-officio members and leadership cooptation in the local bodies have become standard operating procedures, with some differences among the parties. The left-libertarian parties, Greens and Radicals, have more or less escaped that trend since they continued to practice *basis-demokratie* and thus limited the centralization and verticalization of their organization.

The PDS took the name of DS in 1998 and since then began introducing a series of changes in the number, composition, mode of selection, and functions of the national bodies (including the mode of election of the secretary), a set of reforms which ended in the mid-2000s only with its further transformation into the Partito Democratico (Democratic Party [PD]) in 2007. The PDS-DS allowed many degrees of freedom to the local echelons and did not consistently pursue centralization, especially given the repeated modification of its central structures. This whirling alternation in the organizational chart reduced the potential for the hardening of power in leadership's hands.

The center-right parties, Lega Nord (Northern League [LN]), Forza Italia (Go Italy! [FI]), and Alleanza Nazionale (National Alliance [AN]) were much more concerned with the problem of control over central collective bodies and peripheral structures. These three parties have, however, chosen different routes. The LN never had large central bodies and kept this line even after its electoral breakthrough. Moreover, since it was conceived as a federal party (made of the various regional leagues), it has limited access to the executive bodies of each regional league. At the top of everything, the party leader from the beginning, Umberto Bossi, dominates unchallenged, profiting from his charismatic appeal. He pays lip service to the party's democratic and collective decision making, but in fact he is the absolute leader and often uses mass rallies to reinforce his charismatic appeal. In the recent past, attempts by some factions (for example the Venetian league) to challenge the leadership ended in massive expulsions.

FI shares with LN the charismatic nature of its leadership, here pushed to the highest possible level in the person of Silvio Berlusconi. The peculiar formation of this party, by personal initiative of one man and his company's close associates, and the virtual nonexistence of a party organization in the first years have stimulated new and ad hoc definitions for such a party, such as "personal"[22] or "business-firm"[23] or "patrimonialist."[24] Even after its "normalization" in 1998, when a statute with some resemblance to the standard model of party organization was introduced, the locus of power has remained in the hands of one man alone, Berlusconi. His extensive right of nomination in all the bodies, including the regional secretaries, plus his unbounded and ultimate power of decision on every issue are the foundation of the unusual concentration and verticalization of power in FI.

AN's leader has been the same person (Gianfranco Fini) since 1987—with 18 months interruption in 1990–1991—but he cannot be called charismatic. The party has always enjoyed, even in the heydays of its antecedent, the MSI, a very intense democratic life, thanks to its deep factionalization. However, the tendency to inflate the collective bodies in favor of a more efficient executive and secretariat has manifested itself in this party as well. And since the MSI transformation of AN in 1995, the party leader has acquired yet more power vis-à-vis the collective bodies, nominating many members and regional officials to those bodies.[25]

Other parties such as the PPI first, and the Daisy[26] later, both heirs to the Christian Democratic tradition, and the die-hard communist Rifondazione Comunista (Communist Refoundation [RC]) have placed ideology first, downgrading the drive for the concentration of power.

Less and Less Relevance for the Membership and Local Units

The progressive reduction of the relevance of party members over Europe has not been reversed by any Italian party. In the first years of its existence, FI did not implement a "normal" recruitment and was formally devoid of members. The supporters could join the "Clubs Forza Italia," a parallel structure controlled by FI officials, but this gave them no formal linkage with the party. Only after 1998 was normal party recruitment initiated. Nearly 200,000 people enrolled, but the members enjoy limited powers and they cannot even elect their local officials at the regional level. This has been an extreme case; the other parties present a more traditional vision. On the opposite side of FI stands the LN, which offers its membership the kind of role associated with the old-fashioned mass party militant.

On the whole, however, the members of Italian parties do not have much say in the decision-making process. In two cases, AN and FI, members cannot elect regional officials, who are nominated from above. At the other end of the scale, the Greens and the Radicals allow each member to participate in the national congresses with the right of vote. But even in these latter parties, the local echelons do not have the right to select candidates for elections. Members are not effectively involved in the candidate selection, which remains firmly in the hands of the national elites. The leftist parties, DS and the hardliner RC (and to some extent, the Daisy), provide in their statutes mechanisms for local units' involvement in the selection process through primaries or consultations, but they are never enforced. The newly formed PD has "open" primaries only for the choice of the center-left candidate to the premiership and for the election of its general secretary. These two events actually mobilize an amazingly high number of people. Contrary to any expectation, the primary for the center-left candidate premier on October 14, 2005, brought 4.3 million to the center-left parties' self-run booths, with long lines waiting until late at night. The same massive mobilization occurred two years after for the election of the PD party secretary, when around 3.5 million went to the booths. In both cases all citizens were willing to sign a declaration of principles and pay a small fee to participate and vote. Other less structured forms of mobilization were enforced by the center-right parties, too. In autumn 2007, FI promoted a sort of referendum among its supporters on a new name that the party, eventually merging with AN in the 2008 general elections. Although this sort of referendum was run with very loose rules and in open stands in streets and squares, people were positively affected by the novelty and participated to a considerable extent. (But precisely because of that loose organization, no reliable figures on the effective number of participants are available.)

Party membership declined in the 1990s because of the party system shakeup following the Clean Hand investigation, but it then regained momentum, and by the end of the 1990s, party members in Italy totaled the highest number in Europe[27] and reached 2.3 million in 2003.[28] However, the role of party members now has less and less relevance, especially in a new party such as FI. Only very recently have there been some attempts fostered by the center-left parties to establish more open procedures and more involvement in the leadership selection process. But these attempts went beyond party members and included the citizenry at large and thus were not an unambiguous sign of internal party democratization.

Growing Relevance of the Elected Officers

Elected officials have become more important in all parties, and the number of parliamentarians throughout the top echelons of party bodies has increased constantly.[29] Overlapping between MPs and members of the bodies that used to be referred to as the extraparliamentary party is now standard practice everywhere. Even parties with a tradition of separation between elected officeholders and party leaders, such as the RC, the PDS-DS, and to some extent the PPI and Daisy, have brought down the barriers between the two components.

Skyrocketing Personalization

Personalization or party presidentialization of politics is a common feature of many contemporary political systems.[30] In general terms this means that power is sufficiently concentrated in the hands of the party leader, and he or she can ignore or bypass subleaders and activists in communicating with the voters. Plebiscitary modes of communication and mobilization and appealing to the electorate at large eliminate the need to consult the will of the party members and middle-level elites.[31]

Obviously, protocharismatic parties such as FI and LN show the highest level of personalization. This is especially true in the case of Berlusconi, whose control of the media empire guarantees him an unprecedented advantage vis-à-vis the other party leader (if any) and, a fortiori, middle-level elites and members. AN and RC, while at the opposite end of the political spectrum, shared some commonalities as far as the role of the party leader was concerned. In AN the party "president" (according to the new internal terminology) has gained much autonomy and power, as discussed above. Gianfranco Fini used his position to address path-breaking statements (radically condemning fascism, for example) to the mass public rather than to his own rank-and-file, either in order to distance himself from his party (which he perceived as a liability, unsuitable for serving his ambition to take over major roles in the political system) or just for showing off his own power within the party. Similarly, RC secretary Fausto Bertinotti enjoyed massive coverage by the media and bypassed the party organs on many occasions (for example, declaring in an interview that nonviolence was the only plausible—and revolutionary—means of action). Both party leaders have, however, had to face a real and intense party life, with a certain level of factionalism, especially in the case of RC in its most recent years.

Other parties have resisted this tendency. The DS's political culture, in fact, based on collective decision making and accountability to the national bodies, somewhat inhibited a process of strong personalization. Massimo D'Alema attempted to distance himself from the party bodies, creating his own "staff" when he was the party secretary in 1994–1997, but this innovation was very badly received and later abandoned by his successors. In the Daisy, the ample power attributed to the party leader at the moment of its foundation in 2001 was drastically reduced soon thereafter, making the secretary more accountable to the party bodies.

In sum, in many respect Italian parties' internal organization and dynamics have not varied greatly from what they were prior to 1994.

With few exceptions, parties have remained closed, unaccountable, and insensitive to the declining role of membership and local units, albeit able to retain a comparatively large number of members. They have, however, increased their oligarchic and personalized traits, shifting the balance of internal power toward the public officeholders (MPs, regional and local representatives) and the top leadership. None of the innovations introduced by many European parties to counteract their declining legitimacy have been adopted by Italian parties. They have been disinterested in establishing the direct election of leaders, the participation of local units in candidate selection, and the consultation of the rank-and-file on relevant policy issues. Only the center-left parties have, on two occasions, tried to break the oligarchic mold by introducing primaries. But these were ad hoc, isolated, exceptional events, remarkable only for the massive mobilization they inadvertently provoked, itself perhaps indicative of popular hunger for greater participation.

As far as the parties' relationship with the democratic system is concerned, the post-1994 setting presents many differences compared to the previous period. The old antisystem parties (PCI and MSI), which had for long delegitimized the democratic institutions and had already changed considerably in the 1980s, now definitely abandoned their old standings and, more or less radically (the former much more than the latter), transformed themselves. However, whereas these parties had accepted the rules of the game, thus reinforcing the democratic system, the newcomers of the post-1994 system—FI and LN—introduced novel tensions in a democratic system. For a long time, LN intermittently advocated the division of Italy, invoking the right of "secession" of the northern regions. Such a project attacked the integrity of the national community, one of the foundations of a political system, and thus could be inscribed in the antisystem category. Even more, the party has carried on a xenophobic and anti-immigrant discourse, using extremely crude and vulgar language, to the point it would have been fiercely stigmatized in other democratic countries. Finally, the party has emphasized the "will of the people" as the ultimate source of legitimacy, disregarding the representative institutions and the logic of checks and balances. This populist approach represents a further break in the national political culture, since no other party in the pre-1994 party system voiced this approach. In sum, the LN secessionist aim, its xenophobic agenda, and its populist appeal contrast sharply with the ideological and constitutional foundations of the Italian political system (whose institutions, we should remember, never changed, not even after the 1994 party system shakeup).

On a different level, FI has introduced and legitimated a worldview that conflicts with the basis of the Italian system. FI too has displayed a populist appeal, denouncing the inability and superfluousness of party politics to deal with the "real problems" of the country (which could and should be run as "a firm," according to Berlusconi), shown indifference toward the respective domain of the various institutions, and exalts its leader as a deus ex machina who should be freed from institutional constraints in order to display his unique capabilities. Even if FI has avoided the LN's plebeian style and extreme positions, it nevertheless has used its populist appeal to delegitimize the present political rules of the game. In sum, together these two parties are weakening the democratic legitimacy of the Italian political system.

CONCLUSION

In this chapter, a *longue durée* approach to the relationship between parties and democracies has been followed. The development of the "quality of democracy" inside parties and the parties' impact on the democratic system through their discourse and behavior have been traced through 60 years, starting from the end of World War II.

The three phases of the gold, iron, and rust age of parties reflect the different receptions they have received in public opinion in the postwar era. In the golden age, they were seen as agencies of democracy because of the role they played in the war of liberation. They attracted millions of people and granted them a forum of discussion—quite valuable after two decade of dictatorship—rather than decision power. The antisystem patterning by the right-wing parties did not harm the democratic system as much because they worked with the rules of the system and organized themselves accordingly; and, on the other side of the political spectrum, the communist party was, in reality, quite supportive of democracy because it considered the democratic setting its own shelter against any right-wing authoritarian development, even if it did not enforce democracy internally, due to the strict adoption of the principle of democratic centralism.

The iron age started in the very early 1960s when the governing parties dramatically accelerated the colonization of the state. Their hold on the administration, the state economic sector, and the civil society produced a backlash in terms of declining legitimacy. The "cycle of protest" of 1968–1969 was directed against the closed, old, bureaucratic party politics. But the parties did not react to the mounting mood of dissatisfaction. Happy with their high level of membership, strong party identification, and voters' loyalty, they did not change their internal structure or their way of working. On the contrary, what they did went in the opposite direction: They passed a bill on state financing with the declared aim of putting a stop to illegal financing, which in fact gave them access to all but unlimited funds. Public opinion reacted very negatively in the 1978 referendum where 43% of the voters sustained the bill's abolition, despite the fact that almost all parties had supported it. Charges of corruption and selfishness were coupled in that period with the more serious accusation of inability to fight red and black terrorist activity. However, the tough antiterrorist stand adopted by the main parties after the Moro kidnapping temporarily obscured all their other deficiencies and "saved" parties from general disdain and distrust. The 1950s identification of parties with democracy still held.

The rust age lasted throughout the 1980s and continued until the old party system collapsed in 1994. The stalemate of the party system and the rising corruption (in part produced by the same stalemate) increased the public dissatisfaction. Most of the parties introduced some changes to counteract the membership decline and the weakening mobilization, but they were not effective. The Clean Hands investigation showed to what extent parties had become unaccountable and not responsive.

Rather amazingly, the new, post-1994 party system did not introduce significant internal changes in order to increase accountability and responsiveness. On the contrary, most of the parties, starting from FI, denied their members an effective role in party affairs. Centralization, verticalization, and personalization, more or less common to all parties even if more in the right than in the left, deprived the rank-and-file of a say in the decision-making process. The very limited internal democracy in some parties was accompanied by the arrival of two new parties (FI and LN), which displayed a populist and undemocratic profile, not in tune with the Italian system's foundation values.

In the most recent years, the parties' inability to introduce relevant innovations has raised a new wave of public protest. A pamphlet denouncing the incompetence, the sleaze, and, above all, the abuse of power and the privileges of the political class and a blog run by a famous showman (Beppe Grillo) have had popular success: the former sold around 1.5 million copies (an incredibly high number by Italian standards) and the latter is one of the top 10 political blogs in the world.

Antiparty and antipolitics feelings surface again. If one adds to this mood the populist rhetoric by some parties, Italian democracy appears, once more, under stress. Parties are no longer an asset for democratic institutions as they were in the past. Instead, they seem to have become a liability.

APPENDIX: ITALIAN PARTIES ACRONYMS

AN	Alleanza nazionale—National Alliance
Daisy	La Margherita—The Daisy
DC	Democrazia Cristiana—Christian Democracy
DS	Democratici di Sinistra—Left Democrats
FI	Forza Italia—Go Italy!
LN	Lega Nord—Northern League
MSI	Movimento Sociale Italiano—Italian Social Movement
PCI	Partito Comunista Italiano—Italian Communist Party
PD	Partito Democratico—Democratic Party
PDIUM	Partito di Unità Monarchica—Party of Monarchical Unity
PDS	Partito Democratico Della Sinistra—Democratic Party of the Left
PLI	Partito Liberale Italiano—Italian Liberal Party
PPI	Partito Popolare Italiano—Italian Popular Party
PRI	Partito Repubblicano Italiano—Italian Republican Party
PSDI	Partito Socialista Democratico Italiano—Italian Social-Democratic Party
PSI	Partito Socialista Italiano—Italian Socialist Party
RC	Rifondazione Comunista—Communist Refoundation

Spanish Parties and Democracy: Weak Party–Society Linkage and Intense Party–State Symbiosis

Luis Ramiro and Laura Morales

INTRODUCTION

The institutional design of Spain's contemporary political system was based on the premise that political parties indeed play an essential role in democratic politics. This conception was reflected in the 1978 Constitution and other fundamental laws and was not surprising given that parties were the core players in the formulation of the new institutional architecture in Spain. Three decades after the approval of the 1978 Constitution, which has shaped Spanish politics to the present, the critical role of parties can hardly be disputed. However, public opinion regarding the actual performance of their functions in the Spanish democracy is certainly not unanimously positive, and criticism is often directed both at their various misbehaviors and at the resultant consequences for the functioning of the entire democratic system.

What we intend to show in this chapter are the ways Spanish political parties fail to carry out some of the main functions reserved for parties in democratic systems, particularly the representation function and the function of linking society to the state. Specifically, many of the problems that Spanish parties encounter in the implementation of their representative function are primarily related to the bias with which they perform their state—society linkage function. Spanish parties have gradually placed themselves in a position where they are more solidly linked to the state than to society.

In order to make our point clear, we will analyze several of the functions assigned to parties in democratic politics: some that are performed in the electorate, some that are performed as organizations, and some that are performed in government.[1]

After a brief summary of the recent history of the Spanish party system, we offer an overview of the functions of parties in the electorate. We will then examine the capacity of Spanish parties to generate symbols of identification and loyalty, the political support they receive from citizens, and their capacity to mobilize the citizenry. For this purpose we will consider the following indicators: party identification, trust in and evaluation of parties, volatility, and participation in party campaign-related activities. We will observe how in this regard Spanish parties have not been very successful.

After this evaluation of the functions of parties in the electorate, we briefly define the kind of organization that Spanish parties have developed. The peculiarities in the way in which Spanish parties perform their functions as organizations help explain some of the weakness in the performance of the parties in the electorate functions reviewed in the previous section. For this we analyze party membership figures and policies, the type of electoral campaigning, and internal policies of organizational innovation. We will end this overview with a discussion of the performance of Spanish parties with regard to some of their functions in government. In contrast with the weaknesses examined in previous sections, the examination of parties in government produces an image of strong parties. In particular, we will analyze their primacy in the legislative process, their cohesion in the legislative, and, as a consequence, their contribution to government stability.

To conclude we study the intense link that Spanish parties maintain with the state. In this final section we examine three very relevant aspects: party finances, the public regulation of political parties, and party rent-seeking in state structures.

RECENT HISTORY OF THE SPANISH PARTY SYSTEM: 1977 TO THE PRESENT DAY

Since the end of the 1970s, a limited multiparty system emerged at the national level in Spain that has since been consolidated. The Spanish party system is characterized by low ideological polarization, the presence of two large nationwide parties that frequently obtain more than two-thirds of the vote, a third (and in some occasions even a fourth) smaller nationwide party, and a relatively high number of peripheral nationalist and regionalist parties with significant parliamentary representation in the national legislature. Party competition has mostly been structured by two cleavages: the traditional left—right socioeconomic division and the center—periphery divide, the latter particularly intense in the Basque Country, Catalonia, and Galicia where peripheral nationalist parties play a key role.

The largest two nationwide parties in the first two democratic elections (1977 and 1979) were the Unión de Centro Democrático (Union of the Democratic Centre [UCD]), an ideologically heterogenous centrist party (with Liberals, Christian Democrats, Social Democrats, among others) created in the transition to the democracy years around the leadership of Prime Minister Adolfo Suárez, and the Partido Socialista Obrero Español (Spanish Socialist Workers' Party [PSOE]), originally founded in the late 19th century but which underwent a notable process of organizational change and ideological moderation in the 1970s under the leadership of Felipe González. The center party UCD collapsed in 1982 (this electoral space was only temporarily occupied by the small Centro Democrático y Social [Social and Democratic Center (CDS)], which disappeared in 1993) and was replaced as one of the two largest nationwide parties by the Partido Popular (Popular Party [PP]). The PP has its origin in the Alianza Popular (Popular Alliance [AP]), a conservative party created during the transition to democracy. AP had among its founders political personnel linked to the Francoist political elite, which was strongly conservative, and in the first democratic elections was ranked fourth in the nationwide vote. At the end of the 1980s, the AP evolved into the PP, trying to move from conservatism toward a more moderate right of center position. The PP was represented in government under the leadership of José María Aznar between 1996 and 2004. Similarly, the socialists, under González's leadership, moved their party toward a moderate version of European social democracy and governed the country between 1982 and 1996, and then with José Luis Rodríguez Zapatero at the helm since 2004. The electoral space of the radical left was initially occupied by the Partido Comunista de España (Communist Party of Spain [PCE], originally founded in the 1920s) which in 1986 promoted the creation of Izquierda Unida (United Left [IU]). The PCE and then IU have been the third nationwide parties for most of the elections held since 1977, but they have experienced significant electoral and organizational instability.

In addition to these Spanish nationwide parties, several peripheral nationalist parties have played relevant roles and have been significant not only in regional but also in national politics, especially through their contribution to parliamentary majorities when the largest nationwide parties did not obtain absolute majorities. The two most important are the center-right Basque Nationalists of the Partido Nacionalista Vasco (Basque Nationalist Party [PNV], founded in the late 19th century) and the center-right Catalan Nationalists of the Convergencia i Unió coalition (Convergence and Union [CiU], formed by a liberal party created in the 1970s and a small Christian democratic party originally founded in the 1930s).

In sum, the Spanish party system is a complex one, with regional party systems radically different from the national one in certain regions. It is formed by nationwide and peripheral nationalist parties that, in spite of their many differences, tend to share common organizational traits that combine traditional mass party structures, low membership, catch-all strategies, strong linkage with the state, and highly professionalized campaign techniques.

PARTIES IN THE ELECTORATE

Political parties link citizens to the political process through simplifying their electoral choices, educating them politically, generating symbols of identification, and mobilizing them.[2] These functions can only be performed through the establishment of partisan ties with the citizens. Several studies show that these ties are weakening in western countries, resulting in an increase in electoral volatility.[3] The consequence is the incapacity of parties to politically integrate and mobilize citizens. These shortcomings in the performance of these functions are also evident in the increasing levels of antiparty sentiments and the lower levels of electoral turnout and party-related political participation. The Spanish case exemplifies these trends, though with some interesting peculiarities.

Party identification is particularly weak in Spain. The proportion of Spaniards who feel close to or identify with a political party is quite reduced when compared to that of other west European countries, including southwestern European nations.[4] Nevertheless, feelings of proximity to political parties have remained relatively stable over time, with between 35 and 40 percent of Spaniards claiming to feel close to some party.[5] In the context of weak party attachments—and diminishing party identification in Western democracies[6]—there is no evidence of partisan dealignment in Spain (Table 4.1).

In addition to assessing party identification, other indicators may enrich our analysis of partisan ties. The impact of the absence of partisan attachments on citizens' capacity to process political information and to guide their reactions to party competition is reinforced by attitudes of distrust, lack of confidence, or skepticism regarding the role of parties.

Table 4.1 Feels Close to or Identifies with a Political Party (%)

1987	1993	1997	2004	2005
38	38	36	37	36

Source: Various surveys from the Centro de Investigaciones Sociológicas (CIS) and Data93 survey. The Data93 file is available at the CEACS Juan March Institute data archive.

Clearly, antiparty sentiments are an additional source of weakening of party attachments in Spain. As we see in Figure 4.1, antiparty sentiments and feelings of alienation toward parties show a trend toward ambivalence in Spain. While one of the indicators of what Torcal, Montero, and Gunther term "cultural" antiparty feelings[7]—"parties are all the same"—shows a moderate increase in Spaniards' alienation with their political parties since the mid-1980s, the other one—"parties only divide people"—is stable over time. Furthermore, this critical view of Spanish parties by citizens coexists with a clear recognition by an overwhelming and gradually increasing majority that they play a fundamental role in democratic regimes. Hence, as Torcal, Montero, and Gunther argue,[8] cultural antiparty sentiments are closely linked to the more general syndrome of political disaffection, alienation, and passivity that characterizes Spanish political culture. It is certainly not a manifestation of an increasing proportion of "critical citizens"[9]; it is simply a symptom of a lack of robust partisan attachments.

Weak and decreasing party attachments are often blamed for limiting the stability of electoral behavior and, hence, for increasing electoral volatility in contemporary democracies. Yet other possible impacts might be a general reduction of citizens' political engagement in partisan activities; thus, we will also examine the evolution of electoral turnout and participation in campaign activities.

Contrary to what we might assume from the former figures on party identification, volatility has not been particularly high in Spain in comparative terms. The context of new parties and a long dictatorship, together with weak partisan attachments, could have promoted higher

Figure 4.1 Attitudes toward Political Parties.

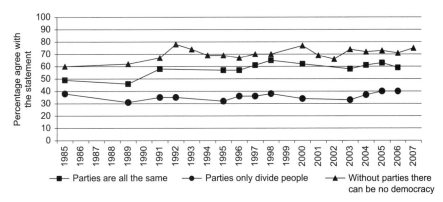

Sources: CIS database, 1987–2007 surveys (http://www.cis.es/cis/opencms/ES/1_encuestas/catalogo.html) and Data93 survey. The Data93 file is available at the CEACS Juan March Institute data archive.

levels of volatility. Yet, volatility has remained largely stable in the past 30 years, most especially aggregate interblock volatility between left-wing and right-wing parties, with the only peak in volatility taking place in the 1982 elections after the socialist landslide and the disappearance of the formerly governing party UCD. This, however, can be attributed not to Spaniards' volatile partisan affiliations but to the shakeup that UCD's crisis meant for the Spanish party system.[10] Nevertheless, individual-level volatility would seem to be steadily increasing amid an apparent stability of voting preferences at the aggregate level, as we can see for the 2008 elections (Figure 4.2).

Certainly, western democracies are experiencing a general, albeit recent, trend of electoral turnout decline.[11] Are weak partisan ties keeping electoral turnout low in Spain? There is not much evidence of this (Figure 4.3). Electoral turnout in Spain has remained mostly stable since the first elections in the 1970s, although a slight declining trend is visible for both regional and local elections since the early 2000s. In any case, the levels of turnout in general elections have been frequently above 70 percent, not a low turnout level when compared to those of other OECD countries.[12]

Figure 4.2 Aggregate and Individual Volatility.

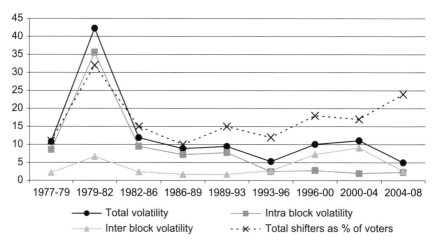

Sources: Mariano Torcal and Ignacio Lago, "Electoral Coordination Strikes Again: The 2008 General Election in Spain," *South European Society and Politics* 13 (2008): 363–375, Table 3, for aggregate volatility; for individual volatility, Richard Gunther, José Ramón Montero, and Joan Botella, *Democracy in Modern Spain* (New Haven, Conn.: Yale University Press), 221, for figures up to 1996–2000; our own extension from the CNEP2004 data set (http://www.cnep.ics.ul.pt/index1.asp) for 2000–2004 and CIS panel survey 7708 for 2004–2008 (http://www.cis.es/cis/opencms/ES/1_encuestas/catalogo.html).

Figure 4.3 Electoral Turnout in Spain by Type of Election.

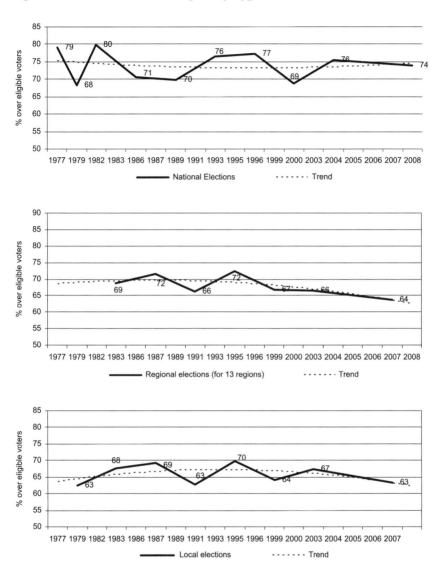

Source: Ministry of the Interior Database. Spanish Elections database, 1977–2008, available at: http://www.elecciones.mir.es/

In addition to its potential effects on electoral turnout, weak(ening) partisan ties may have consequences on other types of party-related political mobilization, such as citizens' participation in electoral campaign activities (Figure 4.4). This form of engagement has seen a general decline in most western societies[13] and has been shown to be

Figure 4.4 Participation in Campaign Activities.

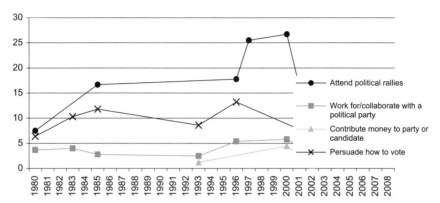

Sources: Several CIS surveys, CIS database, 1980–2008 (http://www.cis.es/cis/opencms/ES/1_encuestas/catalogo.html) and 1993 and 2004 CNEP surveys (http://www.cnep.ics.ul.pt/index1.asp).

negatively affected by the evolution of campaign styles (increasingly professionalized and marketing oriented) and diminishing party membership figures. Spanish parties, as we will see later, are particularly weak membership organizations, and their campaign styles are increasingly professionalized, centralized, and marketing oriented.[14] What are the implications of this situation for citizen participation and mobilization?

Spaniards' participation in campaign activities has been fairly limited throughout most of the democratic period since the early 1980s. In particular, very few citizens collaborate with or work for any political party, and even fewer of them care to contribute money to parties or candidates. In the past, however, Spaniards seem to have been somewhat more active in terms of attending political rallies and persuading other people how to vote. Though the time series are not of good quality, it does seem that in the past decade or so Spanish voters have become much more reluctant to engage even in low-cost campaign activities. Although electoral turnout is comparatively high—yet slightly in decline—citizens' involvement in campaign activities is extremely low and is decreasing.

PARTIES AS ORGANIZATIONS

As organizations, parties perform functions of recruitment of political leaders, training of elites, and articulation and aggregation of political interests. However, party organizations—within which these functions should be developed—have experienced important changes in the past decades that affect their performance in this regard. In fact, the demise of the mass party model entails the reduction of the emphasis in political education, training, transmission of identities, enrollment of citizens, and mobilization more generally. The formation of membership organizations has, therefore, been essential for their capacity to perform their functions as organizations. Thus, one of the most interesting issues is how parties evaluate and conceive of their own membership—and its role within the party—in the context of an ongoing shift away from the mass party organizational style.[15] How are Spanish parties facing and approaching these more general changes?

After four decades of dictatorship, in the 1970s Spaniards regained democracy amid a political environment of limited political mobilization, relative hostility to politics, apathy, and antiparty sentiments. In this adverse context, two additional factors hindered parties' inclination to seek new members. First, since the early transition period, Spanish parties had access to public financing, and this allowed them to sustain their organizational structures in the absence of a vast fees-paying membership. Furthermore, these public subsidies were—and still are—completely dependent on the parties' electoral results, not party membership. Second, Spanish parties were formed or reformed during the 1970s in an era of rapid expansion of the mass media, and this meant that a numerous membership was not essential as a communication tool, given the availability of other channels for the transmission of political messages.[16]

Although during the past three decades of democratic politics the social and political contexts have changed dramatically, this original environment predisposed Spanish parties not to actively pursue the formation of large membership organizations. Spain still has very low levels of associational and party membership and a generalized distrust toward parties. What have the Spanish parties done during the past three decades to increase their social embeddedness and party membership?

The answer is simple: not much.[17] This is the conclusion we reach when we analyze two of the main initiatives that can attract new members to parties: membership drives and internal reforms to increase the role of members in decision making.[18] With regard to the former, although parties have carried out more or less ambitious membership drives, these have never been systematic or intense, but quite sporadic and infrequent. In fact, party officials seem to be skeptical about the efficacy of membership drives and tend to believe more in the usefulness of party structure reform to create a more member-friendly environment that will make membership more attractive. However, Spanish parties have in practice done very little to generate new internal incentives to make membership more appealing.

Spanish parties have tried to increase the inclusiveness of their organizations by reducing the existence of formal barriers to join the party (e.g., having the endorsement of a party member is nowadays a flexible requirement). Simultaneously, some parties have created a new status, that of party supporter, in addition to that of party member, as in the case of Iniciativa per Catalunya Verds (ICV, Initiative for Catalonia Greens), then the PSOE, and more recently the PP. But this initiative, aimed at widening the social and organizational roots of the parties, has remained clearly underdeveloped both in the PSOE and the PP with very slow progress in its implementation.[19]

If we examine the incentives parties have generated to make membership more appealing, we find first that the increase in the opportunities for the participation of members in party affairs has been rather modest. In the drafting and writing of parties' manifestoes, the grassroots involvement is really reduced.[20] The party leadership remains basically in control in this field—as hypothesized by Scarrow, Webb, and Farrell[21]—with minor chances of participation open to party members (e.g., in some forums and debates).[22] Party manifestoes are drafted by formal or informal groups of specialists appointed by the party leadership, and the final document is eventually approved by the party council (in the PSOE, IU, and Convergencia Democratica de Catalunya [CDC, Democratic Convergence of Catalonia]) or by the executive committee (in the PP and PNV). However, some parties have also put in place some procedures of legitimization of the party manifestoes by which members—or their representatives through a system of delegation and party programmatic conferences—can participate. Nonetheless, what is clear from a scrutiny of these procedures is that the functions of interest articulation and aggregation are performed without much involvement of party members.[23]

In the selection of the party leader, the most common procedure in Spanish parties is the election in the national party congress with a vote of congress delegates.[24] There is an almost uniform absence of party primaries to select the party leader—except for some smaller regional parties as the ICV and Esquerra Republicana de Catalunya (ERC, Republican Left of Catalonia)—and there is nothing to indicate that changes should be expected in this regard in the near future.[25] There are certain differences among the parties in the degree to which the process of party leadership selection has been really contested, because in some cases—and especially in the case of the PP—the new leader has oftentimes been appointed by the incumbent party leadership or a personal decision of the incumbent party leader.[26]

Selection of party candidates for election to the national parliament is only rarely in the hands of party members through a process of internal elections or party primaries. The main exceptions refer to its sporadic use for the head of the list for national parliament in the IU and other smaller parties. Most commonly, however, the selection of candidates for the provincial multimember districts for national parliament is done by regional and provincial leaderships directly or through special committees set up for the elaboration of electoral lists. In any case, the last word in the procedure is always formally with the national party leadership, which has veto power in candidate selection. Despite its experimentation with party primaries for the selection of the party candidate to prime minister in the late 1990s, this is also the procedure the PSOE follows.

The latter initiative by the socialists deserves closer inspection because it has probably been the most ambitious recent internal innovation in Spanish party politics and has eventually had interesting implications.[27] The Socialist Party Congress of 1997 decided to introduce internal primaries for the election of the candidates to mayor. However, following a strategy designed by the new general secretary (J. Almunia), the primaries were extended to the selection of the candidate to prime minister. The general secretary intended to revitalize the party organization and to reinvigorate a demoralized party membership, but he also tried to legitimize his own leadership with the purpose of increasing his electoral appeal with the public. However, in a much improvised process of party primaries, the party leader was surprisingly defeated, and the elected candidate (J. Borrell) had no support within the party apparatus in the following months and eventually resigned even before the 2000 elections. The PSOE thus lived through a very traumatic period of internal division and weakness while the public was watching, and the party primaries at the local level also resulted in internal tension. In 2000, the formal procedures of the primaries were adapted with the aim of avoiding damages to the electoral strategies and prospects of the party—for example, by restricting the primaries to the cases where the party was not the executive incumbent. Overall, the primacy of electoral goals has resulted in a formal and informal restriction in the use of primaries in the PSOE. There has been a clearly decreasing trend in the use of primaries during the 1999, 2003, and 2007 local and regional elections and in the general elections of 2004, when the socialists regained control of the national government and no primaries were held to select the party's general secretary (J. L. Rodríguez Zapatero) as its candidate for prime minister. Thus, what once was a very important organizational innovation that gave party members new power and influence in party decision making and could potentially make the party membership more appealing has been a relative fiasco.[28]

In summary, Spanish parties have shown only limited interest in the development of large membership organizations. Although they claim to be interested in attracting new members, they have not developed the policies or the efforts this would require. Organizational reforms and innovations oriented toward making party membership more appealing and to attract new members have been introduced only to a limited degree, and organizational devices that have been implemented by other Western European parties (such as internal party primaries) and that have significantly shifted the distribution of internal party power in favor of the members have not been introduced in Spain.

Given the conditions in which Spanish parties were formed or refounded in the 1970s and their limited attempts to create mass organizations, the low levels of party membership in Spain in comparative terms are hardly surprising. However, what is perhaps more interesting is that despite the rather limited efforts to create mass organizations, to increase membership figures, or to make membership more appealing, party membership in Spain shows no sign of crisis or decline, a pattern common to other southern European countries.[29]

As many scholars have already pointed out, obtaining reliable figures of party membership is often complicated. In countries where the state does not control or monitor membership figures with official and public registers—as is the case in Spain—we can only use two possible sources: the reports provided by the parties themselves and survey data. Most Spanish commentators agree that Spanish parties clearly overreport their membership for two main reasons. On the one hand, parties have not been very efficient in keeping updated membership records and commonly members are not deleted from them once they stop paying their fees. On the other hand, showing constantly increasing membership figures contributes to a positive public image of strength and wide support.[30] Nevertheless, the trends in Figure 4.5 compiled for the two main nationwide parties are interesting because they show a turning point in the mid-1990s when the PP set off to increase its membership base at a much more rapid pace than the PSOE. Even if it is likely that the PP overestimates the annual increase as well, it is clear that the socialists have had a much harder time attracting core supporters.

Figure 4.5 Membership of the Two Main Nationwide Parties (1977–2008).

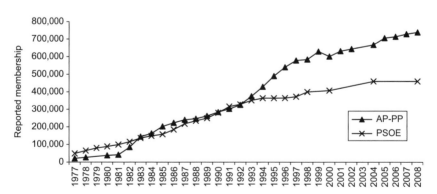

Source: Méndez, Morales, and Ramiro, "Los afiliados y su papel en los partidos políticos españoles," Appendix, updated with party and press reports.

If we observe the figures provided by the parties, the membership growth in the two largest nationwide parties (PSOE and PP) is notable. As we see, the PP also grows in membership, even in the absence of membership empowerment, as it has the most centralized, hierarchical, and least favorable organizational structure in terms of members' empowerment of all the nationwide parties.[31] Hence, the increasing trends, and particularly the one of PP, can partly be explained by the patronage opportunities linked to incumbency, in national but also in regional and local governments.[32]

Survey data, in contrast, provide a consistent picture of stability in party membership nationwide that has oscillated around 3 to 4 percent of the adult population since the mid-1980s. After some euphoria when democracy was regained, Spaniards returned to their traditional passivity and very few of them now care to join political parties at all (Figure 4.6).

In sum, Spanish parties are weak as membership organizations, and this is likely to have negative consequences for their role as agents of socialization, representation, and mobilization. Certainly it could also weaken their legitimacy in the long term. However, this limited social embeddedness has not in itself entailed a decline of parties' overall support and, in fact, their performance of other roles may have even been untouched or reinforced by recent developments. We examine now another of their core roles: their performance as parties in government.

PARTIES IN GOVERNMENT

One of the most important functions of political parties is to structure and organize government. There is hardly any doubt that Spain fulfills

Figure 4.6 Party Membership in Spain (survey data).

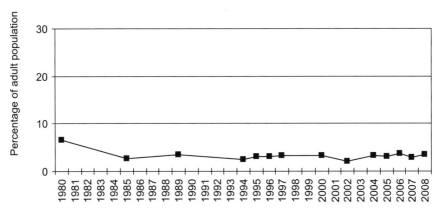

Source: CIS database, 1980–2008 (http://www.cis.es/cis/opencms/ES/1_encuestas/catalogo.html).

the conditions required to be considered a good example of the party government model.[33] The governing party is crucial in the process of government decision making, government policies are defined by the governing party, government personnel are selected through and by the governing party, and electoral competition among parties is the key means of holding politicians accountable to the public. This party government model is also expressed through and reinforced by (1) the party primacy in the legislative process and (2) party discipline in parliament, while these two features have the effect of generating a (3) high government stability. We will discuss how these three aspects unfold in the Spanish case in the next paragraphs.

Party Primacy in the Legislative Process

The primacy of Spanish parties in the legislative process is exerted through their control on the parliamentary parties and the crucial role of the latter in the activity of parliament. There is a very clear chain of dependence: members of parliament are dependent on the parliamentary groups, and parliamentary groups are dependent on the party in its central office, and even on the party leader, given the notable presidentialization of Spanish party politics.[34]

The control over the parliamentary party by the party in its central office is exerted through several mechanisms. There is a substantial overlap of personnel between the party and parliamentary party directorates. It is very common that the party leader will also take on the highest position in the parliamentary party (at least when the party is in opposition) and that the core leaders of the parliamentary parties will also be part of the leadership and directive bodies of the party in central office. The party leadership also takes the leading role in the selection of the parliamentary party directive body (a sort of executive committee) and of its most relevant personalities (the speakers). This party control of their parliamentary branches is also fueled by the hegemonic role of the leadership of the party in central office over the parliamentary party in the selection of party candidates in the Spanish closed party list electoral system. In fact, a very small number of members of parliament control every activity and decision of the parliamentary party: appointments of speakers, legislative action, and votes.[35]

For their part, the parliamentary parties or parliamentary groups in the upper and the lower chambers of parliament are in absolute control of all the parliamentary activity (time, speakers, questions, motions, amendments, funding, and committee posts), while individual members of parliament have very little opportunity to exercise their own initiative.[36]

Party Discipline in Parliament

As a result of parliamentary rules, which give the groups a crucial role in the proceedings of parliamentary debates, and the procedures for candidate selection, which give the parties in central office the power to pick and drop candidates, political coherence of the parliamentary groups is extremely high. Cases of lack of parliamentary discipline in which a member of parliament does not vote according to party instructions are very rare. Parliamentarians generally behave in a very cohesive way and follow party instructions both in the appointment of directive bodies within the parliamentary party or in the appointment of speakers in the different legislative committees and in the direction of their votes in parliament.

What we want to highlight is that both the procedural rules in parliament and the internal rules of parliamentary groups are the result of parties' decisions. It is parties that have chosen to structure parliamentary activity in such a way that the party in central office rules over the parliamentary group and the latter over the individual MPs. The end product is a parties' parliament, in which the leading actors are not the individual MP but the parties, which in this hegemonic setting take for granted the disciplined acceptance of the former.[37]

Stability in Government

As in every parliamentary democracy, the Spanish government depends for its election and survival on the support of a majority in parliament. These successive majorities have been possible thanks to (1) extremely cohesive parties, (2) a particular dynamic of electoral and governmental competition that has constrained the election of voters to a two-party choice set dominated by the two largest centre-right and centre-left parties (PP and PSOE), and (3) certain constitutional provisions that have facilitated the formation of very stable governments.[38] Among these constitutional provisions—chosen by the parties themselves during the transition to democracy—the most important are the electoral system (which overrepresents the winning party in parliament), the procedure of government investiture (which establishes that a mere plurality is sufficient), and the constructive vote of no confidence (which requires an absolute majority around an alternative candidate to prime minister to succeed).

The result of these combined factors is highly stable governments and very low government turnover. In comparative terms, the Spanish political system created in the mid-1970s emerges as one of the most stable in terms of the longevity of its governments.[39] And, leaving aside the personnel changes in the composition of the one-party cabinets, changes in which parties occupy the government are caused only by a call for new elections (Table 4.2).

Table 4.2 Spanish Governmental Terms, 1977–2008

Government	Time in Office	Duration (months)	Party	Majority/ Minority
Suárez I	1977–1979	22	UCD	Minority
Suárez II	1979–1981	22	UCD	Minority
Calvo-Sotelo	1981–1982	21	UCD	Minority
González I	1982–1986	43	PSOE	Majority
González II	1986–1989	40	PSOE	Majority
González III	1989–1993	43	PSOE	Majority
González IV	1993–1996	33	PSOE	Minority
Aznar I	1996–2000	45	PP	Minority
Aznar II	2000–2004	46	PP	Majority
Zapatero I	2004–2008	48	PSOE	Minority

UCD, Unión de Centro Democrático; PSOE, Partido Socialista Obrero Español; PP, Partido Popular.
Sources: Richard Gunther, José Ramón Montero, and Joan Botella, Democracy in Modern Spain (New Haven, Conn.: Yale University Press, 2004), Table 5.10, p. 228, and our extension for 2004–2008.

Therefore, Spanish parties have been successful in their task of organizing and structuring government and, as the literature states,[40] even in a situation in which some other party functions would be in peril, the role of parties in government has not suffered any significant decline. However, this evolution also points to extremely important changes in the nature of Spanish parties that we shall study in the next section.

THE PARTIES-STATE LINKAGE

The weakening of linkages between parties and society and the decline of the mass party model among party organizations in contemporary industrial democracies have resulted in a critical decline in the ability of parties to perform some of their traditional functions such as representation, mobilization, and interest articulation and aggregation. However, the weakening of the representative functions takes place at the same time that parties are able to exert their procedural and institutional functions without the challenges they experience in the social realm.[41] Hence, parties are in a sense becoming detached from society while their linkage with the state increases and approximates a situation of party—state entrenchment.[42]

Van Biezen and Kopecký define three dimensions to analyze in discussing the relation between parties and the state—the extent to which parties depend on the state, the extent to which they are managed by the state, and the extent to which parties themselves control the state—and propose one indicator for each of them: public funding of political parties, public regulation of parties, and party rent seeking within the state.[43] We show in the following sections how for all three indicators the situation in Spain is one of substantial party—state symbiosis.[44]

Public Funding

Generally, how important public funding is for political parties indicates the degree of their dependence on the state for their organizational survival. In the Spanish case, the introduction of public subsidies for political parties has its origin in the very first years of the democratic system established in the 1970s, and this state funding has become the main source of income for parties, which are completely dependent on it for their daily functioning.

Direct public subsidies to parties and parliamentary party groups are combined with a wide range of indirect state support and, also, with private funding.[45] The existence of public funding is justified by the crucial constitutional and political role that the 1978 Constitution reserves, in Article 6, for political parties. State funding is composed of direct and indirect subsidies. The latter include media access—spaces for party advertising in the state media (television and radio) through a system of allocation of time slots according to votes obtained in the previous elections—subsidies for the mailing or postage of party materials during elections; special taxation privileges; and the free use of public buildings (for example, schools) for electoral campaigning.

Certainly, direct state funding is the most relevant of all subsidies, as it is absolutely crucial for parties' survival and for their ordinary functioning. Every year, the general budget of the state (Presupuestos Generales del Estado) includes an amount of money that is distributed among the parties that obtained parliamentary seats in the previous election, according to their number of votes and seats in parliament. The second most important direct state funding is the subsidy that parties receive for electoral campaign expenditures after every election (national, regional, or local). As in the previous case, the distribution of this fund is based on the votes and MPs obtained by the parties that won parliamentary seats (the amount of money that corresponds for each vote and each MP is fixed). Finally, the third component of the direct state funding is the subsidy to parliamentary parties, which consists of a fixed amount to every parliamentary party, the provision of human and material resources for their functioning, and a supplementary quantity distributed among the parliamentary parties according to their size (the number of MPs included in the group).

But, in addition to these, another extremely relevant source of "public" subsidies to parties, without which Spanish parties' dependence from state and public institutions for their survival would not be fully understood and would probably be underestimated, is provided by regional and local institutions. The parties that obtain representation in the regional parliaments of the 17 autonomous regions, as well as those represented in city councils, receive subsidies from the regional and city council budgets. Formally and originally, these subsidies are thought to fund the work of regional MPs and local councilors. However, amid an atypical legal situation (particularly in the case of city councils), these subsidies go far beyond funding parliamentary work and, in fact, have become yet another source of funding for extraparliamentary party structures.[46]

The importance of state subsidies for parties' finances is such that it has been the main party income in most of the cases and throughout the current democratic period: for some parties it is frequently more than 80% of the total party income, as is the case of the nationwide PP and IU. Other sources of party income, such as donations or membership dues, have a minor role both in the financing of routine functioning and in election campaigns.[47] At the same time, the proportion of the subsidies coming from regional parliaments and city councils over the total of all state subsidies has grown intensely and currently is very close to 50 percent.[48] Therefore, one of the main features of the state funding of parties in Spain is its completeness: state subsidies include a diverse catalog of indirect and direct funding both for extraparliamentary organizations (for their daily functioning and for electoral campaign expenditures) and for parliamentary parties.

The second aspect we want to highlight is the involvement in party funding of a full range of national, regional, and local political institutions that not only contribute to the support of the parliamentary parties, but also to the ordinary working of extraparliamentary party organizations. Third, these subsidies are very important for party financial viability: parties' staff and the parties' daily organizational activity fully depend on state subsidies, which are the main party income. Finally, it is important to stress that all this funding is notably biased against parties without parliamentary representation, and that the distribution of subsidies benefits the larger parties—the two biggest nationwide parties or the biggest peripheral nationalist parties—given that the rules applied in the distribution of direct subsidies among parties extend the scarce proportionality of the electoral system to the access to state funding.[49] As a consequence, state funding primarily benefits already successful parties and places additional barriers to the entry of new ones. Though describing this as a "cartelization" of Spanish democracy or of the Spanish party system is an exaggeration—primarily because party subsidies are far from being limited to the largest parties in the regional and local arenas—all the available evidence clearly points to a strong party—state relationship or, at the very least, to the existence of a very strong dependence of parties on the state for their survival.

The Public Regulation of Parties

The public regulation of parties is "part of a process by which their activities become to a growing extent managed by the state."[50] This process seems to have been more intense in recent years, and the state regulation of parties is currently understood as the regulation of a certain kind of public utility.[51] These regulations affect several domains of party activity through different public laws, including the constitution. The constitutionalization of political parties is a clear sign of the fundamental role attributed to parties in the functioning of the political system and is also an important indicator of party—state linkage and of state management of parties.[52]

The Spanish constitution reserves a central role to political parties as the expression of political pluralism and as channels of political participation. Following such postwar constitutions as the Italian (1947), the German (1949), or the French (1958), the Spanish 1978 constitution recognizes the crucial role of political parties in a democracy even to the point of granting them a position of hegemony or qualified privilege in the expression of political pluralism and as channels of political participation.[53] The Spanish constitution declares a clear and strong commitment to representative democracy and to party democracy. As a consequence, the regulation of the procedures and institutions of direct democracy are severely limited and are afforded a very secondary role. All forms of political participation that are not channeled through political parties (or other intermediary actors) were regulated in such a way and were the object of such curtailment, during the constitutional debates, that their relevance in the constitution and in contemporary Spanish politics is rather weak.[54] This includes the referendum, citizen initiatives, popular legislative initiatives, and the right to petition.

Therefore, Spain is an example of strong constitutionalization of political parties: the 1978 constitution identifies them as fundamental vehicles for the political participation of citizens and reserves them a prominent role in its Preliminary Title as basic institutions of the new democratic system. Furthermore, their constitutional strength is all the more enhanced by the constitutional weakening of alternative channels of political participation independent from political parties and linked to direct democracy.[55] In fact, all the parties involved in the process of constitution building, drafting, and debate—with the single exception of the conservative AP—were opposed to these other direct democratic procedures that they judged dangerous for the stability of the democratic system and, what is more important, for the consolidation of the political parties.[56]

On the other side of the constitutional regulation of political parties, the constitution also states that political parties must have a democratic internal functioning but, in clear and informative contrast with other constitutional precepts on the role of parties, this is a mere goodwill rule with hardly any practical or operational consequences. This is very illustrative of the position of parties in the political system because other constitutional principles have indeed had relevant practical consequences. For example, the constitution itself and other laws of constitutional development have led to the regulation of the state funding of parties and to the general regulation of party financing, including private contributions. At the same time, some of these laws of constitutional development have privileged the role of political parties, especially when they assign to parliament the selection of the members of some relevant institutions (see the next section). This has resulted in a party-controlled system of distribution of positions in certain institutions among party members and party supporters. This situation of party control or party colonization of state institutions leads us to another important indicator of party—state linkage that we analyze in the next section: party rent seeking.

Party Rent Seeking within the State

Party rent seeking refers to "the extent to which parties penetrate and control the state and use public offices for their own advantage."[57] The different types of party rent seeking, patronage, clientelism, or corruption entail a distortion of the representation function of parties but are also alternative paths to party formation and to anchoring parties in society. The institutional and social context of party building in the new Spanish democracy of the 1970s made party rent seeking within the state easy, particularly in its generic variety of state control by parties and in the form of party patronage.

The constitutional regulation of political parties in Spain opened the door to interpretations of the role of the parties as monopolistic actors in the performance of certain political functions, and, simultaneously, it also opened the door to the diffusion of party presence in certain institutional spheres.[58] The Spanish constitution gave Parliament the power to participate in the appointment of members of some very relevant public institutions. Among these are the Constitutional Court, the body in charge of the judiciary power (the General Council of the Judicial Power), and the Ombudsman, for example. Through other laws this privilege of parliament was also extended to a long list of institutions that, among others, includes bodies responsible for the supervision or regulation of different policy areas and economic sectors. In practice, the appointment of these bodies has been done by parliament through a system of quotas that distributes the positions among the parties according to their seats.

The obvious consequence is the development of strong party loyalties among the members of the institutions in whose appointment parliament takes part. However, in real terms, the role of parliament in their appointment is above all formal because the real locus of decision is with the parties' central offices and not even with the parliamentary parties.[59] This "partyness" has very negative consequences for the operation of constitutional and regulatory bodies and institutions that should be based in objectivity and independence. Furthermore, this system of party quotas has been transformed into yet another opportunity to distribute party rewards and practice patronage, as key institutional positions are allocated to party members and loyal party supporters. The legal requirement to be vetted by parliamentary committees does not prevent, in practice, the appointment of more than questionable candidates who are eventually approved on the basis of their party backing rather than their professional merits.[60]

In addition to this partisan colonization of institutional positions that should be appointed by parliament (but are in fact more than suggested by the parties), there is also evidence of party colonization of higher public administration positions. The combination of these two dynamics has significantly boosted party colonization of the state and party—state entrenchment. Some scholars have defined the penetration of parties within the higher ranks of Spanish public administration (through the appointment of these positions and of a plethora of collaborators) as a patronage system, a spoil system, or a client-patron system.[61]

In this sense, it is not at all infrequent to witness the appointment of party personnel for high-ranking positions with no regard for their (lack of) professional merits or competence, the appointment of party members or party leaders for positions that require political independence, and the saliency of partisan loyalty over and above any other technical qualifications.[62]

Despite the efforts to professionalize the higher ranks of public administration through legal reforms since the late 1990s, the results have been fairly limited as regards reducing party influence in that field.[63] And, in addition, there is hardly any progress or effective reform in the area of reducing party influence in the appointment of higher positions in constitutional bodies or other relevant institutions. It seems that there is no political will, across parties and successive governments, to change this situation.

Besides this, during the 1970s and the 1980s—the period of democratic transition and consolidation and of regional devolution and decentralization—the political and social conditions were extremely favorable to party patronage and party colonization of the public service and of the public sector. State intervention in the economy through a sizable public sector was considerable, the public administration was weak or was not consolidated as yet—or, as in the case of regional public services during the 1980s, it was in the making[64]—and the prevalence of professional and meritocratic criteria in the selection of personnel was certainly weaker than in later periods.

This context substantially contributed to the development of a quantitatively significant phenomenon of party patronage and colonization of the public administration, particularly at the local and regional levels. Notwithstanding the difficulties in analyzing illegal practices, the evidence that any observer can collect from the news reports and from interviews with key informants tends to consistently support the view that party patronage in public administration and public firms is far from being just something common in the Spanish past. It has been and still is a significant phenomenon. It is relatively frequent to see reports of these practices in the newspapers, as well as the denunciation of these practices by opposition parties and trade unions. The practice of hiring interim public servants and employees at the local and regional levels (both in the public administration and in public firms), which after some years become permanent civil servants without transparent selection processes, has been frequently denounced as party patronage.[65]

Although it is completely impossible to quantify the relative magnitude of patronage within entire regional and local administrations, and although it is entirely possible that only a small proportion of all local and regional public employees are involved, what is not in question is that this practice is quite relevant for the sustenance of party structures. The distribution of these material rewards and incentives helps parties maintain their local and regional structures, while it also allows retaining personnel that are formally paid by public administrations but who devote at least part of their time to party tasks.

Finally, Spanish parties have often been involved in political scandals and have been suspected of corruption since the 1990s. During the 1980s the scandals around party politics were almost exclusively focused on the accusations by the center-right parties and the media around the party colonization exerted by the hegemonic PSOE. However, in the 1990s party scandals and party corruption issues, several of them linked to party funding, reached a peak in public opinion and media attention. During this decade, one deputy prime minister and five socialist ministers resigned amid political scandals of different sorts (state-sponsored antiterrorist death squads, reception of kickbacks, nepotism, fiscal misbehavior), and accusations of illegal practices of party funding linked to the party control of public administration at the national and regional levels affected almost every relevant Spanish party.[66] During the 2000s, a new wave of political scandals has affected the local and regional party elites of very different parties in almost every Spanish region, although at the same time and according to survey results, the salience of the issue of political corruption for public opinion is modest. Many party politicians and members of local and regional governments have been accused of or even sentenced to prison terms for corruption, especially in the management of urban planning where reception of kickbacks, collusion with private interests, and illegal party funding are all quite common.[67]

Furthermore, the policies and the legislation enacted to prevent the types of corruption that more closely affect parties are far from being completely determined or effective. For example, the amendment of the law on party funding (in 2007) has not been ambitious enough, and crucial forms of party misbehavior have not been dealt with. Equally, the parties' internal regulations aimed at avoiding cases of corruption—and especially their limited implementation, the existence of internal ethical codes of practice, and the action of party leaderships when cases of party corruption are denounced—are all aspects in which the attempts of reform by Spanish parties have been clearly insufficient.[68]

CONCLUSION

In this chapter we have reviewed the way in which Spanish parties perform some of the main functions that correspond to parties in contemporary representative democracies and, in doing so, we have examined the very nature of parties in current Spanish politics. With this purpose we have analyzed several of the functions that parties are expected to perform in the electorate, as organizations, and in the government. We have also discussed an extremely relevant issue in every democracy, the link of parties with the state. Our assessment shows that Spanish parties are often deficient in the exercise of their functions in the electorate, that some of their organizational features hamper their capacity to perform some of their functions as organizations, and that it is only their functions in government that they carry out well. In addition, Spanish parties have a particularly intense link with the state in all the dimensions reviewed: party finances, public regulation of parties, and party rent seeking in the state. In this sense, Spanish parties are illustrative of some of the trends parties have experienced in western democracies in the past decades.[69]

Spanish parties have been unable to develop strong partisan identities with the electorate, as the low yet stable levels of party identification indicate. Besides this, there is a significant diffusion and moderate increase of antiparty sentiments and distrust toward parties, although citizens recognize the important role that parties play in democracy. The individual- and system-level consequences of these weak partisan ties and alienation toward parties are complex. Although volatility has been traditionally low and electoral turnout is above 70 percent—albeit, interestingly enough, recently individual-level volatility has been increasing while electoral turnout has slightly decreased—parties are either unable or disinterested in seeking to mobilize citizens in party-related forms of political engagement such as campaign activities.

This last condition is not surprising given that Spanish parties are weak membership organizations in comparative terms—despite the growth of the two largest nationwide parties—and seem not to be particularly concerned with boosting their membership figures. Although Spanish parties are certainly internally more democratic nowadays than they have ever been, they are not following the recent trend among western parties of empowering their membership as a strategy to make membership more appealing and recruit new members. As a result, it is doubtful that Spanish parties have the capacity to perform functions such as politically educating the public, generating symbols of identification, mobilizing the citizenry, or articulating and aggregating interests. It is clear from our analysis that Spanish parties are not excelling in providing participatory linkage.[70]

Although the social functions of parties are in peril, the more institutional or procedural ones that relate to parties as actors that structure and organize government and parliament are performed quite well by Spanish parties, as is also the case for other western democracies. Furthermore, there is a very intense linkage between parties and the state: Spanish parties are significantly regulated by the state and are extremely dependent on state subsidies for their daily functioning, and there is a significant and extended phenomenon of party rent seeking in the state.

The relationships among these circumstances—weak partisan ties, weak membership organizations, problematic performance of social functions, adequate execution of procedural functions, and intense party-state linkage—are possibly mutually reinforcing. Spanish society was hardly inclined to engage in politics during the period of transition to democracy. Consequently, parties had every incentive to find the resources that society did not provide through alternative means and tried to guarantee their survival with state resources. Given the weakness of Spanish civil society and the lack of a substantial mass party heritage, the dependence of parties on the state could only grow. Simultaneously, this strong linkage between party and state—promoted by the decisions of conscious party leaders—widened the gap between parties and society and has not contributed to improve citizens' attachment to their parties. Equally, the limited inclination of Spaniards to engage actively in politics has also favored the rapid transformation of Spanish parties into electoral-professional organizations that are strongly dependent on state subsidies and very rarely promote political participation. Hence, citizens show little interest in participating in parties, and parties show equally little concern for mobilizing Spaniards beyond the polls.

On the other hand, Spanish parties' close linkage to the state, through public subsidies and regulations, has resulted in an abundant amount of party rent seeking. Spanish parties have taken full advantage of their control of state structures and have colonized numerous public institutions. This is a widespread phenomenon and is surely related to the peculiarities of the context of democratization and to the relative youth of its democracy. The state, the new institutions, and the new public administrations were less resistant to party colonization than they normally are in most of the established democracies.[71] Additionally, the close linkage between parties and state and party rent seeking have produced numerous cases of party corruption. The implications of corrupt practices for democracy are multiple and complex, but undoubtedly they hamper parties' social functions, if only because they contribute to an increasing disaffection with them.

When Spain regained democracy, party politics was brought back in after a long involuntary recess. As in every democracy, parties are key for the functioning of Spanish democracy and party government. Spanish parties have been, overall, successful in producing stable and relatively efficient governments, but they have systematically failed to link citizens with politics beyond the strict act of voting. The latter aspect reduces parties' capacity to be responsive to societal needs, while the high levels of party rent seeking and state entrenchment clearly reduce the quality of democratic institutions and limit politicians' accountability.

CHAPTER 5

New Questions for Parties and Democracy in the United Kingdom: Participation, Choice, and Control

Paul Webb

INTRODUCTION: CONTINUITY AND CHANGE IN THE BRITISH PARTY SYSTEM

For 30 years following the end of World War II, it was orthodox to regard the United Kingdom as having one of the most stable and party-oriented political systems in the Western world. Parties penetrated state and society so significantly that it was virtually impossible to conceive of political life in the country without thinking first and foremost of party political life. Since the middle of the 1970s, however, old certainties have been challenged by a continuing and multidimensional debate about the transformation of British party politics. This challenge is predicated on a number of interconnected developments, including the apparent growth of electoral volatility; the spread of partisan and class dealignment; the emergence of nationalist cleavages in Scotland and Wales, which have threatened to fragment the national political culture; the erosion of two-party electoral domination and the concomitant growth of minor parties in the system; and the growing chorus of criticism leveled at the effects of the electoral system. Despite this, the single-member plurality ("first-past-the-post") electoral system continues to ensure that single-party majority governments remain the norm in Westminster.

It is virtually a truism that the United Kingdom is an exemplar of the two-party system. Of course, it is not literally accurate to suggest that only two political parties are represented in the House of Commons, still less that only two parties contest elections for Westminster or receive electoral support. The concept of two-partyism really implies that only two parties "count," as Giovanni Sartori puts it, in understanding the essential dynamics of the system.[1] That is, the major parties in two-party systems receive most of the votes cast in elections and are consequently able to dominate the business of government to the extent of regularly governing alone rather than in coalition. This generally remains the case at Westminster.

Yet it is widely recognized that since 1974 the two-party label has become a simplification that obscures almost as much as it reveals about party politics in the United Kingdom. The reason for this lies in the steady advance of the minor parties since that time. The percentage of the vote jointly accounted for by the Labour and the Conservative parties has dropped significantly from an average of 90 percent between 1945 and 1970 to approximately 75 percent thereafter. In 2005 their combined share of the vote fell to just 67.5 percent.

Minor party progress is further reflected in the greater fragmentation of the party system. The "effective number of parties" is a well-known measure that measures systemic fragmentation, either on the basis of party shares of the popular vote (the effective number of electoral parties [ENEP]), or shares of seats won in parliament (the effective number of parliamentary parties [ENPP]).[2] In the United Kingdom, the ENEP has increased markedly since 1970, from an average of 2.36 between 1945 and 1970, to an average of 3.21 thereafter. The trend is less pronounced for the parliamentary parties due to the disproportional impact of the electoral system. The growing fragmentation of the party system is still apparent, however, as the average ENPP increased from 2.05 to 2.21 periods. In 2005, the increase in both measures became more pronounced, with ENEP jumping to 3.48 and ENPP climbing to 2.44—the highest either measure had been since 1945. In effect, there is now a two-and-a-half-party system in the national legislative arena, but a clear multiparty system in the national electorate. Above all, this change reflects the steady electoral progress of the Liberal Democrats since 1970; indeed, since they won more than a fifth of the popular vote and 60 seats in Parliament in 2005, it is hardly appropriate to continue referring to them as a minor party. In addition, the advance of the nationalist parties in Scotland and Wales (Scottish Nationalist Party and Plaid Cymru, respectively) over the same period, and the long-standing presence of an entirely distinct party system in Northern Ireland, deriving from its peculiar history of ethnic and religious conflict between those with British, Unionist and Protestant or Irish, Nationalist and Catholic identities, means that statements to the effect that "Britain has a two-party system" are in reality gross simplifications that obscure the particular political jurisdictions and arenas of party interaction one is talking about. To put it another way, the United Kingdom actually has more than one party system, and quite different patterns of party interaction may be found within these different systems.[3]

This multiplicity has become an increasingly tangible reality of political life in light of the devolution legislation introduced by the Labour government of Tony Blair in 1997. This introduced a Scottish Parliament and Executive and a Welsh Assembly and Executive, and although the asymmetrical powers of these institutions have made for a curiously idiosyncratic form of quasi-federalism, there can be little doubt that the dynamics of party politics are quite different now in Edinburgh and Cardiff (and Belfast of course) from that in London. In each of these devolved areas of the United Kingdom, multiparty systems and coalition dynamics lend a pronounced accent of consensus democracy to the traditional voice of majoritarian democracy that has so long been associated with Westminster.

So the United Kingdom today displays a steadily evolving complex of party actions and interactions across multiple levels of governance—national, devolved, local, and European—which reflects the multilevel governance typical of a contemporary European country. Where does this leave parties as instruments of democracy in the country?

PARTIES AND DEMOCRACY IN BRITAIN: CRITIQUE AND DEBATE

One thing is quite clear: political parties in the United Kingdom today—as in so many other countries—are widely seen as disappointing in their democratic performance. Those who care about democracy are anxious. There is much talk of disconnect, alienation, and apathy, and the search is on for explanations and for ways to put things right. The blame for this state of affairs is heaped on various targets: the parties and the politicians inevitably lead the way, but somewhat less tangibly, "the political system" is apt to receive sharp criticism from some quarters. Others prefer to level their sights on the role of the mass media and occasionally even on the public itself.

To some extent, this situation dovetails with a long-standing debate between the protagonists of participatory and representative democracy. Whereas the former are inclined to blame the politicians and in some sense or other "the system," the defenders of representative politics as it currently operates are more disposed to say that citizens themselves, and the media on which they depend for political information, are culpable for the low esteem in which politics and its leading protagonists are currently held. From the perspective of this latter school, the radical participationists are unrealistic in their vision of a widespread popular capacity to engage with politics and prone to stray uncomfortably close to the territory of shallow populism in their naive and unreasonable view of the job done by political elites; from the perspective of the participationists, however, their critics appear to be apologists for an anachronistic elitist view of democracy, who take insufficient account of the cognitive revolution that has facilitated a far greater potential for popular political engagement.

THE PARTICIPATIONIST CRITIQUE

It is common for critics to argue that the solution to the perceived problems of contemporary democratic systems lies in an injection of more participatory forms of democracy. Among other things, this approach proposes that, given the particular weakness of parties in terms of representative and participatory linkage, citizens are becoming disaffected and disengaged. Give them more and better forms of democratic linkage, goes the argument, with an emphasis on greater participation, and the disaffection will evaporate. A striking recent example of the argument that participatory reforms can (in part) provide an answer to the problem of democratic disconnect is provided by the report of the Power Inquiry. The Power Report was published in the spring of 2006 as "an independent inquiry into Britain's democracy," funded by the Joseph Rowntree Charitable and Reform Trusts and carried out by a commission headed up by Helena Kennedy. The report is essentially a reaction to what its authors believe is a crisis in British governance. At the heart of this crisis, it suggests, lies a sclerotic system that has failed to keep pace with social change and that is run by elites disconnected from those they are supposed to serve, many of whom are therefore turning away from conventional politics altogether.[4]

In effect, the Power Report counter-poses a people seemingly bursting with pent-up democratic energy with an elitist and bankrupt political system incapable of tapping that burgeoning potential. A good example of this is the report's diagnosis of disengagement and declining turnout in general elections—one of its major preoccupations. The "reality," it seems, is that "the process of formal democracy"—a process about which people feel ill-informed—(1) offers people insufficient influence, (2) is run by parties they think are too similar and that require them "to commit to too broad a range of policies," and (3) involves an electoral system whose procedures are "inconvenient" and whose results are marred by "unequal and wasted votes." The report's solution to these problems is to propose a set of recommendations that will apparently contribute to the "three fundamental shifts" it wants to see, namely (1) "a shift of power away from the Executive . . . and from central to local," (2) "the creation of an electoral and party system which is responsive enough to the changing values and demands of today's population to allow the necessary and organic creation of new political alliances, value systems and organisations which better represent those values and demands," and (3) "the creation of a culture of political engagement in which policy and decision-making employs direct input from citizens."[5]

It is the last of these objectives that most obviously entails the greater deployment of direct and participatory democracy, although some of the detailed proposals designed to weaken the cohesion of parliamentary parties would also be important in paving the way for greater influence of direct democracy insofar as they would likely undermine the representative model's central feature—party government and its attendant chain of accountability. The report contains few recommendations as to the precise forms by which direct participation might be enhanced, although it argues that "citizens should be given the right to initiate legislative processes, public inquiries and hearings into public bodies and their senior management," and expresses its confidence that advances in communication technology will "increasingly allow large numbers of citizens to become engaged in political decisions in a focussed way."[6] Of course there are a number of variants of radical participatory democracy within contemporary political theory, some of which emerge in the British debate from time to time.[7] Although there are few signs that the British state is yet ready for anything as radical as the "realistic utopianism" of deliberative democracy for the masses, in recent years the government has shown some interest in extending elements of what it regards as direct democracy (for instance, through changes in the formal way in which public petitions are dealt with by Parliament).[8] Neither should it go unremarked that there is a further, but quite different, type of supporter of participatory—or at least, direct—democracy. This is populism. Populism is a peculiar variant—many might say pathology—of democracy which is characterized by a number of features including:

- The view that society is "separated into two homogeneous and antagonistic groups, the 'pure people' versus the 'corrupt elite,' and which argues that politics should be an expression of the *volonté générale* (general will) of the people";[9]
- A preference for a direct plebiscitary relationship with a heroic leader, unmediated by the institutions, checks, and balances of liberal and representative democracy;
- The professed aim of defending the established culture, traditions, and rights of "the people" against perceived threats from alien influences, which may be defined in terms of social groups (e.g., immigrants) or political institutions (e.g., the European Union [EU]).

Populism thus constitutes a rejection of representative politics per se. As Gianfranco Pasquino wrote, "in the populist mentality, there is no appreciation at all that some groups of individuals are needed who acquire political and institutional knowledge and apply it to the running of public affairs. Party politicians are always considered an obstacle to the expression of the 'true' will of the people."[10] Populists frequently advocate "more" democracy in the form of referendums that will permit the people to bypass the "self-interested liberal elite that is systematically betraying the interest of ordinary citizens,"[11] at least on issues where they are convinced they have a popular majority (such as capital punishment or immigration). This is illustrated in the United Kingdom by the shared preference of all of the main parties of the radical populist right for referendum democracy; the British National Party (BNP), United Kingdom Independence Party (UKIP), and its short-lived offspring Veritas all vaunted this ambition in their manifestos at the 2005 general election.[12]

THE SKEPTICS' RESPONSE

Broadly speaking, there are two ways in which the participationist critique and prescription have met with a skeptical response: the first is to argue that the problem of disaffection with the central institutions and processes of representative democracy flows in large part from a palpable failure of most ordinary citizens to understand the nature of politics and their role as citizens; the second is to deny that more participation provides a plausible way out of the problem anyway. Logically, the latter position often flows from the former. Since the problem, in the view of the skeptics, is not essentially one of systemic failure or elite shortcomings, the solution should not be to transform our institutions by making them radically more participatory; rather, we should be seeking to understand why so few people really see what politics is about and, therefore, educate them better and eradicate the sources of their incomprehension.

There have recently been a number of outspoken expressions of dismay at the apparent misapprehensions of so many citizens and commentators regarding the nature of democratic politics in the United Kingdom. Representative of this line of argument is Meg Russell's Fabian pamphlet, in which she poses the question "Must Politics Disappoint?," self-consciously taking up the mantle of Bernard Crick's (1962) classic *In Defence of Politics.*[13] She contends that "many of our problems stem from our having forgotten what politics is there for, and why it is beneficial." Starting from Crick's definition of politics as "the activity by which differing interests within a given unit of rule are conciliated by giving them a share of power in proportion to their importance to the welfare and to the survival of the whole community," she laments that politicians and the media too often fail to communicate the essence of politics, "that it is about negotiation and compromise, difficult choices and taking decisions together." Instead, "it is now seen as something largely divorced from everyday life, where politicians are expected to 'deliver,' and increasingly talk their profession down rather than up, within a media environment that is hostile rather than supportive."[14] Culpability for this state of affairs should be shared by citizens, politicians and the media, in her view. Russell identifies a number of causes for the political malaise, chief amongst which is the modern culture of consumerism:

> It is difficult to find anything more antithetical to the culture of politics than the contemporary culture of consumerism. While politics is about balancing diverse needs to benefit the public interest, consumerism is about meeting the immediate desires of the individual. While politics requires us to compromise and collaborate as citizens, consumerism emphasises unrestrained individual freedom of choice. While politics recognises that there are always resource constraints, modern consumerism increasingly encourages us to believe that we can have it all now.[15]

Russell goes on to offer further causes of the crisis of politics, including the adversarial style of British party politics, the advent of modern political campaigning, the nature of media coverage of politics, ideological convergence between major parties, and the growing mutual autonomy of leaders and the parties that should sustain them. While the solutions she proposes contain some elements of enhanced participation (e.g., within political parties), they are largely focused on the need to construct a new, franker, more open and positive culture that emphasizes the value of politics and its central institutions. Politics should come to be regarded as a source of pride, "a cause not for despair, but for celebration."

It should be noted that much in Meg Russell's broad vein of argument is echoed strongly in Gerry Stoker's notable recent addition to the literature, *Why Politics Matters*.[16] Note too that Russell's list of causal factors does include reference to some that are party related, such as ideological convergence between Labour and the Conservatives and the growing mutual autonomy of leaders and the parties. Thus, it would be fair to say that while she is skeptical of some of the criticism leveled at Britain's major democratic institutions, she does not seek to entirely absolve parties of the blame.

The skeptics also reject the view that more participation would work. There is a long tradition of democratic theory, of course, which is generally skeptical of the supposed benefits of participatory democracy. Advocates of elitist representative democracy, such as Joseph Schumpeter, have always regarded the popular control requirement of democracy as satisfied by little more than the electorate's capacity to remove leaders when they are no longer wanted. This is a relatively undemanding criterion for assessing the performance of political elites, which implies that antipathy or disaffection might be based mainly on the ignorant and unreasonable expectations of citizens. In any case, representative democrats would argue, more participation is not the answer to the problem. From the perspective of this school, the solution to the problem of popular disaffection with politics is not to compel citizens to undertake more of it, but rather to find a way of getting them to better understand and appreciate it. This brings us back to Meg Russell's call for a "new culture of politics" and also resonates with the introduction of citizenship education as part of the national curriculum that operates in schools in the United Kingdom (something that owes a considerable debt to the work of Bernard Crick).

The eminent British political scientist and conservative peer (Lord) Philip Norton has cast doubt on the notion that the current structure of representative politics in Britain frustrates citizens and causes a resentment that would only be relieved by institutional reforms designed to bypass party politics by extending participatory democracy. Speaking in a debate on the Power Report in the House of Lords,[17] he cited evidence from the Audit of Political Engagement survey, which shows that, although people tend to claim they want to have a say in the way the country is run and feel they are presently denied that opportunity, when asked what type of activity they would be prepared to engage in, a different picture emerges: "beyond signing petitions, the vast majority of respondents were unwilling to undertake any further action." Furthermore, Norton cites Declan McHugh's argument that more participatory democracy "may only succeed in engaging those already over-represented amongst voters and party members—that is, the educated, affluent and middle class. Mechanisms designed to provide greater opportunities for citizens to participate more directly in decision-making as a means of increasing legitimacy and reducing the perceived democratic deficit may therefore have the opposite effect."[18]

Elsewhere I have suggested that this debate points to the need for considerably more sophisticated empirical research on the British case.[19] We need to know far more about public attitudes toward democratic institutions and processes and their own roles therein. The roles played by political parties need to be part of any such research agenda. In particular, it is important to engage with the challenge to the participationist critics posed by the research conducted in the United States by John Hibbing and Elizabeth Theiss-Morse:

> The last thing people want is to be more involved in political decision-making: They do not want to make political decisions themselves; they do not want to provide much input to those who are assigned to make these decisions; and they would rather not know the details of the decision-making process. . . . This does not mean that people think no mechanism for government accountability is necessary; they just do not want the mechanism to come into play except in unusual circumstances.[20]

Like Russell and Stoker, Hibbing and Theiss-Morse are struck by the naive and unrealistic views about the nature of the political process that many citizens maintain. They discovered a widespread belief that Americans generally shared similar basic goals but were betrayed by elites in areas of "special interests." This was seen to create a cacophonous power struggle based on the pursuit of self-interest, whereas it was felt that an impartial technocratic elite should be able to make policies based on the public interest. There is perhaps more than a hint of populism in all this and in the consequent belief "that the common good is not debatable but, rather, will be apparent if selfishness can be stripped away."[21]

Hibbing and Theiss-Morse summarize the orientations of U.S. citizens as a preference for some kind of "stealth" arrangement, whereby citizens know that democracy exists but expect it to be barely visible on a routine basis, an attitude that they describe as naive and unfeasible. The upshot of the "Stealth Democracy" study is that the authors criticize both the naiveté of popular attitudes toward politics and the insistence of some observers that participatory democracy provides the solution to it. "People need to understand that disagreements can occur among people of good heart and that some debating and compromising will be necessary to resolve these disagreements and come to a collective solution. As such, education designed to increase people's appreciation of democracy needs to be a crucial element of efforts to improve the current situation."[22] The alleged benefits of participatory democracy are derided as "wishful thinking," and they point out that research tends to reveal that it only works under very limited conditions. "Deliberation will not work in the real world of politics where people are different and where tough, zero-sum decisions must be made . . . real deliberation is quite likely to make them hopping mad or encourage them to suffer silently because of a reluctance to voice their own opinions in the discussion."[23] Indeed, they cite a variety of research evidence to debunk three of the major claims of the participationists: that deliberative and participatory democracy produces better decision making; that it enhances the legitimacy of the political system; and that it leads to personal development ("improves people"). Overall, these are bold and important claims that need further substantiation in democratic countries, Britain included.

To summarize, the debate among British observers is typified on the one hand by those who see representative democracy in the country as deeply flawed because of its failure to engage citizens, and on the other by those who see a heavy dose of institutional reform entailing significant elements of participatory or direct democracy as the answer. Political parties are often seen as a major part of the problem of representative democracy by this school. Of late, however, such critics have been countered by a chorus of skepticism about their diagnosis and remedy, although the skeptics do not suggest that parties are beyond criticism.

POLITICAL PARTIES AND DEMOCRACY: THEORETICAL CONSIDERATIONS

Although it is important to understand the main features of the current debate as set out above, we can go further in terms of how this relates to democratic theory. For some "democracy" is a contested concept, subject to rival interpretations, and conclusions about parties are inevitably shaped by normative and theoretical perspectives on democracy.[24] Taking a cue from Alan Ware, we can identify three core elements to democracy. These receive differing emphases in the various treatments of the subject, and the different weight accorded to each element inevitably affects perceptions of party performance. Ware refers to the first democratic element as interest optimalization, the second as civic orientation, and the third as popular choice and control.[25] I will use these three perspectives on democratic theory as a way of organizing my discussion of the current performance of parties in the United Kingdom.

Democracy as Interest Optimalization

For a political system to be democratic, Ware suggests, "rules or procedures employed must bring about results that optimally promote or defend the interests of the largest number of people in the relevant arena."[26] From this perspective, there have broadly been two approaches to the role of parties in fostering democracy, both of which focus implicitly on the articulation and aggregation of interests. Each raises problems of party performance in contemporary democracies such as the United Kingdom.

First, there are pluralists who are not intrinsically hostile to parties as agencies of representative democracy, but who see them as largely secondary to interest groups. There is of course widespread evidence in the United Kingdom and elsewhere of the burgeoning role of interest groups as rivals to articulators of demands, a development seemingly consistent with the pluralist perspective.[27] But this challenge to party is in truth less problematic for the functioning of democracy than the growing problem of aggregation that it poses. Indeed, there is nothing particularly new in this observation, for pluralists themselves were quick to note the problems caused by an explosion of interest articulation that is unmatched by a commensurate rise in a political system's aggregative capacity.[28] Processes of social and political change have almost certainly confronted the parties with new challenges in this respect, as the growing heterogeneity of British society has brought new social group demands and issues on to the agenda of politics to which the parties have sometimes struggled to respond adequately.[29] To be sure, it is hard to see an alternative vehicle to the political party for the aggregation of political demands in a country like the United Kingdom. Single-issue groups may rival parties in the "market for activism,"[30] but they are not in the business of bundling together a multiplicity of interests into ordered and coherent programs of legislative action; interest aggregation, then, remains a core party function. However, this task has become more complex given the growing number of cross-cutting cleavages and issue dimensions which have emerged in the United Kingdom (think of European integration, Scottish and Welsh nationalism, gender politics, environmentalism, and the response to 9/11 for starters); these issues do not always fit easily into the traditional boxes of party politics, which makes it a struggle to build sustainable coalitions of support. Moreover, this struggle may even have undermined the ability of parties to articulate traditional group demands; for Labour at least, the adoption of a more broadly aggregative interclass appeal (the catch-all strategy) since the time of Harold Wilson's leadership in the 1960s has weakened its role as a working-class tribune. In short, in attempting to develop its aggregative capacity, Labour may well have weakened its ability to articulate demands, a phenomenon that reached its apogee under Tony Blair more than 30 years later.

Aggregation is a function that also features highly among the concerns of the second group of "interest optimizers," the social choice acolytes of Kenneth Arrow who argue that the electoral process is destined to be flawed inasmuch as it produces voting "paradoxes" and "cycles."[31] Their conclusion is that it is virtually impossible to satisfy people's wants in an optimal way unless policy is made in homogeneous and consensual communities (which advanced industrial societies like the United Kingdom manifestly are not), or in pure two-party contexts: the latter scenario simplifies programmatic choice to a binary decision-making process and thereby avoids the well-known problem of "cyclical majorities," which arises when three or more alternatives are available. Strictly speaking, all contemporary advanced industrial democracies fail such a test: even the United States, the nearest thing to pure two partyism, does not always guarantee voters a straightforward choice between two candidates, even for presidential office, and as we have already observed, the United Kingdom is less and less purely a two-party system. From this perspective, then, parties do not help avoid this democratic paradox.[32]

Democracy as Civic Orientation

The second element of democracy identified by Ware is that of civic orientation. From this perspective, democracy is not fully realized until citizens express their shared interests as members of the same community, a theme that goes back at least as far as Jean-Jacques Rousseau. Participation in the democratic process is vital to the political education of citizens if they are to develop this civic orientation. Advocates have therefore often placed political participation and education high on their list of criteria for evaluating democracy and its institutions. Implicitly, too, the aggregation of demands into a general will that expresses the public interest is important to this approach. Contemporary political parties are unlikely to fare well by the civic democrat's standards, however.

On normative grounds radical civic orientationists have usually argued, in the Rousseauean vein, that parties are inimical since they tend to articulate and foster narrow group interests to the detriment of the wider community: this is very different from the view of pluralists, who regard pursuit of group interests as central to healthy democracy. It can be readily appreciated that contemporary parties in a country such as the United Kingdom can do little to instill such a demanding notion of civic orientation. It hardly helps to adopt a less demanding version of the concept, so that any kind of community consciousness, including group identity based on region, class, religion, or ethnicity, qualifies. This is because of the widely described demise of cleavage politics and mass parties based on class communities (although Northern Ireland represents an exception to this, with its major parties still being central to the subcultural segmentation of that society).

Furthermore, although it is possible to point to the increased participatory rights that British parties have offered their members in matters of candidate and leadership selection in recent years,[33] it is impossible to overlook the overwhelming evidence of membership and turnout decline. Even allowing for vagaries of accurate data, party membership decline has been little short of precipitous. In 1964, over 9 percent of all registered electors were members of the main three British parties with nationwide organizations; by the time of the 1992 general election, barely 2 percent were (an 80 percent decline in proportional terms).[34] Even allowing for the growth of certain minor parties not included in these calculations (notably the Scottish Nationalists) and the remarkable surge in Labour Party recruitment after Tony Blair was elected leader in the summer of 1994, it is quite evident that a significant trend is apparent. In any case, New Labour's burst of recruitment soon started to reverse itself after the election of May 1997. Moreover, this collapse of membership has a counterpart in declining levels of party activism. In the course of their research on major party membership in Britain, Patrick Seyd and Paul Whiteley uncovered a number of indications of declining activism among members of both the Labour and Conservative parties.[35]

In respect of electoral turnout, this did not follow any clear trend in the postwar period until the past decade. General election turnout was actually higher in the 1992 general election than it was in that of 1945 (77.7% compared to 73.3%), but in 1997 it dropped to its lowest level in any postwar general election up to that point in time (just 71.6%), the greatest decline in national turnout between any pair of elections since 1945. However, this fall was easily outdone in 2001, as turnout plummeted to just 59.5%, a collapse in mass participation that staggered most commentators. There was but a modest recovery in 2005. Overall, then, there can be little doubt that the electorate is notably less likely to engage in active partisan life in Britain, all of which suggests that from the civic visionary's perspective, political parties are at best irrelevant, at worst downright pathological.

Democracy as Popular Choice and Control

By the standards of Ware's third element of democracy—popular control—political parties in the United Kingdom seem less dysfunctional, although still challenged. Even if participation and civic orientation are limited, and interests are not fully optimized, democracy can be regarded as meaningful to the extent that it provides the opportunity for people to exercise a degree of choice and control over public affairs. Ware identifies two distinctive approaches within this tradition. First, there are democratic elitists such as Joseph Schumpeter who see "popular control" as consisting of little more than the electorate's capacity to remove leaders when their governance is no longer wanted. This is probably the least demanding perspective in terms of party performance. In fact, parties may not even be strictly necessary to it, so long as there are rival candidates to contest the major elective offices of state. That said, parties are useful for democratic elitists insofar as they facilitate the necessary process of electoral competition and perform the implicit function of recruiting candidates for office. Thus, democratic elitists should have no serious criticisms of contemporary parties, and one presumes they would regard phenomena such as the decline of party membership and partisan dealignment with relative equanimity. Arguably, however, they should be less sanguine about problems in aggregating group interests, for this is central to the provision of meaningful choice to voters.

The second approach to popular control imposes somewhat higher expectations on parties. Associated with E. E. Schattschneider, this argues that meaningful control can be exerted through mechanisms of popular choice and emphasizes a number of requirements.[36] Crucially, there must be a connection between the competing programs put before the electorate and the policies a government implements. For Schattschneider the best way of ensuring this was to have a two-party system, since this would maximize the chances of single-party government, which he assumed to be less likely than a coalition to dilute its campaign promises in office. In fact, Schattschneider may have exaggerated the virtues of two partyism in this respect, for there is now evidence that two-party systems do not necessarily perform better in producing party effects on governing outputs than coalitional systems, except where the latter arise from very fragmented consociational polities such as the Low Countries.[37]

As opposed to this, however, there is systematic evidence that suggests that parties still have very significant impacts on government. This is crucial to the party government model of democracy, according to which public policy should emanate from party sources that can clearly be identified and held to account by the citizenry.[38] There are a number of potential challenges to this, however, the first of which is breakdown of party cohesion. Noncohesive, fluid, and unpredictable patterns of alignment in parliamentary parties can undermine the capacity of the executive to effect its legislative program and make it difficult for electors to hold accountable specific parties or coalitions of parties that might be regarded as the authors of policy. In the United Kingdom, however, this condition is still largely satisfied by the prevalence of single-party government. It is true that cross-party negotiations and collaboration are not entirely absent and have become more evident, especially in the government of Scotland, Wales, and Northern Ireland. But there is no evidence that such coalitions are especially noncohesive. That said, it is interesting that although party discipline at Westminster is still strong enough for governments to enact most (and often all) of their preferred legislative programs, there is clear evidence of a growth in backbench dissent since 1970.[39] This trend, which has reached its zenith to date under New Labour since 2001, regularly obliges governments to negotiate amendments to its legislative proposals. The growing rebelliousness of the House of Lords has a similar effect.[40] None of this means that public policy can no longer be clearly identified as the policy of a given party or (occasionally) coalition of parties in Britain, but it is evidence that parties and their leaderships are becoming increasingly uncoupled from each other.

This leads us to a related challenge to party government—that of the replacement of parties by individual leaders in the governing process. The possibility that an essentially collegial form of party government is stealthily being usurped by candidate-centered executive leadership is reinforced by evidence of the "presidentialization" of campaigning and voter influences.[41] It should be said that this contention is not in itself novel; a well-known debate on this matter took place in the 1960s.[42] More recently, however, it has been persuasively demonstrated that a powerful prime ministerial department has come to exist "in all but name" as the changing structure of the core executive in the country and the resources available in the prime minister's office and the cabinet offices have brought about transformation of the central state. The traditional fragmentation of the central state in Britain creates a pressing and persistent need for coordination, which is increasingly met by an "integrated core which operates as the central point in the key policy networks."[43] Margaret Thatcher and Tony Blair have been the leaders who most obviously seemed to develop a presidential style of government.[44]

Even so, it must be said that while British prime ministers can often appear firmly in control of the ship of government, they still depend critically on the confidence of their cabinet colleagues and backbench supporters in the Commons, as the reluctant departures from Downing Street of both Thatcher and Blair illustrate. The former lost the confidence of key cabinet colleagues and backbenchers, while her successor John Major's period at the helm of government was devastated by backbench dissent. Even Tony Blair was no monocrat, as his uneasy relationship with Chancellor of Exchequer Gordon Brown attested. I would conclude that while both the nature of modern political communications and the institutional capacity of government are such that the potential for personalized forms of executive leadership is greater than before, the contingent forces of history and circumstance may well still constrain this through the agency of other members of the government, backbenchers, and even extraparliamentary activists. To this extent, party still shapes governing outputs. However, there is a constant tension between partified and personalized forms of leadership, making for an oscillation between the two over time, underlying which is a trend toward the latter.

A related requirement of parties from the popular choice and control perspective is that they should have sufficient control of the state in order to implement their policies once in power. This is essentially a question of personnel in a country like Britain. Evidence suggests that parties in the United Kingdom are important in this respect: if there is one function that parties still dominate it is political recruitment. Party penetration of the British state is generally high and has become higher since 1960.

For one thing, cabinet ministers are, by long-standing convention, obliged to be parliamentarians, and the latter are almost entirely party politicians. In 1997, the former BBC journalist Martin Bell won the seat of Tatton as an independent (on an anticorruption ticket); in 2001, Dr. Richard Taylor, a retired consultant physician angered by government plans to relocate accident and emergency services away from his local hospital, won the Wyre Forest seat on an Independent Kidderminster Hospital and Health Concern ticket (defending it successfully in 2005). Both, however, constitute rare counter-examples to the domination of the House of Commons by party politicians.[45] Even the occasional selection of nonparliamentarians (and, indeed, of nonparty members) for junior governmental posts is something entirely in the hands of the leading party politicians;[46] taken together with evidence that British voters are overwhelmingly concerned with party rather than candidate considerations, this seems to confirm unequivocally that national governmental recruitment is primarily a party-oriented rather than a candidate-centered process.

The same emphasis on party is largely true of local government. Although it was not uncommon for independent nonpartisan councilors to play a significant role in local politics until the major reorganization of local government in the 1970s, this has now become comparatively rare, except at the lowest level of subnational government. To this extent, therefore, there is actually a case for arguing that party penetration of the polity has increased since 1960. The constitutional reforms by which the new Labour government of 1997 introduced devolution and citywide government in London has not altered the essential picture, since candidacies for these new offices are also dominated by party nominees, although it should be said that the first London mayoral election did result in the remarkable victory of a nonparty candidate. Where cities opt to follow London's example of instituting directly elected mayors, some potential for candidate-centered politics may emerge at the subnational level; however, this has not become the norm.

Neither should it be overlooked that there is a whole layer of nonelective public office that is part of the means by which Britain's public institutions are governed and resources allocated—that of the "quangocracy." QUANGOs (an acronym for quasi-autonomous nongovernmental organization) are bodies appointed by ministers to undertake delegated functions outside central Whitehall departments, given budgets and powers by their sponsor departments and then left to get on with their work, accountable to their secretaries of state and occasionally cross-examined in parliamentary committees. Exactly how extensive the quangocracy is, is a matter of some conjecture and dispute, for much depends on the precise definition and methodology used; estimates vary from 500 to several thousand QUANGOs in the United Kingdom, running at a total cost to the taxpayer of anywhere from 64 billion to 123 billion pounds, equivalent to 9.3% of gross domestic product and 21.1% of total public spending.[47] QUANGOs are involved in an enormous range of activity and public provision, including school governorships, Training and Enterprise Councils, local health authorities and hospital trusts, and a variety of funding councils. Many of these positions are in the gift of the political parties, and indeed the increasingly naked exploitation of this vast reservoir of patronage by the Conservative governments between 1979 and 1997 became a subject of some controversy on the 1990s. Often the quangocracy's domain seemed to be enhanced at the expense of elective local authorities, and increasingly the Tories regarded it as vital to the exercise of power that sympathizers—especially from the world of business—outnumbered their rivals' appointees on all these bodies.[48] In opposition, Labour politicians made much of this phenomenon and promised a bonfire of QUANGOs when they came to office; after more than a decade in power, however, similar criticisms are now leveled at Labour by their opponents, who claim that the number and costs of QUANGOs grows steadily.

And there is another reason why QUANGOs tend to survive the axemen: these agencies remain a good way for politicians to reward party stalwarts, old colleagues, friends, and cronies. Many of the best known QUANGOs have Labour supporters employed in their ranks. The former Labour leader Lord Kinnock is now head of the British Council. The Labour-supporting chief executive of the Tate galleries, Sir Nicholas Serota, was already ensconced when Labour came to power, but over the past 10 years he has acquired a knighthood and a new chairman, the Labour-backing business grandee Paul Myners, who partially funded Gordon Brown's leadership campaign in 2009.[49]

It is impossible to say just how partisan the exercise of power within these many and varied bodies is, but public criticism such as outlined above risks creating the impression that representative forms of democratic linkage are being usurped by clientelistic linkages and this does little to enhance the popular reputation of parties or their ability to perform their representative function effectively.

Thus far, I have focused on the questions of party control of government and state that are important from the choice and control perspective on democracy and have shown that by and large party control remains strong. But there is the choice side of the equation to consider as well, and here the picture is far less clear. Indeed, parties are often said to fail to offer citizens the meaningful political choices that Schattschneider identified as crucial to the ability of citizens to exercise control over accountable political elites. This is through their alleged convergence around centrist ideological options. An interesting recent variant of this critique has been developed by Colin Hay who argues that the current political malaise among citizens owes much to the narrowing of political space in Britain around a neo-liberal consensus. This has generated a depoliticization of public life, incorporating privatization, deregulation, the hollowing-out of the British state as responsibilities have been sectioned off from central government to more distant agencies, and a greater emphasis on individual responsibility. The net effect of this has been to restrict the domain in which politicians may act, or state a convincing case for political action. This in turn simply serves to undermine the point of politics in the eyes of many citizens.[50]

What evidence is there to support the contention that the choice of parties makes little meaningful difference in policy outcomes in the United Kingdom? This issue bears directly upon the issue of accountability, for if parties are fundamentally unable to shape public policy, who does (if anyone), and who should be held to account (if anyone)? It is an issue of obvious importance for democratic perform-ance. It is of course well recognized that a variety of macrosocial devel-opments can seriously constrain the scope for autonomous action by party governments, including technological changes, demographic trends, social changes, and economic cycles. Indeed, the whole question of global economic constraints on national governmental autonomy has become one of the defining political themes of the contemporary era and a highly vexed issue for politicians and intellectuals alike. The power of these implacable and impersonal forces can seem daunting, and it is not surprising that commentators should question the ability of parties to make any real difference. In fact, the broad question of whether or not they do breaks down into at least two more specific issues: first, do parties actually offer the electorate reasonably distinct policy alternatives, or are they so convergent as to render the idea of choice meaningless (Hay's point)? Second, irrespective of what they might promise to electors, do they actually generate real differences in terms of policy outputs once they get the opportunity to wield power?

The more straightforward issue to deal with is that of programmatic distinctiveness. Long-term manifesto analyses of shifting party ideolo-gies demonstrate that ideological distance between the major U.K. par-ties tends to fluctuate. There have been times in the past few decades when the gap between Labour and the Conservatives has approximated a gulf, the early 1980s being the most obvious such occasion. However, more than one study shows that this gulf has diminished sharply since 1992, at least in terms of left-right ideology.[51] Ideological convergence is particularly evident in matters of macroeconomic management, and analysis of manifestos suggests that the long-term trend has been one of convergence in the United Kingdom.[52] This should not lead us to the simplistic conclusion that there are no important differences between the major parties; it is not hard to demonstrate sharp contrasts over themes like constitutional reform, Europe, or welfare policy in recent years, but it does suggest that those who struggle to discern the differences have picked up on something tangible.

Does the growing indistinctness of ideological emphases, at least in certain areas, render insignificant party impacts on policy outcomes? The general conclusion has been that parties can and do continue to make a difference, at least to quantitative trends in public expendi-ture.[53] Given the preponderance of single-party governments in the postwar era, Britain is precisely the sort of country in which one would expect to find a definite link between manifesto promises and govern-ment action. Even so, two further points are worth adding. First, quite apart from the quantitative analyses, it is intuitively still obvious to most observers that parties can affect quite distinctive qualitative shifts in public policy once in power. One need only think of the conservative governments' legislative initiatives on trade union powers or social and educational policy in the 1980s; similarly, New Labour's agenda of constitutional reform was less quantitative than qualitative in its implications for the British state, yet it was none the less profound for all that. Second, it should be borne in mind that the longer parties are in power, the greater their policy impact is likely to be. As has often been pointed out, public policy tends to have a momentum of its own, and it can take considerable time and effort to change its direction. This fact may well explain an asymmetry in the party effects discovered by Klingemann, Hofferbert, and Budge:[54] The Conservatives tend to have a greater impact on policy outputs when in office than Labour. When one bears in mind that between 1945 and 1997, the Conservatives enjoyed 35 years in office compared to Labour's 17, including unbroken spells of 18 years and 13 years, compared to Labour's maximum incumbency of 6 years, it is readily apparent that the former have experienced significantly greater opportunities for wielding long-term influence over the development of national policy.

In essence, therefore, the overall conclusion must be that, while there have undoubtedly been significant areas of policy convergence between the parties, they remain central to the provision of meaningful and accountable governing choices in the United Kingdom. However, the (partly justified) perception of many voters that there are no great differences between the major parties probably contributes to the erosion of their popular standing.

CONCLUSION: PARTIES AND DEMOCRATIC REFORM IN THE UNITED KINGDOM

Political parties in the United Kingdom, as elsewhere in the democratic world, attract many expressions of dissent and disapproval. With some reason they can be criticized for offering weaker participatory linkage than was once the case, and certainly weaker than participationist visionaries would desire. It is unsurprising then that one of the major lines of criticism of party democracy in Britain is that it should be supplemented by substantial and radical new forms of participatory or direct engagement by citizens. It is equally hard to make a case that political parties are important to the building of community or civic orientations in the country, except in the most banal sense. Any Rousseauian notion of "community" can be dismissed as unrealistic utopianism in a large, plural, and modern industrial society, and the withering of social class communities has further undermined any claims that parties might be integral to community-building today.

But parties in Britain have probably never thought of making such claims for themselves, even implicitly. The party model of democratic government is premised, instead, on the notion that it affords the citizenry a meaningful degree of choice between and control over political elites, inasmuch as it is crucial to fostering accountability through elections. Weakness in performing this function is a particularly acute issue for political parties in the United Kingdom, and there are two particular problems that emerge in this connection. First, parties suffer from the widespread perception that they fail to offer sufficiently meaningful choice to voters, for one reason or another. For those on the left in particular, this often comes down to the criticism that the major parties share in a neo-liberal consensus, which has narrowed the range of feasible policy options. I have suggested here that this view is simplistic and overlooks the ways in which parties can "make a difference," but this may be beside the point; the fact is that the perception of diminished political choice is widespread and this alone is enough to feed public cynicism about party politics.

Paradoxically, the second problem emerges from what appears to be a strength of party in Britain: the degree of control that parties exert over state personnel and the legislative process. We have seen that this control helps the United Kingdom closely approximate the party government model of accountability. Since the parties are sufficiently cohesive in parliament, single-party governments can get most of their legislative programs enacted, thus redeeming their manifesto pledges. This enables voters to identify clearly the appropriate executive actors who should be held accountable, and these actors can be rewarded or punished at the next election. Even if it is the case that executive leadership and electoral processes are becoming more focused on individual politicians at the expense of parties, this does not present a great problem for the party government model of accountability, since the eviction from office of a particular leader by the electorate necessarily entails the eviction of the party team around him or her as well. However, the extent of party control over the state may be becoming part of the problem in terms of public perception and legitimacy, for it is the features of party control that the public seems to disapprove of. There is ample evidence that voters dislike the quangocracy, cronyism, or anything that strikes them as parties feather-bedding or entrenching their positions. The long-standing debate in Britain about the impact of the single-member plurality electoral system, which underrepresents the liberal democrats in particular and serves as a high representational threshold to new parties, is one aspect of this, although it is not (yet) the case that a majority of voters wish to see proportional representation for Westminster elections. The growing recourse to state funding of parties—regarded as rent-seeking behavior by parties by some political scientists—is another, newer aspect. Although the financial situation of parties in Britain is rarely comfortable, and there may well be a rational case for greater state support, there is little doubt that the public at large is hostile to the idea, regarding it as somehow sleazy and self-regarding. Notwithstanding the extensive reform of the regulatory framework of party funding in the United Kingdom in the past decade, and the efforts of the parties to extend this yet further in the near future,[55] the warning of Peter Mair still seems apposite in this respect:

> On the ground, and in terms of their representative role, parties appear to be less relevant and to be losing some of their key functions. In public office, on the other hand, and in terms of their linkage to the state, they appear to be more privileged than ever.[56]

This suggests that reform efforts somehow need to focus on the perceived problems of excessive party control of the state, without undermining their capacity to enact promised legislative programs. Such an agenda would encompass matters of party funding, electoral reform, and the process of making public appointments. Even so, while such reforms may be intrinsically worthy—and indeed, are on the governmental agenda—it is hard to believe that they would impact radically on public opinion. Neither is there yet convincing evidence to suggest a great appetite among citizens for a radical extension of participation or that it would significantly improve public support for political elites and parties; after all, there are countries around the world where direct and participatory democratic practices already exist but they have not prevented similar trends in public disaffection as those displayed by Britain. Overall, this review suggests that political parties continue to make an important contribution to the functioning of democracy in the United Kingdom, but are more challenged and less appreciated for what they do. Although they strive to find the reforms that will rectify the situation, it is doubtful that any that are envisaged will have a significant impact in the foreseeable future. This is perhaps because the roots of the apparent malaise are less institutional than attitudinal in nature, reflecting the changing nature of advanced industrial societies.

PART II

Scandinavia

CHAPTER 6

The Massive Stability of the Danish Multiparty System: A Pyrrhic Victory?

Christian Elmelund-Præstekær,
Jørgen Elklit, and Ulrik Kjaer

INTRODUCTION

In a European—and certainly in an international—perspective, the Danish political system has been remarkably stable. For more than a century, Denmark has experienced no revolutions, not even velvet ones. Inspired by the Belgian and the Norwegian[1] and to some extent the American and the French constitutions,[2] Denmark wrote its constitution (Grundlov) in 1849, marking the end of absolute monarchy and the beginning of the era of representative democracy.

Moreover, Denmark has for more than a century been ruled by democratic parties that have contributed to rendering the political elite accountable. Even though Denmark has experienced antidemocratic parties, especially in the run-up to and during World War II, such parties never gained substantial political power, far from it. At least since 1920, the political regime, its parties, and the party system have remained rock solid through two world wars, the Great Depression, constitutional amendments, membership in the European Union, and entrance into the nonindustrial 21st century. All along, the people have endorsed the democratic system by turning out to vote in great numbers—between 79.2% and 89.5% of the eligible voters—in each of the 30 national elections held since 1929.

Seen from within Denmark, pundits, observers, and political scientists alike agree that the Danish case is, however, anything but dull. Within the boundaries of this small country, remarkable electoral events have happened, primarily the "earthquake" election in

December 1973 when the numbers of parties in parliament doubled, and more recently the 2001 election where the parties right of center, for the first time in generations, won an absolute majority. So things happen, even though no blood is shed, no coups are plotted, and no regimes have been overthrown in Denmark.

In this chapter we pay special attention to one of the long-lasting building blocks of the Danish democratic system, the political parties, and discuss the stability and the possible change of the Danish party system from 1920 to 2007. This is done by drawing primarily on the theoretical framework of Giovanni Sartori,[3] and to a lesser extent, that of Martin Lipset and Stein Rokkan.[4] Thereby, we are able to differentiate between electoral and institutional change; and we conclude that despite increasing volatility, more parties, and changed patterns of voting among the Danes, the party system has indeed been quite stable. We do, however, point to moments of change and their prerequisites as well as discuss the possibility of a party system change in the near future and the desirability of party system stability when viewed through democratic glasses.

Denmark more than doubled its electorate before the 1918 election, as women and 29-year-olds won the right to vote; further, "dependency" and recent arrival to the constituency were no longer accepted as valid reasons for not allowing people on the voters' roll. At the same time, a mixed member proportional (MMP) representation electoral system was implemented. However, this system was only used once, while the system still used today (with minor modifications) was introduced before the first of the three parliamentary elections in 1920. The last of these three elections—the one in September 1920—was conducted in the same geographic area that is Denmark today (i.e., including the northern part of Schleswig, which was reunited with Denmark after having been lost to Prussia and Austria in 1864). For these reasons, we see the September 1920 election as a good starting point, with the geographical area, the electoral system, the constitution, and the party system all established as they would be functioning during the interwar period.[5]

Denmark has had a multiparty system since the early days of the twentieth century. However, the simple Duvergerian[6] distinction between two-party systems and multiparty systems does not help us understand change and continuity within the Danish party system. Among the various attempts to construct a viable analytical framework for analysis of party systems, we prefer Giovanni Sartori's approach.[7] One advantage of Sartori's framework is the way in which he combines the "format" (i.e., the number of parties) and the "mechanics" (i.e., the nature of the competition among parties) of the analyzed system.[8] We discuss the format of the Danish party system in the next section of the chapter, and then turn to its mechanics in the third section. Finally, we discuss the stability of the present party system, and address the democratic aspects of change or continuity in the Danish party system.

THE FORMAT OF THE PARTY SYSTEM

In a study of the format of the Danish party system we distinguish between two main periods: the first period covers the 50-plus years from 1920 until 1973, while the second period covers the post-1973 years. Figure 6.1 illustrates that in the 1973 election the predominance of the Liberals, Conservatives, Social Liberals, and Social Democrats— the so-called four old parties—was dramatically challenged by a range of new parties.[9] As can be seen from the figure, the four old parties among themselves shared between 80% and 90% of the total vote in the first period, but most often less than 70% in the second.

The first period is characterized by immense stability.[10] Although numerous small parties (e.g., the Communists) repeatedly, and once in a great while successfully, tried to gain access to parliament, the period was dominated by the four old parties.[11] The old parties enjoyed a de facto power monopoly that "In their own words 'kept [the small

Figure 6.1 Percentage of votes obtained by the four old parties (Liberals, Conservatives, Social Liberals, and Social Democrats) taken together and all other parties taken together in Danish parliamentary elections, 1920–2007.

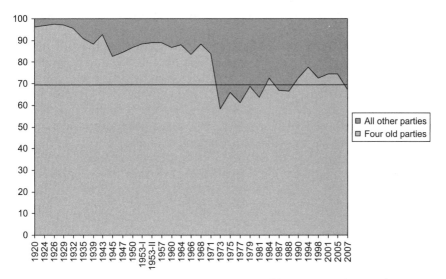

Source: Electoral statistics, various years. Jørgen Elklit, "Denmark," in *Elections in Europe. A Data Handbook*, I–III, ed. Dieter Nohlen, Florian Grotz, and Philip Stöver (Oxford: Oxford University Press, forthcoming 2010).

parties] outside the wall set up by the four old parties around themselves and their work of the Folketing.' [The small parties] did not participate in committees, nor were they allowed to take part in high-level
bargaining in connection with major political compromises."[12]

Counting the number of relevant parties according to Sartori's counting rules yields an average of five to six parties in this period, but in
actual practice the system was a four-party system.[13] After 1966, the
system could, however, be described as a four-plus-one-party system,
as the Socialist People's Party (Socialistisk Folkeparti) gained a firm
footing in parliament and even became the main parliamentarian supporter of the Social Democratic government in 1966–1967.[14]

The story of why the election of 1973 was called and the reasons it
produced so significant a transformation of the Danish party system is
an intriguing one, combining as it does sheer accident and a quest for
change coming from very diverse quarters. First, according to the constitution, the prime minister can call an election at will, but the December election of 1973 was nonetheless entirely unexpected and was only
called because an important bill on housing taxation was rejected by
the parliament. The direct cause of this rejection was that a right-wing
Social Democrat, Erhard Jakobsen, apparently ran out of gas on his
way to Parliament and thus could not make it in time for the crucial
vote. Second, after Parliament was dissolved, Jakobsen announced the
formation of a new party, the Center Democrats (Centrumdemokra-
terne). Initially this party strongly opposed the Social Democratic bill
on new housing taxes in particular and the alleged leftish swing of the
Social Democratic Party in general. After just a few weeks of campaigning, it gained almost 8% of the votes cast. Third, another new party,
the Progress Party (Fremskridtspartiet), also ran for parliament for the
first time. Defining itself as a protest against the "old, traditional and
elitist" parties, and pledging to abolish income taxes and the unneces-
sary paperwork of the public administration, it was able to celebrate an
even larger electoral victory as it won almost 16% of the total vote.[15]
And finally, this was also an election in which many old-timers reen-
tered Parliament, as the Christian Democrats (Kristeligt Folkeparti), the
Communist Party (Danmarks kommunistiske Parti), and the Justice
Party (Retsforbundet) collectively gained more than 10% of the vote. In
sum, as Mogens Pedersen noted, the 1973 election marked the "defeat
of all parties."[16]

The 1973 elections were truly extraordinary, but what happened in
subsequent elections? Did everything go back to "normal" or was the
new situation stable and persistent? The answer is apparent in Figure
6.1: The dramatic and surprising 1973 election was not a breakdown of
the existing system that in time would return to "normalcy." Rather,
the system adapted itself and found a new steady state in the years following.[17] As can be seen from the second period in Figure 6.1, the

group of other parties managed to keep between one-third and one-fourth of the vote during the following decades. The four old parties did regain some strength in the following 20 years, still commanded more than half of the seats in parliament, and never became obsolete in Danish politics.

After 1973, however, these parties could form governments only in cooperation with some of the new parties (also because of the increasing dimensionality of the party system). Thus although the election results and the dramatic changes in the partisan composition of the parliament were shocking to the political system, these were in many ways far greater shocks to the established political parties than to the established representative democracy. The tensions in Danish society were first and foremost resolved by altering the partisan balance in parliament and not by seriously questioning parliamentary democracy as such—the fighting against the established regime was done in the voting booth and not in the streets.

Moreover, the number of relevant parties increased to an average of eight or nine,[18] but the system never became polarized: "It is more to the point to state that the system since 1973 had a central and a peripheral part. The nucleus is composed by the four old parties plus two of the new ones [i.e., the Center Democrats and the Christian Democrats]."[19] In the next section we discuss the configuration of the competition in the party system in more detail. Here we conclude that the format of the Danish party system has changed from one of limited pluralism to one of extreme pluralism since more parties have been represented in parliament after 1973 than before. We also conclude that the system shifted from a "four-party system" to a "four-plus-two-party system."[20]

One question remains, however: Why did the stable Danish party system change—and why did it not return to "normalcy" in subsequent elections? Explaining the election result, Pedersen points to a range of short- and long-term factors:[21] An important long term factor was the changing social structure. In the 1950s many European countries underwent a transition, which changed them from industrial to service and information societies. The rural population was declining, as methods of production changed and the number of farms—and farmers—declined. It was not a new phenomenon for a surplus rural population to find new jobs in the industrial urban sector, but this kind of change now became more pronounced. In addition, expanding welfare programs enabled women to find jobs in the service sector. These factors contributed to increasing wealth in many families and the suburban middle class was expanding as rapidly as the welfare state.

One consequence of this development was a weakening of the link between social classes and political parties: The Social Democrats as well as the Liberals had to refocus their fundamental electoral strategies and start appealing to the new middle class as their traditional support bases among manual workers and farmers, respectively, were vanishing. The societal cleavages dividing voters according to socioeconomic class and urban/rural background were weakening and no longer served as the primary basis for partisan alignment.

Simultaneously, there began to be signs of public distrust of the four old political parties that had for so long been almost the only parties in government. In 1963 the government called a referendum on a land reform bill, but the proposal was rejected by the public. In 1969 this story repeated itself as a government proposal to lower the voting age was turned down at the obligatory referendum. These referenda were not important in and of themselves, but they highlight how the old parties were in many ways out of touch with the voters.

Turning to the short-term factors, Pedersen points to the major municipal reform in 1970 that changed the local political landscapes and made the renomination as well as the reelection of national politicians more unpredictable compared to what it had been. In addition, the expansion of the welfare state required an increase in tax revenue, which together with the introduction of tax collection at the source— making individuals, not families, the objects of taxation—was implemented in just three years around 1970. During the same few years, the total taxation revenue increased from 33% to 44% of gross national product, which annoyed many taxpayers. During the same period, pornography and the right to an abortion were being legalized. Many of the traditional voters of this period's center-right government found the various reforms too far-reaching, while at the same time more progressive forces, partly within the Social Democratic Party, felt that the reforms were not far-reaching enough.

However, long- and short-term factors such as those indicated above do not translate directly into a party system change. A catalyst is needed. The call for the 1973 election was such a trigger event. The founder and leader of the new Progress Party, Mogens Glistrup, made it his mission to fight not just against increasing taxes, but against taxation in general. He also presented himself as opposed to all the established parties and their leaders who, in his view, were out of touch with the common man. The second new party, the Center Democrats, was likewise able to offer relief to the voters: The party represented a kind of third way between the traditional left and right wings that apparently were more concerned with their internal competition than with developing new political solutions for a changed world. Hence, the two new parties both attempted to provide solutions or at least responses to some of the short- and long-term problems or societal changes referred to above. Moreover, because of the long-term factors, the party system did not return to "normalcy" even when the Progress Party and the Center Democrats eventually lost their importance and ultimately their representation in parliament in the 1980s and the 1990s.

The Danish 1973 election is a fine illustration of what Peter Mair has called "the problem of party system change."[22] Mair warns against the tendency to equate electoral change with party system change. The social makeup of a given country and the number and names of its political parties may change without any change occurring in the party system—and vice versa—he argues. In the Danish case, socioeconomic cleavages had been undergoing transformation for almost two decades before anything happened at the party system level. And when something eventually happened, it did not change the system fundamentally. As demonstrated above, the four old parties still run the political show in Denmark, even though since 1973 they have required the support of two smaller (system oriented) parties. Thus, we must be cautious when analyzing the present party system and discussing its stability. New parties may appear and new cleavages may arise, but it remains to be seen whether this necessarily means that "the working Danish multiparty system" is undergoing yet another transformation and perhaps is becoming unstable. We return to this question in the last section of the chapter. First, however, we look at the mechanics of the party system.

THE MECHANICS OF THE PARTY SYSTEM

Obviously the Danish multiparty system became more densely populated after the 1973 election than it was before. However, one must study not only the format of the party system, but also its mechanics, that is the type of competition between the parties in the system. Sartori argues that a limited pluralistic format (up to five or six parties) leads to a moderate pluralistic mechanic (i.e., centripetal party competition), while systems with an extremely pluralistic format (more than six parties) experience a polarized pluralistic mechanic (i.e., centrifugal party competition).[23] Such propositions have troubled scholars of the Danish party system, because it did not polarize permanently as it became extremely pluralistic.

Figure 6.2 shows the relative vote share of different parties and groups of parties in Danish parliamentary elections since 1920. The most interesting feature of the figure is that apparently nothing happened in the aftermath of 1973. Whether or not that shakeup election fractured the existing format of the system, it did not alter the relative strength of the two blocs in the parliament.[24] This changed—interestingly enough—in the 2001 election. First, however, we consider the period between 1973 and 2001.

As illustrated by Figure 6.2, the Social Liberals have had a pivotal role in Danish politics for a long time. Most of the time, none of the

Figure 6.2 Vote percentages obtained by different parties and groups of parties in Danish parliamentary elections, 1920–2007.

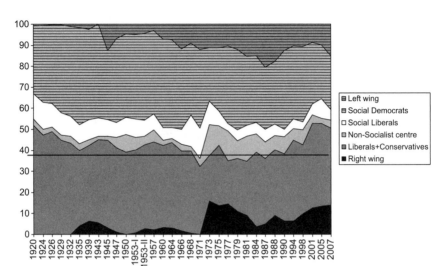

Note: "Left wing" includes Socialist People's Party, Free Social Democrats, Left Socialists, International Socialistic Worker's Party, Marxist/Lenin Party, Communist Worker's Party, Denmark's Communist Party, Red/Green Alliance, the Greens, the Minority Party, the Peace Party, the Humanistic Party, Democratic Renewal, and Common Course. "Non-Socialist Center" includes Center Democrats, New Alliance, Christian Democrats, Liberal Center, Peasant's Party, Industry Party, German Minority Party, Pensioners' Party, the Society Party, the Independence Party, Justice Party, and independents. "Right wing" includes the Progress Party, Danish People's Party, National Socialist Worker's Party, National Cooperation, Farmer's Party, and the Independent Party.

Source: See Figure 1. Jørgen Elklit, "Denmark," in *Elections in Europe. A Data Handbook,* I–III, ed. Dieter Nohlen, Florian Grotz, and Philip Stöver (Oxford: Oxford University Press, forthcoming 2010).

political wings have been able to form a government without this party's acceptance—or at least the absence of resistance. This led to a peculiar situation in the 1980s where a nonsocialist minority government enjoyed the confidence of the Social Liberals on economic and domestic matters, but not in the field of foreign policy. The Social Liberals did not want to move to a vote of nonconfidence and thus bring down the government, but the party enabled the opposition to run the foreign policy of Denmark via specific instructions to the minister of foreign affairs.[25]

However, there are exceptions from the general picture in Figure 6.2, namely 1973 and 1975. The 1973 election yielded only 83 seats in total to the Social Democrats, the left wing, and the social liberals, which put the nonsocialist center parties in a position to choose between a Social Democratic and a Liberal-led government. They chose the latter. In 1975, the nonsocialist coalition and the right-wing again had a majority without support of the Social Liberals, but as the rather inexperienced Progress Party—and Glistrup—did not offer unconditional support to the incumbent Liberal prime minister, the surprising end result was the formation of a Social Democratic minority government.[26] Notwithstanding these exceptions, most of the time since 1929 the Social Liberals have been able to pick and choose governments more or less as they saw fit (alternately the nonsocialist center parties had the same position). This has in turn concentrated the competition in Danish politics around the center of the system, making the system centripetal both prior to and after the 1973 election.[27]

This conclusion is contrary to what Sartori's analysis would lead us to expect. Why did the Danish system not become polarized as it became extremely pluralized?[28] Some scholars argue that only the number of "effective parties" should be counted when determining the format of the system, not the broader category of relevant parties as indicated by Sartori himself.[29] If this point of view is accepted, the Danish party system contained only five or six effective parties in the post-1973 period, which is still a limited pluralistic format.[30] However, Sartori did not explicitly argue that the extreme pluralistic format instantaneously leads to a polarized mechanic. Although Denmark had no genuine antisystem parties on either end of the ideological spectrum,[31] both the right and the left wing have had a relatively considerable popular support (see Figure 6.2) since 1973. In fact, the most important development in the election was the landslide victory of the right-wing Progress Party.[32] In other words, the electoral competition did become polarized to some extent after 1973, but this polarization was not reflected in the parliament. This obviously supports the view that one must treat the "domains of identification" among the voters and the "dimensions of competition" in the parliament as two separate concepts.[33] Doing so, we will argue that at least two factors can improve the general understanding of the persistent centripetal competition in Denmark.

First, the Progress Party was not a traditional party, but an unpredictable and unreliable gathering of very different people with considerable blackmail potential. In the first years, the party had virtually no organization and was largely run by the charismatic Glistrup and his political gut-feelings.[34] The best example of the unpredictability of the party is probably the government formation negotiations in the aftermath of the 1975 election referred to above. Later, Glistrup was imprisoned for tax fraud, making it even more understandable that most politicians were unable to imagine that the Progress Party could ever be a reliable partner in a center-right government.

Second, it takes time to alter a well-established parliamentary culture—or pattern—of conflict and cooperation. Pedersen argues: "The basic characteristic of Danish party politics before 1973—and to some extent also after that year—is the essentially coalescent pattern of decision-making. . . . Unanimous decisions were the typical outcome of the legislative process. . . . In the case of controversial issues the government mostly pursued the goal of 'broad agreement,' meaning that at least the four 'old' parties supported the proposals under consideration."[35]

Besides this norm of consensus, Danish politics has traditionally been quite corporative in nature, and shifting governments have involved the relevant external organizations—often representatives of the labor movement and the various employers' organizations—early on in the legislative process to increase the likelihood of later implementation.[36] When the Progress Party entered this realm of consensus, contributing substantially to the development of an almost institutionalized two-block dogma, it is quite possible that the "congregation" of old parties simply did not (yet) realize how thoroughly the nature of doing politics was changing. They just kept competing around the center as they had done for more than half a century.

This situation to a considerable degree remained stable until the 2001 election. Here the competition turned more "normal," in the Sartorian sense: The party system did not polarize, as there are still no antisystem parties, but the direction of the party competition clearly became more centrifugal in nature. As can be seen from Figure 6.2, the nonsocialist coalition and the right wing won an absolute majority of the vote in 2001 as well as in the two subsequent elections. For the first time in 80 years the Social Liberals, or the group of center parties in combination, were unable to control the political balance in parliament. Also, none of the nonsocialist center parties have passed the threshold and won seats in parliament since 2001 (the new party New Alliance is an exception to which we return)—which they did in every election in the period 1973–2001. This indicates that the direction of the competition within the system did, indeed, change in 2001.

In short, the 2001 election marked the defeat, not of all parties, but certainly of the center parties and the rapid rise of the Danish People's Party (Dansk Folkeparti) on the right wing. The Danish People's Party proclaimed itself in 1995 as a splinter of the Progress Party. A key strategy of the new party was to seek political power and negotiate political deals with other parties, or—in other words—become a more "normal" and responsible party than the Progress Party ever was.[37] The ideas of the Danish People's Party were not very different from those of the Progress Party: one could see it simply as the mature version of that party. It had immediate success in its first election in 1998 with 7.4% of the total vote and its vote share doubled over the three succeeding elections. By 2007, the party had become the third largest party in parliament.

This strengthening of the right wing in Danish politics, the continued stability on the left wing, and the disappearance from parliament of all the nonsocialist center parties except the New Alliance after the 2001 election (as illustrated in Figure 6.2) simply turned the mechanics of the 1973–2001 period on its head: The four old parties are still central to Danish politics, but the "two additional" parties are no longer parties of the center (i.e., the Center Democrats and the Christian Democrats). Instead, the "additional two" parties are now the Danish People's Party and the Socialist People's Party, parties that take more extreme positions than did any of the four old parties.

The power of the Danish People's Party is particularly evident during government formation, annual national budget negotiations, and larger reforms. Here the nonsocialist government often relies completely on support in Parliament from the Danish People's Party.[38] At the other end of the political spectrum, the Socialist People's Party is in a similar manner moving closer toward the Social Democratic Party: The socialists have traditionally been the "opposition to the left" of social democratic governments, but in recent elections the leaders of the party have discussed the possibility of not only supporting, but possibly even joining, a future government under social democratic leadership. The party and its new leader, Villy Søvndal, did very well in the 2007 election, and some media commentators as well as the Social Democrats were positively inclined toward a Socialist-Social Democratic government—for the first time ever.[39] The campaign communication of the Socialists themselves tells a similar story: In the elections of 1994, 1998, and 2001, the party campaigned negatively toward the Social Democrats and the then social democratic government, but in 2005 and 2007 such attacks ceased.[40]

To reiterate, we argue that the 1973 election essentially changed the traditional four-party format of the Danish party system to a "four-plus-two" format, with the two additional parties being nonsocialist center parties. The 2001 election then changed the centripetal mechanic of the system to a more centrifugal one. This happened because the center parties lost their political and parliamentary influence (and representation), which was then taken over by two wing parties—one at either end of the political spectrum. What did not change, however, at any point of time during the past century of Danish parliamentarian politics is its dimensionality, to which we now turn.

Danish politics is fundamentally about left and right, that is about whether the government of the day should be based on (rather vague) versions of socialism or liberalism.[41] Notwithstanding that a Social Democratic Prime Minster Jens Otto Krag claimed that "one has a policy position until one takes another one" and another (Conservative) Prime Minister Poul Schlüter declared the ideologies dead, scholars point out that "Danish politicians have always conducted their campaigns and their debates in terms of a left-right vocabulary."[42] This argument has been empirically proven on a number of occasions. Consulting the volatility figures of parliamentary elections gives the first indication: While the general volatility in periods has been rather high in Denmark, the so-called bloc volatility has been stable and low. The voters tend, in other words, to shift among parties within the same coalition, but not between them, as would be expected if important cross-cutting cleavages did exist.[43] Next, the above mentioned study on party communication finds that two-thirds of all direct attacks among the parties in election campaigns since 1994 have been communicated by a party on the one side and targeted at a party on the other side of the left-right divide.[44] Finally, a recent study of the votes cast in Parliament since 1953 aiming at the exploration of dimensionality of the policy space in which the parties operate was able to identify only one dimension throughout the entire period: the age-old and well-known left-right dimension, which has dominated Danish politics at least for a century.[45]

Although both the format and the mechanics of the Danish party system have been transformed over the past 40 to 50 years, the system still primarily operates in that single dimension. Thus, the fundamental logic of the competition within the system—and therefore also the system itself—has not changed.[46] The driving force in Danish politics is still the socioeconomic worker—owner cleavage, which has been institutionalized in a number of different old and new parties over the course of the past century. In this perspective Denmark is no exception from most other European countries that display rather persistent left-right dimensions.[47]

Hence, Peter Mair's key argument is that Lipset and Rokkan's "freezing" hypothesis is still valid: The modern party systems of Western Europe still look very much as they did in 1920.[48] To explain this stability, Mair notes that it is hard for new cleavages to become institutionalized the same way as the rural—urban, the worker—owner, the center—periphery, and the state—church cleavages did in the 19th century: There simply are no more voters to mobilize.[49]

In the Danish case, the rural—urban cleavage was mobilized by the Liberals (Venstre, literally "left"), representing small farmers on the one side and the Conservatives (the party's first name was Højre, literally meaning "right") representing the bourgeoisie of the cities and the aristocracy in the rural areas on the other. In the first several decades of Danish democracy, these two parties where the only relevant ones in parliament and thus the main competitors. Later on the Social Democrats mobilized the workers and the former left and right joined forces as they both represented the employers, although in different kinds of industry. The Social Democrats were able to activate the latent socioeconomic cleavage because they realized the value of the potential mobilization of a new segment of voters who did not usually vote, either because of tradition, because of the effects of open voting under a first-past-the-post electoral system,[50] or because workers who did not have their own household did not have the right to vote (as mentioned in the introduction these election rules changed only in 1918). It was an indication of the changing patterns of competition that the conservatives previously known as the Right (Højre) in 1915 changed its name to the Conservative People's Party (Det Konservative Folkeparti), as its main opponent in the electoral and parliamentary arena was no longer the Left party (Venstre, i.e., the Liberals).

Since 1920, no Danish party has been able to mobilize a new segment of voters along an already existing or new social cleavage and bring this political line of conflict into parliament—even though such new divisions among the people probably exist. Such an enterprise is tremendously difficult because a new party must first establish itself as a reliable and trustworthy organizational unit, which demands more and more financial resources and thus becomes more and more difficult to create and maintain.[51] Next, this new party must fight to mobilize along an alternative cleavage in competition with the established parties that represent traditional cleavages.

Such fundamental societal changes do not happen overnight, but we shall nevertheless in the subsequent and final section discuss the possible emergence of a new policy dimension among the Danish voters, one that is producing new parties, as we examine the degree of representation that the current, quite stable, Danish party system offers Danes.

CONCLUSIONS

Some aspects of the Danish party system have obviously changed during the past five decades. More parties now fight for electoral support, and new possibilities for coalitions of government and political corporation are evolving. At the same time, however, the system is steady as a rock when the fundamental left-right competition is considered.

At this point a normative—or democratic—question arises: Is this high degree of stability actually a good thing or not? The intuitive response among most scholars and observers tends to be "yes," because stability renders the system reliable, predictable, and thus probably more efficient. The stable party system ensures that some organization is in charge of a responsible government, and some organization is keen to control and criticize the government as well as alert and willing to take over that responsibility, if the public should vote the incumbent government out of office.

An efficient political system might, however, not be a truly representative one.[52] If stability at the parliamentarian level does not reflect a similar "freezing" at the electoral level, the party system and the people might grow farther apart. As described above, the 1973 election was a long-coming protest against the established parties and their way of doing politics—as well as a realignment of the voters reflecting the transition from an industrial society to a service and information society. That the political system found a new equilibrium shortly after the political eruption of 1973 suggests that the change can be seen as some sort of a democratic relief that created a new balance between the political system and the society as it was then. Change and short-term instability can, thus, be good for democracy if they recalibrate the political system and make it more representative of the people.

A central question then arises: Is the current Danish party system capable of representing the Danes? Are there any indications of a mismatch between the representatives and the represented as was the case prior to the 1973 election? Obviously, no working party system can match the voters on a one-to-one basis, but in the following we argue that both short- and long-term factors are at play in 2009 as they were in the period prior to 1973.

Regarding the short-term factors, the present nonsocialist government is constantly criticized for its reliance on so-called bloc politics (i.e., governing on the basis of a narrow center-right majority in parliament).[53] Using this, but also other majority coalition creations, the government has implemented a range of unpopular reforms since it seized power in late 2001. The largest and most debated of these reforms is the so-called structural or municipal reform implemented on January 1, 2007. This reform reduced the numbers of local authorities from 271 to 98 and the number of regional authorities from 14 to 5.[54] At the same time most political and administrative functions at the regional level (e.g., environmental issues, psychiatric care, and local public transportation) were delegated to the local (municipal) level. A main reason behind this immense restructuring of the Danish welfare state was to build stronger and more professional local units—and, one might add, to make it possible for local politicians to rationalize in order to cut costs. The Social Democrats were reluctant in the negotiations, and although the government came very close to negotiating a broad deal on the reform, it ended up by not subscribing to it.[55] The government also reformed the legal jurisdictions and the police, cut the foreign development aid, and made it easier to contract out health care and social services to private operators. Another key issue for the government and the Danish People's Party is the introduction of the so-called "tax-stop," which forbids the the government to increase the level of taxation in any way. Finally, the government made Denmark a dedicated U.S. ally in the war against terrorism in Afghanistan and, publically more problematic, in Iraq. Most of these reforms and policies were implemented by a narrow majority extending to the right (i.e., with the participation of the Danish People's Party), which in turn made them rather unpopular among the half of the public that did not vote for the parties in or behind the current coalition. Using the narrow center-right majority instead of seeking support among a wider range of parties violates the above-mentioned consensus norm in Danish politics[56] and could conceivably destabilize the party system, as similar short-term factors did in 1973.

A short-term factor such as the degree of government popularity is always open for discussion and different interpretations. Less open for discussion is the existence of a second political dimension at the electoral level which is not reflected in the party system at the parliamentarian level, as Danes, like citizens in other Western countries, have realigned during recent decades.[57] Thus, the same kind of long-term factor is now in play as was seen during the late 1960s. Forty years ago, the new suburban middle class had increased rapidly and the four old parties could not accommodate this new group of voters, who were neither traditional industrial workers nor traditional employers, nor were they likely to identify strongly with those traditional classes. Today the new alignment takes place along a new material/postmaterial political dimension.[58] This dimension includes noneconomic issues (e.g., the environment, individual rights, and refugee and immigration related issues) and ranges from a libertarian to an authoritarian position. A liberal position on such so-called "new politics" emphasizes, for example, the protection of the environment and individual rights, while an authoritarian position stresses economic growth, is tough on crime, and is intolerant toward minorities. Such new politics have also been called "value politics," as opposed to the "old politics" or "redistribution politics" of the traditional left–right cleavage.[59] A recent work argues that this new dimension in Danish politics reflects a new societal cleavage between highly and poorly educated people (the highly educated being the most liberal).[60]

Just as in the late 1960s, we can now see that electoral change is not automatically translated into party system change. What is different from the late 1960s—and from the 1973 election in particular—is the absence of a catalyst that can spark a party system change fueled by short- and long-term factors such as those just described. In 1973, two new parties came out of nowhere and were able to represent both the new middle class (i.e., the Center Democrats) and the politically frustrated (i.e., the Progress Party). No such parties are available today, and without such outlets the electoral changes have no institutional vehicle and therefore no chance of challenging the stability of the current party system.

In this perspective a new party that participated in the 2007 election is of great interest. The New Alliance Party (Ny Alliance) was not just another new party with little that was really new about it (compare the Minority Party [Minoritetspartiet] and Democratic Renewal [Demokratisk Fornyelse] appearing in the 2005 and 1998 elections, respectively).

New Alliance was an exponent of the well-educated end of the new educational dimension in the electorate and as such the antipole of Danish People's Party. Its presence was first announced in May 2007, six months before the 2007 election, as a protest against the left-right politics of the established parties. Armed with the slogan, "Enough is enough" (referring to the power of the Danish People's Party), the party presented itself as a bridge builder between the two traditional blocs in Danish politics. The party had very liberal economic policies and hence endorsed tax reliefs as did the conservatives in the government. At the same time, however, New Alliance strongly opposed the tough immigration policies of the government, especially those espoused by the Danish People's Party.

In so doing, New Alliance was indicating a willingness to cut across the established lines of cooperation and conflict in parliament. Until 2007, the Danish People's Party's main adversaries were the parties of the traditional left, even though the party has always been a keen supporter of welfare state expansion and thus in line with the Social Democrats and the other parties on the left wing. But New Alliance was a new kind of opponent for the Danish People's Party. The two parties might have been able to bring the new educational cleavage into the parliamentarian arena, with two parties representing the opposite poles of a new political dimension. Had this occurred, it might have become salient in the same way the traditional left-right dimension did when the Social Democrats entered parliament and gradually became a stronger party, eventually triggering a party system change more than 100 years ago.

New Alliance failed, however. The party did manage to gain representation in the parliament as five of its candidates were elected, but prior to the election of 2007 some polls had forecast it would have as many as 22 seats. The party was not fully prepared for the election, its policies were not all presented, the party had virtually no organization, and only a few candidates were nominated when the election was called. Moreover, the new party and its inexperienced candidates—and leaders—had great trouble communicating the policies of the party. In a heated live debate between Pia Kjærsgaard (the leader of Danish People's Party) and Naser Khader (the spokesperson of New Alliance), Khader could not explain what a flat 40% tax would mean in practice—even though this proposal was one of the central pledges of the party (and Khader is an economist by training). At the same time New Alliance almost by definition was reluctant to publicize the name of its preferred candidate for prime minister, and only in the last phase of the electoral campaign did it become clear that the party would support the incumbent government after Election Day. This made the party the target of criticism from virtually all other parties and did not help to invigorate the party's own campaign.[61] The poor performance and internal disputes continued after the election, and in just six months it had lost three of its five MPs: One of the party founders left both the party and the parliament, another joined the Liberals, while the third was excluded and later joined the Social Liberals. This led to a realignment of the party, marked by a new manifesto and a new name: Liberal Alliance. Just as the dissidents were absorbed into existing parties, the renamed party itself was absorbed into the traditional left-right logic of the existing party system—in a position similar to that occupied by the Center Democrats.

And so, despite a flurry of expectation that real change was in the air, the Danish parties still compete along the same political dimension as they have done for more than 100 years, and a possible party system change is on hold for the time being. Instead, the system broke the new party, and the party in parliament thus continues to differ from the party of the general public. This kind of stability is clearly not contributing to full and democratic representation, but it does help ensure efficient and responsible government.

Nonetheless, some of the factors that led to the surprising results of the election of 1973 continue to be present in contemporary Danish politics. Future short-term instability and realignments of the party system may be a democratic virtue as such events can recalibrate an otherwise frozen party system that has not developed in sync with the electorate it is supposed to represent. It is in this perspective that we ask if maintaining the massive stability of the Danish party system may prove to be some kind of Pyrrhic victory.

However, it must also be emphasized that whatever problems or challenges the political parties have experienced in the time span covered in this chapter, we are dealing with problems that in most countries in the world would no doubt be seen as very minor when measured with a representative democratic yardstick. Not only are the Danes in massive support of representative democracy as the ideal form of government, they are also unquestionably in favor of the political parties as the main players in the game. Although party membership rates are in decline (as in most other European countries), for the moment nobody really challenges the position of the political parties as the main agencies ensuring democratic representation in Danish politics today. As noted, one of the defining elements of the Danish way of conducting democracy is an insistence on continuously service-checking the political system and judging how well it is functioning in democratic terms. In this process the political parties are not seen as part of the problem but rather as a part of the solution.

CHAPTER 7

Parties as Vehicles of Democracy in Norway: Still Working after All These Years?

Elin Haugsgjerd Allern

INTRODUCTION

Norway has a democratic tradition dating back to the early 19th century. After the end of the Napoleonic Wars in 1814, the 434 years of union between Norway and Denmark ended. A codified constitution introduced the principle of separation of powers and a multitude of checks and balances, granting the franchise to approximately one-third of the males. This made Norway one of the most democratic systems in Europe at the beginning of the 19th century.[1] However, the country was soon transferred to its victorious neighbor, Sweden, by the Treaty of Kiel, and within this new union, the head of state became dominated by the dual monarchy.

From the 1870s, liberal forces strived with increasing intensity to introduce cabinet accountability to the Storting (the Parliament). In 1884, they forced this reform upon the conservative cabinet loyal to the king through using the power of impeachment. In parallel, parliamentary representatives gradually organized into different and stable party groups. From 1884 and onward, the power of the monarch was eroded, international and judicial constraints weakened, and the right to vote was gradually extended to new groups. Later the autonomy of local government "was reduced through a series of centralized reforms in education and social welfare policy."[2]

In 1905, Norway separated peacefully from Sweden. After a national referendum confirmed the people's preference for a monarchy, the Norwegian government offered the throne to the Danish Prince Carl. The

Storting unanimously elected him king, and he took the name Haakon VII. So by this point in time, Norway had become a constitutional monarchy with many democratic institutions—and political parties—in place.

Universal suffrage was introduced in 1913. With the introduction of proportional representation in 1920, single candidates and interest groups were largely superseded by multiple well-organized political parties in electoral politics.[3] Apart from the proportional representation (PR) election system and a multiparty system, Norway achieved a Westminster-like regime form of simple and unconstrained political delegation through cohesive parliamentary parties by the middle of the 20th century.[4] Due to a relatively low level of political conflict and extensive cooperation among various institutions, political parties, and social segments, Norway developed into a stable liberal democracy.[5] The political parties became strong in the various functions associated with party-based democracy, enjoying extensive popular support as democracy-providing institutions.

In recent decades, however, the parties' importance to the well-being of democracy has increasingly been questioned in Norway, as in most other established democracies, due to weakening ties between parties and voters.[6] Societal and institutional developments such as the decline of traditional social identities and old cleavages have challenged party-based democracy. According to the Norwegian Study of Power and Democracy,[7] the democratic chain of command from voter to government is disintegrating: Parties are finding it increasingly difficult to recruit members, mobilize constituencies, and get voters to the polling stations. Moreover, an inclination toward minority cabinets has created a more fragile chain of government.[8]

This chapter offers a broad assessment of Norwegian parties as (potential) vehicles of democracy at the beginning of the 21st century. To what extent do parties contribute to making democracy work today? First, I discuss how we can go about systematically analyzing the roles parties play as agencies for democracy in Norway. This involves identifying the major tasks parties are expected to perform to conform to the normative understandings of democracy in Western Europe. Next, Norway's political parties and party system and institutional framework of party politics are briefly presented in turn. Third, I assess the contemporary parties' ability to perform the various tasks associated with party-based democracy. The analysis addresses party roles in both society and government, especially at the national level.

ASPECTS OF DEMOCRACY AND THE ROLES OF PARTIES

Democracy is commonly—and in Norway—defined as a system of government characterized by majority rule, political equality under the law, and the protection of individual rights.[9] However, it could be argued that Norwegian and Western political culture and systems reflect at least three alternative models of what democracy more specifically means: competitive democracy, participatory democracy, and deliberative democracy.[10] Although they are rivals in theory, contemporary Norwegian political institutions embody amalgams of all three. Therefore, when assessing parties' democratic performance, there is good reason to apply a multifaceted set of evaluation criteria. The alternative models partly call for alternative party roles. All expect parties to structure the votes of the electorate: to impose an order or pattern enabling voters to choose candidates according to party labels. But beyond this minimum function, the three perspectives embody quite different expectations as to what makes party-based democracy work.[11]

The competitive (economic/liberal) model of democracy is closely connected with the minimal definition of a liberal, representative democracy: the sovereign individual's freedom from restraint and exploitation of state power.[12] Accountability is crucial and assumed to be supported primarily by the retrospective judgment of voters at elections involving competing parties.[13] Positively, democracy is also about bringing together opposing, prepolitical individual interests by means of preference aggregation, not integration.[14] The crucial mechanism is again party competition. Finally, the competitive model emphasizes government efficiency. Hence, in a competitive perspective, the major roles of parties are seen as vote structuring, preference aggregation and government efficiency, and provision of delegation and accountability. Implicit here is recruitment of political leaders, although the parties do not necessarily need to control the nomination of candidates themselves.

The participatory (communitarian) model of democracy offers a positive concept of democratic government: democracy is primarily about ensuring popular sovereignty through regular and intensive participation of the populace. Participation should be maximized in order to provide self-development and political integration.[15] Consequently, democratic rights need to be extended from the state to other societal institutions.[16] Participatory ideals thus suggest that the major tasks of political parties are to structure votes and link mass opinion to public policy making by aggregation of alternative preferences into policy packages. Party organizations are, of course, also to promote mass participation. Even if parties lead to institutionalization of conflict and represent hierarchical structures, some participatory democrats highlight political parties as realistic options for mass participation in relation to the state.[17] Although recruitment of political leaders is not at the forefront, parties are expected to promote variety in terms of preferences, experience, and resources at the elite level.

Advocates of deliberative democracy acknowledge that modern societies are heterogeneous and functionally differentiated,[18] but they hold that decision making is not simply about preference aggregation. Opinion formation and revision take place in the public sphere.[19] Thus, accountability—elections, majority votes, and bargaining—has to be legitimated by prior deliberation—that is, by debate open to affected and competent persons under conditions promoting reasoned reflection.[20] Deliberation is also seen as having an educational effect,[21] and some argue that inclusive deliberative arenas are needed.[22] According to Jürgen Habermas, parties are particularly suited to mediate between the public and other deliberative spheres, enabling citizens to deliberate with decision makers on a range of political issues.[23] Hence, parties should offer vote structuring, representation of diverging perspectives, and a balanced recruitment of leaders. Party organizations are furthermore expected to be open for mass participation in deliberative forums, but also to promote deliberation among institutional elites to ensure accountability.

The question now is to what extent today's Norwegian political parties are able to perform the functions assumed to make different aspects of democracy work: vote structuring, mass participation and deliberation, recruitment of political leaders, preference aggregation and government efficiency, and finally, provision of delegation and accountability. Some of these tasks may be interdependent, but I will keep them apart analytically in assessing the democratic performance of Norwegian parties. First, however, a brief presentation of the Norwegian political parties and their institutional setting is needed.

POLITICAL PARTIES AND PARTY SYSTEM

Norway's party system[24] is usually dated back to the 1880s, that is, to the struggle over constitutional reform and parliament democracy and to the establishment of the Conservatives and the Liberals.[25] According to Stein Rokkan's model for sociopolitical cleavages, the first party establishments reflected both a territorial center—periphery cleavage and a sociocultural conflict over language, between the elites of the capital and the national bureaucracy, and an alliance between a rural, populist-nationalist movement protecting traditional values and a radical urban opposition to the political hegemony of the civil service. Later, other cross-cutting cleavages appeared. The main division emerged within the labor market: a left-right axis, dividing the socialist and nonsocialist parties.[26] Between the 1930s and until the early 1970s, Norway had one of the most stable party systems in Western Europe. Eventually all parties developed national headquarters and membership organizations.[27]

Following the end of the Labor Party's predominant position in the 1960s, the Norwegian party system comprised, in terms of government alternatives, two blocs divided along the left-right axis. Between 1961 and 2005, the government was in the hands of either the Labour Party minority or center-right or centrist minority coalitions. Today, the system still reflects old cleavages, but recent political changes have led to new conflict dimensions and a more open and fluid party system.[28] The parties currently represented in the Storting are, from the left to the right of the political spectrum: the Socialist Left (SV), the Labor Party (DnA), the Center Party (Sp),[29] the Christian People's Party (KrF), the Liberals (V), the Conservatives (H), and the Progress Party (FrP).[30] Only the Socialist Left and the Progress parties were formed after 1960.

INSTITUTIONAL SETTING AND STATE REGULATIONS

The main features of political parties institutional setting are the territorial organization of the state, the structure of the executive, the parliament, and the civil service.

Norway is a unitary state characterized by a fairly strong degree of decentralization,[31] but the constitutional status of subnational government—counties and municipalities—is weak.[32] In recent years, the central government has tightened its control over local government, introducing measures like standardization, more detailed reporting systems, and individual rights legislation.[33] Yet parties still operate in a setting of multilevel government.

All legislative authority is exercised by the people through the national assembly, the Storting. The legislative/executive relations conform to most key features of parliamentary government. However, Norwegian government formation "is best described as 'free-style bargaining',"[34] and the main procedural rule is "negative parliamentarism": A prospective or sitting government does not need the explicit support of a parliamentary majority, but merely the absence of a majority against it.[35] There is no formal vote of investiture, the prime minister is not obliged or expected to hand in his resignation at the end of a parliamentary term, and the common interpretation of confidence and no-confidence votes is permissive.[36] Legislative terms are fixed (four years), the assembly cannot be dissolved earlier, and cabinet members may not simultaneously hold parliamentary seats.

The judicial review of public decision making is fairly weak, and there is no constitutional court in Norway.[37] In the civil service, the administration is formally professional and nonpartisan, reflecting the Weberian ideal of administrators as neutral and removed from politics.[38] In recent years, structural devolution has taken place through establishment of more autonomous agencies and state-owned enterprises,[39] but Norway usually ranks high on international measures of centralization, encompassment, and collective bargaining.[40]

The Norwegian Constitution remained silent on parties until 1983.[41] As far as other types of direct regulations are concerned, the electoral formula is still that of PR in 19 relatively small multimember districts. Voters may alter the lists by crossing out the name of one or more candidates, but such changes rarely have an impact, as a large number of voters would have to make the same move in order to overrule the default ranking.[42] Votes are transformed to seats on the basis of the modified Laguë system. In 2005, the total number of seats in the Storting was expanded from 165 to 169, with "adjustment seats" (introduced in 1988) increasing from 8 to 19. This has helped to moderate the overrepresentation of sparsely populated rural areas, but has not eliminated it.

As elsewhere throughout Scandinavia, there are only soft constraints on party financing.[43] The level of state subvention of parties is high, but parties were not required to make income accounts publicly available until 1998, and there is still no cap on donations.[44] However, broadcasting of political advertising is restricted: Political advertisements are not permitted on television, only in the newspapers, on radio, and on the cinema screen.

As far as indirect regulations go, agreements existed to regulate party influence on and representation in the television debates of the Norwegian Broadcasting Corporation (NRK) before elections, but there are no such constraints today.[45] Existence of corporatist institutions strengthens the position of interest groups vis-à-vis the state. The degree of corporatism is fairly strong in Norway,[46] despite a partial decline and increase of lobbyism in recent decades.[47] Also numerous voluntary organizations outside the labor market are linked with the state apparatus.[48]

To conclude, the political system includes elements of both "majoritarian" and "consensus" democracy. Norway has never been a prime example of the "party government" model. But the position of political parties in society and public office had grown strong by the 1960s. On this background, the question now is how political parties perform in contemporary democratic politics.

THE PERFORMANCE OF PARTIES IN CONTEMPORARY DEMOCRATIC POLITICS

When asked if parties are necessary to democracy toward the end of the 20th century, 89% of the Norwegian public responded affirmatively, confirming that the demand for more direct democracy—in terms of referendums—is limited. However, nearly 40% reported that they were skeptical as to whether the existing parties cared about their interests.[49] The European Social Survey indicates that the average degree of trust in parties is relatively high, but the proportion stating that they have confidence in political parties and their public officials is not stable.[50] Also, nonparty members are reported to be skeptical regarding the internal democratic qualities of party organizations.[51] But how do parties actually perform as agencies for democracy in Norway?

Vote Structuring

In the narrowest sense, vote structuring means that voters respond to the labels the parties present.[52] In a system where mainly organized groups contest elections—not individual candidates or ad hoc lists—a persistently low voter turnout and frequent shifts of party preferences would indicate a relatively weak vote structuring capacity: under such circumstances, voters apparently find it hard—or irrelevant—to choose according to party labels. In Norway, the level of voter turnout has historically been fairly high and the level of volatility relatively low. Is this still the case?

In the first decade of the 21st century, on average more than three-fourths (about 77%) of the Norwegian electorate participated in elections (Figure 7.1): That is a sizable turnout level, approaching the mean score of West European countries during the early 2000s.[53] Moreover, although nonpartisan lists receive some support at the municipal level, old parties still present lists across the country, and alternative lists are hardly visible in national politics.[54]

Figure 7.1 Percentage of Voter Turnout in National, Regional, and Local Elections, 1945–2007.

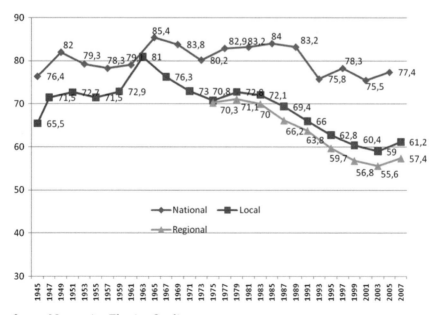

Source: Norwegian Election Studies.

And yet the vote structuring capacity of parties is not as good as it once was. Although voter turnout in the Scandinavian countries rose during the 1950s, it has since 1960 declined from more than 80% to about 75% in 2001. In 2005 turnout at the national level rose again to about 77%, probably because of the presence of two clear-cut government alternatives. Voter turnout now seems to have stabilized at a lower, but not low, level in national elections since 1989. At the regional and local levels, the decline has been steeper.

During roughly the same period, aggregate electoral volatility—the average change in party vote shares between consecutive elections[55]—has been increasing (Figure 7.2). From a record high 20.4% in 1973, following the European Community membership referendum in 1972, the system returned to the "normal" postwar level of around 4% (average) in 1977. But since then, aggregate electoral volatility has been rising, in 2005 reaching about 19%—which is a comparatively high level of fluctuation.[56] Panel data confirm this pattern at the individual level.[57] The tendency goes hand in hand with a long-term decline in class-based voting.[58] Moreover, since 1965 the proportion of voters who make their party choice during the election campaign has soared from 15% to more than 40%.[59] A long-term increase in net volatility has also been identified in local elections.[60]

If successful vote structuring also means opinion structuring—not only that parties are able to make voters respond to their labels[61]—the development of party efficiency seems even less impressive. The correlation between ideological dimensions and party choice is still strong,[62] but parties' role as activators of predispositions and as political

Figure 7.2 Percentage of Aggregate Volatility in Storting Elections, 1945–2005.

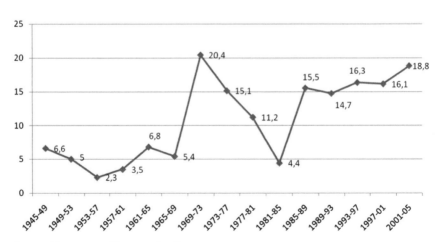

Source: Norwegian Election Studies.

reference groups is weaker than in the first half of the 20th century. The decline of the party press, the rise of a range of alternative media channels, and numerous new interest groups have reduced party control over, if not dominance within, the public sphere.

Mass Participation and Deliberation

Do parties make mass participation in politics and political debates possible? Although some were established as parliamentary elite groups, Norway's political parties all came at some point to resemble what Maurice Duverger termed the "mass party model" in Europe.[63] Local party branches and formally representative internal democracy were eventually established across the board. Hereby, parties opened up for popular participation and debate: For many years, about 15% of Norway's voters were dues-paying members, according to party archives.[64]

Today's political parties can be argued to mirror a "faded" mass party model. In terms of formal organizational structures, few radical changes have been observed—internally and externally—since the 1960s. Despite recent debates on membership ballots, the formal empowerment of rank-and-file members at the expense of the mid-level elite activists, seen in some other European countries,[65] is evident only to a very limited extent.[66] Data indicate that members were reasonably satisfied with their leaderships both in 1991 and 2000. Modern technology offers virtual debating forums on party Web pages and intranet, but Norwegian parties have not made pioneering use of this technology so far.[67] As regards external relations, traditional links with particular interest groups have become weakened but not eroded. The historically most prominent example of close relationships—between the Labor Party and the Confederation of Trade Unions—is no longer based on collective membership of union branches, but an influential joint committee and leadership overlaps remain.[68]

That said, today's party politics is increasingly played out in the mass media and party headquarters, and parliamentary groups have been professionalized by means of increased income from public subventions.[69] As a consequence—and in the wake of a series of weak minority governments—there is little doubt that politics has gradually become more centered on the parliamentary activity and party leadership in Norway, as in other established democracies.[70] Moreover, in recent years many parties have blurred the distinction between the central organization and its surroundings by opening their internal manifesto making—yet not candidate selection—processes to external participants.[71] Interest groups have also started to spread their donations across a wider range of parties, and enjoy contacts not limited to traditional party allies.[72] In summary, today's parties try to engage both members and nonmembers, but the membership organization seems—as a whole—somewhat disempowered in practice, especially regarding national politics.

At the individual level, parties' performance is less impressive and more radical changes have materialized, although Norwegian parties still recruit members. Data from the national Elections Studies and Values Studies indicate that broader political engagement—in terms of political interest, political discussion, and political action—has increased since the mid-1960s, including activities related to political influence through parties and interest groups.[73] Also, younger voters now belong to conventional political organizations in Norway.[74] However, in terms of membership figures and intraparty activity, political parties are—like most other traditional organizations—less able to inspire political engagement in the electorate than previously. The total party membership has declined since the 1960s.[75] Figure 7.3 shows the dramatic drop

Figure 7.3 Party Membership Figures, 1990–2007.

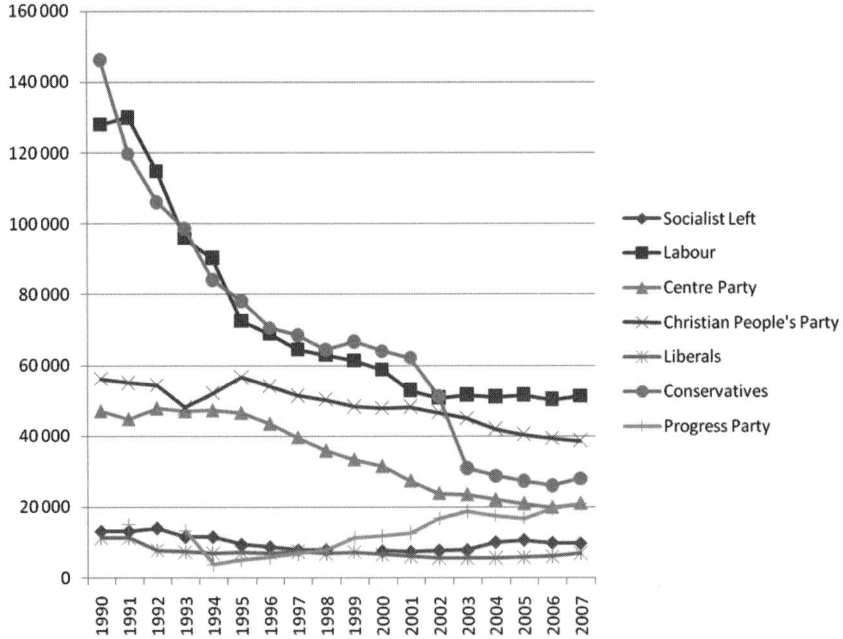

Note: Figures refer to the turn of the year (i.e., 1998 = December 31, 1998). Membership in youth organizations is included in the figures of the Center Party, the Christian People's Party, and the Conservatives, but not in the other cases. Corporate members are included in the case of Labor until 1995. The Progress Party does not consider its figures reliable until 1994. For these and other reasons, one should be careful when comparing figures, across parties and over time.

Sources: Knut Heidar and Jo Saglie, Hva skjer med partiene (Oslo: Universitetsforlaget, 2002); Party annual reports or membership archives.

in membership figures in recent decades, particularly for the larger parties. The seven major parties put together have lost more than half of their members since 1990: The total membership figure declined from about 402,000 in 1990 to about 171,000 in 2006. By 2008, the curve seems to have, more or less, leveled off.

On average, as Figure 7.4 shows, the membership/electorate ratio has dropped from about 16 to less than 10% since the mid-1960s according to national election surveys, yet not linearly. In 2001 and 2005, only 8% of those surveyed claimed to belong to a political party. Moreover, we see that lower membership figures are echoed by a long-term decline in the share of voters who say they identify themselves with a particular party. Surveys of party members reveal that party members have become a socially more exclusive group, and the share of middle-aged members (50−64 years) has increased.[76]

The level of intraparty activity is far from overwhelming. More than half of the party members reported spending no active time in an average month, according to the above-mentioned surveys.[77] The figures also indicate that parties do not function very well as deliberation forums for the grass roots. In 2000, about 8% of Norwegian party members reported that they had participated in "a study circle arranged by the party" during the past year.[78] A larger share of Norwegians are involved in less conventional and ad hoc political activities, such as protest marches and petitions, than in the postwar era.[79] True, the

Figure 7.4 Trends in Party Membership and Party Identification, 1965−2005. Percentage of shares of the electorate. Party identification includes both strong and weak identifiers.

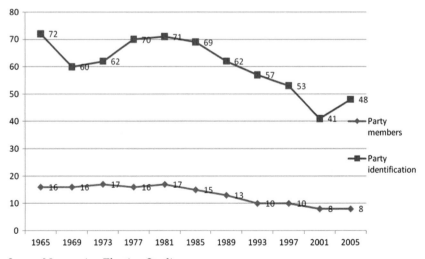

Source: Norwegian Election Studies.

decline in party membership has not led to a change in the share of active members. And party branches are regularly involved in public decision making at the local level. But the total number of party activists has fallen significantly over time.[80]

Hence, Norway's parties offer valuable arenas in terms of formal organizational structures for popular involvement, and by diluting institutional boundaries they enhance the capacity to promote deliberation in terms of open debates. However, the parties' ability to stimulate mass participation and debate at the individual level has clearly declined in a long-term perspective, especially at the national level of politics.

Recruitment of Political Leaders

To what extent do parties actually control the selection of candidates for parliamentary office? And what kinds of political leaders do they select? From a participatory and perhaps deliberative perspective, ensuring a range of preferences, experiences, and resources is crucial, while emphasis on party competition analogous to a market of commodities would require leaders to be highly professional.[81] Historically, mass membership parties like the Norwegian ones have been associated with firm control of nominations and the participatory pattern of leadership recruitment.[82] Yet, despite a widespread norm of list balancing, the Norwegian Parliament has historically been characterized as "a social elite."[83]

Today, Norwegian parties do undoubtedly control the political recruitment process to public office. It is virtually impossible for independent individuals and loosely organized groups to run for office. The requirements of the Nomination Act of 1920—prescribing a decentralized, representative selection process—were not mandatory, but parties had to abide by the rules to get their expenses covered by the state. Although these rules have since been abolished, decentralized decision making remains the norm in Norway, and parties control the selection of candidates more strongly than in any other Nordic country: Nominations are restricted to local party branches, and candidate selection is the result of closed conventions.

As far as the nature of party nominations is concerned, empirical studies indicate political experience is virtually an absolute requirement and that lists are balanced. In line with participatory norms, common list balancing criteria are (still) experience in local and provincial government, territorial affiliation, gender, age, political views, social background, and to some extent organizational affiliations.[84] Due to changes in voting behavior and mass media capacities, efficient media communicators have become more important for political recruitment over time. But on the whole, the selection criteria have been remarkably stable since the 1960s.[85]

The result is a less "elitist" national assembly than in many other European countries. The decentralized, closed nomination processes tend to favor loyal party workers with political experience from the local and regional levels.[86] But the social background of (elected) candidates has become both more and less representative over time. On the one hand, women's average share of seats increased from about 5% in 1945 to about 38% in 2005,[87] partly because the leftist and center parties have introduced gender quotas. So like all the Scandinavian countries, Norway stands out in terms of female representation.[88] Since Gro Harlem Brundtland's first government of 1981, Norwegian cabinets have been characterized by virtual gender parity.[89]

On the other hand, ethnic minorities have barely been represented in the Storting to date. The share of MPs with higher education (university and college) is not particularly high, but has increased significantly over time, reaching 76% in 2005, as opposed to about 24% in the electorate as a whole.[90] In terms of occupation, professionalization is the keyword, perhaps reflecting that public subvention has allowed parties to hire more people to work for them: In 1945, only 3% of the MPs came from positions within the party organization or from partisan positions at the national, local, or regional level of the state. In 2005, this share peaked at 33%.[91] Also, cabinet members have been increasingly drawn from inner party circles.[92]

Thus, parties do control the recruitment of public officials today in the same way as they used to, but there is a clear tendency toward "academization" and "professionalization" of the candidate selection process over time. In other words, we are witnessing a shift from a participatory pattern of recruitment toward the competitive norm of selecting formally skilled political leaders.

AGGREGATION OF POLITICAL PREFERENCES AND GOVERNMENT EFFICIENCY

To aggregate interests in terms of preferences implies that parties must take account of, accommodate, and convert a range of political views into policy packages.[93] Implicit is a degree of interest articulation as different parties represent alternative policy programs. Through government efficiency, the policy programs are realized as public policies. Various types of organizations can perform the act of aggregation in its various guises. But unlike interest groups, parties usually mediate between interests across a broad range of issues. This happens in two major ways: Individual parties aggregate preferences as organizations by producing policy platforms, often based on membership involvement. However, since party members are in the minority and not necessarily representative of voters, parties' ability to take the electorate's policy views into account also depends on how the competition between parties works.

Historically, membership organizations have provided parties in Norway with a significant instrument for determining opinion. Numerous internal debates at different organizational levels of parties have led to fairly detailed but wide-ranging electoral platforms transforming diverse preferences into manageable packages.[94] This phenomenon has in fact been especially pronounced in Norway.[95] Moreover, being moderately pluralist, the Norwegian system of parties has tended to promote genuine interest aggregation, not consensus building, across major voter groups.[96] And policy studies show that—despite corporatist arrangements—parties have mattered for government output.[97]

Today, there is no doubt that Norwegian parties, as organizations, accommodate and convert interests into policy packages. Thanks to generous public subventions, the policy-making capacity of party headquarters has increased in recent decades. The party manifestos today cover a wider range of topics—and hereby interest spheres—than ever before.[98] The survival of intraparty democracy suggests that parties are still able to map and articulate the grievances of the voting public themselves.[99] And party leaders have seemingly attempted to compensate for the decline in membership figures by approaching a more open model of party organization.[100] Party headquarters use opinion polling and other professional methods to capture voter opinions,[101] and in most cases the party's central organization is in contact with various interest groups when preparing the manifesto.[102] However, this behavior might also signal a development where genuine aggregation of interests is replaced by the mere collection of interests (captured by others).[103]

The next question is how the party system works as an aggregative mechanism. Does party competition for votes produce policy alternatives that take account of the preference structure of major voter groups? According to the much-quoted—and theoretically disputed—cartel party (hypo)thesis, established parties have in fact started to distort competition for votes in the wake of rising costs of communication and declining participation, fiscal crises, and economic globalization. Through selective institutional arrangements and by imposing constraints on "feasible" policy options, they have apparently established "cartels" of parties.[104] In other words, parties are hypothesized to temper their aggregative performance at the system level.

The relatively modest level of party fragmentation in Norway—with only two new persistent parliamentary parties since the 1960s—could indicate such a limited responsiveness toward the electorate's policy views.[105] Yet, even if we concentrate on two simple proxy indicators—public subvention regimes and ideological development—the evidence for a cartel-like party system does not seem particularly strong in the case of Norway. Parties must be able to present lists in national elections and be supported by a minimum 2.5% of the voters to receive basic financial support. This system handicaps new small parties competing for votes. But the threshold is lower than the 4% electoral threshold at the national level (for adjustment seats) and the majority of the support is distributed proportionally according to votes.[106] The emergence of the Socialist Left and above all the Progress Party can be argued to mirror a deep-seated protest against established (cartel-like) party politics, but their relative parliamentary success nevertheless indicates the old parties have not really distorted competition through selective institutional arrangements.

Ideologically, there is no strong and persistent process of policy convergence, suggest that the parties no longer reflect diverse and conflicting preferences in major issues. Although analyses based on data from the Manifesto Project[107] show that the parties did converge during the 1970s and in the 1990s after World War II along the important left-right axis, voting records on economic issues have revealed significant policy distances in Parliament.[108] In fact, the frequency of dissent in the Storting has grown considerably since the mid-1970s.[109] And even more important, the ideological changes revealed by manifesto analyses may well reflect an adaptation to new demands in the Norwegian electorate.[110]

That said, a new broad consensus has developed among old parties in major economic and social issues in the wake of, for example, economic globalization. No doubt this limits the range of what is regarded as "feasible" public policies by political elites. But a more meaningful interpretation of this ideological "hegemony" than "collusion" is probably that the parties' preference aggregation has become alarmingly uniform regarding certain policy fields: Only exceptionally do voter groups with less centrist (more radical) views in socioeconomic issues receive attention from parliamentary parties in the public sphere.[111] In this particular sense, major Norwegian parties are perhaps less representative for the electorate as a whole than they once used to be.

In terms of government efficiency, it still matters for government output what kind of party or parties occupies the parliament and the executive. But, in spite of declining corporatism, the governing parties are not as dominating as they once were. A series of weak minority governments has certainly constrained their capacity to transform platforms into public policy. Furthermore, governments seem to have a hard time convincing voters that they are efficient producers of public goods: There is a clear, and increasing, tendency for parties in position to suffer—not benefit—in terms of votes. The state's generous income from the oil sector does help incumbent parties, but it probably also strengthens the expectations toward government policy output.[112]

To conclude, parties' policy-making capacity has improved, and they do still aggregate preferences as organizations—but not to the extent they used to. At the system level, the relative stability seems to indicate that surviving parties are fairly adaptable, but there are also signs of decline both within and outside government.

PROVISION OF DELEGATION AND ACCOUNTABILITY

A democratic regime must contain mechanisms by which the people can select and control their representatives.[113] Accountability means that the people have the right to demand information and to impose sanctions.[114] Parliamentary government tends to rely on mechanisms by which "principals" seek to control "agents" before, not after, a delegation relationship has been established.[115] Voters delegate authority through prospective voting, and accountability is assumed to be supported by the retrospective judgment of voters at elections. The existence of organized party groups makes the accountability of control collective and more distinct.[116] Here I focus on the first two links in this chain: the relationships between voters, parliament, and the cabinet as a whole, and the role of the parties in this.

In Norway, the constitutional chain of governance has been relatively simple, and firmly organized political parties have had free and regular contested elections.[117] No doubt this is still the case, but how do parties more specifically affect people's ability to select and control their representatives today? Several aspects of party structure and behavior may impinge on these relationships.

As regards the relationship between voters and the Storting, parties' performances are clearly ambiguous before elections in terms of political communication. First, the Internet has provided a new party-controlled information channel to voters during election campaigns, and parties still produce extensive manifestos. Thus, voters have ready access to party platforms and can give MPs distinct political mandates.[118] Second, a higher level of education among voters, increased involvement of interest groups through "voter guides" to party policies,[119] and more critical (nonpartisan) journalism have made more "neutral" political information available to voters. These developments suggest an electorate able to use its right to vote prospectively and retrospectively more efficiently than ever.

But on the other hand, the parties' capacity to communicate personally with voters has diminished with the decline in membership figures. And changes in media structure have also challenged the parties' ability to transmit their messages. The major parties once owned their own daily newspapers, but these have all become independent and formally nonpartisan.[120] Television has become the main type of mass media for political issues—without being subject to strict regulations regarding form and content. The rise of television access makes it easier to reach the electorate as a whole, but media studies indicate that increasing attention is paid to party tactics, instead of policies, in the public media sphere.[121] When editorial staff invite politicians and select topics for debate before elections, maximizing television ratings often seems a prime consideration, and "newsworthiness" becomes the prevailing selection criterion, at the expense of representativeness.[122]

In this way, the parties' ability to communicate policy views has been put on trial: A recent survey indicates that a large and growing part of the Norwegian electorate finds only small differences among today's parliamentary parties: in 2001, this was the response of 68% of those surveyed.[123] The share fell to 53% in 2005, when a red–green preelectoral coalition was established and voters again had two clear government alternatives.[124] But many voters seem to misread the actual distances between parties in terms of policies: Numerous voters prefer coalition alternatives that are completely unrealistic in terms of policy.[125] Thus, despite improved direct access to political information about parties, voters apparently find it increasingly hard to choose, difficult to give parties a distinct political mandate, and challenging to hold them accountable for public policies.

In contrast, candidate selection has not changed much as an institutional mechanism: Voters may still scrutinize their potential representatives in advance, but only party members can take part in nominations—and among these, few get involved.[126] Membership ballots have barely been used, and the ballot structure leaves illusive room for voters to influence the rank order of candidates at the national level. On the other hand, the fact that legislative turnover has increased in recent years does suggest that parties tend to treat incumbents less gently than before.[127] Following several modifications of the election system made by the parties (see above), the partisan proportionality has improved and the overrepresentation of rural areas has been lessened. In this sense, it could also be argued that the individual voter's ability to delegate power to MPs through parties has been strengthened (by the parties).

After the election, the key issue is whether voters are able, through parties, to control the parliamentary groups and individual representatives. In a competitive perspective, parties are primarily supposed to be sanctioned by means of elections. But in systems based on extensive party platforms, party members may contribute to accountability by scrutinizing the behavior of parliamentary party groups.[128] Hence, the documented decline in membership figures—and the informal shift of power from extraparliamentary parties to parliamentary party groups— may have reduced the parties' ability to serve as efficient counter-powers to political elites and hold public office holders accountable.

The relationship between parliament and the executive involves cabinet formation/dissolution and various mechanisms aimed at enabling scrutiny of the party or parties in government (ex post). To make this aspect of democracy work, parties may not only strengthen the chain by organization and disciplined behavior in parliament and government—they can also introduce means of parliamentary oversight for opposition parties, such as standing committees and parliamentary questions.[129] In Norway, both mechanisms have traditionally been in place. The "negative version" of parliamentarism has encouraged the formation of numerically weak governments.[130] Cabinet formation has been characterized by a limited number of minority (center/right or centrist) coalitions and coalition avoidance by Labor and others. But detailed party manifestos and high cohesion in the legislature and executive in terms of party discipline have made the executive—legislative relationship work in line with the ideal-typical model of parliamentary government.[131] Most minority governments have relied on ad hoc parliamentary support, but by means of pragmatic negotiations and compromises. Nonsocialist coalitions have applied a range of coordination mechanisms to avoid overt conflict in the Storting.[132]

Today, this description represents a partial truth only. The party discipline of MPs remains high and makes accountability of control collective and more distinct.[133] Moreover, in recent years, parliamentary scrutiny of the Norwegian executive has formally been sharpened through an increasing number of effective institutional vehicles, including a "spontaneous" (unscripted) question session every week. All this has strengthened the ex post control of opposition parties over the governing party or parties, perhaps encouraged by increased media focus and demands for the involvement of politicians in executive decisions.[134]

But to what extent are opposition parties able to control the executive in practice? In a comparative perspective, Thomas Poguntke and Paul Webb argue that the internationalization of modern politics and expanded steering capacities of state machineries have produced an "executive bias" that has strengthened the role of the executive political top elites toward their parliamentary groups and/or their parties.[135] However, in the wake of increased fragmentation of the party system, we see that numerically weak Norwegian cabinets face significant challenges—as vehicles of government—in their relationship with the legislative assembly. First, they have experienced a growing number of parliamentary defeats.[136] Second, the Storting is an active working parliament, not primarily a debating forum—and there has been a measurable increase in the general activity level of its MPs. Accordingly, the government parties' agenda control seems to have declined, which has led "to a more fragile chain of delegation and accountability," seen from the executive point of view.[137] The Westminster-like features of the regime have certainly been challenged.[138] On this background, and after a disastrous election result in 2001 (24.3%), the Labor Party formed, for the first time, a (majority) coalition government in 2005, together with the (originally agrarian) Center Party and the Socialist Left Party.[139]

As regards the cabinet and its relationship with public administration, parties enjoy little ex post control over civil servants. The latter are still expected to be professional and loyal to whatever parties are in office. Yet, over the past 15 years, agencies in the central administration have gained greater managerial autonomy through a process of structural devolution, partly inspired by the doctrine of New Public Management (NMP). Consequently, it could be argued that cabinet members' political discretion and control have declined,[140] even if the reforms have also been initiated by the parties themselves. However, it should be added that legislation designed for greater scrutiny concerning the administration has also strengthened the ex post and third-party controls, by means, for example, of the Office of the Auditor General.[141]

Thus, on the whole, the parties' traditional governing role as vehicles of delegation and accountability is challenged. However, whether increasing delegation of power and the growth of governance networks at the expense of hierarchical structures means that the parties themselves are failing to provide delegation and accountability in government, or whether what is needed is institutional reform in the party setting, is open to debate.

CONCLUDING REMARKS

Voters may be skeptical about the extent to which today's political parties care about their interests, but there is no simple answer to whether these parties perform the major tasks associated with party-based democracy in its various guises. The evidence is mixed; parties show signs of both success and failure. Their performance has declined in some significant respects, but not in all—quite to the contrary. For example, as far as preference aggregation is concerned, parties' policy making seems clearly improved due to a significant growth in party headquarters in recent decades. Hence, the democratic chain of command from voter to government through parties is not generally disintegrating in Norway.

That said, there is no doubt that the parties' democratic performance suffers in significant respects. What seems to suffer the most is the provision of mass participation and deliberation. In general, Norwegian parties appear to struggle more with their representative functions than with their institutional (procedural) roles. Given the relative emphasis of various party tasks associated with each normative perspective, we may conclude that the parties' ability to facilitate the participatory and deliberative aspects of democracy is less than their capacity to perform in line with the competitive model. Increased institutional openness and elite autonomy might benefit aspects of deliberative democracy. But by and large, we see a gradual shift toward the competitive understanding of democracy: free and regular elections between professional party elites.

Moreover, the findings of my stepwise analysis also indicate that party ability to sustain representative democracy in all its three guises can be questioned. The ability to perform the common task of preference aggregation suffers, among other things, from the decline of parties as membership organizations. To what extent parties are able to reflect new issues and conflict dimensions is still open to debate. Moreover, with the number of party employees increasing, the question arises whether parties might turn into a sealed, self-recruiting sphere—with leaders constituting a detached political class. As far as delegation and accountability are concerned, voters are struggling to identify sufficiently distinct party alternatives in Norway. Increased volatility implies that voters are able to punish political parties more efficiently than before, but it also seems to indicate that the electorate to some extent finds it hard to assess credit and blame. Increased autonomy and professional independence generally challenge the performance of political accountability and democratic transparency.

Furthermore, the tension between the representative and institutional tasks of parties in democracy seems to have increased in recent years. First, the governing role of parties is not readily combined with social movement-like structures that more voters demand. Second, for parties chasing increasingly unfaithful voters, it may appear tempting to behave short-sightedly, by presenting public policy as something that can easily be "fixed" while, at the same time, the parties' ability to govern nationally is challenged by, for example, strengthened international constraints, local autonomy, and increased party fragmentation. Hence, parties alternating in government appear to experience a negative dynamics between their role in opposition and in office. The gradual shift of power from the executive to the legislative adds yet another dimension to this dilemma.

Obviously, parties are not to blame for all negative tendencies; exogenous factors also play a part. But whatever the verdict on the question of guilt, parties certainly have a more dubious reputation as instruments of representative government than they once had in Norway. If they are to avoid becoming de-democratized semistate agencies, key challenges are the balance between their representative and governing role and communication with voters—within the framework of a long-established party system, multilevel structures, weakened collective identities, other available channels of political participation—and modern media politics.[142]

PART III

Eastern Europe

CHAPTER 8

Political Parties and Democracy: The Polish Case

Hieronim Kubiak

INTRODUCTION

The democratic political system of modern Poland and its party system span a relatively long period of time, but their actual history is brief. Although the first legal acts paving Poland's way toward democracy date back to the 14th century, it is only since the end of World War I that the history of modern democracy in Poland really got under way. Furthermore, this long-term democratization process was interrupted four times by what Samuel Huntington has termed "waves of reversal"[1]: The first of these took place in 1653–1772, the second in 1795–1918, the third in 1926–1939, and the fourth in 1947–1989. Although each of these periods was characterized by a different set of causes and effects, they all left clear imprints on the Polish will and ability to continue as a national state with the ability to foresee and react to change. These traces are clearly manifested in the systems of values; in symbolic, civic, and political culture; as well as in social awareness, including active and dormant stereotypes, individual models of Polish religiousness, and mutual interference on the part of the church and state. Some of the variables that generated waves of reversal from democratization were caused by internal matters (e.g., class conflicts or group interests), others by external conditions (e.g., political system differences between neighboring countries, irregular economic development, ethnic or national conflicts and wars).

THE HISTORICAL BACKGROUND OF THE POLISH
CONSTITUTIONAL SYSTEM: MOVING TOWARD DEMOCRACY

Establishing the democratic process took at least six centuries in Poland and began in 1385 when Polish nobility was given the right to approve a member of the reigning dynasty as king. In 1529 the principle of *vivente rege* elections (the right to choose a successor while the ruling monarch was still alive) was established, and in 1573 the *viritim* principle introduced the practice of having a convention to elect the king that could be attended personally by each member of the nobility. Although the majority of the population was excluded from this right, by 1653 Poland had "more electors than . . . France."[2] However, during the ensuing period (1653–1764), the aristocracy increasingly dominated political life.

Attempts to halt this process between 1764 and 1795 (a period that included the passing of Europe's first written constitution on May 3, 1791, considerably expanding the civic rights of townsmen) ultimately ended in failure, and in 1795 Poland lost its independence to the three partitioning states of Russia, Prussia, and Austria.[3] The evolution of the democratic process was interrupted for 123 years.

From 1918 to 1939

The rebuilding of the sovereign Polish state between 1918 and 1935 was characterized by one electoral statute and three constitutions,[4] each improving the level of democracy. The electoral statute of 1918 guaranteed that members of parliament were chosen through universal, secret, direct, equal, and proportional voting, with the right to vote given to all persons over 21, including women. The first constitution established a republican form of government, complete with separation of powers and other important democratic principles, including formal guarantees of law and order, the independence of courts and judges, and a guarantee of civic rights and liberties. Political parties, those already in existence at the end of the 19th century and those established at the time of World War I, as well as immediately after 1918, were given the right to participate in parliamentary elections. Unfortunately, the principle of the electoral statute of 1918, which in many respects was analogous to the Declaration of Criteria for Free and Fair Elections (Inter-Parliamentary Union 1994), did not survive for long. The 10 articles of the March Constitution met the same fate. After the wars in the early twentieth century (not only World War I but also the Polish-Soviet War in 1920), battles for the establishment of state boundaries, measures leading to the integration of regained territory, unification of the legal system (each of the three partitioned parts of Poland had been governed under different systems and legal customs), as well as the violent exacerbation of social, ethnic, and religious conflicts and interparty disputes, all made the situation more tense. Party and political fragmentation (contemptuously referred to as *partyjniactwo* [petty party politics]) was accompanied by a lack of integrated public opinion. Under the influence of 123 years of partition rule, there was a clear indication that the ability to organize as a state was lacking; this was accompanied by passivity (mainly among the peasants who constituted a majority of the Polish population). On December 16, 1922, the president of the Republic of Poland, Gabriel Narutowicz, who had been elected a week earlier by the left, peasant activists, and national minorities, was assassinated by the radical nationalist Eligiusz Niewiadomski. According to the right wing, including the National Democrats (Narodowa Demokracja), the election was "decided by non-Polish voices."[5] An armed clash between police and army forces against workers in November 1923 in Cracow left 18 civilians and 14 soldiers dead.

Two and a half years later, on May 12, 1926, Józef Piłsudski led a military coup d'état, resulting in amendments (August 1926) that drastically reduced the democratic components of the Polish constitution.[6] The role of the legislative body (Sejm) was severely limited, and greater powers were granted to the executive authorities (the president and the government), paving the way toward an authoritarian government. The parliamentary elections of 1930 took place under a prevailing "atmosphere of intimidation and contempt for the law" and were almost certainly rigged.[7] In August 1930, the Sejm was dissolved and its prominent members, mostly those who were connected with the group who had formed the center—left coalition (Centrolew) in 1929, were arrested and jailed during the night of September 9, 1930.[8] In 1934, a new prison was established to house political prisoners and a new constitution, the so-called April Constitution, was enacted in 1935 and became the normative basis of the new order, far closer to an outright authoritarian system than to a parliamentary democracy. Passed in the absence of opposition members of parliament and without the required quorum, the new constitution made practically all institutions of power subordinate to the president (in particular the Sejm and the Senate, the government, the courts, the army and state control).[9]

From 1945 to 1989

The end of World War II, the Treaty of Yalta, and the Potsdam Agreement led to the physical and political division of Poland for more than 40 years and imposed the ideological, military, economic, and political influence of the Soviet Union. There was no question of any return to the previous phases of democracy. In Poland reference to democratic institutions and the legal standards of the early 1920s could still be seen in the Constitutional Act of 1947, but political practice continued to diverge ever more from these assumptions, backed up by acts and decrees of government introduced in 1949 and 1950.

The Polish political system experienced particularly harsh Stalinization from 1948 to 1955.[10] The Constitution of the Polish People's Republic was passed on July 22, 1952, abolishing the office of president (replacing it with the State Council). The political system was now defined as a socialist democracy, and despite the claim in Article 3 of the Constitution that authority was vested in "working people in towns and villages," the same article made clear that sovereign power was in fact vested in the Polish United Workers' Party (PZPR), established in 1948 and supported by two parties licensed by the PZPR: the Polish Peasants' Party (PSL) and the Democratic Party (SD).[11] All the components of "red totalitarianism" were in place.[12]

However, democratic cracks appeared in this system long before the 1990s. Following Stalin's death (March 5, 1953), the events of Berlin (June 1953), and the 20th Congress of the Communist Party of the USSR (February 1956), the process of change began. Slowly but surely totalitarianism evolved into a more traditional authoritarianism.[13] The workers' rebellion in Poznań (June 1956) and the return of Władysław Gomułka (earlier removed and imprisoned for "right wing nationalistic deviation") as first secretary of the Central Committee of the Polish United Workers' Party (KC PZPR) in October of the same year were high points in this atmosphere of change.

In March 1968, a new wave of political anti-Semitism swept the country. In December 1970, a series of strikes, demonstrations, and bloody confrontations between workers and the police and army led to the dismissal of Gomułka and his replacement by Edward Gierek. The 1970s saw continuous demands for change in the form of workers' strikes, the formation of the Workers' Defense Committee (KOR) in 1976, and the establishment of the Founding Committee of Independent Trade Unions and the Young Poland Movement in 1978. The role of the Catholic Church increased under the leadership of Karol Wojtyla, Pope John Paul II, as early as 1978. In August and September 1979, the Confederation of Independent Poland (KPN) was established, which was the first illegal radical party with a pro-independence orientation. Shipyard strikes in Gdańsk and Szczecin led to the emergence of the Independent Self-Governing Trade Union "Solidarity" (NSZZ "Solidarność") in 1980.

The communists were, of course, not yet ready to give up. Meeting in July 1981, the Ninth Extraordinary Congress of the PZPR, inspired by movements in the so-called horizontal structures of the party, committed itself to making a strong effort at grass-root reform and attempted to solve the Polish socioeconomic and political crises without the use of force. Three months later General Wojciech Jaruzelski was elected as PZPR first secretary. Beginning in mid-December 1981, there followed a nearly two-year period of martial law,[14] during which many were interned, imprisoned, injured, or killed.[15] As a sign of protest 850,000 PZPR members returned their party identification cards.[16] The country began drifting in an unpredictable manner.

In 1983, however, the granting of the Nobel Peace Prize to Lech Wałęsa, the leader of Solidarity, and Soviet Premier Mikhail Gorbachev's initiatives of perestroika and glasnost, which allowed increased freedom and introduced some aspects of parliamentary democracy, gave the Polish movement toward democratization greater strength.[17] Roundtable talks were finally held in the spring of 1989, resulting in the announcement of parliamentary elections for June 4 of that year. These were not yet fully free elections (65% of the seats in the Sejm were reserved for the ruling party block), but results showed nonetheless that Poland was at last firmly set on the path toward "escape from socialism."[18]

Democratization of the Polish System after 1989

The early 1990s saw the start of state and social transformation in Poland. Through a sequence of legal regulations and nationwide debates, there was a return to traditional democracy. The Polish People's Republic was replaced by the Third Republic and a parliamentary cabinet political system. The new constitution, adopted by national referendum in May 1997, states that "The Republic of Poland shall be a democratic state ruled by law and implementing the principles of social justice" (Chapter I, Article 2), with supreme power vested in the nation, exercising power through its representatives or directly through referenda (Chapter I, Article 4).[19] Public power is decentralized and the inhabitants of territorial units throughout the country constitute by law a self-governing community and participate in its management (Chapter I, Articles 15 and 16). Importantly, citizens of the Third Republic of Poland were permitted to engage in the "creation and functioning" of political parties and trade unions, nongovernmental organizations (NGOs), citizens' movements, foundations, and so forth (Chapter I, Articles 11 and 12).[20] Elections to the Sejm are "universal, equal, direct and proportional and shall be conducted by secret ballot," while those for election to the Senate are universal, direct, and by secret ballot (Chapter IV, Articles 96 and 97). All persons aged 18 and over who fully retain their civic rights have an active right to vote.

HISTORICAL BACKGROUND OF POLISH POLITICAL PARTIES AND PARTY SYSTEMS

The first signs of political parties in Poland came in the 16th century when Polish nobility and business magnates began to form into groups for the purpose of presenting their opinions and arguments regarding the course of government. Those holding similar views were known as a *stronnictwo* (party), a word that is still used as synonymous with *partia*. However, modern political parties did not make their appearance until toward the end of the 19th century. We turn now to a consideration of the evolution of Polish parties as they moved toward playing an active role in the democratization of Poland. To do so, we divide the history of modern parties prior to the present era into four periods: the final decades of the partition period (1880–1918), the interwar period (1918–1939), the immediate postwar period (1945–1948), and the years of the Polish People's Republic (PRL, 1952–1989).

First, however, in order to have in place the criteria for judging how successful the parties have been at various stages of their history, we begin by laying out, in general terms, what we consider to be the functions of democratic parties.

The Functions of Parties

Although the preparation of candidates—placing them on party lists and organizing and supporting their campaigns—are functions that define parties as distinct from other political organizations in modern participatory and deliberative democracies, political parties (providing they are not ephemeral in nature) also engage in other, often long-term activities.[21] A more comprehensive list of the functions of political parties includes: (1) stimulating citizens to participate in political power in a pluralistic society, both at the local government and central government levels, (2) influencing the development of civic and political culture by actively shaping the skills of participation in public life, (3) inspiring analyses of the political system, (4) expressing interests (not only economic, but also political, cultural, and, in certain specific situations, referring to one's outlook on life), (5) building alternative programs for solving problems, taking into account not only group interests but also the common good, (6) shaping public opinion, (7) forming leaders (including potential heads and state activists), and (8) forming shadow cabinets.

Political parties that fulfill these functions and that are interested not only in immediate success but also in mid- and long-term results generate their own specific immune system, which helps them resist wandering vagabonds, who treat party affiliations as yet another trampoline to help them develop their own career. Such members join parties en masse at the time when they are successful, when the parties start governing, or as part of a governing coalition. But when things change, they leave immediately, looking for new banners, mottos (which more often than not are slogans), and organizational structures.

But of course one party alone does not make a democracy. We must also consider the party system, the combination of parties that contest a nation's elections and the rules and customs that govern their behavior.[22]

Does this system function to ensure that power is exercised in keeping with public opinion? Does the combined activity of the parties "constitute an emanation of society and at the same time an indispensable mechanism for transforming the will of society into the will of the state"?[23]

The Final Decades of the Partition Period (1880–1918)

The first modern political parties came into being in Poland in the final decades of the 19th century. Their structures, programs, and names, however, were not stable. Strongly influenced by political moods and conflicts specific to each of the three partitioned parts of Poland, personal animosity among the elite, and European ideological and political quests, these parties divided rather quickly into factions and joined coalitions or left them. As a result, some parties were seasonal in character and quickly left the political scene, while others, although changing their name, evolved around social characteristics and problems and with time formed the permanent political currents— left-wing, centrist, and right-wing—exhibiting class interests for the common good, regional within the partitioning states, or based on the concept of rebuilding an independent Polish national state.

The agrarian social structure of the inhabitants of Poland at the end of the 19th century meant that there was relatively strong influence, particularly in Galicia, among the peasant political movement, also known as a folk movement. Almost at the same time in the Russian and Prussian parts of partitioned Poland, worker movements appeared, while all three partitioned areas saw the emergence of other social layers, whose programs went beyond the social class layer divisions. The dominant feature of programs and movements arising over and above class and regional divisions, particularly in the period 1908–1914, contained aspirations toward independence.[24]

The peasant movement tradition began over 100 years ago and has taken various organizational forms such as the Peasants' Party (Stronnictwo Ludowe), established in 1985. After 1903, it was known as the Polish Peasants' Party (PSL). Its program demanded political equality for peasants, access to schools, and social solidarity.[25]

The history of Polish left-wing parties goes back to 1882 when in Warsaw the International Social-Revolutionary "Proletariat" Party came into being and operated for four years. It was from this background that the future founders of the Second Proletariat (1888) and Third Proletariat (1890) came. These parties sought the overthrow of capitalism, the establishment of a socialist system, and an alliance with workers from other countries.

In 1892, in Paris, another extremely important left-wing current emerged, namely, the Polish Socialist Party (PPS). The ideological and political principles of this party concentrated primarily on the battle for the independence of Poland, political freedoms, and improvement in the economic standing of workers.

Finally, the merger of the Polish Workers' Union (ZRP, formed in 1889) and the worker circles of the Second Proletariat saw the birth in 1893 in Warsaw of yet another important Polish left-wing orientation, namely, the Social Democrats of the Kingdom of Poland, transformed in 1900 into the Social Democrats of the Kingdom of Poland and Lithuania (SDKPiL), with a membership of around 30,000 in 1905–1907. It represents the strongest Marxist faction in the Polish workers movement. Following Poland's return to independence on December 16, 1918, the SDKPiL and PPS-Lewica set up the Communist Workers' Party of Poland (KPRP). Delegalized in 1919 by the then state authorities, it became a section of the Comintern (Third International), and after 1925 it changed its name to the Communist Party of Poland (KPP).

The third current of Polish political parties, which merged in the late 19th and early 20th centuries (significant in terms of future development), was the National Democratic orientation, also referred to as the National Democratic camp or, colloquially and in journalistic jargon, endecja (from the initials ND), which was closely associated with Roman Dmowski (1864–1939). For this movement, national interest is the prime factor in the system of values and conduct. The nation must be independent and for this reason the prime objective of Poles was the struggle to regain independence. The effectiveness of this struggle depends primarily on working every day for the nation and providing ideological and educational training for children and adolescents, rural areas included. Its followers must prepare for armed struggle because, as past experience has shown, the nation has lost its best forces through uprisings, and, finally, the economy should be nationalized.

The purpose of successive national democratic parties was to Polonize the minorities occupying the eastern and southeastern borders, regarded merely as ethnic elements and not fully formed national communities. Given the strong anti-Semitic tradition of many leaders and advocates of the National Democratic camp, Jews were required to assimilate definitively by breaking links with their former community and its cultural models.

Following independence and formed from a variety of national democratic currents, the Peasant-National Union (Stronnictwo Narodowo-Demokratyczne) came into being in 1919 and was strongly represented in the first Sejm. Its place was taken after 1928 by the National Party (Stronnictwo Narodowe), which came into being in 1928.[26]

The Interwar Period (1918–1939)

Following World War I, Poland started rebuilding its independence as a republic (Rzeczpospolita) with a parliamentary cabinet political system of government. Transitory regulations[27] gave citizens, among other things, the right to form associations and unions, including political parties and coalitions, and it was not long before the political scene was full of these. Although part of the orientation and political structures representing them could already boast a long-term history and its own clientele, others were only just emerging as an answer to the challenges of revived statehood. The situation they faced after the war was dire: catastrophic infrastructure and economy, great poverty and unemployment, ethnic conflicts and the problems of national minorities, as well as developments in the international surroundings of the Second Republic, including those of two neighboring countries—the Union of the Soviet Socialist Republics and Germany (Weimar Republic, 1919–1934 and the Third Reich from 1934).

In this context a multiparty system was formed consisting of the right-wing (the National Democratic camp), the center (Christian Democrat party and the "Piast" Peasants' Party[28]), and left-wing circles united by the National Workers' Party, which later led to the Labour Party (Stronnictwo Pracy) and the left wing (Polish Socialist Party, "Liberation" Polish Peasants' Party, and the Komunistyczna Partia Polski (KPP; Communist Party of Poland). The main actors on the national minority political scene were Jewish, Ukrainian, Belarus, and German groupings, as well as regional and local groups. Some of these were represented in the Sejm, others were not. However, no political orientation had a majority in the Sejm. Parliamentary debates, even those concerning matters of fundamental importance for the state and society, such as the agricultural reform and the constitution, dragged on with no resolution.

In the Sejm's second term of office (1922–1928), the position of the two new political forces, the National Minority Block (BND) and the Christian Democrats, deserves special mention. The growing strength of the BND was undoubtedly due to the ethnic structure of Polish society during the interwar period. Much the same as during the First and Second Republics, the country was still multinational, and national minorities in those times constituted approximately one-third of all citizens.[29] The cultural and political ambitions of each of these minorities were expressed in their political conduct. Furthermore, the politics of the neighboring countries also had an impact (particularly that of the USSR and Germany) as did Poland's international obligations, stemming from the so-called Little Treaty of Versailles of June 28, 1919. The Polish government was obliged, among other things, to grant all inhabitants of the country, irrespective of their place of birth and parents, nationality, language, race, and religion "total and complete protection of life and freedom" (Little Treaty of Versailles, Chapter 1, Article 2).

It is more difficult, however, to explain the situation of the Christian Democratic parties. Taking into consideration that Poles were and continue to be primarily Catholics and hold their religious identity in great esteem, one could expect that Christian Democratic parties would develop rapidly, and that the Catholic social program, which included the Encyclical Rerum Novarum of Leo XIII of 1891, would be the basis of their political activity.[30] But this was not the case, probably because the church itself was and remains a very strong political institution in Poland, and the secularization of Polish society is not sufficiently advanced.[31] Furthermore, Polish Catholics were already active in many other political parties, including the National Democrats.

In the elections to the Sejm of the third term of office (1928–1930), a new and previously unknown political force emerged and won. Although it functioned as a party, its actual name was Non-Party Government Cooperation Block (BBWR). This specific bloc comprised a variety of political currents and options, oriented around the charismatic leadership of Józef Piłsudski, and came into being in 1928. The main purpose of this political force was to consolidate social support for governments that emerged after the May coup d'état and to strengthen executive power at the expense of legislature. Following the Sejm elections of 1928, the BBWR became the largest parliamentary grouping (with 28.1% of all mandates), although far short of a majority. However, it won no less than 55.6% of all mandates during the 1930 Sejm election only two years later. Before and during its term in office, the Piłsudski camp strove to change the legal status and the impact of political parties, convinced that the Sejm was still too independent and resistant toward the government.[32]

In order to come to grips with the Sejm, the governing bloc made the decision to change the constitution radically and did so in 1935.[33] The essential changes to electoral law and corresponding procedures involved: (1) reducing the number of deputies from 444 to 208 and the number of senators from 111 to 96, (2) transferring from proportional elections to majority voting, (3) creating 104 electoral districts, in each of which out of a total of four candidates two deputies were elected, (4) granting the so-called regional assemblies, themselves comprised of representatives of various self-governing bodies—territorial, economic, vocational, trade unions, women's organizations and colleges—the sole right to nominate candidates as deputies and to decide the final electoral roll, and (5) recognizing as valid voting cards where voters had failed to cross anything out (in such cases the first two candidates on the card were chosen).[34]

The opposition, both left and right wings, called for the elections to be boycotted and in fact only half of those with the right to vote turned out on Election Day.[35] Despite the low turnout, those who had initiated changes in voting regulations were still successful in attaining their objectives. From then until the outbreak of war and the suspension of all political party activity, the rule forbidding opposition parties to put forward their own candidates ensured that the Sejm of the Fifth (1935–1938) and Sixth (1938–1939) terms of office contained just two political groupings: the BBWR and national minorities.

The Postwar Years (1945–1948)

Immediately after World War II and the period of Nazi domination ended, Poland entered a brief transition period when the old system norms of the Second Republic of Poland were no longer fully binding and the new, typically Soviet "Socialist realist" values had not yet been conclusively imposed on the nation. Some political parties survived the war, continuing their activities—at least symbolically—abroad; others, under the impact of war losses and the death of their leaders, as well as political repression, ceased being active or went underground. Other parties merged, changed their programs and names, or, retaining the same ideological orientation, started from scratch.

Of particular importance for future events, the Polish Workers' Party (PPR) was established in 1942. Shortly afterward, this party had a fundamental impact on the events of 1945–1947. The party was inspired by former members of the Communist Party of Poland and small organizations associated with it, as well as groups of radical socialists and peasant activists. The wartime program of the PPR, apart from its armed struggle against the Nazis and reconstruction of the social system and the economy after the war, also included alliance with the USSR.

Examples of other initiatives include the clandestine organization Freedom, Equality, Independence (Wolność, Równość, Niepodległość), which came into being in 1940, set up by former activists of the Central Executive Committee of the PPS, and the Freedom and Independence Association (Wolność i Niezawisłość [WiN]), which was created in 1945 by part of the staff of the Home Army (Armia Krajowa). During the first postwar election campaign, this political orientation supported the idea of parceling out large landed properties, limited nationalization of the economy, and simultaneous comprehensive development of the cooperative movement and private industry and trade.

In order to understand the Polish party system in 1945–1948, it is not enough to simply describe the main players that created the system. It must be remembered that the end of World War II brought changes to Poland that were not only the result of decisions made by Poles. New state borders were delineated (the border shifted significantly to the west and at the same time the surface area of the country became smaller). The composition of the population radically changed from multiethnic and multifaith to single nationality (Polish) and virtually single faith (Roman Catholic), and internal and external migration of the population became more intense. And finally, 1945 brought the takeover of Poland by the Soviet Union as the Red Army moved into Polish territory and so-called Soviet "advisers" were installed in the new state apparatus. Contacts with countries in the West were broken. Repression and political processes took over. Death sentences were dealt out.

The fundamental adversaries in the conflict were those who, on the one hand, were against the loss of full state sovereignty, and, on the other, those who believed in the authenticity of socialist mottos and visions of the system. There were also those (and these constituted the majority) who perceived reality much the same as during the partition period, in other words, through the eyes of the positivist: it was, they believed, necessary to live and be creative in all kinds of situations so that later favorable conditions, both domestic and international, could be best used to attain the required system changes.

To foreign observers, everything seemed to move forward in keeping with the rules and regulations of democracy. Formally, politics were regulated by the March Constitution.[36] In June 1946, the so-called Polish People's Referendum took place. Citizens were to say whether they were in favor of abolishing the Senate, agricultural reform, nationalization of the fundamental branches of the industry, and the state borders including the Baltic, the River Oder, and the Lusatian Neisse River. According to currently available sources, the results of the referendum were rigged. The remains of the Polish multiparty political system made themselves known once again in January 1947 during elections to the legislative Sejm. Of the 444 mandates the PPS gained 116, the PPR, 114, the Peasants' Party, 109, the Democratic Party, 41, the PSL, 27, and the Labour Party, 15.

The elections of 1947 constituted a final turning point for the existing political parties, not only right-wing and centrist parties but also left-wing parties. Under the pressure of events, the multiparty system of the Second Republic of Poland, even in its reduced form, was replaced by a hybrid constituting a specific merger of a single-party system with certain elements of a hegemonic system.[37]

The dominant parties became the PZPR, which emerged after the Unification Congress (December 1948) from the PPR (with a membership of 900,000, according to officially given figures), and the PPS, which was forced to surrender (although having more than 500,000 members). The leader of the former was Władyslaw Gomułka, and Józef Cyrankiewicz led the latter. In the early period of the party's existence, about 60% of members were workers. In the tempestuous year of 1980, this figure dropped to close to 40%. The final formula that standardized the political and party system, together with the new name of the state, was the Constitution of the Polish People's Republic (PRL) of 1952. Work on the final phrasing of this document took five years (from 1947 to 1952). A single-chamber parliament was introduced, and the number of mandates, following amendments in 1956, was set at 460. It is notable that system implications of the new constitution (including regulation of political party activities and electoral rights and procedures) no longer referred to the spirit of the March Constitution of 1921 but to the April Constitution of 1935.

The Polish People's Republic (1952−1989)

Apart from the PZPR, the party system of the time also constituted the United Peasants' Party (Zjednoczone Stronnictwo Ludowe [ZSL]), the Democratic Party (Partia Demokratyczna [PD]), and four legal associations of lay Catholics.[38] Although none of these associations held the status of political party, each of them under the Polish socialist realist model held functions that could be defined as party functions and possessed its own parliamentary circles.

The PZPR, following subsequent program amendments and partial democratization of internal norms (in particular in 1956, 1971, and 1981), remained the governing (leading) party for 42 years. At the end of the 1970s, the peak period of development, the party had approximately 3 million members. In the year in which the party itself ceased operations (on the strength of a democratic decision taken at the Eleventh Convention, January 1990), it still had a membership of about 1 million.[39]

The ZSL was established in December 1949, following the merger of the Peasants' Party and the PSL.[40] When it was first founded, it was a typical class party, representing the interests of Polish peasants, constituting in the later half of the 1940s approximately 50% of the population of Poland.[41] The ZSL program did not constitute an alternative to that of the PZPR. Because of the binding principles of the system and political practice, the ZSL was an alliance party, recognizing the hegemonic role of the PZPR. After 1956, both parties signed two important documents. The first of these (1956) was the Declaration on the Principles of Cooperation. The second (1957, following the withdrawal of the PZPR from the forced collectivization of rural areas), together with other jointly approved resolutions, constituted the basis of state agrarian policy. At the turn of the 1970s, the ZSL had a membership of almost 500,000.

The SD was yet another clientelistic party. It came into being in 1938−1939 as the emanation of democratic groupings active, at the time, in Poland's larger cities. Following its underground activities in 1940−1945, after the war, it joined ranks with the democratic parties bloc. From the mid-1950s it was also joined by members of the Labour Party. In politics the SD primarily represented part of the intelligentsia, craftsmen, petty manufacturers, and other professions offering services. During the tempestuous 1981−1982 period, SD party membership, according to official statistics, oscillated at a membership level of around 110,000.

The four Catholic associations, mentioned briefly above, also played their part now. Although their formal status was analogical (i.e., they all existed in keeping with and within the bounds of binding law), they differed in character and each had a different social base. PAX, already in existence from 1945,[42] was linked with some interwar activists of ultra-radical groupings and the new Catholic circles concentrated around the weekly Today and Tomorrow (Dziś i jutro).[43] The basic political function of PAX, which in its heyday (1981) had approximately 21,000 members, was to stimulate pro-system attitudes among Catholics. It was represented by five members in the Sejm.

The Christian Social Association (Chrześcijańskie Stowarzyszenie Społeczne [ChSS]) and the Polish Catholic-Social Union (Polski Związek Katolicko-Społeczny [PZKS]) were considerably smaller than PAX. In its prime (1982), the former had a membership of about 10,000, while the latter, also in 1982, had around 3,000 members. The ChSS was established in 1957 as an attempt to create and broaden the sociopolitical space for believers in order to develop religious culture and pro-ecumenical attitudes.[44]

The PZKS came into being as a result of social agitation accompanying the political events of 1981. In the Sejm the PZKS held a five-person Member Circle (Koło Poselskie). At the end of the 1980s, its membership was around 10,000.

Yet another phenomenon of the times was the All-Poland Catholic Intelligentsia Club (Ogólnopolski Klub Inteligencji Katolickiej [KIK]), which came into being in 1956 and was transformed one year later into four clubs created in Warsaw, Cracow, Poznań, and Wrocław. The parliamentary representative of KIK circles was, from January 1958, an independent five-member Circle of Catholic Members (Koło Posłów Katolickich [Znak]). KIK represented Poland's top Catholic intellectuals and politicians.[45]

All parties and associations belonged to the Front of National Unity (Front Jedności Narodu [FJN]; created in 1952 as the National Front [Front Narodowy], it was finally transformed into the FJN in 1956).[46] In reality this institution was in many ways reminiscent of the interwar BBWR. Its basic tasks involved the preparation of a single list of election candidates, as well as equivalent lists for elections to the national councils at all levels. However, all important issues were decided by the ruling party committees. For this reason, election results throughout the entire period of the existence of the Polish People's Republic were not an expression of the free will of voters and honest democratic procedure, but rather of the decision to divide mandates before the elections in the offices of the prime political actor: the leadership of the PZPR. The fundamental decision was always the same: Those in power had to have the kind of majority in the Sejm over others that would make it impossible for any parliamentary coalition of allied parties and Catholic circles to threaten the PZPR position. Therefore, election results, including the number of mandates obtained by the PZPR, the ZSL, and the SD, as well as the four Catholic circles, were always known before voting even took place.[47]

In this situation citizens could do practically nothing if they were against participation in this kind of election. All that the authorities wanted was mass participation in the elections as an expression of legitimization of the entire political system. At the same time, refusing to vote was seen as an act of political opposition.

POLITICAL PARTIES IN THE THIRD REPUBLIC OF POLAND (1989 TO PRESENT): CONTINUITY AND CHANGE

The internal rhythm that gave Poland the opportunity to move toward democratization beginning in 1989 was determined simultaneously by four mutually conditioned processes: (1) the overcoming of political inertia inherited from the Polish People's Republic, (2) the spontaneous self-organization of society, (3) the transformation from a centrally based, state enterprise—dominated economy to a free market, and (4) radical change of Poland's position within the international community (membership in NATO and accession to the European Union).

These were the forces that combined to make change possible, when the need for change finally became overwhelmingly clear. The legacy of the 44-year period (1945–1989) was rife with systemic flaws. The lack of legal opposition within the system forced continued auto-amendment of the political system. The dividing line between the party and the state was thoroughly blurred, generating a "party state" syndrome and making it impossible for a body of qualified staff serving the state (and independent of political parties) to emerge. State services were politicized and under control of what came to be known as the "internal circle of the party," the "party within the party," the "real party." The ruling elite had no need to search for legitimization and relied on conviction in its own "historical mission"; no effective mechanism for creating and exchanging the elite (both managerial and political), based on the principle of relatively open rivalry, existed. Instead of an effective political culture, manifested by negotiation skills in solving conflicts, the social coexistence of people with different systems of values, and the rational viewing of one's surroundings and organizing oneself in specific groups (including political parties acting within the law), a two-tier logic prevailed, characterized by the mentality of barricades and of fortresses under siege, faith in slogans as the prime mover, coupled with the blocking of free thinking. These were the conditions that helped make change inevitable once external conditions made it possible.

The New and Revived Political Parties after 1989

However, overcoming this syndrome, by now deeply embedded, turned out to be far more difficult than simply establishing a formal basis for the political self-organization of society. In the realm of political parties, the first problem was an embarrassment of riches. Following the approval of the Political Parties Act of July 28, 1990, which gave rights to each group comprising "at least 15 persons holding full capacity to engage in legal activities" (Act of July 28, 1990, Article 4(3)), new parties started springing up virtually every day.

Chapter I, Article 13, of the Constitution of the Republic of Poland of 1997 only deprives those parties the right to register and act legally whose "programs are based upon totalitarian methods and the modes of activity of Nazism, fascism and communism, as well as those whose programs or activities sanction racial or national hatred, the application of violence for the purpose of obtaining power or to influence State policy, or provide for the secrecy of their own structure or membership."[48]

According to data held by the Regional Court in Warsaw (Civil Registration Section VII), by 1992 there were already 132 registered parties, in 1994 approximately 200, in 1995, 270, and in 1996, 300. In the following years, partly as a result of the statutory changes of 1997, which stated that the founding groups of political parties must contain a minimum membership of 1,000 (Political Parties Act of June 27, 1997, Chapter III, Article 11) and that all of the already-existing parties must also have at least 1,000 members, the number of parties diminished. According to the same source in the autumn of 2007, 116 political parties (former and newly registered parties included) complied with statutory requirements, while 37 were in the process of completing registration documentation. The remaining previously existing parties either disbanded, were struck off the register, or merged with other parties.

In the early phase of system transformation, yet another reason for the formation of new parties, apart from the wish to make the most of regained liberty and to become organized in order to settle or promote (sometimes defend) one's own interests or system of values, was the disintegration of Solidarity. Up to the legislative elections of 1989 and 1991, millions of citizens were united through resistance to the common adversary—the PZPR. But when Solidarity gained power, it soon turned out that the costs (both material and psychosociological) and the interests (as well as systems of values) of the various emerging groupings were different, and sometimes even diametrically so. Under the pressure of these contradictory forces, the Solidarity civic movement shrank dramatically and transformed into a reclaiming trade union, frequently losing even to other unions.

The many parties that appeared after 1989 followed a variety of historical paths to achieve the right to participate in the new system. Survivor parties were those with the longest histories and included the left-wing PPS, the peasant PSL, and to some extent the Christian Democrats and National Democrats. Successor parties were the continuation of parties from the time of the Polish People's Republic such as the Democratic Left Alliance. Post-Solidarity parties were those that emerged from Solidarity and included Law and Justice (Prawo i Sprawiedliwość [PiS]), the Democratic Party, the Citizens' Movement for Democratic Action, and others. And, finally, the majority of the 116 parties that were registered in June 1997 were entirely new parties.

The new parties took many different forms (from club to movement to catch-all)[49] and could be found across the ideological spectrum. By the beginning of 2008, there were at least eight left-wing parties, ranging from radical left-wing, left-wing, and center-left, the strongest being the Democratic Left Alliance. The Democratic Party of the intelligentsia was an influential centrist party, although it had little chance of gaining electoral success without forming a coalition with other parties. On the right, there have been dozens of small and very small parties, usually not participating in parliamentary elections on their own. Other groups are harder to classify: The conservative PiS, for example, combines social solidarity and a range of left-wing mottos with nationalism and views of the most conservative faction of Polish Catholicism. The Citizens' Platform (Platforma Obywatelska [PO]) is liberal in its economic views but at the same time adheres to a conservative code of customs, in some cases synonymous with standards propagated by the episcopate of the Catholic Church. The PSL has formed a ruling coalition since 2007 with the PO and is concerned with social class divisions. The peasants' party, Self-Defence of the Republic of Poland (Samoobrona Rzeczpospolitej Polskiej) has been described by its founder Andrzej Lepper as the "party of working people, of the impoverished, of the injured."[50] For some parties and groups, such as the Catholic Electoral Committee "Homeland" (Katolicki Komitet Wyborczy "Ojczyzna"), the Christian-National Union (Zjednoczenie Chrześcijańsko-Narodowe), and various Catholic family movements, religious devotion constitutes a sufficient ideology.

Concerning international politics and the European Union, the Democratic Left Alliance (Sojusz Lewicy Demokratycznej [SLD]) belongs to the Socialist International (in the European Parliament, the Party of European Socialists), and the PO to the Christian Democratic International (in the European Parliament, the European People's Party—European Democrats). The PiS participates in the Union for a Europe of the Nations, which acts as a group at the European Parliament. And finally, the PSL belongs to the Christian Democrat International. At the

European Parliament—similar to the PO—it cooperates with the European People's Party—European Democrats.

The Socioeconomic Context

To understand the evolution of the Polish party system and the conduct of Polish voters in recent years, it is of course also important to examine the socioeconomic context, that is, the restructuring of a centrally steered economy to a free market economy. The significance of this restructuring, carried out under the Leszek Balcerowicz Plan, had its negative effects. Among other things, it led to sudden growth in unemployment (halted and then gradually reduced only after Poland's accession to the European Union), increased the number of excluded persons (in particular older citizens and persons representing low human capital), and, last but not least, initiated the polarization of Polish society. The equal distribution of poverty, typical of the Polish People's Republic (PRL), was now replaced (under the Third Republic of Poland) by the drastically disproportionate distribution of material, human, and social capital.

Social inequality in Poland—the concentration of capital and differentiation in revenue—grew rapidly after 1989. By 2005, the value of the Gini index for Poland was 0.31–0.33; by 2008 it had risen to 0.34.[51] The significance of this index is compounded by the fact that the majority of Polish families have absolutely minimal (or nonexistent) resources other than those incorporated in the index.[52]

The image of the increasingly sharp division into the rich and poor (as well as what divides Poles and what unites them) is deeply embedded in the consciousness of the Polish population, well aware of the many analyses systematically carried out by published economists, sociologists, and social psychologists.[53] However, perceiving one's own situation does not always lead to rational conclusions. Frequently, particularly among the less educated and older members of society, the response is to shift the burden of blame incorrectly, a tendency that can make the problems worse and cause those who, for so many reasons, should be partners in seeking solutions to become, on the contrary, bitter enemies.[54] The social exclusion generated by poverty can enhance a deformed concept of reality and facilitate the intergeneration transfer of exclusion, and this can be translated into electoral behavior. The strategic question—Poland but what kind of Poland?—is then likely to be answered in accord with what has been termed a barricade mentality: "it's us or them."[55]

Electoral Results

The first fully free legislative elections held in 1991 filled the Sejm with 25 parties whose candidates had often been combined in electoral coalitions, concentrating the weaker actors on the political scene. Furthermore, 6.18% of valid votes were cast for parties that failed to reach the electoral threshold (5% of valid votes for parties entering independently and 8% for coalitions). Two years later, in the 1993 elections, the majority of votes went to only seven parties. However, approximately one-third of the valid votes were cast for a dozen or so parties and coalitions that failed to reach the electoral threshold. This tendency continued in subsequent parliamentary elections: seven parties took most of the seats in the Sejm in 2005; five in 2007.

Yet another factor worth noting was the uneven distribution of votes for parties given a parliamentary mandate. The clear leaders were: the left-wing SLD in 2001, two right-wing parties—PiS and PO—in 2005, and the PO in 2007. However, none of these parties has successfully secured a majority, permitting the formation of an independent government. The coalition partners have been the PSL for the SLD, "Self-Defence" and the League of Polish Families for the PiS, and finally, once again the PSL but this time with the PO. It is notable that none of the dominant parties went on to be the governing party in the election that immediately followed. Apparently none of them was able to implement its electoral program to a degree that would satisfy the electorate, and so electoral retribution followed.

Overall, the number of political parties in Poland capable of exceeding the 5% electoral threshold is decreasing dramatically, and their ranks are also shrinking. In the beginning of 2008, the SLD and three other parties forming the Left and Democrats coalition—according to their own declarations—had a membership of approximately 81,800, the PO approximately 33,920, the PiS approximately 16,900, and the PSL approximately 60,000.[56] In addition, each of these parties contains its own groups of young activists (popularly referred to in Poland as *młodzieżówka*). The number of members of such entities is small and changes rapidly.[57]

Explaining the Results: Voter Response

Voter turnout in all of the parliamentary elections of the Third Republic of Poland was exceptionally low. In 1991, only 43.2% of all citizens with voting rights went to the polls, in 1993, 52.08%. Similar voting levels were registered by the State Election Committee (PKW) at the beginning of the 21st century: only 40.57% in 2005 and 53.88% in 2007, the highest turnout in elections since 1989. Furthermore, voting behavior and political preferences differed from region to region.[58]

An opinion poll carried out on a representative nationwide sample of 1,038 persons in mid-2008 that assessed voter support for Poland's four strongest parties found 48% support the PO, PiS, 28%, SLD, 9% and PSL, 6%. Eight percent of respondents were either still undecided or supported different parties. In the same poll, voters were asked for which of the top seven parties they had the most negative opinion. To this question 48% of the respondents named the PiS, whereas "Self-Defence" came in second with 35%, and the others followed: LPR, 24%, SLD, 23%, PO, 18% and PSL, 4%.[59]

Taking into account both views expressed by respondents (i.e., support and rejection indicators taken together), it is notable that voters are far more polarized toward the PiS than toward the PO. In this case we have a clear indication of two different Polands facing each other: the first, the Poland of poverty represented by the PiS, and the second, the party of the affluent or those who simply believe in the new opportunities offered by the progress of civilization.[60] In between these two polarized groups there is usually a large middle class. In Poland, however, this structural space is virtually empty. The modern middle class still remains in statu nascendi. The voters of the first Poland (i.e., Poland of poverty) will continue to vote for the PiS in future parliamentary elections (in particular if at least part of them are not recaptured by the new program of the SLD). The second Poland (i.e., Poland of affluence) constitutes PO voters who organize themselves, among other things, into political parties (even if they support such parties only through the electoral act and not through formal membership), in order to, as Florian Znaniecki stated, "organize oneself towards creative tasks" so as to consider change as one's opportunity.[61]

Under these circumstances, the following question must be asked: Is it possible to find a new center-left or center-right formation, capable of offering to this electorate an alternative possibility of existing, which complies with the basic principles of the Charter of Fundamental Rights of the European Union? At present the PO is taking measures aimed at guaranteeing itself a wider electorate without relinquishing, particularly in its verbal declarations, its conservative-Christian democratic inclinations. The PO sees the attainment of this by amending its principles regulating the financing of political parties, increasing the number of members of parliament elected in a single constituency, and finding new ways to translate valid votes into mandates.

However, the ruling PO is also envisioning reforms. It wants to deprive parliamentary parties of remuneration by the state of eligible expenses incurred by them during the election campaign and also deprive parliamentary parties from state aid earmarked to cover part of the costs related to their activities. The PO proposes that parties—including those represented at parliament—gather their own means through member contributions, donations, wills, and so forth. Multimandate constituencies should become single-mandate, while the principles of calculating votes should be changed from proportional representation to majority representation. It is difficult not to notice that all of these proposals—if they were implemented—would improve the standing of the large parties representing the interests of affluent society, but at the same time would fundamentally limit the possibility of the remaining parties to continue on the political stage, in particular the small parties. Their relevance for the ability of Polish parties to serve as agencies of democratization seems self-evident.

Civil Society: Strong Enough to Supplement the Parties as Agencies of Democratization?

The shrinking number of citizens who belong to political parties is asymmetric to the increasing number of NGOs and foundations and the number of citizens committed to their activities. On the basis of law in force in Poland in the 1989–1994 period, more than 47,000 NGOs and foundations came into being. However, only about 17,000 of these were active.[62] Up to 2006, the number of registered NGOs and foundations grew to more than 63,000. But of these, much the same as in the previous case, only half of them are visible in everyday public life. It is rare for any of these to enter directly into competition with political parties.[63] Most often, they either never participate in organized political life or constitute—in particular during parliamentary elections and self-government (regional and local) elections—a kind of civic wrap, permitting parties to penetrate various circles otherwise difficult to access. In this manner networks of sociopolitical interaction are helping to create a semblance of civic society and participatory democracy. But, as is demonstrated by the latest investigations, during the past five years the number of newly organized NGOs has been drastically decreasing (in the 2003–2008 period by approximately 25 percent).[64]

Furthermore, when we analyze the actual voluntary commitment of units and groups in civic activities, the conclusions are not so optimistic. As demonstrated by the European Social Survey of July 2008, only 1.7 of Poles participate in activities of political parties and civic groups (while in the remaining European Union [EU] countries this value stands at 3.9%), 4.5% of Poles participate in different types of organizations (EU, 13.6%), 6.1% contact politicians or officials (EU, 13.8%), 5.5% sign petitions (EU, 25.1%), 1.4% participate in legal demonstrations (EU, 6.2%) or wear badges supporting an important campaign or action (EU, 7.7%). Undoubtedly, this is to a large degree a cumulated syndrome that Father Józef Tischner, following in the footsteps of Alexander Zinoviev, referred to as homo sovieticus.[65]

CONCLUSIONS

Social anger during the Polish People's Republic found its outlet in the form of cyclically repeated crises. The climax of these was the Solidarity movement and the peaceful takeover of power following the

Roundtable talks of 1989. But what will the various categories of citizens who lost out during the period of system transformation do now? At present their main form of protest is abstaining from voting and withdrawing from public life. Sometimes this way of escaping from freedom and civic responsibility is dressed in slogans of primitive nationalism, xenophobia, and demonstrative religiosity.

The evolution of the Polish party system is unforeseeable, at least for the time being. Conditions stimulating the transformation of the Polish multiparty system into a two-party system are already there. Looking at the results of this type of system in Great Britain and the United States, one may presume that present shifts do not constitute a threat to democracy. Can one, therefore, without taking into account historical context, the cultural foundation, and the degree of social structure polarization, imagine that a bipolar party system is really the best solution for countries like Poland? But what would happen in Poland if the only alternative to the PO turned out to be the PiS, and that as a result of the cumulated anger of those who lost out and were alienated, it gained a majority at the general election, permitting it to form a one-party government and implement the PiS vision of the Fourth Republic of Poland, which it has spoken about, including a change of constitution? What will happen in the absence of a party that could offer a considerable group of citizens, which neither supports the PiS system of values and the manner of thinking nor the techniques it employs when in power, not only the chance of casting a negative vote (on, for instance, the PO's list), but also to vote for meaningful positive alternatives? Is it not likely that the mechanism of self-destruction of democracy would then emerge? The history of interwar Europe reminds us only too well of at least one such case.

Let us imagine instead that the Polish people decide to move in a different direction and that they are capable of doing so. After all, human nature and democracy are an accumulated effect of human actions, although these actions are never free from "given structural conditions inherited from the past." It is people who "at the same time reinforce or modify these conditions for their future successors."[66] Homo creator and homo sociologicus determine their societies—civil ("the nonstate sphere of social activity"), political ("the representative sphere of social activity"), state ("the administrative-coercive sphere of social activity"), and public ("the informational sphere of social activity")—and the growing sovereignty of individuals is one of the most important advances of humankind.[67] Sovereignty enables people to make choices and enables them to "run away from the gulag of religion, race, region and nation."[68] Human nature and democracy are congruent. If human nature is "free, end-oriented, and calculating/rational/reasonable," then only democratic order is able, by its rules, devices, and procedures, "to overcome the consequence of human freedom, sociability and conflict."[69] Participation, direct or through freely chosen representatives, of free and equal citizens in politics, acceptance of the rules of the game, and trust in social contracts are crucial factors for democracy.[70]

If this optimistic analysis is correct, then it is necessary to know how and to have a means and a will through rational behavior to halt—or at least limit—the processes that lead to the self-generation of poverty through poverty. It is necessary to interrupt the cause-and-effect sequence of events, whose end product means the exclusion of millions. And this needs to be done before they and their children start voting. For in a democracy—and Poland is at present a democracy—it is the leaders of the victorious parties who will decide.

SUPPLEMENTARY REFERENCES

Almond, Gabriel A., and S. Verba. *The Civic Culture: Political Attitudes and Democracy in Five Nations.* Princeton, N.J.: Princeton University Press, 1963.

Encyklopedia Powszechna PWN [PWN Universal Encyclopaedia]. Vol. 1 (1973), Vol. 2 (1974), Vol. 3 (1975), Vol. 4 (1976). Warsaw: Państwowe Wydawnictwo Naukowe (PWN).

Encyklopedia Powszechna Gutenberga 1931–1935 [*Gutenberg Universal Encyclopaedia 1931–1935*] Vol. XIII, Vol. XIX, Vol. XXI. Warsaw: Wydawnictwo Guttenberga.

European Social Survey. United Kingdom: Center for Comparative Social Surveys, 2008.

Gross, Feliks, and Z. Gross. *Socjologia partii politycznej* [*The Sociology of Political Parties*]. Kraków: Czytelnik, 1946, 47.

Lawson, Kay, ed. *How Political Parties Work.* Westport, Conn.: Praeger, 1994.

Rocznik Statystyczny 1983 [*Statistical Yearbook 1983*]. Warsaw: Główny Urząd Statystczny, 1983.

The Act of 28th July, 1990, "On Political Parties," in *Polish Constitutional Law.* Warszawa: Bureau of Research of the Sejm, 1996, 443–447.

"Ustawa z dnia 27 czerwca 1997 r. o partiach politycznych" ["The Act of 27th June 1997 on Political Parties"]. In *Dziennik Ustaw Rzeczypospolitej Polskiej* 98. Warszawa, 19 sierpnia 1997, 604.

Wiatr, Jerzy J. "Election and Voting Behaviour in Poland." In *Essays in the Behavioral Study of Politics,* ed. A. Ranney (Urbana: University of Illinois Press, 1962).

Wielka Encyklopedia PWN [*PWN Great Encyclopedia*] 21. Warszawa: Wydawnictwo Naukowe PWN, 2004, 559.

CHAPTER 9

The Relationship between Parties and Democracy in Hungary

Attila Ágh

INTRODUCTION

In the past two decades, Hungary has developed a consolidated democratic system, and the Hungarian parties have played a central role in this democratization process. This chapter focuses on two issues. It analyzes first the general features of the Hungarian party system with its strength and weaknesses and, second, the recent populist turn in Hungarian politics. The chapter examines the reasons for similarities and dissimilarities in the new East-Central European democracies, since the Hungarian parties have the same organizational weaknesses and small membership base, yet unlike the other parties in the new democracies they have very low electoral volatility and great stability. Again, the populist turn in the new democracies has a wide range of similarities, but it has some very specific Hungarian features as well. In Hungary a rather large, stable, and well-organized center-right party has emerged with clear populist and Euroskeptic tendencies. This chapter offers a social and cultural explanation for this special trend in the development of Hungarian democracy.

THE FOUNDATIONS OF THE HUNGARIAN POLITY

The historical kingdom of Hungary was formed in the 10th century based on western Christianity and state architecture. After the Turkish invasion in the 16th century, Hungary became a relatively autonomous part of the Habsburg Empire with its own constitution. It became independent but was partitioned among its neighbors after World War I under the terms of the Versailles Peace Treaty. Its territory was reduced to a third of its former size, with 4 million Hungarians living in the neighboring countries, a situation which still has an impact on Hungarian domestic politics and party competition. In the following interwar period, Hungary had a moderate authoritarian regime with a multiparty parliament, but voting rights were restricted at some parliamentary elections. After World War II, the Yalta Agreement and the Paris Peace Treaty brought Hungary into the Soviet sphere of influence, and between 1949 and 1989 Hungary belonged to the Soviet "external" empire as a member of the Warsaw Pact and Council for Mutual Economic Assistance. However, Hungary was the only Soviet-dominated country that organized a robust revolution against the communist regime and Soviet rule. Although the 1956 revolution was crushed by the Red Army, following the restoration of the old order the tough Hungarian resistance to Soviet rule forced János Kádár, the new party leader, to produce the most liberal version of state socialism in the region. Hence, in the 1960s and 1970s, some elements of a market economy were introduced in Hungary. The Hungarians were allowed to travel to the West, and they returned from the West with the ideas and skills of western society.[1]

In the 1980s, some further socioeconomic liberalization took place, including the first steps of democratization, the political crisis became ever more manifest, and the transition process began. In 1985, the parliamentary elections were partly free and competitive, and parliament assumed a more active role. New parties continued to emerge. In 1987, the first opposition party—the national-conservative Hungarian Democratic Forum (Magyar Demokrata Fórum [MDF])—was formed, followed in 1988 by two liberal parties: the Alliance of Free Democrats (Szabad Demokraták Szövetsége [SZDSZ]) and the Alliance of Young Democrats (Fiatal Demokraták Szövetsége [Fidesz]). During the same period the two leading historical parties also returned, namely, the countryside-based Smallholders Party (Kisgazda Párt [FKGP]) and the more urban-based Christian Democratic Peoples Party (Kereszténydemokrata Néppárt [KDNP]).

At the 1988 conference of the ruling party, the Hungarian Socialist Workers Party (Magyar Szocialista Munkáspárt [MSZMP]) removed the ailing János Kádár from power. In 1989, the reform wing of the MSZMP convened a party congress, legally liquidating the old ruling party and forming a small new party, the Hungarian Socialist Party (Magyar Szocialista Párt [MSZP]). Thus by 1989, all the new parliamentary party actors had appeared, and the Party Act in October 1989 legitimized and regulated the Hungarian multiparty system.[2]

In the late 1980s, the deep crisis of the communist world system broke out, and the bipolar world system collapsed in 1989–1990. But the Hungarian economic and political transformations largely preceded this process and to some extent also contributed to the weakening of the Soviet external empire. Pro-market and democratization legislation had already been passed, earlier than in any of the other communist countries. In the summer of 1989, the negotiated transition began, and on June 13, 1989, the National Roundtable was convened. It was the most important institution of democratic transition and was composed of the representatives of the ruling party, the opposition parties, and some social organizations like the trade unions. The National Roundtable finished its work on September 17, 1989, by signing an agreement on democratic transition between the main political and social actors, thereby laying the foundation for the new constitution that was passed and then promulgated on October 23, 1989, the day of the 33rd anniversary of the October 1956 Revolution. The formal turning point came only in the spring of 1990 when the first free and fair election was held. Between May 1989 and May 1990, the interim government of Miklós Németh managed the political transition and prepared the "founding elections."

The negotiated transition was completed by the spring 1990 elections. The fact that this deep political change, a "revolution" without bloodshed or violence, had been peacefully negotiated was a great historical achievement. However, this was not simply an "elite transition" created by negotiating elites on both sides. In the second half of the 1980s, the entire Hungarian society was on the move. Civil society movements organized large mass demonstrations and scores of nonparty organizations. On March 15, 1989, on the national holiday remembering the March 1848 Revolution, hundreds of thousands of Hungarians held a peaceful demonstration in Budapest and expressed their support for systemic change. This was the "movementist" period of the Hungarian civil society when social movements dominated the political scene, and it was followed by an organizational period in the early 1990s when thousands of new voluntary organizations emerged. These social movements made possible the emergence of an active counter-elite and legitimized its demands at negotiations with the ruling party. The ruling party was also deeply split in the late 1980s, and its reform wing, a well-organized faction that largely supported the opposition demands against the ailing party leadership, received increasingly greater popular support.

The social transformation was also spurred on by the fact that in the 1980s millions of Hungarians visited Western Europe. Public opinion surveys during this era clearly demonstrated the westernization of the Hungarian population and its public discourse. Thus the communist ruling elite in Hungary had lost the ideological and cultural hegemony long before it lost its political monopoly: a "psychological" and cultural transition preceded the final political transition when power was transferred from old to new political elites.

Due to strong popular support, the long transition in Hungary produced a consensual polity, a parliamentary democracy with a weak, representative president and a strong prime minister. Legally, the new Hungarian Constitution was created by amending the 1949 Constitution. The amendments relied both on the traditions of the 1946 democratic constitution and on the principles drawn from the current West European constitutions. After the first free elections, the new parliament made some additional amendments in 1990, first introducing the prime ministerial government of the German type (a "chancellor's democracy"), also in use in Spain and elsewhere, as a means of stabilizing the democratization process. The constitution has been further amended more than 20 times in some details, but this has been in a context of high consensus: the fundamental acts still need a two-thirds majority vote for their amendment. Occasionally someone proposes the idea that a new constitution is needed in order to establish a coherent and unified structure. However, the present constitution has worked well so far, and the parties cannot agree upon a new structure. Therefore, the well-designed but somewhat improperly structured constitution may stay in force for many years to come.

The Hungarian polity can also be characterized as an extended "checks and balances" system. Since January 1990, a powerful Constitutional Court has exercised a wide range of competencies. The judiciary is independent, with both the Supreme Court and the State Procurator Office separated from the Ministry of Justice and from the executive branch in general. The same applies to the National Bank, which is responsible for monetary policy and is supervised by parliament. The implementation of the budget is monitored by the independent State Audit Office, which has regularly presented its reports to parliament. Finally, citizens' complaints are handled by the Ombudsman Office and its supervision also falls into the competence of the parliament. All these democratic institutions still bear the mark of the long, negotiated transition and have greatly contributed to the successful consolidation of the Hungarian democratic system, including the multi-party system.

The post-transition record of continuous political stability has its foundation in the particular Hungarian electoral system developed during the negotiated transition. This mixed—"personal" and proportional—system was also the result of the National Roundtable negotiations concluded on September 17, 1989. Voters now cast two votes, one for a specific candidate in the 186 individual districts and one for the party lists in the 20 territorial units. In the individual districts, there is a majority system, with a second round if there is no absolute majority in the first round (186 seats). In the 20 territorial lists—19 counties and Budapest as the capital—there is a proportional system with voting for the party lists. In both parts of the electoral system the parties are compensated for the "lost votes" (i.e., for all votes not producing a parliamentary seat) on the national list. Within the proportional, territorial and national lists, there are 210 seats. Altogether the unicameral Hungarian Parliament has 386 seats with the MPs coming partly from the individual districts, where candidate-party competition exists, and partly from the proportional lists, with an exclusive party competition. This electoral system has proven to be well balanced because it has provided both a personal touch for the political elite and a rather proportional result, with a slight distortion effect to create a stable governing majority in the parliament. In 1990, the 4% threshold required for the parliamentary parties successfully eliminated the smaller parties. The threshold was increased in 1994 to 5%, but it has had no practical significance, since the gap has widened between the nonparliamentary and the parliamentary parties.

Given these stable constitutional foundations of the Hungarian polity, there has been remarkable political stability as well. In fact, Hungary is the only newly democratized country where regular elections have taken place only at the conclusion of the full mandate (i.e., every four years). There have been no early elections. This political stability has also appeared in the party system, as shown by the fact that the five parties that emerged first in 1988–1989 (see above) have all remained parliamentary parties for the past 20 years, and other parties have made few inroads into their domination. The Hungarian Life and Justice Party (Magyar Élet és Igazság Pártja [MIÉP]) formed by splitting away from the MDF managed to become a parliamentary party for one term (1998–2002). After the decomposition of the MDF as an umbrella organization and the rise of Fidesz, the three parties on the right (MDF, Fidesz, and KDNP) have from time to time formed an electoral coalition, but they have appeared in parliament as separate party factions (currently the case with the Fidesz and KDNP). This dynamic stability with the same party actors can be considered the first basic feature of the Hungarian party system, whereas its second basic feature is the ongoing deep political polarization and the tendency toward a quasi—two-party system (see below).

The Hungarian Constitution also stipulated freedom for meso- and micropolitics (i.e., it created elbow room for social and territorial actors within mesogovernments or as organized interests of various kinds, including business representations and trade unions). A National Interest Reconciliation Council was created as well, and the government is supposed to consult it in all important decisions concerning fiscal questions in general and the world of labor in particular. In the same way, the Constitution has separated state administration from public administration. On one hand, the vertical state administration has developed a great degree of "deconcentration" in the implementation of the central government decisions. On the other hand, the horizontal—county

and municipal—levels of the elected public administration have represented a robust "decentralization" of the decision-making process
based on the principle of subsidiarity (i.e., taking the decisions at the
level closest to those concerned). Intergovernmental relations have
emerged between the different levels of state administration as well as
public administration, although democratic institution building is somewhat more complete at the national level. Yet the democratic system
has nevertheless been working rather well at the lower levels, as has
been confirmed and legitimated by the municipal elections.

The first fully democratic municipal elections in Hungary were in
September and October 1990. Since 1990, there have been municipal
elections every four years, in the autumn of the years in which parliamentary elections are held (in the spring). The two electoral campaigns
have usually merged, yet sometimes they have led to the opposite political results. In the municipal elections it is very difficult to identify
the "winner" parties because there are many contenders and elected
posts, and usually all parties get some of the posts through the parallel
elections at settlement and county levels. In the settlements 3,200
mayors and about 40,000 councilors are elected, and another 100 are
elected in the counties (including in the larger county councils and in
the smaller county governments). The municipal elections have usually
produced some kind of balancing effect vis-à-vis the parliamentary
elections. In general, this effect contributes to the democratic consolidation, since the opposition parties in the parliament have some strong
positions in the municipalities. In Hungary, the leftist and liberal parties (MSZP and SZDSZ) have usually been strong in Budapest and in
the other bigger cities, except for Debrecen, the second-largest city and
the "capital" of Eastern Hungary. The rightist and conservative parties
(first MDF and FKGP, nowadays Fidesz), in turn, have been strong in
the smaller settlements and middle-sized cities. Thus, in many cases
the bigger cities as the centers of the 19 counties have been controlled
by the left-liberal parties, but the surrounding countryside in the same
counties has been governed by the conservatives.

HUNGARIAN PARTY HISTORY AS DEMOCRATIZATION

The recent political history in Hungary has been formed by simultaneous external pressures and internal demands. Democratization and
Europeanization have been both an outside challenge and a domestic
necessity. Yet, democratization may reflect the domestic processes
better, while Europeanization indicates the processes of structural
adaptation to the external pressures. I will discuss the party history in
this order, although in fact we will be talking about two sides of
the same coin, since the Great Transformation in the early 1990s meant
not only a structural accommodation to the European Union (EU)

constitutionally but was in fact a general democratization process, and these general features of democratization were at the same time an anticipative Europeanization (i.e., an indirect preparation for EU membership), which was in turn followed after 1998 by adaptive Europeanization to prepare more directly for joining the EU.[3]

As already shown, the democratization process began with the constitution making in the late 1980s, laying the foundation for a democratic polity in Hungary. It was above all a political operation, choosing from among the Western European constitutional solutions to create a proper transfer of institutions. The new constitution in the first stage of the institutional development also outlined the major direction for further changes, continuing institution building from macropolitics through meso- to micropolitics. But the consensual politics of the transition period came to an end abruptly at the time of the spring 1990 parliamentary elections, when the first completely free and fair multiparty elections were held.

The 1990 spring parliamentary election produced the victory of the national conservative parties (MDF, FKGP, and KDNP) with József Antall as prime minister, but the liberal party (SZDSZ) was a close second and played the role of a strong opposition party cooperating with the then liberal Fidesz, which was its ally in the First Parliament (1990–1994). The leftist, social-democratic party (MSZP), one of the prime movers of the democratic transition, became a rather small opposition party in the First Parliament.

Since then there have been four additional free elections, an electoral history marked by several common features (Tables 9.1 and 9.2). First, government stability has been strong in Hungary, and there have only been two government reshuffles within the same party coalition. Between 1990 and 1993, József Antall was the prime minister heading a national-conservative government (MDF, FKGP, and KDNP), and after his death his minister of interior (Péter Boross) completed the term. Between 1994 and 1998 there was no change at the top of government, and Gyula Horn was the prime minister of the socialist-liberal government (MSZP and SZDSZ) for the whole term (Table 9.3). The situation was the same between 1998 and 2002 when Viktor Orbán was the prime minister of a new national-conservative government (Fidesz, FKGP, and MDF) as Fidesz shifted in its political orientation from market liberalism to national conservatism. In the 2002–2006 cycle, there was again a socialist-liberal coalition (MSZP and SZDSZ) with a change in 2004 between Péter Medgyessy and Ferenc Gyurcsány at the post of prime minister, but both prime ministers came from MSZP and led the same coalition. The government of Gyurcsány was reelected in 2006 with a large majority and formed the second Gyurcsány government on June 9, 2006 (Tables 9.4 and 9.5). The renewed socialist-liberal coalition broke up on May 1, 2008, when the SZDSZ left the government

Table 9.1 Elections to the Hungarian Parliament (%)

Year	MSZP	SZDSZ	Fidesz	MDF	FKGP	KDNP	MIÉP	Others
1990	11	21	9	25	12	6	—	16
1994	33	20	7	12	9	7	2	10
1998	33	8	29	3	13	2	5	7
2002	42	6	41[1]	—	1	—	4	6
2006	43	7	42[2]	5	—	—	2	1

Notes: Fidesz, Magyar Polgári Szövetség (Hungarian Civic Alliance); FKGP, Független Kisgazdapárt (Independent Smallholders Party); KDNP, Kereszténydemokrata Néppárt (Christian Democratic Peoples Party); MDF, Magyar Demokrata Fórum (Hungarian Democratic Forum); MIÉP, Magyar Élet és Igazság Pártja (Party of Hungarian Life and Justice); MSZP, Magyar Szocialista Párt (Hungarian Socialist Party); SZDSZ, Szabaddemokraták Szövetsége (Alliance of Free Democrats).
[1]Common list with MDF.
[2]Common list with KDNP.
Source: For the data on the governments and party composition see Gabriella Ilonszki and Sándor Kurtán, "Hungary," *European Journal of Political Research, Political Data Yearbook* (1992–2007). See also Péter Sándor, László Vass, and Ágnes Tolnai, eds., *Magyarország politikai évkönyve* (Political Yearbook of Hungary on 2006), (Budapest: Hungarian Center for Democracy Studies Foundation, 2007). All data are also available at the National Election Office (www.valasztas.hu).

over a disagreement about health care reforms. Nonetheless, the SZDSZ supported the minority MSZP government, which fell short of a majority by only four seats.

In the first period of anticipative Europeanization (1990–1998), there were two government cycles, focusing first on political institution

Table 9.2 Allocations of the Party Seats in the Hungarian Parliament

Year	MSZP	SZDSZ	Fidesz	MDF	FKGP	KDNP	MIÉP	Others
1990	33	92	21	164	44	21	0	11
1994	209	69	20	38	26	22	0	2
1998	134	24	148	17	48	0	14	1
2002	178	20	164	24	0	0	0	0
2006	190	20	141	11	0	23	0	1

Notes: Fidesz, Magyar Polgári Szövetség (Hungarian Civic Alliance); FKGP, Független Kisgazdapárt (Independent Smallholders Party); KDNP, Kereszténydemokrata Néppárt (Christian Democratic Peoples Party); MDF, Magyar Demokrata Fórum (Hungarian Democratic Forum); MIÉP, Magyar Élet és Igazság Pártja (Party of Hungarian Life and Justice); MSZP, Magyar Szocialista Párt (Hungarian Socialist Party); SZDSZ, Szabaddemokraták Szövetsége (Alliance of Free Democrats).
Source: For the data on the governments and party composition see Gabriella Ilonszki and Sándor Kurtán, "Hungary," *European Journal of Political Research, Political Data Yearbook* (1992–2007). See also Péter Sándor, László Vass, and Ágnes Tolnai, eds., *Magyarország politikai évkönyve* (Political Yearbook of Hungary on 2006), (Budapest: Hungarian Center for Democracy Studies Foundation, 2007). All data are also available at the National Election Office (www.valasztas.hu).

Table 9.3 MSZP Voting Support

Year	Number of voters on the party list	Percentage on the party list	Electoral turnout in percentage
1990	534,897	10.9	65.09
1994	1,781,504	33.0	68.92
1998	1,497,231	32.9	56.26
2002	2,361,997	42.0	70.53
2006	2,336,705	43.2	67.83

Note: MSZP, Magyar Szocialista Párt (Hungarian Socialist Party).
Source: For the data on the governments and party composition see Gabriella Ilonszki and Sándor Kurtán, "Hungary," European Journal of Political Research, Political Data Yearbook (1992–2007). See also Péter Sándor, László Vass, and Ágnes Tolnai, eds., Magyarország politikai évkönyve (Political Yearbook of Hungary on 2006), (Budapest: Hungarian Center for Democracy Studies Foundation, 2007). All data are also available at the National Election Office (www.valasztas.hu).

building, and second on completing economic transition to a functioning market economy. The initial democratic transition came to an end around 1998, and early consolidation as well as EU accession negotiations began. From 1998 to 2006, Hungary moved into the stage of adaptive Europeanization as it made the specific democratic structural adjustments necessary to join the EU. During the third government (1998–2002), the main job of the Orbán government was to manage the EU accession negotiations that were concluded in December 2002 in Copenhagen under the Medgyessy government. The Medgyessy government and then the first Gyurcsány government (2002–2006) made the necessary direct preparations, with further structural adjustments and the initial domestic accommodations. The first Gyurcsány government (2004–2006) then carried over into a third, postaccession period, with the same coalition (2006–2010) responding to EU pressure for further tough structural and socioeconomic reforms.[4]

Table 9.4 Presidents of Hungary

Election year	President	Party support
1989	Mátyás Szűrös	Interim
1990	Árpád Göncz	Liberals
1995	Árpád Göncz	Liberals, Socialists
2000	Ferenc Mádl	Conservatives
2005	László Sólyom	Conservatives

Source: For the data on the governments and party composition see Gabriella Ilonszki and Sándor Kurtán, "Hungary," European Journal of Political Research, Political Data Yearbook (1992–2007). See also Péter Sándor, László Vass, and Ágnes Tolnai, eds., Magyarország politikai évkönyve (Political Yearbook of Hungary on 2006), (Budapest: Hungarian Center for Democracy Studies Foundation, 2007). All data are also available at the National Election Office (www.valasztas.hu).

Table 9.5 Governments of Hungary

Year	Prime minister	Party composition
1990	József Antall	Conservatives, Smallholders, Christian Democrats
1993	Péter Boross	Conservatives, Smallholders, Christian Democrats
1994	Gyula Horn	Socialists, Liberals
1998	Viktor Orbán	Conservatives, Smallholders, Christian Democrats
2002	Péter Medgyessy	Socialists, Liberals
2004	Ferenc Gyurcsány	Socialists, Liberals
2006	Ferenc Gyurcsány	Socialists, Liberals
2008	Ferenc Gyurcsány	Socialists

Source: For the data on the governments and party composition see Gabriella Ilonszki and Sándor Kurtán, "Hungary," *European Journal of Political Research, Political Data Yearbook* (1992–2007). See also Péter Sándor, László Vass, and Ágnes Tolnai, eds., *Magyarország politikai évkönyve* (Political Yearbook of Hungary on 2006), (Budapest: Hungarian Center for Democracy Studies Foundation, 2007). All data are also available at the National Election Office (www.valasztas.hu).

What was the role of the parties during these stages of democratization and Europeanization? Analyzing the recent political history of parties as the agents and products of democratization, one has to note first that the emergence of the Hungarian parties has also gone through several stages. Initially they appeared as social movements, then they created rather wide spectrum, heterogeneous "forum" parties formed by the intellectual or social elites. After the founding elections, when party leaders and representatives were selected and elected, the successful parties went through a parliamentarization process, a process that introduced party discipline, created professional party leadership and MPs, generated party programs, and led to the building of loose constituencies among the population at large. In a very narrow, traditional, or textbook meaning, the emergence of the Hungarian parties came to an end basically in the second half of the 1990s. By the founding elections of 1989–1990, three kinds of parties had come into being: (1) the new parties based on the opposition movements (MDF, SZDSZ, Fidesz), (2) the reformed ruling party (MSZP), and (3) the reborn historical parties (FKGP, KDNP) that had existed until 1949. Actually, the new parties and the MSZP were the main actors even at the beginning of democratization, since in Hungary the historical parties were weak and did not play a significant role in the first period and have since survived as intraparty units in Fidesz.

The electoral history of the new democracies in Eastern and Central Europe has been described as a move from general mobilization to demobilization, resulting in low electoral participation or in nonrepresentative elections. However, in Hungary this general tendency has appeared much less in low turnout at elections and much more in the decreasing trust in the parties and the increasing political passivity of the majority of population. Systemic change began in Hungary as elsewhere as a "movementist" aspect of civil society, with the mobilization of the masses through social movements creating a breakthrough in politics to democratic transition. But after this breakthrough, the Hungarian parties managed to demobilize civil society associations and build up a system in which the parties acted as quasi-monopolistic political actors. Since then there has been a participation paradox: The opportunity of participation at the free and fair elections has opened for the Hungarians, but many have turned away from the electoral forms of participation. As a result, electoral and other participation has become socially asymmetrical and dominated by the winners of systemic change, leaving at least one-third of the population outside the electoral game. Thus, the initial large mobilization drive at the very beginning of systemic change has not yet generated a civic culture and participatory democracy as a new tradition in Hungary.[5]

The basic weakness of the Hungarian parties is that they are "small-sized mass parties." The memberships of the Hungarian parliamentary parties are usually between 10,000 and 30,000, so the party membership is small compared to the number of voters for each party, approximately 1 to 100 as an average, with further erosion of party memberships in the 2000s. The social base of the Hungarian parties has been very weak. The parties are elitist, top-down organizations and have a high level of leadership centralization. In addition, they live on state subsidies as cartel parties. It has often been mentioned that their organizational linkages with society are weak and that they have a high number of party employees in their headquarters compared to the size of membership. Efforts to improve mobilization by initiating national referenda regularly or organizing frequent party congresses have thus far not succeeded in changing this imbalance.[6]

There has been a long and controversial process of change everywhere in Europe from the party systems of industrial society based on materialist values and class cleavages to those of postindustrial service society based on postmaterialist values and culturally oriented social cleavages. The party landscape in the EU can briefly be characterized as a mixture of the two kinds of party systems, and both the remnants of the industrial society and the new elements of the service society have had a deep impact on the Hungarian party landscape. This has led to the characterization of the New Left and New Right parties as basic transformations in party politics. The New Left has differed from the Old Left because of its rejection of class-based politics and because it has embraced the participatory and decentralized forms of party membership. The main issues on the agenda of the New Right have been taxation, immigration, and radical regionalism, in addition to the antipolitical and antielitist forms of protest that have clearly indicated the sense of crisis in the declining industrial society and its social strata and have led to social and national populism. The description of European party developments as resulting in parties somewhere between irrelevance and omnipotence applies even more to Hungarian parties, which are seriously impacted by these western conditions of radical transformations on both left and right. Of course domestic conditions and the internal logic of party building have also been important, but adaptation to western requirements has been dominant.[7]

From the late 1980s, four main tendencies can be identified in the development of the Hungarian party system:

1. The continuous reduction in the number of parties through the elections (although Hungary had a rather concentrated party system from the very beginning). The first turning point came in 1994 when the two leading parties of the early systemic change—MDF and SZDSZ—lost their dominant positions, and the second turning point in 1998 produced the present bipolar party system. So far the winning parties have usually received a relative majority of seats (the only exception being the MSZP in 1994) and have formed coalition governments to respond to popular pressure for consensual politics.[8]

2. Moving from the original chaos of forum type parties, the left-right divide has steadily become the dominant principle in the Hungarian party system, marked by the affiliation of the Hungarian parties to the appropriate EU transnational parties. MSZP declared itself a social-democratic party from the very beginning in October 1989, but the titles of rightist and conservative became common only in the mid-1990s. Fidesz moved to the right side of the party spectrum in 2003–2004, and it has unified the rightist parties—FKGP, KDNP, and a fraction of MDF—into one big catchall party. Hence, a bipolar party system has come into being. While in 1990 the two biggest parties gained only 46.1% of the total votes, by 2006 it rose to 85.2%, which offered a picture of a concentrated bipolar party system. The number of effective parties declined from 6.7 to 2.7 between 1990 and 2006.[9]

3. The voters' volatility decreased from 28.4% in 1994 to 8.4% in 2006, thus reaching the Western European average level. An impressive 89% of MSZP voters in 2002 supported this party in 2006, and 85% of Fidesz supporters in 2002 did the same in 2006. The percentage of lost votes for all parties decreased from 15.8% to 3.2% between 1990 and 2006. The widespread social dissatisfaction produced alternating governments between left and right in most elections until 2006, when the first government was reelected, which can also be a sign of consolidation.[10]

4. The latest tendency is the strong populist turn of parties as a result of the long-term declining trust in parties, which has led both to the general delegitimization of the parties and to the increase in unconventional forms of political participation such as street demonstrations and civil disobedience movements.[11]

HUNGARIAN PARTY HISTORY AS "EUROPEANIZATION"

The impact of external, global forces has increasingly appeared in Hungary through the EU. Although this accommodation process has been full of conflicts, the strong impact of the EU on domestic developments has not been felt as an alien force, since the values in Hungary—despite the decades of Soviet rule—have been basically of western origin. Hungarians have developed a western cultural identity, and the domestication of western achievements has always been part of their historical program. The Central European democratic traditions in general have also had their cultural legacy in the systemic change. The most characteristic national tradition of Hungary has been to adopt western institutions and patterns of behavior, since Hungarians have not considered these as "alien" but as desired targets. The historical routine of structural accommodation to the West in the postcommunist developments is seen by most as a "return to Europe." Furthermore, the external adaptation pressure has been apparent first and foremost in the emergence and functioning of the Hungarian party system, since Europeanization at the political level has appeared more strongly and directly in the "particization"—including the transnational elite socialization—than in any other field of political transformation. Actually, finding EU partners has been the only dependable guarantee of legitimacy and survival for the Hungarian parties. Parties have been formed by Europeanization and have been at the same time the chief political actors of the Europeanization process themselves, as manifested in the changing positions of the government and opposition.[12]

There has been a long debate in the European studies on the relationships between the national parties and the EU level parties. At first the dominant view was that the impact was limited, but this has changed somewhat recently. For instance, Robert Ladrech has pointed out that the impact of the EU on the national parties can be observed in policy contents and programs, organization, patterns of party competition and party-government relations, and even beyond, in the party-society relationships. However, so far little attention has been paid to the participation of the Hungarian parties in the European party system, and therefore the limited impact approach has survived to a great extent, a tendency exacerbated by the failure to make a distinction between the external and internal Europeanization of the East-Central European (ECE) parties, since Europeanization has been very direct or hard on one side and very indirect or soft on the other. As I understand it, external Europeanization is an elite-based process through contacts with and membership in international party organizations that has resulted in evident changes in the Hungarian parties' programs, values, and public discourses. As a result, the parties have shaped a western-type image or outlook for themselves (as an "international" party).

Internal Europeanization, on the other hand, has been a process of transforming the membership, the constituency of the Hungarian parties, and their relationship to the civil society, changing the internal party organizations and popular beliefs accordingly. Internal Europeanization as a mass-based process is the transformation of the basic party features such as membership and organization to resemble more closely western-type parties with respect to internal structures, including the relationship to the party constituency and the civil society as a whole.[13]

So far external Europeanization has only scratched the surface of the Hungarian parties. Europeanization has mostly appeared through the established official contacts and the informal meetings of only a few party leaders with their western counterparts. The bulk of party membership—and even more the population at large—has not been informed or consulted regarding discussions of the EU left and right within international social democracy or Christian democracy. The reason is simple: The opportunities and threats have been so different in Hungary that most of the population cannot decode them. The lack of social consolidation has meant that most Hungarians are still focused on their domestic difficulties and material needs. Nevertheless, EU membership and exposure to the problems shared throughout the EU are likely to provoke a complex and controversial process of internal Europeanization of the Hungarian parties.

Hence the analysis of external and internal Europeanization offers a general approach for discussing the ECE polities with the thin Europeanization of the ECE parties as a model. In fact, external Europeanization has proceeded in the above-mentioned two stages—anticipatory and adaptive—and also had a limited but increasing impact on internal Europeanization. During these initial stages, European integration has, however, produced a split between the external and the internal Europeanization of the Hungarian parties, with a growing contrast between their international and domestic activities. At present, after Hungary's entry into the EU, this conflict has sharpened, and the activities of the Hungarian MEPs (members of the European Parliament) have provoked an acute conflict between these representatives and the domestic parties, unleashing a reform drive at home. We can expect that during the next parliamentary cycle, beginning in June 2009, Europeanization will penetrate more deeply into the domestic structures of the parties, and shaping EU alternatives will become a more important aspect of each party's national strategy.

In sum, all these arguments point in the same direction: The Hungarian parties are not yet completely prepared for assuming the rights and duties of membership in the EU level parties. Given the low degree of their external Europeanization and even slower progress with internal Europeanization, the Hungarian parties have been lagging behind in both policy cooperation and strategy making in the EU. This thin

Europeanization is, however, well known in most cases of the former new member states from Greece to Spain. But there are two big differences. First, when the south European states entered, the EU still operated at a level of much less complexity. Today the main political actors in new member states face a tremendously increased demand for both policy coordination and strategic thinking with respect to party elites and party programs. Second, the western sister parties offered active assistance to the Spanish and Portuguese parties, and, despite the significant assistance of some western party foundations, there has been nothing of similar size in the case of the Hungarian parties.

Although, as noted, the "anticipative" Europeanization of the Hungarian parties could be observed in the early 1990s, the real specificity of Europeanization as a special accommodation to the EU party systems was not felt or demanded until after membership was achieved. At that point Hungarian MEPs had to adapt to the fact that domestic policy issues would be treated according to EU cleavage lines. This in turn resulted in changed relationships between MEPS and their party factions at the EU level, entailing a long and painful learning process for the party elites. So far the EU transnational organizations as well as EU level party factions have been successful to some extent in the Europeanization of the individual Hungarian parties at home, but not yet been able to Europeanize the Hungarian party system (i.e., the basic relationships between the parties at home). Establishing illegitimate and constructive roles for the governing and opposition parties is still extremely difficult because the political game is still about delegitimizing the other party group and blocking the activities of government while in opposition, even in the field of necessary reforms.

Altogether, the Hungarian parties have been the most important agencies of both democratization and Europeanization, but their role has been very controversial. On the external side, the Hungarian parties have performed below expectation and have produced only a thin Europeanization, with some stronger external and weaker internal Europeanization. On the domestic side, the parties have both facilitated and impeded democratization by promoting their own democratic institutionalization but damaging the participatory democracy with their exclusivist behavior. By working hard to change themselves to meet EU and democratic expectations regarding the role elected party representatives play in governments, they have made important contributions. However, Hungarian society has paid a high price for the emergence and consolidation of the parties. The parties have neglected the party-society relationship to a great extent, thereby helping to produce a postaccession crisis that has led at the same time to a general crisis for the parties themselves.

THE MATRIX OF THE PARTY SYSTEM AND THE
POSTACCESSION CRISIS

As we have seen, the Hungarian parties have been formed under two kinds of pressure: external and internal. Beyond the usual divide of left and right in the party systems, the demand for Europeanization has also produced two kinds of party profiles according to their relation to EU. Thus, the Hungarian parties can be described according to the two axes of left and right on one side, and Europeanization and nation-centrism (or traditionalism) on the other. This typology gives us four basic types of Hungarian parties: Europeanized left and Europeanized right, and nation-centric left and nation-centric right. The motives and actions of political leaders can also be described in this matrix, thus giving us as well a typology for politicians. In both cases of party organizations and party leaders, all four boxes can be filled. However, in the Hungarian bipolar party system, at present only two parties are really important: the Europeanized left (MSZP) and the nation-centric right (Fidesz). The same goes for the two party leaders. With the personalization of politics, there have only been two main actors in Hungarian politics: Ferenc Gyurcsány (MSZP), the impatient modernizer, and Viktor Orbán (Fidesz), the populist leader.[14]

Upon closer examination, the internal cleavages have appeared in a more complicated way than the classical terms of left and right would express, since the basic divide is between Westernization-Europeanization and "Nationalization-Traditionalization." After the collapse of the communist regime, the two main tendencies of "return to Europe" and "return to History" have confronted each other. Most people have supported both, but they have clashed forcefully in the question to what extent they have to be implemented in a strategic "policy mix." Half the population has opted more for Europeanization-Westernization as accepting, following, and implementing imported western models, but the other half of the population has preferred the "Hungarianization" of development to westernization by putting more emphasis on Hungarian traditions and specificities. Both tendencies have their own justification because after the decades of "Easternization" and de-Europeanization, and especially in the period of the EU accession, there has been an urgent need for the "return to Europe." In the same way, after decades of oppression of national traditions causing terrible damage not only to minds and mentalities but also to the economy by imposing alien models on Hungary, there has been a popular demand to return to the development based on national capacities and specificities.

The party polarization in Hungary has taken place according to this divide of "Europe" and "Nation." Although the confrontation of these tendencies appeared at the very beginning of the democratization process, this conflict greatly deepened later when Fidesz became the leading party on the right. In the early 1990s, MDF, as a forum-type party or umbrella organization, represented the "national" line with FKGP and KDNP, while SZDSZ, MSZP, and Fidesz were on the "European" side. Since the mid-1990s, Fidesz and its dependent partner, KDNP, have been on the "national" side, with some incorporated vestiges of FKGP, and in a constant family quarrel with the more EU-oriented MDF, whereas MSZP and SZDSZ have stayed on the Europeanization side. Altogether, the Hungarian right is much more national populist and Euroskeptic than the western right, since it favors the "Europe of nation-states" much more than its sister parties in the West. The Hungarian left supports EU integration more, but it has been constantly frustrated in its efforts to get significantly closer to the model of "Social Europe," so its leftist character has often been questioned by friends and foes alike. Accordingly, this dual divide has distorted both types: the center-left suffering from the trap of materialist needs due to the severe economic crisis management, and the center-right struggling with the contradictions of Europeanization. This has produced blurred and uncertain identities on both left and right, and it is hardly possible to find a real pro-European center-right party in Hungary nor is it possible to identify a center-left party with a marked leftist program.[15]

The formation process of the Hungarian parties has not proceeded along the classical cleavage lines of social stratification and economic status, not even in the emerging deep social polarization. The process has been basically relying on the age-old cultural cleavages, although it also reflects the new winner-loser divide as well, since the winners have usually supported Europeanization and the relative and absolute losers have in turn demanded more national protection. The cleavages between the Hungarian parties has not been based on the social strata but much more on the cultural images and values (cultural divide: Europe-Nation), on the relationships to the former regime ("anticommunist" divide: former "communists" and oppositions), or on the new social tension (privatization divide: winners and losers). As Renata Uitz argues, the difference between the two larger parties is primarily due to the cultural and historical factors and has little to do with their social and economic policies. Most analysts agree that the relationship between economic status and party preferences is weak in Hungary, since both big parties have all the social strata among their supporters in similar proportions. Due to these cleavage lines, the Hungarian party system has a relative consolidation with the stable bipolar party system, and at the same time there has been an increasing political deconsolidation with the populist mobilization of the relative or absolute losers by Fidesz.[16]

This paradoxical situation has emerged after two decades of controversial history of civil society. In the first half of the 1990s, there was a robust development of voluntary associations and nongovernmental organizations in Hungary. But this process lost momentum in the second half of the 1990s. The overly strong influence of parties *(particization)* in political life and the economic difficulties in the everyday lives of the citizens were equally responsible for this decline. The political space was almost fully occupied by parties on one side and the time of average citizens was fully absorbed by overwork on the other. The social background of this controversial process is that two generations of losers have emerged in Hungary so far. The first generation of losers were those affected by the mass unemployment in the early 1990s due to privatization, the second generation of relative losers in the early 2000s were those who have been unable to compete in the new context of EU membership. In general, the standard of living has returned to the 1989 level only through an increasing social polarization that has damaged most of the Hungarian population. People have also suffered to a great extent from the decreasing social security and poor public services. In a word, there is no social consolidation in Hungary but rather a "social shock" effect after two decades of economic and political systemic change.[17]

Accordingly, mass dissatisfaction with the new democratic order and market economy has triggered at the political level a demand for populist sloganeering and has provided a fertile ground for national and social populism. In the first stage of the new Hungarian populism, Fidesz introduced modern political communication techniques in the mass media in the 1998 elections, winning by promising the end of the transition misery. During the 2002 election cycle there was unprecedented high turnout as a reaction to the "return to the Past" by the Fidesz government, so the national-conservative line of Fidesz lost by a narrow margin. In the second stage of Hungarian populism (2002–2006), Fidesz turned to the mass mobilization of its supporters by organizing "civic circles" and large street demonstrations in order to put pressure on the government. They claimed they alone represented the "nation," emphasizing that the nation cannot be a loser. They considered their party leader Viktor Orbán to be the "prime minister of the Hungarian nation," in an opposition of "nation" to the "country." So he was supposed to be the leader of the "15 million Hungarians" at home and abroad (i.e., also in the neighboring countries). Since then there has been a deepening or sharpening paradox in the party-society relationship in Hungary, now characterized by a very highly mobilized and polarized society with a very low level of real political participation (i.e., a negative or anomical participative democracy). The high mobilization has occurred through mass street demonstrations and mass meetings of the Fidesz, often accompanied by the violent street actions of the extreme rightist mob.[18]

Fidesz lost the 2006 elections, again, and this ushered in the third stage of the Hungarian populism. Thus, parties and party systems have recently been transformed again, as the vital issue of political mobiliza-tion-demobilization has come to the fore in this all-party crisis. Hence the second Gyurcsány government has meant both consolidation and deconsolidation of democratic politics. Certainly, it has been a step to-ward consolidation, since the incumbent government was reelected for the first time in Hungary. At the same time, it has brought the deconso-lidation of the Hungarian party system, since Fidesz has not been ready to accept its second failure at the elections and has begun a general attack on the government through both parliamentary and nonparlia-mentary means by stigmatizing the government as antinational and representing foreign interests. Instigated by this inimical political atmosphere, the radical right organizes violent actions on national holi-days and all other possible occasions. Although Fidesz has halfheart-edly officially condemned these violent street demonstrations, in fact it has supported them by the national-social populist public discourse with a mantra of "we have been living worse and worse in Hungary due to the misdeeds of the government." This "crisis discourse," with an antiparliamentary approach of "voting against the government in the streets," has instigated popular dissatisfaction and has gone beyond the democratic rules by declaring the incumbent government elected at free and fair elections as "illegal," "illegitimate," and "bolshi-libi" (Bolshevik-liberal with a reference to Jews) traitors of the nation. In addition, Fidesz has kept a constant public discourse going regarding "police brutality" against the demonstrators, although just to the con-trary, it is the demonstrations that have been very brutal and in all cases many more police than extreme right demonstrators have been wounded.[19]

Thus the main danger now for the democratization of the Hungarian party system is populism and Euroskepticism combined. There has been a deep split in Hungary in the political life between the Hungar-ian Socialist Party and Fidesz, and this bipolar party structure has impeded the creation of party consensus on Hungarian national strat-egy in the EU. A diffuse party resistance against EU membership may be larger in some other new member states, but Fidesz is, by far, a larger and better organized soft Euroskeptic party than any other center-right party in the ECE and produces greater concern. Many center-right parties play both sides, supporting EU integration abroad, including within the European Parliament, but issuing ambiguous dec-larations on the EU at home in order to keep the anti-EU voters among their supporters. However, in Hungary democracy is seriously under siege, since Fidesz has regularly organized pseudo-mobilizations as "national referendums" by the party or its "civic circles" plus street demonstrations that have deconsolidated democratic order and parlia-mentary democracy. In Fidesz itself, with an almighty president in the party statute, these mass mobilizations have at the same time served as a substitute for party membership, which is relatively small and hierarchically organized without intraparty democracy.[20]

Altogether, the historical turning point of the entry to the EU provoked a crisis in the Hungarian party system. The postaccession crisis has been caused by dual pressure from inside and outside. From inside there has been a cumulated social crisis that has caused reform fatigue, and a negative participative democracy has emerged as an anomical mobilization of society. From outside there has been a continued EU demand for further reforms, including the preparations for the introduction of the euro, that have demanded deep cuts in the state budget. As a result, Hungary is one of the most pessimistic countries in the EU. The postaccession crisis can be briefly characterized as producing sociopolitical senility in parties and party leaderships after a mere 20 years, a phenomenon aggravated if not caused by the shocking effects of the EU membership. The Hungarian governments and parliaments, as well as the parties and political elites, have been programmed for democratization and EU accession, and both goals have been attained. These actors, however, have shown no sensitivity to the genuine popular demands in the form of long-term social consolidation. Nor have they demonstrated any sensitivity to the new phenomena of EU membership. They have neither new strategic programs nor new messages for the current postaccession period with a proper EU competence. The political elites in general have become—at least mentally and sociopolitically—"old," tired, and extremely unpopular and have been busily promoting their private business interests from their political positions. Even many relatively younger politicians are in fact very "old," since they have been oversocialized by former generations of politicians and have developed the same kind of outdated or old-fashioned patterns in political culture as the outgoing first generation.[21]

CONCLUSIONS

Altogether, the main characteristics of the Hungarian parties are: (1) they have been small-sized mass parties or catchall parties, since the people have not joined parties in great numbers as earlier in the West, so the parties have a "head" but no "body"; (2) they can be qualified, therefore, as "office-seeking" cadre parties, since the small membership is just enough to provide the political elite; (3) their structuring principle has been based much more on cultural than socioeconomic cleavages, since cultural traditions and "camps" matter most; (4) they have still been much more politically ideologically than policy oriented, hence the necessity of dealing with the EU policy universe by entering the EU has caused serious problems; and finally (5) there has been a bigger divide between left and right or between the pro-EU and Euroskeptic parties than in the West, which has almost completely excluded compromises, coalition making, and national consensus among them. In their increasing propensity to create old-fashioned spoils systems, the governments have had a series of political purges at all changes of governments, particularly in public administration.[22]

In sum, at first Hungarian democratization was a party-based development, but with the emergence of weaker parties than in the west. All in all, the party-based democracy in Hungary has been stable and weak at the same time. The individual parties as agents of democratization have been formed and Europeanized to some extent, but the party system is still far from both democratization and Europeanization, since the legitimate roles of government and opposition have not yet appeared. The main difficulty in Hungary is that the typical western actors have not yet been formed. The Europeanized rightist party Fidesz has not been able to avoid the dual trap of national-social populism and Euroskepticism and MSZP has been stronger in Europeanization than in elaborating its leftist character, since crisis management and seeking to promote socioeconomic reforms have kept it from becoming a western type of leftist party. As one can foresee the ongoing tendencies, on one hand the Hungarian parties will be facing within the EU further drastic transformations in the main direction of the internal Europeanization of parties. The specific Europeanization pressure upon them will increase to a great extent in the new cycle of the European Parliament (2009–2014). On the other hand, however, the left may be weakened by its failure to achieve social consolidation, and national and social populism may be the main line of the Hungarian right for some years to come.

SUPPLEMENTARY BIBLIOGRAPHY

Ágh, Attila. "The Role of ECE Parliaments in EU Integration." In *Democratic Governance and European Integration: Linking Societal and State Processes of Democracy*, ed. Ronald Holzhacker and Erik Albaek (Cheltenham: Edward Elgar, 2007), 249–268.

Burnell, Peter, ed. *Globalising Democracy: Party Politics in Emerging Democracies* (London: Routledge, 2006).

Delwit, Pascal, ed. *Social Democracy in Europe* (Brussels: Université Libre de Bruxelles, 2005).

Holzhacker, Ronald, and Erik Albaek, eds. *Democratic Governance and European Integration: Linking Societal and State Processes of Democracy* (Cheltenham: Edward Elgar, 2007).

Ilonszki, Gabriella, and Sándor Kurtán. "Hungary." *European Journal of Political Research*, Political Data Yearbook (1992–2007), 966–973.

Merkel, Wolfgang. "Embedded and Defective Democracies." *Democratization* 11 (2004), 33–58.

Sándor, Péter, László Vass, and Ágnes Tolnai, eds. *Magyarország politikai évkönyve* [*Political Yearbook of Hungary on 2006*] (Budapest: Hungarian Center for Democracy Studies Foundation, 2007).

Sikk, Allan. "How Unstable? Volatility and the Genuinely New Parties in Eastern Europe." *European Journal of Political Research* 44 (2005), 391–412.

Tavits, Margit. "On the Linkage between Electoral Volatility and Party System Instability in Central and Eastern Europe." *European Journal of Political Research* 47 (2008), 537–555.

Tóka, Gábor. "A magyarországi politikai tagoltság nemzetközi összehasonlításban" ["The Hungarian Political Structure in an International Comparison"]. In *Törések, hálók, hidak: Választói magatartás és politikai tagozódás Magyarországon* [*Cleavages, Nets, Bridges: Voter Behavior and Political Structure in Hungary*] ed. Róbert Angelusz and Róbert Tardos (Budapest: Hungarian Center for Democracy Studies Foundation, 2005), 243–322.

CHAPTER 10

The Czech Party System and Democracy: A Quest for Stability and Functionality

Miroslav Novak

INTRODUCTION

The transition to democracy in Central and Eastern European countries was not only a significant event but also a welcome laboratory for political sociologists and constitutional lawyers. It has stimulated them to think about which democracies are more or less successful, what kinds of models are best for countries undergoing democratization, and the degree to which the new democracies have actually been inspired by existing models. There has been debate, for example, on parliamentary versus presidential systems,[1] proportional versus first-past-the-post systems of voting and the related political party systems, and the consensus versus the Westminster model of democracy.[2]

A decision in favor of one or another system of electing a parliament also has important consequences for the political life of the country and the success of democratization. From the very beginning (first within the Czech and Slovak Federal Republic) the Czech Republic chose the electoral system of proportional representation with multimember districts and a 5% legal threshold. In addition, unlike most other postcommunist countries, which have had a tendency to establish semi-presidential regimes, the Czech Republic introduced a pure parliamentary regime (only Hungary and the Czech Republic among postcommunist countries have presidents elected indirectly by parliament and not directly by the people). These institutional characteristics, and especially the system of electing the lower chamber, are connected with the type of government that is formed, how it functions, and how it is maintained or how it possibly fails: with governmental stability or instability, capacity for action or paralysis, and ultimately with the character of democracy in the nation and its prospects.

This chapter is divided into three sections after this brief introduction. In the next section I consider key developments in the post-transition era (1989–1992): The emergence and development of the all important Civic Forum movement, the response of the Czech Communist Party to the removal of Soviet rule, the development of cleavages around which these and other parties and movements would form, an overview of the early postcommunist parties and party system as of the 1992 elections, and the breakup of Czechoslovakia that took place subsequent to (and in part due to the results of) that election. The next section (1992 to the present) focuses heavily on the elections to the Chamber of Deputies in 1996 and the subsequent formation of a minority government, a key turning point in recent Czech history, but also summarizes the history of party development up to the present time. A brief concluding section summarizes the relationship between Czech parties and democracy today.

POSTTRANSITION DEVELOPMENT OF THE CZECH PARTY SYSTEM (1989–1992)

The first question in relation to the postcommunist systems of Central and Eastern Europe was whether their democracies could be "consolidated." To the extent that some achieved such consolidation at the end of the 1990s, the issue then became how effective the newly consolidated democracies would be.[3] The emergent party system was of key importance both for the consolidation of democracy and for its later efficiency and quality.[4] As Scott Mainwaring and Timothy R. Scully[5] have noted vis-à-vis Latin American systems, for new democracies it is very important that their party system should become "institutionalized."[6]

Research on the development of the Czech party system can usefully employ standard methods of analysis of party systems (on the basis of criteria such as the degree of fragmentation) but only from the parliamentary elections of 1992 forward.[7] Prior to these elections, the political differentiation of the Civic Forum (Občanské Fórum [OF]) was the dominant issue, and so we begin with that.

The Civic Forum, 1989–1992

The first phases of the development of the party system in the Czech Republic were significantly influenced by the broad OF movement, which came into existence not through electoral and parliamentary processes but as a result of the protest movement against an existing communist regime in November 1989.[8] The Social Democrats (ČSSD), led by Jiří Horák, and the miniature Christian Democratic Party (KDS), led by Václav Benda, were originally part of this movement, but they left the OF even before the first democratic parliamentary election, and another mini-party, the Liberal Democratic Party (LDS) of Emanuel Mandler, separated from OF immediately thereafter.

The assembly in October 1990, during which Václav Klaus, the minister of finance, was elected chairman of the OF, was an important landmark for its future. Before his election the OF was only a conglomerate of various trends and orientations, but Klaus had a clear conception that he sought to push through energetically and succeeded in convincing a majority of its members. The new chairman wanted to change the OF into a political party, and this proposal was adopted by the next OF assembly on January 12, 1991.

Meanwhile, various currents inside OF became institutionalized. First, as early as October 1990, the Inter-Parliamentary Club of the Democratic Right came into being with a founding announcement signed by 37 deputies of the Federal Assembly and 21 deputies of the Czech National Council (ČNR) in October 1990 on the initiative of Daniel Kroupa and his friends. The second stream was represented by the Liberal Club, created in December 1990 with a founding declaration signed by 33 deputies of the Federal Assembly and 36 deputies of the ČNR.

The third stream, which in January 1991 founded the Club of Social Democrats led by Rudolf Battěk (who had been expelled from the ČSSD because he had run on the OF ticket in the election of 1990 as a member of the ČSSD), was much weaker than the other two. According to its secretary, Bohuslav Ventura, it came into existence as a reaction against the "irresponsible attempt" to change the OF into a right-wing party with exclusive membership. Finally, some of the deputies of the OF, especially those in ČNR (about a quarter of whose members were in the OF), did not join any of the rival groups but instead founded an "independent" OF.

By the end of 1990, there were three conceptions (scenarios) of the near future of the OF:

1. OF should continue to be a broad movement. This view was especially prevalent in the Liberal Club.
2. OF should become a serious political party with a clear program (a majority opinion, especially typical of the supporters of Klaus).
3. OF should become a cultural foundation only, an umbrella for interactions between the various parties and movements derived from the OF. This idea was promoted particularly by Daniel Kroupa, chairman of the Inter-Parliamentary Club of Democratic Right.

In the end there was no choice but to divide OF into two groups at its next, farewell assembly in February 1991. The criterion for division was the recognition or nonrecognition of the decision of the previous assembly of the OF. Should the OF be transformed into a political party in line with conclusions of the assembly (the Civic Democratic Party [ODS]), or should it continue to develop as a broad residual movement (the Civic Movement [OH])?

In April 1991, 40 federal deputies of the ODS founded their own parliamentary group. Six deputies of the former OF, led by Valtr Komárek, joined the Social Democrats and in May an eight-member club of social democratic orientation (SDO) was established. Also, the founding assembly of the ODS took place at the same time. Klaus was elected chairman, and surveys of electoral preferences performed by AISA (a Czech marketing research group) in the same month showed the ODS to be the strongest political formation by far, with the support of 19% of respondents. The ODS maintained this position consistently both in elections and in electoral preferences until the beginning of 1997.

A star-studded founding assembly of the OH was also held with pomp in April 1991.[9] Prestigious foreign guests, German Minister of Foreign Affairs Hans-Dietrich Genscher, French Ministre d'Etat Lionel Jospin, and NATO Secretary General Manfred Wörner, attended. The subsequent development of this residuum of the OF, however, did not live up to the expectations of its friends. It won no seats in the 1992 parliamentary election and never recovered from the defeat.

The development of Josef Lux's Czechoslovak People's Party (ČSL), its relation to OF, and its successive entities were very important. Analysis of the declarations of their chairmen shows that they both accused the other (Lux accused OF, and Klaus the ČSL) of a lack of "profiling." At the same time, the ČSL was undergoing a complicated process.[10] One aspect that deserves mention is the role of its Christian social faction, expressed, for example, in its manifesto of March 1991. At the beginning of the 1990s, the ČSL was regularly cooperating, namely with the social democrats, Moravian autonomists, and even the reform communist Obroda Club; together they produced documents that strongly criticized government policy. On the issues of restitution and privatization, however, the ČSL, like the Civic Democratic Alliance (ODA) and the KDS, was more radically to the "right" than Klaus and his supporters.

The ČSL at the time was in a government coalition on the Czech level only, not on the federal level, and its more "social" members suggested that the ČSL should leave the Czech government and join the opposition. Furthermore, the party advocated a social market economy, which was rejected by Klaus, even though the term originally related to the liberal economic policy of postwar Germany.[11]

The Role of Communists in the Czech Transition

Meanwhile, Czech communists were following their own path. Indeed, one of the key differences between the kind of transition from

Soviet rule that took place in the Czech case and in other Central European countries was the role played by the Communist Party and its supporters.[12]

Jerzy Wiatr has suggested that we distinguish between (1) transition by "capitulation," (2) transition by a "contract" establishing coregulation, and finally (3) transition by "controlled opening," or a granted or conceded transition.[13] Hungary comes close to the model of "granted" transition, Poland to a significant extent embodies "coregulated" transition, while Czechoslovakia and the former German Democratic Republic (GDR) are closest to transition by "capitulation."[14] This kind of transition had a strong impact on the fate and direction of the Communist Party.

The Hungarian and Polish postcommunists converted themselves into social democratic parties, alternating in power several times with their conservative rivals. In the Czech case, the Communist Party of Bohemia and Moravia (KSČM), its character already changed by the gradual "normalization" following the Soviet invasion in 1968, became the only significant communist party in Central Europe after 1989 to refuse to convert to social democracy. In both of the first two parliamentary elections (in 1990 and 1992), the communists were the second largest political power in the Czech Lands, although in both elections they finished far behind the winner. The result was that no political alternative was possible: such a large communist party opposing the system could not be a legitimate alternative to the government of the time. The "exceptionalism" of the Czech case thus was not due to weakness but rather to the strength of the communists after 1989. The Czech Republic was in fact the only country in Central Europe where a comparatively strong[15] and to a certain extent dogmatic communist party prevented a healthy alternation of governments for quite a long time.

This also explains why a historical (not postcommunist) social democratic party has gradually succeeded in occupying a key position in Czech political life. Communist survival and social democratic revival are actually related to each other. Although the Social Democratic Party (ČSSD) did not take many votes from former communists, as did the KSČM, the preference for the ČSSD began to rise after the KSČM showed itself incapable of making the transformation into a moderate left party.[16] The ČSSD obtained only 6.5% of the vote in the election to the Czech National Council (ČNR) in 1992, but in the next election to the Chamber of Deputies its vote increased by 20% to a total of 26.4%. This made alternation possible, and in the 1998 election to the Chamber of Deputies, it became a reality.

Kinds of Cleavages in the Developing Czech Party System

A third key development in the early post-Soviet era was the emergence of contemporary cleavages around which the new party system could coalesce. There is no doubt that in the countries of Central Europe cleavages more or less similar to those in Western Europe are gradually appearing, and this is true of the Czech Republic as well. The process is slowed down by the fact that the communist regime was something more than a mere external political coating or "superstructure" under which social, economic, cultural, religious, and national life pulsed almost intact. This is particularly evident in economic life, which must undergo a much longer, more difficult, and more painful transformation than the political sphere. On the other hand, social differences undoubtedly existed under the communist regime, and conflicts of interest were not solved but only suppressed. The emergence of clear cleavages, old and new, might take a while, but it would happen.

In the region's first democratic elections (with the exception of Hungary, which was far ahead of the other countries) the Czech Republic encountered two basic "issues": (1) a totalitarian party versus a mediator of democratic forces (which Daniel-Louis Seiler, following Jean and Monica Charlot,[17] calls the state–civic society cleavage); and (2) a movement for independence or autonomy against an existing political center of power (the center–periphery cleavage). In other words, either a broad democratic anticommunist alliance (in a movement like the OF) or a no less broad national movement for independence formed (both goals could of course be combined). Only after one or both of these objectives had been attained did the broad movements begin to undergo differentiation, usually on the basis of the social–liberal cleavage that represents (albeit in more or less embryonic form) the classic left–right cleavage.[18]

The social–liberal cleavage begins to gain ground only later, in the second stage of the transition. The oft-repeated claim that it is meaningless to speak of a left–right cleavage in postcommunist countries applies only to the first stage of broad movements and by no means to the second stage of the differentiation and disintegration of those movements, and still less to the following stage of the crystallization and stabilization of a "normal, standard" democratic political scene.

What was the situation in the Czech Lands and in the former Czecho-Slovak Federation? During the first free elections in 1990, the most important decision at stake was between the outgoing communist power on the one hand and the incoming democratic opposition on the other (in other words the provisional issue of state–civic society cleavage). As early as the second democratic elections in 1992, what played the decisive role in the Czech Lands was the social–liberal cleavage or the left–right cleavage (at least in an embryonic form). At the same time, for the first time a center–periphery cleavage became evident at the federal level (Czecho-Slovak) and partly also at the Czech level.[19] Here too there was a temporary combination of the two cleavages. The difference in the social impact of the first years of economic transformation in Slovakia and the Czech Lands (the rate of unemployment was roughly three times higher in Slovakia) reinforced the efforts of Slovak politicians to increase the powers of Slovak national institutions (the government and parliaments) vis-à-vis federal institutions, so as to be able to push through a different economic policy in Slovakia. The Czech left, weak in comparison to the right at the time, supported the Slovak campaign for decentralization because it shared with Slovak politicians a repugnance for the Czech right and its neo-liberal economic rhetoric.[20]

According to Szelényi et al., in the postcommunist countries of Central Europe, the terms left and right have been gradually becoming more meaningful as the "politics of interest" have begun to gain the upper hand with the associated institutionalization of political parties.[21] This is also leading, as Petr Matějů and Blanka Řeháková have rightly pointed out, to the consolidation of the relationship between social class and choice of party.[22] As many sociological surveys have shown, the importance of the social-liberal dimension has been increasing rapidly in the Czech Lands, where the left–right axis is dominant, compared with other countries such as Slovakia. Research has shown that in Czech society, self-placement on the left–right scale has been quite stable in a bell-shaped distribution with a slight deflection to the right since 1991. On a 10-point left–right scale, the average value since 1991 has been around 6 and the mode at the value of 5.[23]

Behind this stability of self-declared political leanings, however, a significant development of attitudes related to the left–right axis has taken place. In their attitudes and values, Czechs have leaned slightly to the left for several years.[24] Hence some of those who profess to support the right adhere to socioeconomic values and attitudes on the left. As Vlachová and Matějů comment, this discrepancy may reflect the presence of noneconomic values toward which only the right is open.[25] Especially in the first half of the 1990s, the right was associated with the freedoms and values of Euro-Atlantic civilization much more than the left, which tended to be associated with the sinister communist past. The pro-market euphoria, so strong at the beginning of the 1990s in all social categories, has also gradually evaporated. The biggest discrepancy between declared political orientation and value-based orientation was recorded in 1990, while in the following years their correlation has increased.

In sum, in Czech politics the trend in the 1990s was clearly in the direction of the increased importance of the left–right dimension, not only in party competition, but also in voter identification. Although naturally (in view of the different starting point) in some aspects this trend has been in the opposite direction to that of most of the advanced western democracies (the left–right cleavage becoming pronounced in the Czech Republic just when it is diminishing and becoming less clear in the western countries, in the same way as class identification, which has been becoming sharper for a certain time just as it is declining in the West), differences between the advanced western democracies and the Czech Republic are not increasing as a result, but decreasing. By the beginning of the breakup of the Czecho-Slovak Federation in 1993, party competition in the Czech Republic could be characterized by "one-dimensional simplification," as defined by G. Sani and G. Sartori.[26]

Parties and Movements Emerging after the Fall of Communism

With an understanding of the crucial roles played by the OF and the communists, plus the nature of cleavages emerging and reemerging, we can now take a broader look at the various types of political forma-tions that appeared after the fall of the communist regime at the end of 1989. We classify them by origin, as follows:

1. *The former hegemonic party—the communists.*[27] The Czech communists have been present in all elections since 1989 and have regularly won about 10% to 20% of the seats in the Chamber of Deputies. The KSČM is the only party with mass membership in the Czech Republic. However, the number of members has been slowly decreasing since the fall of communism. From more than 560,000 members in 1990, the membership dropped to less than 94,000 in 2005[28] and to about 88,000 in 2006.

2. *Historical and traditional parties that existed in the interwar democracy of the First Czechoslovak Republic*, which were domesticated, castrated, and forced to play the role of "satellites" subject to the Communist Party after the Putsch in 1948. After 1989, their collaborating leadership was replaced, they enjoyed a mass influx of new members, and they could again play a normal democratic role. Two Czech parties fall into this category: the Czechoslovak Socialist Party (ČSS), later called the National Social Liberal Party (LSNS), and above all the ČSL (later the Christian Democratic Union—Czechoslovak People's Party [KDU-ČSL]). The ČSL has won seats in every posttransition parliament (1990, 1992, 1996, 1998, 2002, and 2006), while the ČSS managed to get into parliament only in 1992 as part of a coalition of three parties called the Liberal-Social Union (LSU), which registered as a movement because the minimum vote required for "coalitions" to enter parliament was higher than for "movements." The ČSL, and later the KDU-ČSL, has the second highest membership after the KSČM; it is more thoroughly organized than the parties founded more recently and not only has a stable electorate, but from the point of view of electoral geography, it also has maintained its electoral bastions (especially South Moravia) over the long term. Along with the communist party, it might still be considered a "mass" party. In addition, it has become the party with the greatest coalition poten-tial in the Czech political spectrum.

3. *The ČSSD*, which differs from the preceding category and has numerous and heterogeneous roots. The ČSSD might schematically be defined as a

renovated traditional, historical party, which, unlike the preceding two, was not made into a "satellite" by the communists, but was merged with, or rather absorbed by, the communists, bearing in mind that most of the then social democrats disagreed with the fusion. In the first parliamentary election after the fall of the communist regime in 1990, the restored ČSSD, led by Jiří Horák, did not manage to get into either of the two chambers of the Federal Parliament or into the Czech Parliament (ČNR) because it failed to reach the 5% threshold. Nevertheless, many deputies of a social democratic orientation were active in parliament and the government under the mantle of the OF during that legislative term. To sum up, it could be said that the ČSSD is a historical or traditional party, but its origins cannot be identified only in its former domestic and exiled members and sympathizers who had refused fusion with the Communist Party and who tried to restore it in 1968 (vainly) and again in 1989 (successfully). Its restoration also owed something to the small but influential left wing of the OF and "liberal" communists who joined the party after various vain attempts at reformation of the communist party.

4. *The parties that had started as small unofficial or dissident groups before November 1989.* These include the ODA and the KDS, which had developed from the dissident group Movement for Civic Freedom (HOS), and the LDS, which had developed from the dissident group Democratic Initiative (DI). Both ODA and LDS won seats in parliament on the ticket of the OF in the first legislative election. These small parties—with the temporary exception of ODA—did not play an important role in the Czech party system.

The ODA, a party that professed conservative policies and advocated Friedrich von Hayek's ultraliberal economics, failed to reach the 5% threshold needed to win seats in either chamber of the Federal Parliament in 1992, but was saved by the breakup of the Czech and Slovak Federation, after which the ČNR, which included members of the ODA, declared itself the Chamber of Deputies of the new Czech state. In 1997, the ODA (like the ODS) suffered an internal crisis, related among other things to financial scandals, and fielded no candidates for the Chamber of Deputies in the election of June 1998. Nor did the ODA remain for long in the framework of what was known as the Coalition of Four (Čtyřkoalice), whether for the official reason (its debt) or because its larger partners the KDU-ČSL[29] and the Freedom Union-Democratic Union (US-DEU) were afraid that, with the ODA being a liability, they would not manage to reach the 5% threshold.

The KDS stood as part of the Christian Democratic Federal Coalition in the first parliamentary elections (1990), and in the second parliamentary elections in 1992 it stood as part of a coalition with the ODS, with which it merged in March 1996.

5. *The broad democratic movement, OF, and its successor political entities.* The OF was the clear victor in the first free parliamentary elections in 1990. Immediately afterward, however, a process of internal differentiation began that led first to the establishment of parliamentary groups of various orientations (the most notable being Daniel Kroupa's Inter-Parliamentary Club of the Democratic Right and Jiří Dienstbier's Liberal Club). As already noted, following an open split in February 1991, the OF formally split in April 1991

into two parts: Václav Klaus's ODS and the Jiří Dienstbier's OH. Other political entities that also emerged from the defunct OF included the ODA, whose origin went back to the time before the formation of OF, and two social democratic associations.[30]

6. *Entirely new parties.* Prior to 1992, these included most notably the extreme right-wing nationalist Association for the Republic—Republican Party of Czechoslovakia (SPR-RSČ), led by Miroslav Sládek, which first won seats in parliament in the election of 1992. Other important and continuing new parties, including the Freedom Union, founded after an internal crisis in the ODS in 1998, will be discussed in the next section.

The 1992 Elections and the Breakup of the Czecho-Slovak Federation

The 1992 parliamentary election was a significant landmark for two reasons: It was one of the key stages in the development of the Czech party system and it was a starting point for the process of splitting the Czech and Slovak Federation quickly and comparatively peaceably into two separate states. The configuration of political parties on the federal level played a significant role in this process. It is important to remember that for a long time prior to the breakup of the Czecho-Slovak Federation, and even before the parliamentary elections of 1992, no "Czechoslovak" party system had existed. There had been no common "umbrella" movement (in the Czech Lands this role had been played by the OF, and in Slovakia by the Public against Violence). Divergent development of the (post)communist parties in the Czech Republic and Slovakia meant that not even the formal federation of the Czech KSČM and the Slovak Party of the Democratic Left (SDL) survived for long. Not even the ODS, whose chairman Václav Klaus was the only Czech party leader to mount a genuine electoral campaign in Slovakia as well, managed to put down deep enough roots in Slovakia to become a relevant party there. Even under the federation, in 1992, the Czech political parties formed an independent party system, just as the Slovak parties formed an independent Slovak party system.

The clear victory in 1992 of Klaus's ODS in the Czech Lands and the even more overwhelming triumph of Mečiar's Movement for Democratic Slovakia (HZDS) in Slovakia made the two chairmen the decisive actors in the Czech and Slovak negotiations. As Karel Vodička stated, Klaus's ODS, which won in the Czech Lands, had no choice: Mečiar's HZDS was "the only conceivable coalition partner for the ODS."[31] While Klaus's ODS preferred a working federation, Mečiar's HZDS favored a confederation. No way was found to solve the incompatibility of these two objectives other than the compromise of splitting the Czecho-Slovak Federation into two separate states. The Slovak effort to change the federation into a confederation was associated with the significantly more negative impact of the economic transformation in Slovakia compared with the Czech Lands. The Slovak politicians reacted to the victory of Klaus's conception of economic transformation by endeavoring to get as much sovereignty for the Slovak Republic as possible. In other words, the liberal–social cleavage strengthened the center–periphery cleavage.

CZECH PARTIES, 1992 TO PRESENT

This section will trace the fortunes of the principal parties as they have evolved over the course of the 1990s and the first years of the 2000s and then conclude with a discussion of problems related to the Czech party system.

Eight formations of parties and movements gained seats in the new Czech Parliament[32] following the elections of June 1992. Among the successful parties, Klaus's ODS emerged by far the strongest, obtaining 29.73% of the votes and 38% of the seats. Only this party could be considered in any way as being large or strong. The distant second place was secured by the Communist Party of Bohemia and Moravia (KSČM), which had run on the Left Bloc ticket, obtaining 14.05% of the votes and 17.5% of the deputies. Far behind the communists came six small parties or movements, with each winning about 6% of the votes and between 7% to 8% of the seats.[33] One of these was the extreme right-wing and xenophobic SPR-RSČ. Thus two antisystem parties (the KSČM and the SPR-RSČ), at opposite ends of the political spectrum, were able to obtain parliament seats. We can, however, pose the question of whether or to what extent these two parties (or at least one of them) fulfilled a "tribune function," that is, the *fonction tribunitienne*, as identified by Georges Lavau.[34]

Although the ODS, which could be characterized as the "party of the voters" (or *parti d'électeurs* as defined by Jean Charlot or "catch-all party" as defined by Otto Kirchheimer), gained only 29.73% of the votes and 38% of the seats.[35] At that time the disproportion was still quite serious, because the 5% threshold excluded many parties, including the OH (although with 4.59% of the votes the OH nearly made it).

The coalition government, ideologically quite homogenous, was formed from the ODS, the ODA, and the KDU-ČSL and had a majority (105 of the 200 seats, 52.5%). The ODS was not yet a party with a "majority mission," but it was a "dominant" party in the sense defined by Maurice Duverger, that is, a party that is in power for a certain period of time[36] (strictly speaking this should be three successive legislative terms, but obviously no Czech party could yet fulfill such a condition), far stronger than any other party within the given system.

Beginning with the parliamentary elections in 1996, however, the ODS found a real rival in the ČSSD. The latter subsequently defeated the ODS not only in the parliamentary elections of 1998 (which was understandable given the preceding crisis in the ODS and the establishment of the Freedom Union), but surprisingly even in the next parliamentary elections in 2002. Klaus not long afterward resigned from the chairmanship of the ODS. His unexpected election as president of the republic in 2003 was balm for him personally and for his party.[37] As in the preceding legislative term, in the period since the 2002 parliamentary elections, the ODS has been the most frequent leader in polls and won the 2006 parliamentary elections.

As early as 1992, the ČSSD aspired to becoming a party of middling size like the KSČM. In preelectoral surveys, it more than once reached 10% of the votes and thus seemed to be in second place to the ODS and ahead of the communist party. Its actual result in the 1992 parliamentary elections (6.53% in the Czech National Council) was therefore a serious disappointment to its supporters.

Voter preference for the ČSSD began to rise after the replacement in February 1993 of its chairman Jiří Horák by Miloš Zeman, a proponent of a tougher left policy who had made himself famous by saying that he wanted "to go for the government's throat." This rise in the fortunes of the social democrats was confirmed at the elections to the Chamber of Deputies in May–June 1996, when the ČSSD (26.44%) was already close on the heels of the ODS (29.6%) in terms of votes. Thus the Czech political scene seemed to be approaching a bipolar system of two relatively moderate political forces, with the prospect of future peaceful alternation. The growth in support for the ČSSD was not at the expense of the communists, whose electoral base remained significantly stable.

In the early elections to parliament in June 1998 the ČSSD successfully defended the role of the frontrunner and with 32.31% of the votes overtook the ODS, which had recovered quite rapidly from its internal crisis at the end of 1997 to take 27.74%. Thanks to a written agreement between the ČSSD and the ODS, in which the ODS agreed not to table or support any proposal for an expression of nonconfidence, the ČSSD was able to form a minority government and remain in power for an entire legislative term. Shortly before the parliamentary elections in 2002 the ČSSD distanced itself from the "opposition agreement" (although it was its main beneficiary) and rather surprisingly managed to emerge the victor again in the 2002 parliamentary elections.

The KSČM went into the elections to legislative bodies in 1992 as part of a pseudo-coalition called the Left Bloc composed of the communists and a group known as the Democratic Left. The attempts on the part of the chairman of the KSČM Jiří Svoboda to change the name and orientation of the party failed in the face of opposition from its orthodox party base. In June 1993, the communist congress played a decisive role when it replaced the relatively liberal film director Svoboda with the more orthodox apparatchik Miroslav Grebeníček. Another result of this congress was the formation of two more miniature reform post-communist parties: the liberal communist SDL (Party of the Democratic Left) and the Left Bloc (SLB).[38]

Orthodox communists represented not only the vast majority of members of communist parties, but also the majority of communist voters. The elections to the Chamber of Deputies in 1996 therefore offered an opportunity for revenge for former federal communist deputies at the cost of their colleagues from the ČNR. Only the KSČM exceeded the 5% threshold (with 10.3% the vote), while the SLB (1.4%) and the SDL (0.1%) failed woefully. In the parliamentary elections of 1990 and 1992, the communists took second place, but in the elections to the Chamber of Deputies in 1996, they came in third. Furthermore, they were far behind the ČSSD, which with 26.4% of the vote was only three percentage points behind the ODS (29.6%). According to a poll taken 24 hours before the election of May 1996, the communists were still the least liked party. They did not attract voters from other parties. This changed, however, in 1999, when the communists began to attract former social democratic voters. The most likely explanation is that while the ČSSD had been in opposition, it had attracted a large part of the dissatisfied public. After the ČSSD had started to govern, some of its supporters deserted it to the benefit of the KSČM. The KSČM achieved its best result yet in the parliamentary elections of 2002, when it finished third with 18.51% of the votes behind the ČSSD (30.2%) and the ODS (24.47%). Following these elections it obtained places in the leadership of the Chamber of Deputies for the first time since 1989 and its member Vojtěch Filip even became the Deputy Chairman of Parliament. The KDU-ČSL obtained 6.28% at the elections to the Czech National Council in 1992. At the elections to the Chamber of Deputies in 1996, it won 8.08% of the votes.

Although during the first half of the decade the KDU-ČSL moved right in both economic and social areas, in the late 1990s it began to shift toward the left, which was especially appreciated by the chairman of the ČSSD Miloš Zeman, who began to see it as a potential coalition party. Indeed, the KDU-ČSL became the party with the highest coalition potential. On the other hand, in 1997 its former chairman, Josef Lux, became one of the main architects to the fall of Václav Klaus's cabinet, in which he was deputy prime minister. The electoral base of the party had remained stable: 72.8% of those who voted for it in 1992 supported it again in the 1996 election to the Chamber of Deputies (according to the research agency SC&C/ARC;[39] for web-pages of this research agency see http://www.scac.cz/).

The ODA, as discussed above, temporarily survived only because of the breakup of the Czecho-Slovak Federation, to which its chairman Josef Kalvoda had contributed with his irreconcilable policy toward the Slovaks. In 1992, the party barely passed the 5% threshold in the national Czech elections to the ČNR (with 5.9% of the vote). In 1993, according to surveys of voting preferences, the ODA and the ČSSD were found to be the two parties whose electoral support increased the most, to more than 10% of the vote, but in the 1996 election to the Chamber of Deputies, however, the party won only 6.4%. In contrast to the KDU-ČSL, the ODA with its strongly ideological neo-liberal character, could not play the role of a "hinge small party" able to "tip the scales."[40] Its electoral base was also extremely unstable.[41] On the Czech political scene, the ODA was the party closest to Duverger's cadre party type, or perhaps to Katz and Mair's cartel party type.[42]

The Moravian autonomists (Movement for Autonomous Democracy-Association for Moravia and Silesia [HSD-SMS]), a regionalist Moravian party, just barely managed to pass the 5% threshold (with 5.8% of the vote) and entered the ČNR as the weakest party in 1992, but before long it almost evaporated from the Czech political scene. First, it changed its name to the Movement for Autonomous Democracy of Moravia and Silesia (HSDMS) in 1993 and to the Czech and Moravian Centre Party (ČMSS) in 1994. In December 1994, the remnants of the parliamentary groups of the ČMSS and LSU merged to create the ČMUS parliamentary group. In 1996, three Moravian parties participated in the parliamentary elections, the "most successful" winning only 0.45% of the vote and the second 0.3%.

The nationalist xenophobic right was represented in the Czech spectrum by the Association for the SPR-RSČ, which could perhaps have been defined as a "small party of a political minority"[43] if it had not so much revolved around its chairman Miroslav Sládek and his family.

Of the parties that did not pass the threshold for entering the parliament in 1992, the most important was the OH, chaired by former Federal Minister of Foreign Affairs Jiří Dienstbier and unofficially favored by the Head of State Václav Havel.

After the elections of May–June 1996, only six parties remained in the Chamber of Deputies: the large ODS and its small sister ODA represented the liberal and conservative right, the ČSSD the socialist left, the KDU-ČSL the Christian democratic center, the not-renamed and fairly orthodox neo-communist KSČM, and finally the SPR-RSČ, the nationalist extreme right. The crystallization process of the Czech political scene seemed to be almost complete. Serious change did not result even after an internal crisis in the two moderate right parties at the end of 1997 and the beginning of 1998 (caused partly by financial scandals and leading to the fall of the second Klaus government). The disintegrated ODA was more or less replaced in the party spectrum by the Freedom Union, which came into existence in 1998 with the secession of some former ODS deputies. The ODS, in which chairman Václav Klaus temporarily further strengthened his own position, nonetheless managed, after a few months of stumbling, to keep its place as the strong moderate right party. The ODS, although founded after 1989, was already a party with "somewhat stable roots in society," a quality considered by Mainwaring and Scully to be an important criterion for the "institutionalization" of a party system.[44]

What Kind of Party System

The preceding history of the fortunes of the parties during the 1990s and in the beginning of the 2000s highlights the fact that the ongoing process of differentiation and crystallization of the Czech party scene was still far from complete. However, as of February 1995 the ČSSD (with only 6.5% of the vote in 1992) was becoming the second largest party in the Czech spectrum alongside the ODS, and within the communist and postcommunist formations, only the orthodox communist core (KSČM) had a significant electoral basis. Although the centrist Left Bloc had the most communist deputies in the ČNR from 1992 to 1996, in 1996 it obtained only 1.4% of the vote! The elections to the Chamber of Deputies in 1996 put an end to the division between parliament and public opinion.

The maintenance of the strong position of the moderate right ODS and the unusually substantial strengthening of the moderate left ČSSD may be considered the main benefits brought by the 1996 election. Thanks to this election, the Czech political scene approached a desirable bipolarity with two comparatively moderate forces having the prospect of alternating in power. Fragmentation diminished (only six parties entered the Chamber of Deputies, and the effective number of parliamentary parties was 4.15). The process of crystallization of the party scene advanced strikingly on the right of the political spectrum thanks to the merger of the KDS with the ODS, and even more on the left, which was thoroughly dominated by the ČSSD. In its distinctive features, however (above all the presence of two antisystem parties), the Czech Republic still remained dangerously close to "polarized pluralism," as described by Giovanni Sartori.[45]

Furthermore, the political scene after the elections of 1996 paradoxically became considerably less "governable" than after 1992. The fear that the seemingly very stable 1992–1996 coalition government of the right center was in fact exceptional has been confirmed.[46] As things have turned out, the probable medium (or even long-term) future of the Czech political scene is likely to be one of government weakness (or even powerlessness).

The explanation of the paradox that the process of reducing fragmentation and approaching bipolarity leads not to higher but to lower governability can be found in the process of gradual increase in the proportionality of elections in the Chamber of Deputies. As voters gradually became accustomed to the 5% legal threshold, they voted "more rationally"—they did not vote for parties that had no chance of getting into parliament according to the polls.[47] Therefore, to obtain an absolute majority of parliamentary seats it became necessary to win a considerably higher percentage of the vote (about 45%) than had been the case in the 1992 election. This has made the establishment of comparatively homogeneous governing majorities much more difficult.

In 1992, the coalition of the moderate right (ODS-KDS, ODA, KDU-CSL) obtained an absolute majority (52.5%) of the seats with only 42% of the vote. In that election, 19.1% of the vote was lost and reallocated. By contrast, in the next parliamentary election only 11.2% of the vote was lost, and not even 44% of the vote was enough for the coalition (ODS,[48] ODA, KDU-ČSL) to obtain an absolute majority. It won only 49.5% of the seats and had to function with a minority government. A minority government, in the absence of a dominant party, is very vulnerable. Hopes expressed before the end of the 1992–1996 term that the two largest Czech parties (the ODS and the ČSSD) would recognize that it was in their best interests—and in the interests of the Czech Republic and its long-term governmental efficiency—to adjust the electoral law for the Chamber of Deputies to facilitate the formation of governments capable of action were not realized.[49] The difficulties connected with the formation of governmental coalitions have only gradually brought these parties (first the ODS and then later the ČSSD as well) to this understanding.[50]

Early elections to the Chamber of Deputies in 1998 led to an "opposition agreement," which was concluded by the two largest parties (ČSSD and ODS) and which enabled the minority cabinet to govern the whole legislative term (1998–2002). Most important, both large parties agreed to change the electoral law in a way to favor large parties. However, the Constitutional Court unfortunately repealed all the decisive features of this bill.[51]

The fate of the electoral law can be seen as symbolic of the slow advancement of the Czech party system toward attaining the level of institutionalization and moderate competitiveness that permit parties to play a positive role in the process of democratization. Some developments have been very positive, but there have been setbacks as well.

On the positive side, there has been a further decrease in the number of parties managing to get into the Chamber of Deputies (only five after the 2006 elections, while after the elections of 1996 it was six and after elections to the ČNR in 1992 it was eight). If instead of the number of parties in the lower house we use the index of the effective number of parliamentary parties, we can say that from 4.8 (after the 1992 elections to the ČNR) it fell to 4.15 in 1996, 3.71 in 1998, 3.67 in 2002, and finally to 3.09 in 2006. It is important to note that Sládek's extreme right-wing xenophobic SPR-RSČ has failed to retain a presence in the Chamber of Deputies, meaning an important decline in fragmentation and in ideological polarization, especially because no party in the Czech Parliament has represented the extreme right again since the 1998 elections to the Chamber of Deputies.

Also encouraging is the fact that with the formation of a minority government by the ČSSD a certain form of political alternation was finally achieved in the Czech Republic, albeit one limited by the "opposition agreement." Political alternation was repeated after the 2006 elections, which brought a center-right government to power.

More mixed has been the role played in recent years by the smaller parties in the evolution of a democratic party system. The small parties that did not wish to enter a coalition with the ODS (KDU-ČSL), or even with either the ODS or the ČSSD (Jan Ruml's Freedom Union, even though Miloš Zeman had offered it four ministerial chairs), were very much taken aback by the opposition agreement and formed what was known as the Coalition of Four, which tried to paper over its lack of political homogeneity by concentrating its campaign rhetoric on preparation for entry to the European Union (although every parliamentary party apart from the KSČM had this in its program, including the "euro-realist" ODS), and on the populist demand for direct election of the president. The strategy worked in that in the Senate elections of November 1998 the Coalition of Four managed to gain the most seats (13, while the ODS won 9, the ČSSD only 3, and the KSČM 2). This development seriously weakened the constitutional majority of the two large parties in the Senate.

Disagreement with the opposition agreement was also expressed, in 1999 and at the beginning of 2000, in the emergence of the initiative Impulse 99 (led by Tomáš Halík and Jiří Pehe) and the Thank You Now Leave! Association (founded with a petition of the same name by former student leaders including Martin Mejstřík and Šimon Pánek). Neither of these protest initiatives succeeded in transforming themselves into a relevant political issue, although their criticisms of the state of politics, the economy, and morality in the Czech Lands found a response in the media and among some famous intellectuals and broader civic circles for a certain period.

The 2002 Elections to the Chamber of Deputies

The 2002 elections to the Chamber of Deputies, held on the basis of a slightly amended electoral law (drawn up after the basic elements of the electoral law pushed through by the ODS and the ČSSD had been rejected by the Constitutional Court), more or less confirmed the trend that had already been evident for several years.[52] It should be noted that 28 political formations took part in these 2002 elections—many more than in the two preceding elections to the Chamber of Deputies (in 1998 there were 18 political formations and in 1996 only 13).[53]

This increase was associated with the fact that as a result of the decision of the Constitutional Court the threshold necessary for parties to obtain a state contribution to their campaigns had been reduced. Although this did not lead to any serious increase in party fragmentation,[54] it somewhat raised the index of exclusion (the percentage of votes that were lost).[55] The ČSSD came first, the ODS second, just as in the preceding early elections in 1998. This could be regarded as a success for the ČSSD, which in the opinion polls had been getting dangerously low results, while for the ODS the result was undoubtedly a disappointment. Nor did the KDU-ČSL and US-DEU coalition have much reason to be satisfied with their results, while the KSČM, whose results were better than those of the former two's coalition, obtained its best ever percentage of the vote since the establishment of the Czech Republic. I would, however, offer a word of caution against drawing hasty conclusions from this growth in the number of communist seats. The rise in the number of KSČM seats may be considered a movement in the direction of Sartori's "polarized pluralism" based only on the assumption that the KSČM is remaining at the very least as ideologically dogmatic as before.[56]

In any case, the Czech Republic is one of those countries whose party system cannot be fully characterized as polarized pluralism or as moderate pluralism, but rather as something in between these two categories.[57]

CONCLUSIONS

The process of party system development was launched later in the Czech Republic than in other states such as Hungary, and it involved a "detour" caused by the temporary need for a broad movement (the OF) to counterbalance a comparatively dogmatic communist party. Nonetheless, a party system has formed in which the left–right dimension has clearly prevailed for several years; it is one of the Central and Eastern European systems that is most similar to those of West European continental democracies, and following the concepts developed by Angelo Panebianco and Herbert Kitschelt, one of the most institutionalized and structured.[58] We may also consider it a positive feature that for the moment the Czech party system is even closer in its characteristics to a "balanced" party system, as defined by Gordon Smith, who regards such systems as typical of most Western European democracies.[59] If we then look at the results of all the elections to the Chamber of Deputies (including the 1992 elections to the Czech National Council held before the breakup of Czechoslovakia), what is most striking is the remarkable stability of electoral preferences for the ODS.

The Czech party system no longer faces excessive fragmentation or volatility (both have declined since the elections to the Chamber of Deputies in 1996, establishing thus a trend that successfully continued with the early parliamentary elections of 1998 and was confirmed by the next elections to the Chamber of Deputies—in 2002 and in 2006). However, the ideological distance between the relevant parties has remained significantly wide, and it is becoming difficult to form governments capable of action, representing a weak point in the progress of Czech democratization. There is still a relatively high degree of polarization (the ideological or other distance between relevant political subjects).[60] Nonetheless, there are grounds for believing that starting with the elections to the Chamber of Deputies in 1998, polarization is diminishing in the Czech Republic (the SPR-RSČ dropped out of parliament and—as I pointed out above—not even the growing support for the KSČM can be mechanically interpreted as an increase in polarization).

Ideological polarization is related to another weakness of the Czech party system, the low coalition potential of the parties (naturally this applies above all to the KSČM). This diminishes the number of majority coalitions that are mathematically possible. It restricts the possibility of a bipolar multipartitism associated with the alternation of two moderate and relatively stable alliances. It also somewhat diminishes the likelihood of another alternative that Jean Blondel[61] calls a two-and-a-half-party system or imperfect bipartisanism of the German kind (and which compared to the latter mentioned form has the disadvantage of reducing "accountability").[62] Here the ČSSD and the ODS would most probably be the two large parties, while the role of "tipper of the scales" would be played by the KDU-ČSL. Such a change is hard to imagine without a change in the electoral law, especially as the KSČM, which has stood outside the government for a long time, has recently obtained the votes of the dissatisfied and has been increasing its support since 1999.

A major modification of the law regulating the elections to the Chamber of Deputies (similar to the reform agreed on by a joint ODS-ČSSD committee) would have to be passed by both chambers of parliament. This would require a substantial increase in the parliamentary weight of the two major system parties. It would also have to survive scrutiny by the Constitutional Court. However, such a change represents a necessary but by no means sufficient condition for the future smooth functioning of the Czech party system. A substantially reformed electoral law would potentially facilitate—not only in the translation of votes for seats in individual elections to the Chamber of Deputies but above all from the long-term perspective and in its psychological effect—the formation and maintenance[63] of (a) homogeneous[64] majority coalitions (in the best case), or (b) at least functioning minority governments.

Unfortunately, under the current electoral law, we can expect the contrary: heterogeneous and nonfunctional government coalitions and perhaps the growth of the influence of the KSČM. The last election to the Chamber of Deputies in 2006 illustrates this clearly. It gave rise to the constellation of 100 MPs of the left (social democrats and communists) on the one hand, and 100 MPS of right center (ODS, KDU-ČSL, and Green Party[65]) on the other hand. Moreover, it took no less than 7 months for the right-center government to receive the necessary vote of confidence in the Chamber of Deputies, especially owing to the defection of two social democratic members of parliament who supported the government. (In the epilogue below I mention the conditions under which this cabinet ended in the spring of 2009.)

To sum up, the last majority and politically homogeneous government was formed after the 1992 elections. In contrast, the parliamentary elections of 1996, 1998, 2002, and 2006 led to weak governments that were either minority cabinets or majority cabinets with heterogeneous political programs. Hence, their efficiency was substantially curtailed.

If we start from the premise that a party system is generally created above all by "interactions" between parties, it is hard to avoid the pessimistic conclusion that "the Czech party system cannot be considered consolidated" as it continues to lack stable models of interaction.[66] The relationship between parties and democracy in the Czech Republic is thus a complicated one. No party system is perfect, so our demands must be suitably modest. There is no question that tremendous progress has been made after November 1989, but without greater stability, efficiency, and smoother relationships between the parties themselves, it is also clear that it is too soon to be sure that the gains that have been made will endure.

EPILOGUE

At the time I was making corrections to this text (in March 2009) the Czech cabinet lost a vote of no confidence in the Chamber of Deputies by 101 votes to 96. The coalition was voted down due to the defection of four coalition MP at a very awkward moment: right in the middle of the six-month period when the Czech Republic held the presidency of the European Union. However, although the Czech Republic suffered a loss of prestige, democracy itself was not in danger and the Czech Republic remains a consolidated, albeit poorly functioning, democracy.[67] As noted above and in other earlier works, the consensual model is not generally and everywhere better. A simple majority model may work better, as would probably be the case in the Czech Republic, a culturally relatively homogeneous country (in contrast to the Czecho-Slovak Federal Republic or the interwar first Czechoslovak Republic).[68] The move toward majority democracy could best be achieved through an amendment of the electoral law for the Chamber of Deputies, but it is unlikely that any such change will be made in the foreseeable future. Therefore, the problems related to government formation, which began in the Czech Republic after the 1996 parliamentary elections, will continue to plague the Czech Republic, even as democracy itself survives relatively unscathed.

Notes

INTRODUCTION, POLITICAL PARTIES AND DEMOCRACY: THREE STAGES OF POWER

1. Having only indigenous authors is a unique and important characteristic of *Political Parties and Democracy* and thus well worth mentioning. As the word "indigenous" has two senses, it is perhaps also worth mentioning that here it is used in its primary sense: "living in a particular area or environment; native" to describe all authors and all co-editors, none of whom lives outside the countries he or she writes about. Authors of specific chapters occasionally use the words "indigenous" and "native" in their secondary sense, to refer to specific ethnic groups. Both usages are correct and the reader will find that the usage intended is always clear in context.

CHAPTER 1, POLITICAL PARTIES AND DEMOCRACY IN FRANCE: AN AMBIGUOUS RELATIONSHIP

1. Colette Ysmal, "The Evolution of the French Party System," in *The Organization of Political Parties in Southern Europe*, ed. Piero Ignazi and Colette Ysmal (Westport, Conn.: Praeger, 1998); Paolo Pombeni, *Introduction à l'histoire des Partis* (Paris: Presses Universitaires de France, 1992), 9–25.

2. Gilles Le Béguec, "Le Parti," in *Histoire des Droites en France*, ed. Jean-François Sirinelli (Paris: Gallimard, 1992), 13–59.

3. Florence Haegel, "Parties and Organizations," in *Developments in French Politics 3*, ed. Alistair Cole, Patrick Le Galès, and Jonah Lévy (London: Palgrave, 2005), 18–34.

4. Yves Mény, "La Faiblesse Des Partis Politiques Français: Une Persistante Exceptionnalité," in *De la Ve République à l'Europe*, ed. François D'Arcy and Luc Rouban (Paris: Presses de Sciences Po, 1996), 77–94; Florence Haegel and Marc

Lazar, "France: Anti-System Parties vs. Governmental," in *When Parties Prosper: The Uses of Electoral Success*, ed. Kay Lawson and Peter H. Merkl (Boulder, Colo.: Lynne Rienner, 2007), 295–311.

5. Stefano Bartolini, "Collusion, Competition and Democracy (Part I)," *Journal of Theoretical Politics* 11 (1999), 435–470; Stefano Bartolini, "Collusion, Competition and Democracy (Part II)," *Journal of Theoretical Politics* 12 (2000), 33–65.

6. Maurice Duverger, *Les Régimes Semi-Présidentiels* (Paris: Presses Universitaires de France, 1986); Robert Elgie, *Semi-Presidentialism in Europe* (Oxford: Oxford University Press, 1999).

7. John D. Huber, *Rationalizing Parliament. Legislative Institutions and Party Politics in France* (New York: Cambridge University Press, 1996).

8. Anne-Marie Cohendet, *Le Président de la République* (Paris: Dalloz, 2002).

9. Emiliano Grossman and Nicolas Sauger, "The End of Ambiguity? Presidents versus Parties or the Four Phases of the Fifth Republic," *West European Politics* 32 (2009), 420–434.

10. The issue of the president's judicial responsibility has in fact been raised only recently. During its term, the president cannot be prosecuted for acts anterior to his terms, although he may, in principle, be prosecuted after the end of his term. However, the penal responsibility of the president can still be put into question by a specific—largely political—court, the High Court of Justice. No president has actually ever been prosecuted by the Court, and the likelihood of its evolution toward some form of impeachment is currently small.

11. Christine Pütz, "Die Partis Présidentiels in Der V. Republik: Politische Institutionen und Parteienwandel," PhD thesis, University of Mannheim, 2001.

12. Giovanni Sartori, *Parties and Party Systems: A Framework for Analysis* (Cambridge: Cambridge University Press, 1976).

13. Jean-Luc Parodi, "Le Nouvel Espace Politique Français," in *Idéologies, Partis Politiques et Groupes Sociaux*, ed. Yves Mény (Paris: Presses de Sciences Po, 1991), 49–59.

14. Gérard Grunberg and Florence Haegel, *La France Vers Le Bipartisme? La Présidentialization Du PS et de L'UMP* (Paris: Presses de Sciences Po, 2007).

15. Amir Abedi, *Anti-Establishment Parties: A Comparative Analysis* (London: Routledge, 2004).

16. Peter Mair, *Party System Change: Approaches and Interpretations* (Oxford: Clarendon Press, 1997).

17. Stefano Bartolini, "Institutional Constraints and Party Competition in the French Party System," in *Party Politics in Contemporary Western Europe*, ed. Stefano Bartolini and Peter Mair (London: Franck Cass, 1984), 103–127.

18. Pierre Bréchon, *Les Partis Politiques Français* (Paris: Montchrestien, 1999); Howard Machin, "Stages and Dynamics in the Evolution of the French Party System," *West European Politics* 12 (1989), 59–81.

19. Ben Clift, "Dyarchic Presidentialization in a Presidentialized Polity: The French Fifth Republic," in *The Presidentialization of Politics—a Comparative Study of Modern Democracies*, ed. Paul Webb and Thomas Poguntke (Oxford: Oxford University Press, 2005), 219–243; Nicolas Sauger, "Un Système Électoral Vecteur D'instabilité? L'impact Du Système Électoral Sur la Structuration du Système Partisan Sous la Cinquième République," in *Les Partis Politiques En France*, ed. Florence Haegel (Paris: Presses de Sciences Po, 2007) 359–391.

20. Bartolini, "Collusion, Competition and Democracy (Part I)"; Bartolini, "Collusion, Competition and Democracy (Part II)"; G. Bingham Powell, *Elections as Instruments of Democracy: Majoritarian and Proportional Visions* (New Haven, Conn.: Yale University Press, 2000); Nicolas Sauger, "Les Systèmes Partisans en

Europe: Équilibre, Changement et Instabilité," *Revue Internationale de Politique Comparée* 14 (2007), 229–242.

21. These signatures have furthermore to be geographically dispersed.

22. Richard S. Katz, "Why Are There So Many (or So Few) Electoral Reforms?," in *The Politics of Electoral Systems*, ed. Michael Gallagher and Paul Mitchell (Oxford: Oxford University Press, 2005), 57–78.

23. Jean-Luc Parodi, "Proportionnalization Périodique, Cohabitation, Atomization Partisane: Un Triple Défi Pour Le Régime Semi-Présidentiel De La Cinquième République," *Revue Française de Science Politique* 47 (1997): 3–4.

24. Ben Clift and Justin Fisher, "Party Finance Reform as Constitutional Engineering? The Effectiveness and Unintended Consequences of Party Finance Reform in France and Britain," *French Politics* 3 (2005), 234–257; Ben Clift and Justin Fisher, "Comparative Party Finance Reform: The Cases of France and Britain," *Party Politics* 10 (2004), 677–699; Abel François and Nicolas Sauger, "Groupes d'Intérêt et Financement de la Vie Politique en France: Une Évaluation des Effets de L'interdiction des Dons de Personnes Morales," *Revue Française de Science Politique* 56 (2006), 227–254.

25. Graham White, "One-Party Dominance and Third Parties," *Canadian Journal of Political Science* 6 (1973), 399–421.

26. In fact, the merger was even larger. It encompassed also the Liberal Democracy (which came out of the UDF in 1998) and part of the RPF (Pasqua's Eurosceptic Party).

27. The government was furthermore quasi-monopartisan since only one member of the UDF (G. de Robien) participates in it. Since 2007, the splinter New Center from UDF (now labeled MoDem for Democratic Movement) has taken over this role of auxiliary of the UMP and still participates in government. The New Center is, however, hardly a genuine political party.

28. The members of the Constitutional Council are nominated by the president of the Republic, the president of the Senate, and the president of the National Assembly.

29. The UMP lost this majority of local government in the 2004 local and European elections, which gave control to the socialists of almost all the regions. The municipal and departmental elections of 2008 confirmed this tendency of dominance of the Socialist Party at the infra-national level.

30. This majority was the result of the merger of two groups (RPR and Independent Republicans, which gathered members of either UDF or Liberal Democracy). However, the UMP majority has been now transformed now to a plurality since the results of the 2004 senatorial elections.

31. George Tsebelis and Jeannette Money, *Bicameralism, Political Economy of Institutions and Decisions* (Cambridge: Cambridge University Press, 1997).

32. Colette Ysmal, "Incumbency in France: Electoral Instability as a Way to Legislative Victory," in *The Victorious Incumbent, a Threat to Democracy?*, ed. A. Somit et al. (Aldershot: Dartmouth, 1994), 190–217.

33. Olivier Costa and Eric Kerrouche, "MPs under the 5th Republic: Professionalization within a Weak Institution," *West European Politics* 32 (2009), 327–344.

34. Martial Foucault, "How Useful Is the Cumul des Mandats for Being Re-Elected? Empirical Evidence from the 1997 French Legislative Elections," *French Politics* 4 (2006), 292–311.

35. Abel François, "Testing the 'Baobab Tree' Hypothesis: The Cumul des Mandats as a Way of Obtaining More Political Resources and Limiting Electoral Competition," *French Politics* 4 (2006), 269–291.

36. Florence Haegel, ed., *Partis Politiques et Système Partisan en France* (Paris: Presses de Sciences Po, 2007).

37. Grunberg and Haegel, *La France Vers le Bipartisme?*.

38. Arthur Lupia, "Delegation and Its Peril," in *Delegation and Accountability in Parliamentary Democracies*, ed. Kaare Strom, Wolfgang C. Müller, and Torbjörn Bergman (Oxford: Oxford University Press, 2003), 33–54.

39. The Commission Nationale des Comptes de Campagne et des Financements Politiques recapitulates each year the organizations which have registered with it. In 2003 (last available year), 244 organizations wanted to be registered, among which 195 actually were. Among these parties, 68 had benefited from public funding.

40. Nicolas Sauger, "The UDF in the 1990s: The Break-Up of a Party Confederation," in *The French Party System*, ed. Jocelyn Evans (Manchester: Manchester University Press, 2003), 107–120.

41. David Hanley, "Compromise, Party Management and Fair Shares: The Case of the French UDF," *Party Politics* 5 (1999), 171–189.

42. Andrew Knapp, "France: Never a Golden Age," in *Political Parties in Advanced Industrial Democracies*, ed. Paul Webb, David M. Farrell, and Ian Holliday (Oxford: Oxford University Press, 2002), 107–150.

43. Markku Lakso and Rein Taagepera, "Effective Number of Parties: A Measure with Application to West Europe," *Comparative Political Studies* 12 (1979). This index is the inverse of the index of fragmentation proposed by Rae (Douglas W. Rae, *The Political Consequences of Electoral Laws* (New Haven: Yale University Press, 1969), 3–27, i.e. $N = 1/\sum si^2$, where s is the proportion or seats or votes gained by the ith party or candidate.

44. Clift, "Dyarchic Presidentialization in a Presidentialized Polity."

45. Gary W. Cox, *Making Votes Count: Strategic Coordination in the World's Electoral Systems* (Cambridge: Cambridge University Press, 1997).

46. Parodi, "Proportionnalization Périodique, Cohabitation, Atomization Partisane."

47. André Blais, "Strategic Voting in the 2002 French Presidential Election," in *The French Voter: Before and After the 2002 Elections*, ed. Michael Lewis-Beck (Basingstoke: Palgrave, 2004), 93–109.

48. Jean-Luc Parodi, "Les Effets Pervers D'une Présélection Annoncée," *Revue Française de Science Politique* 52 (2002), 485–504.

49. Claire Durand, André Blais, and M. Larochelle, "The Polls of the French Presidential Election: An Autopsy," *Public Opinion Quarterly* 68 (2005), 602–622.

50. Raymond Kuhn, "The French Presidential and Parliamentary Elections, 2002," *Representation* 39 (2002): 44–46.

51. Pascal Perrineau, ed., *Le Désenchantement Démocratique* (La Tour d'Aigues: Editions de l'Aube, 2003).

52. Philip M. Williams, *Crisis and Compromise: Politics in the Fourth Republic* (Hamden: Archon Books, 1964), 215–216.

53. Ergun Ozbudun, "Party cohesion in Western democracies: A causal analysis." *Sage Professional Papers in Comparative Politics*, 1 (1970).

54. For this classical approach of social choice, see Amartya Kumar Sen, *Collective Choice and Social Welfare* (Amsterdam: North-Holland, 1984); Kenneth J. Arrow, *Social choice and individual values*, 2nd ed. (New York: Wiley, 1963) (1951).

55. The Rice Index is calculated as the "proportion of the group comprising the group majority on a roll call *minus* the proportion comprising the group

minority." Thus if members of one party split evenly, it is: 50% − 50% = 0. If all members vote in one way, then it is: 100% − 0% = 100. Total cohesion is thus represented by a score of 100.

56. Frank L. Wilson and Richard Wiste, "Party Cohesion in the French National Assembly: 1958–1973," *Legislative Studies Quarterly* 1 (1976), 467–490.

57. The index has been computed so that parties and not parliamentary groups were taken into account. This is important since a few groups have associated with different parties for administrative reasons, because of the existence of a given threshold to form a group.

58. Nicolas Sauger, "Party Discipline and Coalition Management in the French Parliament," *West European Politics* (2009), 307–323.

59. Michael L. Mezey, *Comparing Legislatures* (Durham, N.C.: Duke University Press, 1979); Klaus Von Beyme, *Political Parties in Western Democracies* (New York: St. Martin's Press, 1985).

60. Sona Golder, "Pre-Electoral Coalition Formation in Parliamentary Democracies," *British Journal of Political Science* 36 (2006): 193–212.

61. André Blais and Indridi Indridason, "Making Candidates Count: The Logic of Electoral Alliances in Two Round Legislative Elections," *Journal of Politics* 69 (2007): 193–205.

62. ESS Round 3: European Social Survey Round 3 Data (2006). Data file edition 3.2. Norwegian Social Science Data Services, Norway–Data Archive and distributor of ESS data.

63. Ian Budge et al., *Mapping Policy Preferences* (Oxford: Oxford University Press, 2001).

64. François Petry and Paul Pennings, "Estimating the Policy Positions of Political Parties from Legislative Election Manifestos, 1958–2002," *French Politics* 4 (2006), 100–123; Ian Budge and Michael D. McDonald, "Choices Parties Define: Policy Alternatives in Representative Elections, 17 Countries 1945–1998," *Party Politics* 12 (2006): 451–466.

65. Pascal Perrineau et al., "L'espace Politique des Électeurs Français À La Fin Des Années 1990: Nouveaux et Anciens Clivages, Hétérogénéité des Électorats," *Revue Française de Science Politique* 50 (2000): 463–487.

66. Ronald Inglehart, *Modernization and Post-Modernization: Cultural, Economic and Political Change in 43 Societies* (Princeton, N.J.: Princeton University Press, 1997).

67. Gérard Grunberg and Etienne Schweissguth, "Vers Une Tripartition De L'espace Politique," in *L'électeur a Ses Raisons*, ed. Daniel Boy and Nonna Mayer (Paris: Presses de Sciences Po, 1997), 179–218.

68. Robert Andersen and Jocelyn Evans, "The Stability of French Political Space," *French Politics* 3 (2005), 282–301.

69. Céline Belot and Bruno Cautrès, "L'Europe, Invisible Mais Omniprésente?," in *Le Nouveau Désordre Électoral*, ed. Bruno Cautrès and Nonna Mayer (Paris: Presses de Sciences Po, 2004), 119–141.

70. Jocelyn Evans, "The European Dimension in French Public Opinion," *Journal of European Public Policy* 14 (2007): 1098–1116.

71. Nicolas Sauger, "Sur La Mutation Contemporaine des Structures de la Compétition Partisane en France : Les Partis de Droite Face à l'intégration Européenne," *Politique Européenne* 16 (2005), 103–126.

72. Michael Laver, Kenneth Benoit, and John Garry, "Extracting Policy Positions from Political Texts Using Words as Data," *American Political Science Review* 97 (2003): 311–331.

73. Michael Laver, Kenneth Benoit, and Nicolas Sauger, "Policy Competition in the 2002 French Legislative and Presidential Elections," *European Journal of Political Research* 45 (2006), 667–697.

74. Andrew Knapp, *Parties and the Party System in France: A Disconnected Democracy?* (Basingstoke: Palgrave Macmillan, 2004); David S. Bell, *Parties and Democracy in France: Parties under Presidentialism* (Adlershot: Ashgate, 2000).

75. Knapp, *Parties and the Party System in France.*

76. Nicolas Sauger, Sylvain Brouard, and Emiliano Grossman, *Les Français Contre L'Europe? Les Sens du Référendum du 29 Mai 2005* (Paris: Presses de Sciences Po, 2007).

77. Nicolas Sauger, "The French Legislative and Presidential Elections of 2007," *West European Politics* 30 (2007): 1166–1175.

78. Kay Lawson and Peter H. Merkl, eds., *When Parties Fail: Emerging Alternative Organizations* (Princeton, N.J.: Princeton University Press, 1988).

79. Yohann Aucante and Alexandre Dézé, eds., *Les Systèmes de Partis Dans les Démocraties Occidentales* (Paris: Presses de Sciences Po, 2008).

CHAPTER 2, THE DEVELOPMENT OF A MULTIPARTY SYSTEM IN GERMANY: A THREAT TO DEMOCRATIC STABILITY?

1. Jürgen W. Falter, "Kontinutität und Neubeginn. Die Bundestagswahl 1948 zwischen Weimar und Bonn," in *Politische Vierteljahreschrift* 55 (1981): 236–263.

2. This clause is called a constructive vote of no confidence "because the chancellor of the Federal Republic can only be discarded if at the very same time a successor is voted into office by a majority of the parliament."

3. Markus Klein and Jürgen W. Falter, *Der lange Weg der Grünen: eine Partei zwischen Protest und Regierung* (München: C. H. Beck, 2003).

4. The NATO Double-Track Decision "is the decision of NATO from December 12, 1979 to offer the Warsaw Pact a mutual limitation of Medium-range ballistic missiles and Intermediate-range ballistic missiles combined with the threat that in case of disagreement NATO would deploy more middle range nuclear weapons in Western Europe" (see wikipedia.org, "Nato Double-Track-Decision").

5. Seymour M. Lipset and Stein Rokkan, *Party Systems and Voter Alignments: Cross National Perspectives* (New York: Free Press, 1967).

6. "Alliance 90 (German: *Bündnis 90*) was an alliance of three non-Communist political groups in East Germany. It merged with the German Green Party in 1993 to form Alliance '90/The Greens. Bündnis 90 was formed in February 1990 by Neues Forum, Demokratie Jetzt and the Initiative Freiheit und Menschenrechte. It received 2.9% of the vote in the 1990 Volkskammer elections. For the first all-German elections it formed a joint list with the East German Green Party. It was this coalition that merged with the West German Green Party in 1993" (see wikipedia.org, "Alliance 90").

7. Jürgen W. Falter, *Wer wählt rechts? Die Wähler und Anhänger rechtsextremistischer Parteien im vereinigten Deutschland* (München: C. H. Beck, 1994); Jürgen W. Falter and Markus Klein, "Die Wähler der Republikaner zwischen sozialer Benachteiligung, rechtem Bekenntnis und rationalem Protest," in *Wahlen und politische Einstellungen in westlichen Demokratien*, ed. Oscar W. Gabriel and Jürgen W. Falter (Frankfurt A.M./Bern: Peter Lang, 1996), 149–173; Richard Stöss,

Rechtsextremismus im Wandel (Berlin: Friedrich-Ebert-Stiftung, 2007); Oliver Decker et al., *Ein Blick in die Mitte. Zur Entstehung rechtsextremer und demokratischer Einstellungen in Deutschland* (Berlin: Friedrich-Eber-Stiftung, 2008); Andreas Hallermann and Michael Edinger, "Rechtsextremismus in Ostdeutschland: Struktur und Ursachen rechtsextremer Einstellungen am Beispiel Thüringens," in *Zeitschrift für Parlamentsfragen* 32 (2001): 588–612.

8. Falter, *Wer wählt rechts*; Harald Schoen and Siegfried Bühler, "Feinde im Inneren: Politischer Extremismus im vereinigten Deutschland," in *Sind wir ein Volk? Ost- und Westdeutschland im Vergleich*, ed. Jürgen W. Falter, Oscar W. Gabriel, and Harald Schoen (München: C. H. Beck, 2006), 188–211; Kai Arzheimer, Harald Schoen, and Jürgen W. Falter, "Rechtsextreme Orientierungen und Wahlverhalten," in *Rechtsextremismus in der Bundesrepublik Deutschland. Eine Bilanz*, ed. Wilfried Schubarth and Richard Stöss (Bonn: Bundeszentrale für politische Bildung), 220–245; Kai Arzheimer, "Die Wahl extremistischer Parteien," in *Der gesamtdeutsche Wähler. Stabilität und Wandel des Wählerverhaltens im wiedervereinigten Deutschland*, ed. Hans Rattinger, Oscar W. Gabriel, and Jürgen W. Falter (Baden-Baden: Nomos), 67–86.

9. Allbus (German General Social Survey). The German General Social Survey (ALLBUS) collects up-to-date data on attitudes, behavior, and social structure in Germany. Every two years since 1980 a representative cross section of the population is surveyed using both constant and variable questions. It is distributed by GESIS (see note 19).

10. Statistisches Bundesamt, see their Web page at: http://www.bundeswahl leiter.de/en/europawahlen/ (for voter turnout in East and West Germany).

11. Statistisches Landesamt Baden-Württemberg, see their Web page at: http://www.statistik.baden-wuerttemberg.de/Wahlen/Landesdaten/Kommunal wahlen/LRGrW.asp (for time series of local election results).

12. Amt für Statistik Berlin Brandenburg, follow the link at their Web page at: http://www.wahlen-berlin.de/wahlen/wahldatenbank/tabellen/tabellen.htm (for local election results).

13. Hessisches Statistisches Landesamt, see their Web page at: http://www. statistik-hessen.de/themenauswahl/wahlen/daten/kw01/ergebnisse-1946-2001/ index.html and http://www.statistik-hessen.de/subweb/k2006/EK1.htm (for local election results).

14. Statistisches Landesamt Baden-Württemberg, see their Web page at: http://www.statistik.baden-wuerttemberg.de/Wahlen/Landesdaten/Landtags- wahlen/LRLTW3.asp (for time series of voter turnout in state parliament elections).

15. Statistisches Bundesamt, see their Web page at: http://www.bundeswahl leiter.de/en/landtagswahlen/ergebnisse/ (for voter turnout in state parliament elections).

16. Statistisches Bundesamt, see their Web page at: http://www.bundeswahl leiter.de/en/bundestagswahlen/ (for voter turnout in federal elections).

17. Oskar Niedermayer, *Parteimitglieder in Deutschland: Version 2008* (Berlin: Arbeitshefte aus dem Otto Stammer-Zentrum, 2008).

18. Elmar Wiesendahl, "Keine Lust mehr auf Parteien. Zur Abwendung Jugendlicher von den Parteien." In *Aus Politik und Zeitgeschichte* (B 10/2001), 2–3.

19. The "Politbarometer" surveys are performed since 1977 at about monthly intervals by the Forschungsgruppe Wahlen (Institute for election research) for the ZDF (Second German TV network). Since 1990 it is also available for the newly formed German states. The data from the usual 11 monthly polls per year is integrated, documented and archived in one cumulative data record at the GESIS Central Archive in Cologne. The data and documents from the annual cumulations from 1977 up to 2005 are available on two CD-ROMs for further analytical research. Available are currently: Politbarometer 1977 to 2002 (with retrieval system) and Politbarometer 2002 to 2005.

20. Jürgen W. Falter and Harald Schoen, *Handbuch Wahlforschung* (Wiesbaden: VS Verlag für Sozialwissenschaften, 2005), 375.

21. Harald Schoen, "Den Wechselwählern auf der Spur: Recall- und Paneldaten im Vergleich," in *Die Republik auf dem Weg zur Normalität? Wahlverhalten und politische Einstellungen nach acht Jahren Einheit*, ed. Jan van Deth, Hans Rattinger, and Edeltraut Roller (Opladen: Leske and Budrich, 2000), 199–226.

22. Walther Müller-Jentsch, *Strukturwandel der industriellen Beziehungen. 'Industrial Citizenship' zwischen Markt und Regulierung* (Wiesbaden: VS Verlag für Sozialwissenschaften, 2007), 37.

23. *Politbarometer* 1991 and 2005 (for further details see note 19).

24. Andreas Kost, *Direkte Demokratie in den deutschen Ländern: eine Einführung* (Wiesbaden: VS Verlag für Sozialwissenschaften, 2005).

CHAPTER 3, THE THREE AGES OF PARTY POLITICS IN POSTWAR ITALY

1. Pietro Scoppola, *La repubblica dei partiti* (Bologna: Il Mulino, 1988).

2. This period is concisely described by Santo Peli, *La resistenza in Italia* (Torino: Einuadi, 2006). A more in-depth analysis is in the masterful work by Claudio Pavone, *Una guerra civile* (Torino: Bollati Boringhieri, 1991).

3. See Angelo Maria Imbriani, *Il vento del Sud Moderati, reazionari e qualunquisti (1943–1948)* (Bologna: Il Mulino, 1991); Piero Ignazi, *Il polo escluso. Profilo del Movimento Sociale Italiano* (Bologna: Il Mulino, 1989).

4. Giorgio Galli, *Il difficile governo* (Bologna: Il Mulino, 1972).

5. For a general account see Maurizio Cotta and Luca Verzichelli, *Political Institutions in Italy* (Oxford: Oxford University Press, 2007); Piero Ignazi, *I partiti italiani* (Bologna: Il Mulino, 1997); Paolo Farneti, *Il sistema dei partiti in Italia 1946–1979* (Bologna: Il Mulino, 1983).

6. Emilio Gentile, *La via italiana la totalitarismo. Il partito e lo Stato nel regime fascista* (Roma: Carocci, 2008).

7. Stein Rokkan, *Citizens, Elections, Parties* (Oslo, Universitetsforlaget, 1970).

8. Donatella Della Porta, (a cura di) *Lo scambio occulto. Casi di corruzione politica in Italia* (Bologna: Il Mulino, 1992).

9. Otto Kirchheimer, "The Transformation of the Western European Party System," in *Political Parties and Political Development*, ed. Joseph La Palombara and Myron Weiner (Princeton, N.J.: Princeton University Press), 177–200.

10. Luciano Bardi and Leonardo Morlino, "Tracing the Roots of the Great Transformation," in *How Parties Organize*, ed. Richard Katz and Peter Mair (London: Sage, 1994), 242–277; Leonardo Morlino, "Le tre fasi dei partiti italiani," in

Partiti e caso italiano, ed. Leonardo Morlino and Marco Tarchi (Bologna: Il Mulino, 2006), 85–102.

11. Piero Ignazi, *Il potere dei partiti. La politica in Italia dagli anni Sesanta agli anni Novanta* (Roma-Bari: Laterza 2002).

12. Delia Baldassarri, "Sinistra e destra. La dimensione ideologica tra prima e seconda repubblica," in *Gli italiani e la politica*, ed. Marco Maraffi (a cura di) (Bologna: Il Mulino, 2007), 105–130.

13. Franco Cazzola, *Della Corruzione, Fisiologia e patologia di un sistema politico* (Bologna: Il Mulino, 1988), 138–139.

14. Donatella della Porta and Alberto Vannucci, *Mani Impunite. Vecchia e nuova corruzione in Italia* (Roma-Bari: Laterza, 2007).

15. Gabriele Calvi, *Indagine sociale italiana. Rapporto 1986* (Milano: Franco Angeli, 1987), 60.

16. Luciano Bardi and Gianfranco Pasquino, "Politicizzati e alienate," in *Sulla soglia del cambiamento*, ed. Arturo Parisi and Hans Schadee (Bologna: Il Mulino, 1995), 17–41.

17. Paolo Bellucci, "All'origine delle identità politiche," in *Sulla soglia del cambiamento*, ed. Arturo Parisi and Hans Schadee (Bologna: Il Mulino, 1995), 194.

18. Luciano Bardi and Gianfranco Pasquino, "Politicizzati e alienate," 41.

19. Thomas Pogunkte, "The 'New Politics Dimension' in European Green Parties," in *New Politics in Western Europe: The Rise and Success of Green Parties and Alternative Lists*, ed. Ferdinand Muller-Rommel (Boulder, Colo.: Westview, 1989), 175–193.

20. Gianfranco Baldini, "The Failed Renewal: The DC from 1982–1994," in *The Organization of Political Parties in Southern Europe*, eds. Piero Ignazi and Colette Ysmal (Westport, Conn.: Praeger, 1998), 110–133.

21. Paolo Bellucci, Marco Maraffi, and Paolo Segatti, *PCI, PDS, DS* (Roma: Donzelli, 2002); Piero Ignazi, *Dal PCI al PDS* (Bologna: Il Mulino, 1992).

22. Mauro Calise, *Il partito personale* (Roma-Bari: Laterza, 2000).

23. Caterina Paolucci and Jonathan Hopkin, "The Business Firm Model of Party Organization; Cases from Spain and Italy," *European Journal of Political Research* 35 (1999): 307–339.

24. Marco Maraffi, "Forza Italia," in *La Politica italiana. Dizionario critico 1945–1995*, ed. Gianfranco Pasquino (Roma-Bari: Laterza, 1995); Piero Ignazi, *Partiti politici in Italia* (Bologna: Il Mulino, 2008).

25. Marco Tarchi, *Dal MSI ad AN* (Bologna: Il Mulino, 1997).

26. The Daisy (La Margherita) was created in 2000. It comprised the former PPI plus some other fringes of Catholic and secular groups. It gained 14.5% of the votes in the 2001 elections and then it merged with the DS in the PD in 2007.

27. Peter Mair and Ingrid van Biezen, "Party Membership in Twenty European Democracies, 1980–2000," *Party Politics* 7 (2001): 5–21.

28. Luciano Bardi, Piero Ignazi, and Oreste Massari, *I Partiti Italiani. Iscritti, Dirigenti, Eletti* (Milano: Università Bocconi Editore, 2007).

29. Richard Katz and Peter Mair, "Changing Models of Party Organization and Party Democracy: The Emergence of the Party Cartel," *Party Politics* 1 (1995): 5–28.

30. Thomas Poguntke and Paul Webb, *The Presidentialization of Politics* (Oxford: Oxford University Press, 2000).

31. Ibid., 9.

CHAPTER 4, SPANISH PARTIES AND DEMOCRACY: WEAK PARTY–SOCIETY LINKAGE AND INTENSE PARTY–STATE SYMBIOSIS

1. V.O. Key, *Politics, Parties and Pressure Groups* (New York: Crowell, 1964); Russell J. Dalton and Martin P. Wattenberg, "Unthinkable Democracy: Political Change in Advanced Industrial Democracies," in *Parties without Partisans. Political Change in Advanced Industrial Democracies*, ed. Russell J. Dalton and Martin P. Wattenberg (Oxford: Oxford University Press, 2000), 3–16.

2. See Dalton and Wattenberg, *Parties without Partisans*.

3. See Russell J. Dalton, "The Decline of Party Identification," in *Parties without Partisans*, ed. Dalton and Wattenberg, 19–36; and Russell J. Dalton, Ian McAllister, and Martin P. Wattenberg, "The Consequences of Partisan Dealignment," in *Parties without Partisans*, ed. Dalton and Wattenberg, 37–63.

4. Laura Morales, "¿Existe una Crisis Participativa? La Evolución de la Participación Política y el Asociacionismo en España," *Revista Española de Ciencia Política* 13 (2005): 51–87.

5. On this point we differ with Verge's conclusions about a curvilinear trend of party identification, with an increasing trend until the mid-1990s and a downward trend since. We think that her conclusions are contaminated by the indicators she uses to measure party identification/closeness, which are not appropriate. She uses a multiresponse item in which each respondent needs to specify how close they feel to a specific political party; hence, her measurements are tapping the more variable element of electoral support rather than the more stable notion of party identification. See Tania Verge, "¿Crisis de los partidos en España? Una revisión crítica," *Revista de Investigaciones Políticas y Sociológicas* 5 (2006): 105–127.

6. Dalton, "The Decline of Party Identification."

7. Mariano Torcal, José Ramón Montero, and Richard Gunther, "Anti-Party Sentiments in Southern Europe," in *Political Parties: Old Concepts and New Challenges*, ed. José Ramón Montero, Richard Gunther, and Juan J. Linz (Oxford: Oxford University Press, 2002), 257–291; and Mariano Torcal, José Ramón Montero, and Richard Gunther, "Los Sentimientos Antipartidistas en el Sur de Europa," in *Partidos Políticos. Viejos Conceptos y Nuevos Retos*, ed. José Ramón Montero, Richard Gunther, and Juan J. Linz (Madrid: Trotta, 2007), 245–266.

8. Torcal, Montero, and Gunther, "Los Sentimientos Antipartidistas en el Sur de Europa."

9. As suggested by Pippa Norris, "Conclusions: The Growth of Critical Citizens and Its Consequences," in *Critical Citizens*, ed. Pippa Norris (Oxford: Oxford University Press, 1999), 257–272.

10. See Richard Gunther, José Ramón Montero, and Joan Botella, *Democracy in Modern Spain* (New Haven, Conn.: Yale University Press, 2004).

11. Martin. P. Wattenberg, "The Decline of Party Mobilization," in *Parties without Partisans*, ed. Russell and Wattenberg (Oxford: Oxford University Press, 2000), 64–76.

12. Wattenberg, "The Decline of Party Mobilization," 72.

13. See Dalton, McAllister, and Wattenberg, "Anti-Party Sentiments in Southern Europe," 54–59.

14. Detailed analyses on these characteristics can be found in Luis Ramiro and Laura Morales, "Latecomers but 'Early-Adapters'. The Adaptation and

Response of Spanish Parties to Social Changes," in *How Parties Respond to Voters. Interest Aggregation Revisited*, ed. Kay Lawson and Thomas Poguntke (New York: Routledge, 2004), 198–226; Mónica Méndez, "Turning the Page: Crisis and Transformation of the Spanish Socialist Party," in *Party Change in Southern Europe*, ed. Anna Bosco and Leonardo Morlino (New York: Routledge, 2007), 86–104; and Javier Astudillo and Elena García-Guereta, "If It Isn't Broken, Don't Fix It: The Spanish Popular Party in Power," in *Party Change in Southern Europe*, ed. Anna Bosco and Leonardo Morlino (New York: Routledge, 2007), 67–85.

15. See Susan Scarrow, "Parties without Members? Party Organization in a Changing Electoral Environment," in *Parties without Partisans*, ed. Russell and Wattenberg (Oxford: Oxford University Press, 2000), 79–101.

16. For a full account, see Ramiro and Morales, "Latecomers but 'Early-Adapters.'"

17. Full details can be found in Mónica Méndez, Laura Morales, and Luis Ramiro, "Los afiliados y su papel en los partidos políticos españoles," *Zona Abierta* 108–109 (2004): 153–207; and Ramiro and Morales, "Latecomers but 'Early-Adapters.'"

18. We observe here some of the dimensions on the role and status of party membership proposed by Susan Scarrow, *Parties and Their Members* (Oxford: Oxford University Press, 1996).

19. See Méndez, Morales, and Ramiro, "Los afiliados y su papel en los partidos políticos españoles."

20. See Méndez, Morales, and Ramiro, "Los afiliados y su papel en los partidos políticos españoles," and Ramiro and Morales, "Latecomers but 'Early-Adapters.'"

21. Susan Scarrow, Paul Webb, and David Farrell, "From Social Integration to Electoral Contestation. The Changing Distribution of Power within Political Parties," in *Parties without Partisans*, ed. Russell and Wattenberg (Oxford: Oxford University Press, 2000), 129–153.

22. See Ramiro and Morales, "Latecomers but 'Early-Adapters'"; and Luis Ramiro and Laura Morales, "European Integration and Spanish Parties Elite Empowerment amidst Limited Adaptation," in *The Europeanization of National Political Parties, Power and Organizational Adaptation*, ed. Thomas Poguntke et al. (London: Routledge, 2007), 134–161.

23. See Méndez, Morales, and Ramiro, "Los afiliados y su papel en los partidos políticos españoles," for more details on this.

24. Ibid.

25. However, in some smaller regionally based parties the leader is elected, through diffrent procedures, by the entire membership. This is the case of the PNV (Basque Nationalist Party), the left-wing Catalan nationalist ERC (Republican Left of Catalonia), or the Catalan Greens ICV (Initiative for Catalonia Greens).

26. In the Spanish case another of the hypotheses proposed by Scarrow, Webb, and Farrell "From Social Integration to Electoral Contestation," referred to the growing role of party members in the selection of party leaders, is not confirmed. In any case, these procedures are obviously affected by other internal factors as the level of internal conflict and factionalism. In general terms, the role of the MPs is also relatively small in Spain and when they play a significant one it is normally due more to their positions within the party leadership than to their own condition of members of parliament. For a specific analysis of the

main center-right party, see Luis Ramiro, "Programmatic Adaptation and Organizational Centralization in the AP-PP," *South European Society and Politics* 10 (2005): 207–223.

27. See some discussions by Carles Boix, "Las elecciones primarias en el PSOE," *Claves* 83 (1998): 34–38; and Johnatan Hopkin, "Bringing the Members Back In? Democratising Candidate Selection in Britain and in Spain," *Party Politics* 7 (2001): 343–361.

28. In other fields, organizational innovation has had ambivalent results. Spanish parties have created sectorial structures with the purpose of widening the posibilities of participation and to attract certain groups of professionals. The results have not been remarkable and these structures remain substantially underdeveloped. In contrast, there have been several initiatives to increase the presence of women in the party directive bodies that have had good results—particularly in the PSOE and in IU, but not in the PP, which opposes this kind of policy. See Tania Verge, "Representación política y modelos de partidos en España: los casos de IU, PSOE y PP," in *Partidos políticos. Viejos conceptos y nuevos retos*, ed. José Ramón Montero, Richard Gunther, and Juan J. Linz (Madrid: Trotta, 2007), 209–244.

29. See Anna Bosco and Leonardo Morlino, "What Changes in South European Parties? A Comparative Introduction," in *Party Change in Southern Europe*, ed. Anna Bosco and Leonardo Morlino (London: Routledge, 2007), 1–28.

30. The reliability of the membership figures is doubtful. In the PSOE and IU there have been several moments in which it has been evident that the real membership figures are lower than the ones declared by the party. At the end of the 1990s, during the primaries to select the candidate to prime minister, the party recognized the need to reelaborate its census of members. In the case of IU the doubts have been persistent, and in 2008 even the party general secretary (G. Llamazares) said that the party congress of that year was manipulated due to the exaggeration of the membership figures.

31. See Ramiro, "Programmatic adaptation and organizational centralization in the AP-PP," and Astudillo and García-Guereta, "If It Isn't Broken, Don't Fix It."

32. See Bosco and Morlino, "What Changes in South European Parties?," 23.

33. Richard Katz, "Party Government: A Rationalistic Conception," in *The Future of Party Government: Visions and Realities of Party Government*, Vol. 1, ed. Francis G. Castles and Rudolf Wildenmann (Berlin: Walter de Gruyter, 1986), 31–71; Ian Holliday, "Spain. Building a Parties State in a New Democracy," in *Political Parties in Advanced Industrial Democracies*, ed. Paul Webb, David Farrell, and Ian Holliday (Oxford: Oxford University Press, 2002), 248–279.

34. See Manuel Sánchez de Dios, "Parliamentary Party Discipline in Spain," in *Party Discipline and Parliamentary Government*, ed. Shaun Bowler, David Farrell, and Richard Katz (Columbus: Ohio State University Press, 1999), 141–162; Ingried van Biezen, "On the Internal Balance of Party Power: Party Organizations in New Democracies," *Party Politics* 6 (2000): 395–417; and Ingrid van Biezen and Johnatan Hopkin, "The Presidentialization of Spanish Democracy: Sources of Prime Ministerial Power in Post-Franco Spain," in *The Presidentialization of Politics*, ed. Thomas Poguntke and Paul Webb (Oxford: Oxford University Press, 2005), 107–127.

35. See Pablo Oñate, "Congreso, grupos parlamentarios y partidos," in *El Congreso de los Diputados en España: funciones y rendimiento*, ed. Antonia Martínez (Madrid: Tecnos, 2000), 95–139.

36. See de Dios, "Parliamentary Party Discipline in Spain," and Holliday, "Spain. Building a Parties State in a New Democracy."

37. See Oñate, "Congreso, grupos parlamentarios y partidos," 139.

38. See Gunther, Montero, and Botella, *Democracy in Modern Spain*, 227.

39. See Thomas Bruneau et al., "Democracy, Southern European Style," in *Parties, Politics, and Democracy in the New Southern Europe*, ed. Nikiforos Diamandouros and Richard Gunther (Baltimore: Johns Hopkins University Press, 2001), 16–82; and Gunther, Montero, and Botella, *Democracy in Modern Spain*.

40. See, for example, Kaare Strom, "Parties at the Core of Government," in *Parties without Partisans. Political Change in Advanced Industrial Democracies*, ed. Dalton J. Russell and Martin P. Wattenberg (Oxford: Oxford University Press, 2000), 180–207.

41. See Stefano Bartolini and Peter Mair, "Challenges to Contemporary Political Parties," in *Political Parties and Democracy*, ed. Larry Diamond and Richard Gunther (Baltimore: Johns Hopkins University Press, 2001), 327–343.

42. Richard Katz and Peter Mair, "Changing Models of Party Organization and Party Democracy: The Emergence of the Cartel Party," *Party Politics* 1 (1995): 5–28.

43. Ingrid van Biezen and Petr Kopecký, "The State and the Parties. Public Funding, Public Regulation and Rent-Seeking in Contemporary Democracies," *Party Politics* 13 (2007): 235–254.

44. Some scholars, though with no systematic empirical evidence, directly define the Spanish system as a partitocracy, for example, Manuel Ramírez, *Consenso, Constitución y partidos políticos. Una reflexión crítica 26 años después* (Barcelona: Institut de Ciències Polítiques i Socials WP 248, 2006), 15.

45. See Pilar del Castillo, "Financing of Spanish Political Parties," in *Comparative Political Finance in the 1980s*, ed. Herbert E. Alexander (Cambridge: Cambridge University Press, 1989), 172–199; Santiago González-Varas, *La financiación de los partidos políticos* (Madrid: Dykinson, 1995); Pilar Cortés, *Recursos públicos y partidos políticos* (Madrid: Centro de Estudios Políticos y Constitucionales, 2003); and María Holgado, *La financiación de los partidos políticos en España* (Valencia: Tirant lo Blanch, 2003).

46. The institution in charge, among other tasks, of the examination of party financing (Tribunal de Cuentas) has frequently warned in its annual reports of the distortion or bending of the law on party funding that these practices entail.

47. Ingrid van Biezen, "Party Financing in New Democracies: Spain and Portugal," *Party Politics* 6 (2000): 329–342.

48. To complete this picture of party financing and state subsidies we should add that Spanish parties are significantly indebted and have large bank loans. The public is every so often reminded of this whenever the media report that parties enjoy special conditions for these loans and that some of them have had their loans condoned in the past.

49. Luis Ramiro, "Del privilegio constitucional de los partidos a la promoción del multipartidismo moderado," in *Las sombras del sistema constitucional español*, ed. Juan Ramón Capella (Madrid: Trotta, 2003), 107–127.

50. See van Biezen and Kopecký, "Party Financing in New Democracies," 239.

51. Richard Katz, "The Internal Life of Parties," in *Political Challenges in the New Europe: Political and Analytical Challenges*, ed. Kurt Richard Luther and Ferdinand Müller-Rommel (Oxford: Oxford University Press, 2002), 87–118; Ingried van Biezen, "Political Parties as Public Utilities," *Party Politics* 10 (2004): 701–722.

52. See van Biezen and Kopecký, "Party Financing in New Democracies," 240.

53. Manuel Ramírez, "Partidos políticos en España: hegemonía constitucional, práctica política y crisis actual," in *Régimen jurídico de los partidos políticos y Constitución*, ed. Manuel Ramírez et al. (Madrid: Centro de Estudios Constitucionales, 1994), 13–31.

54. Manuel Ramírez, *La participación política* (Madrid: Tecnos, 1985).

55. Ángel Rodríguez, *Transición política y consolidación constitucional de los partidos políticos*. (Madrid: Centro de Estudios Constitucionales, 1989).

56. According to the procedures defined in the Constitution, the parties have a relevant role even in certain direct democracy procedures as the referendum or less mediated procedures as the popular legislative initiative. See Manuel Ramírez, *Partidos políticos y Constitución. Un estudio de las actitudes parlamentarias durante el proceso de creación constitucional* (Madrid: Centro de Estudios Constitucionales, 1989).

57. See van Biezen and Kopecký, "Party Financing in New Democracies," 240.

58. Manuel Ramírez, *España de cerca: reflexiones sobre 25 años de democracia* (Madrid: Trotta, 2003).

59. See Ramírez, *Consenso, Constitución y partidos políticos*, 14.

60. Spanish parties are also extremely influential in the appointment of the directorates of some regional savings banks through the intervention that regional governments and parliaments have in the selection of some savings bank executives. As a result, some notorious party politicians have been appointed as savings bank executives, some executives are sometimes decided by agreement among the main parties, and even party conflict and factionalism affect the selection of savings bank executives.

61. Roberto Blanco-Valdés, *Las conexiones políticas. Partidos, Estado, sociedad* (Madrid: Alianza, 2001).

62. Ibid., 142.

63. Ibid., 138.

64. Yves Mény and Martin Rhodes, "Illicit governance: corruption, scandal and fraud," in *Development in West European Politics*, ed. Martin Rhodes, Paul Heywood, and Vincent Wright (Basingstoke: Macmillan, 1997), 95–113.

65. This is a subject for which it is extremely difficult to obtain empirical evidence. However, news reports where the media, the unions or the opposition parties denounce practices of party patronage in public administration abound, as noted, for example, in some articles in the newspaper *El País* in 2007 on December 4 (p. 20), 14 (p. 4, Galicia Edition), and 17 (p. 3, Valencia Edition); in 2008 on May 16 (p. 1, Valencia Edition), June 19 (p. 13), September 17 (p. 2, Valencia Edition) and 18 (p. 2, Valencia Edition), October 8 (p. 5, Andalucía Edition), 9 (p. 4, Andalucía Edition), 17 (p. 7, Andalucía Edition) and 27 (p. 3, Andalucía Edition), November 6 (p. 1, Andalucía Edition), December 12 (p. 5, Galicia Edition), 14 (p. 3, Valencia Edition) and 17 (p. 2, Galicia Edition); and in 2009, January 7 (p. 4, Valencia Edition), and February 25 (p. 12).

66. See Paul Heywood, "Sleaze in Spain," *Parliamentary Affairs* 48 (1995): 726–737; and Fernando Jiménez, "Political Scandals and Political Responsibility in Democratic Spain," *West European Politics* 21 (1998): 80–99.

67. Fundación Alternativas, *Informe sobre la democracia en España 2006* (Madrid: Fundación Alternativas, 2007).

68. Fundación Alternativas, *Informe sobre la democracia en España 2007* (Madrid: Fundación Alternativas, 2008).

69. Paul Webb, "Conclusion. Political Parties and Democratic Control in Advanced Industrial Societies," in *Political Parties in Advanced Industrial Democracies*, ed. Webb, Farrell, and Holliday, 438–458.

70. Kay Lawson, "When Linkage Fails," in *When Parties Fail*, ed. Kay Lawson and Peter H. Merkl (Princeton, N.J.: Princeton University Press, 1988), 13–38.

71. See van Biezen and Kopecký, "The State and the Parties."

CHAPTER 5, NEW QUESTIONS FOR PARTIES AND DEMOCRACY IN THE UNITED KINGDOM: PARTICIPATION, CHOICE, AND CONTROL

1. G. Sartori, *Parties and Party Systems: A Framework for Analysis* (Cambridge: Cambridge University Press, 1976).

2. Laakso and Taagepera, "Effective number of parties: a measure with application to Western Europe," *Comparative Political Studies* 12 (1979): 3–27.

3. Paul Webb, *The Modern British Party System* (London: Sage, 2000), chapter 1.

4. For a more detailed account and critique of the Power Inquiry's report, see Tim Bale, Paul Taggart, and Paul Webb, "You Can't Always Get What You Want: Populism and the Power Inquiry," *Political Quarterly* 77 (2006): 195–216; Charles Pattie and Ron Johnston, "Power to the People through 'Real Power and True Elections'? The Power Report and Revitalising British Democracy," *Parliamentary Affairs* 60 (2007): 253–278.

5. *Power to the People: The Report of Power, an Independent Inquiry into Britain's Democracy* (London: Power Inquiry, 2006), 20–25.

6. Ibid., 24, 229.

7. Paul Webb, *Democracy and Political Parties* (London: Hansard Society, 2007).

8. James Fishkin and Bruce Ackerman, *Deliberation Day* (New Haven, Conn.: Yale University Press, 2004); *The Governance of Britain* (CM7170, London: Stationery Office, 2007).

9. Cas Mudde, "The Popular Zeitgeist," *Government and Opposition* 39 (2004): 543.

10. Gianfranco Pasquino, "Populism and Democracy," in *Twenty First Century Populism: Structure and Agency of the Unwelcome Guest of European Democracy*, ed. Daniele Albertazzi and Duncan McDonnell (Basingstoke: Palgrave Macmillan, 2007), 15–29.

11. Gerry Stoker, "Immature Democrats," *Prospect* (January 2006). See also Paul Taggart, *Populism* (Milton Keynes: Open University Press, 2000), 10–11.

12. Paul Webb, "The Continuing Advance of the Minor Parties," in *Britain Votes 2005*, ed. Pippa Norris and Christopher Wlezien (Oxford: Oxford University Press, 2005), 101–119. Note that this entire section of the chapter draws on

my article "The Continuing Advance of the Minor Parties," *Parliamentary Affairs* (October 1, 2005).

13. Meg Russell, *Must Politics Disappoint?* (London: Fabian Society, 2005); Bernard Crick, *In Defence of Politics* (London: Weidenfeld and Nicolson, 1962).

14. Russell, *Must Politics Disappoint?*, 4.

15. Ibid., 10.

16. Gerry Stoker, *Why Politics Matters: Making Democracy Work* (Basingstoke: Palgrave Macmillan, 2006). A very similar argument about the failure of so many citizens and commentators to recognize the essential nature of politics can be found in Bale et al., "You Can't Always Get What You Want."

17. House of Lords Debates, June 15, 2006, available at http://www.publications.parliament.uk/pa/ld200506/ldhansrd/vo060615/text/60615-04.htm#60615-04_spnew1.

18. Declan McHugh, "Wanting to Be Heard but Not Wanting to Act? Addressing Political Disengagement," *Parliamentary Affairs* 59 (2005), 546–552.

19. Webb, *Democracy and Political Parties*.

20. John Hibbing and Elizabeth Theiss-Morse, *Stealth Democracy: Americans' Beliefs About How Government Should Work* (Cambridge: Cambridge University Press, 2002), 1–2.

21. Ibid., 9.

22. Ibid., 10.

23. Ibid., 207.

24. Paul Webb, "Conclusion: Political Parties and Democratic Control in Advanced Industrial Democracies," in *Political Parties in Advanced Industrial Democracies*, ed. P. Webb, I. Holliday, and D. Farrell (Oxford: Oxford University Press, 2002), 438–460.

25. Alan Ware, *Citizens, Parties and the State* (Oxford: Polity Press, 1987).

26. Ibid., 8.

27. K. Aarts, "Intermediate Organizations and Interest Representation," in *Citizens and the State*, ed. H. D. Klingemann and D. Fuchs (Oxford: Oxford University Press, 1995); P. Byrne, *Social Movements in Britain* (London: Routledge, 1997), 227–257.

28. M. Crozier, S. P. Huntington, and S. Watanuki, *The Crisis of Democracy: Report to the Trilateral Commission on the Governability of Liberal Democracies* (New York: New York University Press, 1975).

29. Webb, *The Modern British Party System*, chapter 1.

30. Jeremy Richardson, "The Market for Political Activism: Interest Groups as Challenge to Political Parties," *West European Politics*, 18 (1995), 116–139.

31. K. J. Arrow, *Social Choice and Individual Values* (New York: Wiley, 1951).

32. That said, Kenneth A. Shepsle and Mark S. Bonchek, *Analyzing Politics: Rationality, Behavior, and Institutions* (New York: Norton, 1997), calculate that, in a three-voter, three-candidate election, only 12 preference arrangements of 216 possible arrangements lead to intransitive group preferences under plurality voting (as used in the United Kingdom).

33. Webb, *The Modern British Party System*, chapter 7.

34. Paul Webb, "Are British political parties in decline?" *Party Politics* 1 (1995), 306; Patrick Seyd and Paul Whiteley, "British Party Members: An Overview" *Party Politics* 10 (2004), 356–357.

35. Patrick Seyd and Paul Whiteley, *Labour's Grass Roots* (Oxford: Clarendon Press, 1992), 202, and Patrick Seyd, Paul Whiteley, and Jeremy Richardson, *True Blues* (Oxford: Clarendon Press, 1994), 223–224.

36. E. E. Schattschneider, *Party Government* (New York: Rhinehart, 1942).

37. H. D. Klingemann, R. Hofferbert, and I. Budge, *Parties, Policy and Democracy* (Boulder, Colo.: Westview, 1994), 260.

38. Richard S. Katz, "Party Government: A Rationalistic Conception," in *The Future of Party Government: Visions and Realities of Party Government*, Vol. 1, ed. Francis G. Castles and Rudolf Wildenmann (Berlin: Walter de Gruyter, 1986), 43.

39. P. Norton, *Dissension in the House of Commons: Intra-Party Dissent in the House of Commons Division Lobbies 1945–74* (London: Macmillan, 1975); P. Norton, *Conservative Dissidents: Dissent Within the Parliamentary Conservative Party 1970–74* (London: Temple-Smith, 1978); P. Norton, *Dissension in the House of Commons 1974–79* (Oxford: Oxford University Press, 1980); Philip Cowley and Mark Stuart, *Dissension amongst the Parliamentary Labour Party, 2001–2005: A Data Handbook*, available at: http://www.revolts.co.uk/DissensionamongstthePLP.pdf; Philip Cowley and Mark Stuart, *Dave's Dissidents? The Conservative Parliamentary Party in the 2005 Parliament*, available at: http://www.revolts.co.uk/Daves%20Dissidents%2005-07.pdf

40. Meg Russell and Maria Sciara, "Why Does the Government Get Defeated in the House of Lords? The Lords, the Party System and British Politics," *British Politics* 2 (2007): 299–322.

41. A. Mughan, *The Presidentialization of Elections in Britain* (Basingstoke: Palgrave, 2000); Richard Heffernan and Paul Webb, "The British Prime Minister: Much More Than 'First among Equals,'" in *The Presidentialization of Democracy: A Study in Comparative Politics*, ed. Richard Heffernan, Paul Webb, and Thomas Poguntke (Oxford: Oxford University Press, 2005), 26–62.

42. J. Mackintosh, *The British Cabinet* (London: Stevens, 1962); R. H. S. Crossman, "Introduction," in *The English Constitution*, ed. W. Bagehot (London: Watts, 1964), 1–57; G. W. Jones, "The Prime Minister's Power," *Parliamentary Affairs* 18 (1965): 167–185.

43. M. Burch and I. Holliday, "The Prime Minister's and Cabinet Offices: An Executive Office in All but Name," *Parliamentary Affairs* 52 (1999): 43.

44. M. Foley, *The Rise of the British Presidency* (Manchester: Manchester University Press, 2000); D. Kavanagh and A. Seldon, *The Powers Behind the Prime Minister: The Hidden Influence of Number 10* (London: HarperCollins, 1999); P. Hennessy, "The Blair Style of Government: An Historical Perspective and an Interim Audit," *Government and Opposition* 33 (1998): 3–20.

45. Even then, both men's successes depended in part on decisions by the Liberal Democrats (and Labour in Bell's case) to withdraw their own candidates in the constituencies concerned.

46. Tony Blair demonstrated a certain proclivity for this practice, on assuming office in 1997, in appointing one or two prominent businessmen with little or no background in party politics to junior ministerial posts: examples include Lord Simon, Lord Sainsbury, and Lord MacDonald. In order to maintain constitutional tradition, however, these men took their places on the Labour benches in the House of Lords.

47. Ben Farragia, *The Unseen Government of the UK* (London: Taxpayers' Alliance, 2008); Chris Leslie and Owen Dallison, *You've Been Quango'd! Mapping Power across the Regions* (London: New Local Government Network, 2008).

48. S. Jenkins, *Accountable to None: The Tory Nationalization of Britain* (London: Penguin, 1995), 264–265.

49. Rob Watts, "Quangos: The Runaway Gravy Train," *Daily Telegraph* (August 20, 2007).

50. Colin Hay, *Why We Hate Politics* (Cambridge: Polity Press, 2007).

51. Judith Bara and Ian Budge, "Party Policy and Ideology: Still New Labour?," in *Britain Votes 2001*, ed. Pippa Norris (Oxford: Oxford University Press, 2001), 26–42.

52. Miki L. Caul and Mark M. Gray, "From Platform Declarations to Policy Outcomes: Changing Party Profiles and Partisan Influence over Policy," in *Parties without Partisans: Political Change in Advanced Industrial Democracies*, ed. R. S. Dalton and M. P. Wattenberg (Oxford: Oxford University Press, 2000), 208–237.

53. B. Hogwood, *Trends in British Public Policy* (Buckingham: Open University Press, 1992).

54. Klingemann, Hofferbert, and Budge, *Parties, Policy and Democracy*.

55. Hayden Phillips, *Strengthening Democracy: Fair and Sustainable Funding of Political Parties. The Review of Funding of Political Parties* (London: Stationery Office, 2007).

56. Peter Mair, "Political Parties, Popular Legitimacy and Public Privilege," *West European Politics* 18 (1995): 54.

CHAPTER 6, THE MASSIVE STABILITY OF THE DANISH MULTIPARTY SYSTEM: A PYRRHIC VICTORY?

1. Ditlev Tamm, "Hvorfor skal grundloven revideres?" *Politica* 33 (2001): 12.

2. Inge Adriansen, *Nationale symboler i det Danske Rige 1830–2000* (København: Museum Tusculanums Forlag, 2003), 110–112.

3. Giovanni Sartori, *Parties and Party Systems: A Framework for Analysis* (Colchester: ECPR Press, 2005 [1976]).

4. Seymour Martin Lipset and Stein Rokkan, "Cleavage Structure, Party Systems, and Voter Alignments: An Introduction," in *Party Systems and Voter Alignments: Cross-National Perspectives*, ed. Seymour Martin Lipset and Stein Rokkan (New York: Free Press, 1967), 1–64.

5. Three elections were called in 1920, two because of the 1915 constitution's requirements for constitutional amendments. For further details on the constitution and its history, see Jørgen Elklit, "The Politics of Electoral System Development and Change: The Danish Case," in *The Evolution of Electoral and Party Systems in the Nordic Countries*, ed. Bernard Grofman and Arend Lijphard (New York: Agathon Press, 2002).

6. Maurice Duverger, *Political Parties: Their Organization and Activities in the Modern State* (London: Methuen, 1959 [1951]), Book 1, chapter 1.

7. For a short overview, see Peter Mair, "Party Systems and Structures of Competition," in *Comparing Democracies. Elections and Voting in Global Perspective*, ed. Lawrence LeDuc, Richard Niemi, and Pippa Norris (London: Sage Publications, 1996), 83–106.

8. Sartori, *Parties and Party Systems*, Chapters 5 and 6.

9. The four old parties are: the Liberals (Venstre) founded in the parliament 1870; The Conservatives (Det Konservative Folkeparti) founded in parliament in 1881; The Social Democrats (Socialdemokratiet) founded as part of the labor movement in 1871; the Social Liberals (Det Radikale Venstre) founded in 1905 as a splinter from the Liberals, see Jørgen Elklit, "Det klassiske danske partisystem bliver til," in *Valg og vælgeradfærd: Studier i dansk politik*, ed. Jørgen Elklit and Ole Tonsgaard (Århus: Politica, 1986).

10. Erik Damgaard, "Stability and Change in the Danish Party System over Half a Century," *Scandinavian Political Studies* 9 (1974), 103–126; Mogens N. Pedersen, "The Danish 'Working Multiparty System': Breakdown or Adaptation," in *Party Systems in Denmark, Austria, Switzerland, the Netherlands, and Belgium*, ed. Hans Daalder (London: Frances Pinter, 1987), 1–60; Mogens N. Pedersen, "The Defeat of All Parties: The Danish Folketing Election, 1973," in *When Parties Fail: Emerging Alternative Organizations*, ed. Kay Lawson and Peter H. Merkl (Princeton, N.J.: Princeton University Press, 1988), 257–281.

11. Damgaard, "Stability and Change in the Danish Party System over Half a Century."

12. Pedersen, "The Danish 'Working Multiparty System'," 8–9.

13. Jacob Christensen, "Tilpasning eller krise? Det danske partisystem 1953–1998," in *Valg, vælgere og velfærdsstat: Festskrift til Hans Jørgen Nielsen*, ed. Peter Kurrild-Klitgaard, Lars Bille, and Tom Bryder (København: Forlaget Politiske Studier, 2000), 43–44.

14. Damgaard, "Stability and Change in the Danish Party System over Half a Century."

15. Lars Bille, "Tre nye partier?" *Politica* 35 (2003), 391–401.

16. Pedersen, "The Defeat of All Parties," 1.

17. Ibid.

18. Christensen, "Tilpasning eller krise? Det danske partisystem 1953–1998," 43.

19. Pedersen, "The Danish 'Working Multiparty System'," 17.

20. One might argue that the Socialist People's Party became an additional important party as it gained substantial public support and political power in 1966, and that the pre-1973 thus should be termed a "four-plus-one" system, see Damgaard, "Stability and Change in the Danish Party System over Half a Century." Following this line of reasoning, the post-1973 system would be a "four-plus-three" system. The Social Democrats did not, however, consider the Socialists a critical parliamentarian source of support as the two new nonsocialist center parties often were considered by the Liberals and the Conservatives (1966–1967 is an exception, see note 39). Thus, we prefer the terms "four" and "four-plus-two" systems in this respect.

21. Pedersen, "The Defeat of All Parties," 265–272.

22. Peter Mair, "The Problem of Party System Change," *Journal of Theoretical Politics* 1 (1989), 251–256. See also Peter Mair, "Myths of Electoral Change and the Survival of Traditional Parties," *European Journal of Political Research* 24 (1993), 121–133.

23. Sartori, *Parties and Party Systems*, 110–113.

24. Pedersen, "The Danish 'Working Multiparty System'," 4.

25. Nikolaj Petersen, "Sikkerhedspolitikken og 1988-valget," in *To folketingsvalg*, ed. Jørgen Elklit and Ole Tonsgaard (Århus: Politica, 1989), 305–327. For a

broader and critical discussion of the role of the Social Liberals, see Christoffer Green-Pedersen, "Det Radikale Venstres betydning i dansk politik. Er den så stor, som vi går og tror?," *Politica* 35 (2003), 274–286.

26. Tage Kaarsted, *Regeringen, vi aldrig fik: Regeringsdannelsen 1975 og dens baggrund* (Odense: Odense Universitetsforlag, 1988); Jørgen Elklit, "Party Behaviour and the Formation of Governments: Danish Experiences from the 1970s and 1980s," in *Policy, Office, or Votes? How Political Parties in Western Europe Make Hard Decisions*, ed. Wolfgang C. Müller and Kaare Strøm (Cambridge: Cambridge University Press, 1999), 63–88.

27. Compare Christensen, "Tilpasning eller krise? Det danske partisystem 1953–1998."

28. An exception is Lars Bille, "Denmark: The Oscillating Party System," *West European Politics* 12 (1989), 42–58, who argues that the system was in fact polarized in the period 1973–1975 and again from 1987 and some years ahead. Note also that the Danish system after all is more centrifugal than the similar systems of Finland and the Netherlands, see Christoffer Green-Pedersen, "Center Parties, Party Competition, and the Implosion of Party Systems: A Study of Centripetal Tendencies in Multiparty Systems," *Political Studies* 52 (2004), 324–341.

29. Sartori, *Parties and Party Systems*, 107–110.

30. Christensen, "Tilpasning eller krise? Det danske partisystem 1953–1998," 42–44.

31. Bille, "Denmark: The Oscillating Party System."

32. Jørgen Elklit and Mogens N. Pedersen, "Decembervalget 1973: 30 år efter," *Politica* 35 (2003), 365–376.

33. Giacomo Sani and Giovanni Sartori, "Polarization, Fragmentation and Competition in Western Democracies," *Western European Party Systems: Continuity and Change*, ed. Hans Daalder and Peter Mair (Beverly Hills, Calif.: Sage, 1983), 330.

34. For example, Pedersen, "The Defeat of All Parties," 40.

35. Pedersen, "The Danish 'Working Multiparty System'," 6–7. Other studies have demonstrated that more than 75% of the bills in the parliament are supported by a broad (i.e., oversized), majority, see Christoffer Green-Pedersen and Lisbeth Hoffmann-Thomsen, "Bloc Politics vs. Broad Cooperation? The Functioning of Danish Minority Parliamentarism," *Journal of Legislative Studies* 11 (2005), 153–169.

36. Pedersen, "The Danish 'Working Multiparty System'," 7. See also Peter Munk Christiansen and Asbjørn Sonne Nørgaard, *Faste forhold—flygtige forbindelser. Stat og interesseorganisationer i Danmark i det 20. århundrede* (Aarhus: Aarhus Universitetsforlag, 2003).

37. Elizabeth P. Klages, "Populisme eller hvad? Fremskridtspartiet og Dansk Folkeparti som reaktioner på 'politics as usual,'" *Politica* 35 (2003), 402–412; Tor Bjørklund and Jørgen Goul Andersen, "Anti-Immigration Parties in Denmark and Norway: The Progress Parties and the Danish People's Party," in *Shadows over Europe: The Development and Impact of the Extreme Right in Western Europe*, ed. Martin Schain, Aristide Zolberg, and Patrick Hossay (New York: St. Martin's Press, 2002), 105–134. For a different classification of the two parties, see Jens Rydgren, "Explaining the Emergence of Radical Right-Wing Populist Parties: The Case of Denmark," *West European Politics* 27 (2004), 474–502.

38. Karina Kosiara-Pedersen, "The 2007 Danish General Election: Generating a Fragile Majority," *West European Politics* 31 (2008), 1040–1048.

39. In 1966 the Social Democrats formed a single party minority government supported by the Socialist People's Party. This arrangement, called the "Red Cabinet," was similar to the present form of cooperation between the nonsocialist government and the Danish People's Party, but it lasted for less than a year due to internal disputes. At the same time a splinter, the Left Socialists, broke away from the Socialist People's Party as a protest of the arrangement. Thus, this left-wing wooing did not end up in a red marriage; more likely it warned the party leaders not to repeat the experiment any time soon, see: Erik Mader, *SF under 'det røde kabinet'* (Odense: Odense Universitetsforlag, 1979). In 1987, the socialists once more explicitly supported an alternative Social Democratic government, but when one was finally formed in 1993, it was solely on the basis of the center parties, see Bille, "Denmark: The Oscillating Party System," 47.

40. Christian Elmelund-Præstekær, *Unoder og kammertoner i dansk valgkamp. Partiernes positive og negative, person- og politikfokuserede kampagner 1994–2007* (Odense: Syddansk Universitetsforlag, 2009), chapter 11.

41. Asbjørn Skjæveland, *Government Formation in Denmark 1953–1998* (Aarhus: Forlaget Politica, 2003).

42. Pedersen, "The Danish 'Working Multiparty System'," 10.

43. Hans Jørgen Nielsen and Søren Risbjerg Thomsen, "Vælgervandringer," in *Politisk forandring. Værdipolitik og nye skillelinjer ved folketingsvalget 2001*, ed. Jørgen Goul Andersen and Ole Borre (Århus: Systime Academic, 2003), 61–74; Hans Jørgen Nielsen, "The Danish election 1998," *Scandinavian Political Studies* 22 (1999), 67–81. For international comparison, see Stefano Bartolini and Peter Mair, *Identity, Competition, and Electoral Availability: The Stabilization of European Electorates 1885–1985* (Cambridge: Cambridge University Press, 1990), 96–124.

44. Elmelund-Præstekær, *Unoder og kammertoner i dansk valgkamp. Partiernes positive og negative, person- og politikfokuserede kampagner 1994–2007*, chapter 11.

45. Martin Ejnar Hansen, "Reconsidering the Party Distances and Dimensionality of the Danish Folketing," *Journal of Legislative Studies* 14 (2008), 264–278.

46. Mair, "Party Systems and Structures of Competition," 97–98.

47. Peter Mair, *Party System Change: Approaches and Interpretations* (Oxford: Oxford University Press, 1997), 24–27.

48. Compare Lipset and Rokkan, "Cleavage Structure, Party Systems, and Voter Alignments: An Introduction."

49. Mair, *Party System Change*, 7–8.

50. Jørgen Elklit, "Mobilization and Partisan Division: Open Voting in Frederica, Denmark," *Social Science History* 7 (1983), 235–266.

51. See the discussion of the "Cartel Party" type in Richard Katz and Peter Mair, "Changing Models of Party Organization and Party Democracy. The Emergence of the Cartel Party," *Party Politics* 1 (1995), 5–28.

52. Robert A. Dahl, *Dilemmas of Pluralist Democracy: Autonomy vs. Control* (New Haven, Conn.: Yale University Press, 1983).

53. Bloc politics is nothing new in the Danish parliament. The proportion of bills passed using one particular bloc was equally high in the mid-1980s, in 1993–1994, and post-2001, see Green-Pedersen and Hoffmann-Thomsen, "Bloc Politics vs. Broad Cooperation? The Functioning of Danish Minority Parliamentarism," 153–169; Peter Kurrild-Klitgaard, Robert Klemmensen, and Martin E.

Hansen, "Blokpolitik og det samarbejdende folkestyres fire gamle partier, 1953–2005," *Økonomi og Politik* 79 (2006), 79–85. The post-2001 right-wing majority might, however, conduct more bloc politics than earlier governments did in major reforms and other important votes, see Kosiara-Pedersen, "The 2007 Danish General Election: Generating a Fragile Majority," 1040–1048.

54. The former number was 16, if Copenhagen and Frederiksberg—the two capital municipalities, which were not formally counties as the 14 other regional authorities—are included.

55. For a more detailed discussion on the reform, see Peter Munk Christiansen and Michael Baggesen Klitgaard, *Den utænkelige reform. Strukturreformens tilblivelse 2002–2005* (Odense: Syddansk Universitetsforlag, 2008).

56. For a wider discussion of the erosion of the consensus norm, see Tim Knudsen, *Fra folkestyre til markedsdemokrati—Dansk demokratihistorie efter 1973* (København: Akademisk Forlag, 2007).

57. Russell J. Dalton, Scott C. Flanagan, and Paul Allen Beck, *Electoral Change in Advanced Industrial Democracies. Realignment or Dealignment* (Princeton, N.J.: Princeton University Press, 1984).

58. Ronald Inglehart, *The Silent Revolution. Changing Values and Political Styles among Western Publics* (Princeton, N.J.: Princeton University Press, 1977). For the Danish development see Ole Borre, "Old and New Politics in Denmark," *Scandinavian Political Studies* 18 (1995), 187–205; Ole Borre, "To konfliktdimensioner," in *Politisk forandring. Værdipolitik og nye skillelinjer ved folketingsvalget 2001*, ed. Jørgen Goul Andersen and Ole Borre (Århus: Systime Academic, 2003); Ole Borre, "Issue voting i Danmark 2001–2005," in *Det nye politiske landskab. Folketingsvalget 2005 i perspektiv*, ed. Hans Jørgen Nielsen et al. (Århus: Academica, 2007), 177–194; Christian Albrekt Larsen and Henrik Lolle, "Vælgernes mentale kort over partierne fra 1994 til 2005: Én venstre-højre dimension og én protest/ekstremist dimension," in *Det nye politiske landskab. Folketingsvalget 2005 i perspektiv*, ed. Nielsen et al, 233–256; Hans Jørgen Nielsen, "Hvor mange dimensioner er der?" in *Det nye politiske landskab. Folketingsvalget 2005 i perspektiv*, ed. Nielsen et al., 213–233.

59. Borre, "Old and New Politics in Denmark."

60. Rune Stubager, *The Education Cleavage: New Politics in Denmark* (Aarhus: Politica, 2006).

61. Tim Knudsen, "Et resumé: Valget til Folketinget den 13. November 2007," *Tidsskriftet Politik* 11 (2008), 3–9; Lars Bille, "Politisk kronik," *Økonomi og Politik* 81 (2008), 63–73; Kosiara-Pedersen, "The 2007 Danish General Election: Generating a Fragile Majority," 1040–1048.

CHAPTER 7, PARTIES AS VEHICLES OF DEMOCRACY IN NORWAY: STILL WORKING AFTER ALL THESE YEARS?

1. The Norwegian Constitution is the second oldest codified constitution in the world. Øyvind Østerud, "Introduction: Peculiarities of Norway," *West European Politics* 28 (2005): 706; Hanne Marthe Narud and Kaare Strøm, "Norway: An Unconstrained Polity," in *Democratic Institutions in Decline?*, ed. Torbjörn Bergman and Kaare Strøm (Ann Arbor: University of Michigan Press, forthcoming in 2010).

2. Østerud, "Introduction: Peculiarities of Norway"; Narud and Strøm, "Norway: An Unconstrained Polity."

3. Ulf Torgersen, "Interesseorganisasjonene og partilivet," *Nytt Norsk Tidsskrift* 1 (1984): 46–48.

4. Kaare Strøm, Hanne Marthe Narud, and Henry Valen, "A More Fragile Chain of Governance in Norway," *West European Politics* 28 (2005): 785–786; Narud and Strøm, "Norway: An Unconstrained Polity."

5. See Harry Eckstein, *Division and Cohesion in Democracy: A Study of Norway* (Princeton, N.J.: Princeton University Press, 1966).

6. Knut Heidar, *Partidemokrati på prøve: Norske partieliter i demokratisk perspektiv* (Oslo: Universitetsforlaget, 1988); Øyvind Østerud and Per Selle, "Power and Democracy in Norway: The Transformation of Norwegian Politics," *Scandinavian Political Studies* 29 (2006): 37; Peter Mair, "Democracy Beyond Parties," working paper, Center for the Study of Democracy, University of California, Irvine (2005), available at: http://repositories.cdlib.org/csd/; Kay Lawson, "When Parties Dedemocratize," in *When Parties Prosper: The Uses of Electoral Success*, ed. Kay Lawson and Peter H. Merkl (Boulder, Colo.: Lynne Rienner, 2007); Peter Mair, "The Challenge to Party Government," *West European Politics* 31 (2008).

7. In 1997, the Storting decided to launch a power and democracy study to analyze the state of Norwegian democracy at the dawn of the 21st century. An independent steering committee of five researchers was appointed (see Østerud and Selle, "Power and Democracy in Norway").

8. Østerud and Selle, "Power and Democracy in Norway," 37ff; Strøm, Narud, and Valen, "A More Fragile Chain of Governance in Norway," 79ff.

9. As far as Norway is concerned, see "Makt and demokrati: Sluttrapport fra Makt- og demokratiutredningen," *NOU* (2003): 19, 14.

10. David Held, *Models of Democracy* (Cambridge: Polity Press, 1987); Erik O. Eriksen and Jarle Weigård, *Understanding Habermas* (New York: Continuum, 2003).

11. See Elin H. Allern and Karina Pedersen, "The Impact of Party Organizational Changes on Democracy," *West European Politics* 30 (2007): 69–92 for a more elaborate discussion of relevant democratic theory.

12. See, for example, Anthony Downs, *An Economic Theory of Democracy* (New York: Harper and Row, 1957); William Riker, *Liberalism Against Populism* (Prospect Heights, Ill.: Waveland, 1982); Joseph A. Schumpeter, *Capitalism, Socialism and Democracy* (London: Routledge, 1996 [1943]). There are several traditions within this competitive perspective, see, for example, Richard S. Katz, *Democracy and Elections* (New York: Oxford University Press, 1997), for an overview.

13. Schumpeter, *Capitalism, Socialism and Democracy*, 269ff.

14. See, for example, Downs, *An Economic Theory of Democracy*; and Robert Dahl, *A Preface to Democratic Theory* (Chicago: University of Chicago Press, 1956). The difference between aggregation and integration is probably not crystal clear in practice, but this conceptual problem cannot be followed up here.

15. John Stuart Mill, *On Liberty* (New York: Meridian, 1962 [1859]); Carol Pateman, *Participation and Democratic Theory* (Cambridge: Cambridge University Press, 1970), 43.

16. Held, *Models of Democracy*, 259.

17. Ibid., 262.

18. Amy Gutmann and Dennis Thompson, *Democracy and Disagreement* (Cambridge, Mass.: Belknap Press of Harvard University Press, 1996); Jürgen Habermas, *Between Facts and Norm. Contributions to a Discourse Theory of Law and Democracy* (Cambridge, Mass.: MIT Press, 1996).

19. Habermas, *Between Facts and Norms*; John S. Dryzek, *Deliberative Democracy and Beyond* (Oxford: Oxford University Press, 2000).

20. Gutmann and Thompson, *Democracy and Disagreement*, 15–16, 128–164.

21. Bernard Manin, *The Principles of Representative Government* (Cambridge: Cambridge University Press, 1997).

22. Kasper Møller Hansen, *Deliberative Democracy and Opinion Formation* (Odense: University Press of Southern Denmark, 2004), 107.

23. Habermas, *Between Facts and Norm*, 171.

24. For a more detailed presentation of the Norwegian party system, see Nicholas Aylott, "Parties and Party Systems in the North," in *Democratic Institutions in Decline?*, ed. Torbjörn Bergman and Kaare Strøm (Ann Arbor: University of Michigan Press, forthcoming).

25. The conservatives did not fully accept the principle of parliamentary government until 1905. See Trond Nordby, *I politikkens sentrum: Variasjoner i Stortingets makt 1814–2000* (Oslo: Universitetsforlaget), 96.

26. Stein Rokkan, "Geography, Religion, and Social Class: Crosscutting Cleavages in Norwegian Politics," in *Party Systems and Voter Alignments: Cross-National Perspectives*, ed. Seymour Martin Lipset and Stein Rokkan (New York: Free Press, 1967), 372ff; Henry Valen and Stein Rokkan, "Norway: Conflict Structure and Mass Politics in a European Periphery," in *Electoral Behavior: A Comparative Handbook*, ed. Richard Rose (New York: Free Press), 318–321.

27. Elin H. Allern, "Parties, Interest Groups and Democracy: Political Parties and Their Relationship with Interest Groups in Norway," doctoral dissertation, University of Oslo, Oslo, 2007, 5.

28. Knut Heidar, "Norwegian Parties and the Party System: Steadfast and Changing," *West European Politics* 28 (2005): 807–833; Oddbjørn Knutsen, "Voters and Social Cleavages," in *Nordic Politics: Comparative Perspectives*, ed. Knut Heidar (Oslo: Universitetsforlaget); Bernt Aardal, ed., *Norske velgere. En studie av stortingsvalget 2005* (Oslo: N. W. Damm & Sønn, 2007).

29. Over time, the Center Party has moved from the right to the left side of the political spectrum, see Hanne Marthe Narud and Henry Valen, *Demokrati og ansvar: Politisk representasjon i et flerpartisystem* (Oslo: N. W. Damm & Sønn, 2007), 148.

30. For the translation of Norwegian party names, I apply the terms used in Thomas T. Mackie and Richard Rose's *The International Almanac of Electoral History* (Washington, D.C.: Congressional Quarterly, 1991) and in the yearbook of *European Journal of Political Research*. However, it should be noted that *Kristelig Folkeparti* (KrF) itself employs the label Christan Democratic Party, not the literal translation Christian People's Party.

31. Arend Lijphart, *Patterns of Democracy: Government Forms and Performance in Thirty-Six Democracies* (New Haven, Conn.: Yale University Press, 1999), 189.

32. Kaare Strøm and Hanne Marthe Narud, "Norway: Virtual Parliamentarism," in *Delegation and Accountability in Parliamentary Democracies*, ed. Kaare Strøm, Wolfgang C. Müller, and Torbjörn Bergman (Oxford: Oxford University Press, 2006), 525.

33. Øyvind Østerud, Fredrik Engelstad, and Per Selle, *Makten og demokratiet* (Oslo: Gyldendal Akademisk, 2003), 106ff.

34. Strøm and Narud, "Norway: Virtual Parliamentarism," 548, 533.

35. Torbjörn Bergman, "Formation Rules and Minority Governments," *European Journal of Political Research* 23 (1993): 55–66.

36. Strøm and Narud, "Norway: Virtual Parliamentarism," 533.

37. Lijphart, *Patterns of Democracy*, 223ff.

38. Strøm and Narud, "Norway: Virtual Parliamentarism," 544–545.

39. Tom Christensen, "The Norwegian State Transformed," *West European Politics* 28 (2005), 728–730.

40. Jon Erik Dølvik and Torgeir Aarvaag Stokke, "Norway: The Revival of Centralised Concertation," in *Changing Industrial Relations in Europe*, ed. Anthony Ferner and Richard Hyman (Oxford: Blackwell, 1998), 127.

41. Knut Heidar, "Should the Parties Be Incorporated in the Written Constitution?", in *The Role of Constitutions in a Changing Society* (Oslo: Norwegian Academy of Science and Letters, 1991), 299–315.

42. In local elections, personal votes can be given to individual candidates.

43. Karl-Heinz Nassmacher, ed., *Foundations for Democracy: Approaches to Comparative Political Finance* (Baden-Baden: Nomos, 2001).

44. Jon Pierre, Lars Svåsand, and Anders Widfeldt, "State Subsidies to Political Parties: Confronting Rhetoric with Reality," *West European Politics* 23 (2000): 12; Ot. prp. (parliamentary bill) nr. 84 (2004–2005): Om lov om visse forhold vedrørende de politiske partiene (partiloven). [On the Law Concerning Certain Conditions Regarding Political Parties (the 'Party Law')].

45. Sigurd Allern, "Fra politikermakt til journalistmakt," in *I valgkampens hete*, ed. Bernt Aardal, Anne Krogstad, and Hanne Marthe Narud (Oslo: Universitetsforlaget, 2004), 147FF. However, a recent addition to NRK's rights and duties require a "broad and balanced coverage of national elections", and that "all parties and lists beyond a certain size should usually be included in the election coverage" (St. meld. Nr. 18 2008–2009: 2, my translation).

46. Lijphart, *Patterns of Democracy*, 181.

47. Peter Munk Christiansen and Hilmar Rommetvedt, "From Corporatism to Lobbyism? Parliaments, Executives, and Organized Interests in Denmark and Norway," *Scandinavian Political Studies* 22 (1999): 195–220; Hilmar Rommetvedt, "Norway: Resources Count, but Votes Decide? From Neo-corporatist Representation to Neo-pluralist Parliamentarism," *West European Politics* 28 (2005), 740–763; Østerud and Selle, "Power and Democracy in Norway," 33.

48. Per Selle and Tommy Tranvik, "Civil Society in Transition," in *Nordic Politics: Comparative Perspectives*, ed. Knut Heidar (Oslo: Universitetsforlaget, 2004), 83, 88.

49. Russell J. Dalton and Steven A. Weldon, "Public Images of Political Parties: A Necessary Evil?," *West European Politics* 28 (2005): 934.

50. Strøm, Narud, and Valen, "A More Fragile Chain of Governance in Norway," 792; Bernt Aardal, "Oljerikdom og mistillit," in *Norske velgere. En studie av stortingsvalget 2005*, ed. Bernt Aardal (Oslo: N. W. Damm & Sønn, 2007), 347–351.

51. Knut Heidar and Jo Saglie, *Hva skjer med partiene?* (Oslo: Gyldendal Akademisk, 2002), 42.

52. Anthony King, "Political Parties in Western Democracies: Some Skeptical Reflections," *Polity* (Winter 1969): 120–123.

53. Michael Gallagher, Michael Laver, and Peter Mair, *Representative Government in Modern Europe* (New York: McGraw-Hill, 2006), 291.

54. Jacob Aars and Hans-Erik Ringkjøb, "Party Politicisation Reversed? Nonpartisan Alternatives in Norwegian Local Politics," *Scandinavian Political Studies* 28 (2005): 16–79.

55. Mogens Pedersen, "The Dynamics of European Party Systems: Changing Patterns of Electoral Volatility," *European Journal of Political Research* 7 (1979): 1–26.

56. Gallagher, Laver, and Mair, *Representative Government in Modern Europe*, 294.

57. Bernt Aardal, *How to Lose a Walk-Over Election? A Preliminary Analysis of the 2005 Parliamentary Election in Norway*, Report no. 6 (Oslo: Institute for Social Research, 2006), 12.

58. As measured by Alford's index, see Narud and Strøm, "Norway: An Unconstrained Polity."

59. Narud and Valen, *Demokrati og ansvar*, 340.

60. Tor Bjørklund and Jo Saglie, *Lokalvalget i 1999: Rekordlav og rekordhøy deltakelse*, Report 1 (Oslo: Institute for Social Research, 2000).

61. Sigmund Neumann, "Toward a Comparative Study of Political Parties," in *Modern Political Parties*, ed. Sigmund Neumann (Chicago: University of Chicago Press, 1956); Giovanni Sartori, "Party Types, Organisation and Functions," *West European Politics* 28 (2005): 5–32.

62. Bernt Aardal, "Gir store velgervandringer nye mønstre," in *Norske velgere. En studie av stortingsvalget 2005*, ed. Aardal, 97–103.

63. Maurice Duverger, *Political Parties. Their Organization and Activity in the Modern State* (London: Methuen, 1954, 1972).

64. Heidar and Saglie, *Hva skjer med partiene?*, 33ff.

65. See, for example, Katz and Mair, "Changing Models of Party Organization and Party Democracy", 5–28; Susan Scarrow, Paul Webb, and David Farrell, "From Social Integration to Electoral Contestation: The Changing Distribution of Power within Political Parties," in *Parties without Partisans: Political Change in Advances Industrial Democracies*, ed. Russell J. Dalton and Martin P. Wattenberg (Oxford: Oxford University Press, 2002), 138FF.

66. Heidar and Saglie, *Hva skjer med partiene?*

67. Karina Pedersen and Jo Saglie, "New Technology in Ageing Parties. Internet Use in Danish and Norwegian Parties," *Party Politics* 11 (2005): 359–377.

68. Allern, "Fra politikermakt til journalistmakt," chapter 14.

69. Hilmar Rommetvedt, *The Rise of the Norwegian Parliament* (London: Frank Cass, 2003), 59; Rune Karlsen, "Fear of the Political Consultant: Campaign Professionals and New Technology in Norwegian Electoral Politics," *Party Politics*, available at http://ppq.sagepub.com/cgi/rapidpdf/1354068809341055v1, p. 8.

70. See for example Richard S. Katz and Peter Mair, "Changing Models of Party Organization and Party Democracy: The Emergence of the Cartel Party," *Party Politics* 1 (1995): 5–28.

71. Allern, "Fra politikermakt til journalistmakt," chapter 14.

72. Allern, "Fra politikermakt til journalistmakt," chapter 14; Rommetvedt, *The Rise of the Norwegian Parliament*, 759.

73. Ola Listhaug and Lars Grønflaten, "Civic Decline? Trends in Political Involvement and Participation in Norway, 1965–2001," *Scandinavian Political Studies* 30 (2007): 272–299.

74. Compare Marc Hooghe and Yves Dejaeghere, "Does the 'Monotorial Citizen Exist'? An Empirical Investigation into the Occurrence of Postmodern Forms of Citizenship in the Nordic Countries," *Scandinavian Political Studies* 30 (2007): 249–271.

75. Peter Mair and Ingrid van Biezen, "Party Membership in Twenty European Democracies, 1980–2000," *Party Politics* 7 (2001): 5–21.

76. Heidar and Saglie, *Hva skjer med partiene?*, 100ff.

77. Ibid., 766–768.

78. Ibid., 770.

79. Kristin Strømsnes, *Folkets makt. Medborgerskap, demokrati og deltakelse* (Oslo: Gyldendal Akademisk, 2003); Frode Berglund and Bernt Aardal, "Politisk deltakelse—håp for nye generasjoner?," in *Norske velgere. En studie av stortingsvalget 2005*, ed. Aardal, 307ff.

80. Knut Heidar and Jo Saglie, "A Decline of Linkage? Intra-Party Participation in Norway 1991–2000," *European Journal of Political Research* 42 (2003): 761–786.

81. Compare Allern and Pedersen, "The Impact of Party Organizational Changes on Democracy," 74.

82. Sartori, "Party Types, Organisation and Functions."

83. For example, Ottar Hellevik, *Stortinget—en sosial elite?* (Oslo: Pax forlag); Heidar and Saglie, *Hva skjer med partiene?*; Narud and Valen, *Demokrati og ansvar*.

84. Henry Valen, "Norway: Decentralization and Group Representation," in *Candidate Selection in Comparative Perspective: The Secret Garden of Politics*, ed. Michael Gallagher and Michael Marsh (London: Sage, 1988); Henry Valen, Hanne Marthe Narud, and Audun Skare, "Norway: Party Dominance and Decentralized Decision-Making," in *Party Sovereignty and Citizen Control: Selecting Candidates for Parliamentary Elections in Denmark, Finland, Iceland and Norway*, ed. Hanne Marthe Narud, Mogens N. Pedersen, and Henry Valen (Odense: University Press of Southern Denmark, 2002).

85. Narud and Valen, *Demokrati og ansvar*, 78.

86. Heidar and Saglie, *Hva skjer med partiene?*, 71–72; Narud and Valen, *Demokrati og ansvar*, 82–83.

87. Narud and Valen, *Demokrati og ansvar*, 89.

88. Ibid., 82, 89–90.

89. Narud and Strøm, "Norway: An Unconstrained Polity."

90. Hanne Marthe Narud and Henry Valen, "The Norwegian Storting: People's parliament or coop for 'political broilers'," *World Political Science Review* 4 (2008): 16; for statistics on Norway's data on education for 2004, see the Statistisk sentralbyra Web site: www.ssb.no

91. Narud and Valen, *Demokrati og ansvar*, 85.

92. Narud and Strøm, "Norway: An Unconstrained Polity."

93. King, "Political Parties in Western Democracies," 138.

94. Compare Heidar, *Partidemokrati på prøve*; Thomas Poguntke, "Do Parties Respond? Challenges to Political Parties and Their Consequences," in *How*

Political Parties Respond. Interest Aggregation Revisited, ed. Kay Lawson and Thomas Poguntke (Oxon: Routledge, 2004), 4.

95. Christoffer Green-Pedersen, "The Growing Importance of Issue Competition: The Changing Nature of Party Competition in Western Europe," *Political Studies* 55 (2007): 607–628. One possible explanation is perhaps that election dates are fixed and hereby long-term preparations are always possible in Norway.

96. Sartori, "Party Types, Organisation and Functions," 31.

97. Hans Keman, "Policy-making Capacities of European Party Government," in *Political Parties in the New Europe*, ed. Kurt Richard Luther and Ferdinand Müller-Rommel (Oxford: Oxford University Press), 217FF; Jan Sundberg, "Scandinavian Party Model at the Crossroads," in *Political Parties in Advanced Industrial Democracies*, ed. Paul Webb, David M. Farrell, and Ian Holliday (Oxford: Oxford University Press), 203–204.

98. In other words, there has been a shift from parties articulating the aggregated interests of specific social segments toward parties mediating between various social groups.

99. E. E. Schattschneider, *Party Government* (New York: Rinehart, 1942), 60; Giovanni Sartori, *The Theory of Democracy Revisited*, Vol. I (Chatham: Chatham House, 1987), 151.

100. Otto Kirchheimer, "The Transformation of the Western European Party Systems," in *Political Parties and Political Development*, ed. Joseph LaPalombara and Myron Weiner (Princeton, N.J.: Princeton University Press).

101. Hanne Marthe Narud and Rune Karlsen, "Organisering av valgkampen— 'tradisjonell' eller 'moderne'?," in *I valgkampens hete*, ed. Bernt Aardal, Anne Krogstad, and Hanne Marthe Narud (Oslo: Universitetsforlaget, 2004), 120–121.

102. Allern, "Parties, Interest Groups and Democracy," chapters 7–14. Interestingly, the increased organizational openness does not seem to have made parties significantly less responsive to their own grass roots. A recent survey suggests that only a very small minority of party congress delegates have contact with people *outside* the party during the final deliberations, see Heidar and Saglie, *Hva skjer med partiene?*, 221.

103. Poguntke, "Do Parties Respond?," 5.

104. Richard S. Katz and Peter Mair, "Changing Models of Party Organization and Party Democracy: The Emergence of the Cartel Party," *Party Politics 1* (1995): 5–28; See, for example, Ruud Koole, "Cadre, Catch-all or Cartel?," *Party Politics* 2 (1996): 507–523; Susan Scarrow, "Party Subsidies and Freezing of Party Competition: Do Cartel Mechanisms Work?," *West European Politics* 29 (2006), 619–639.

105. Bernt Aardal, "Velgere på evig vandring? Hva skjedde ved stortingsvalget i 2005?," in *Norske velgere. En studie av stortingsvalget 2005*, ed. Aardal, 15.

106. Ot. prp. (parliamentary bill) nr. 84 (2004–2005).

107. See, for example, Andrea Volkens and Hans-Dieter Klingemann, "Parties, Ideologies, and Issues: Stability and Change in 15 European Party Systems 1945–1998," in *Political Parties in the New Europe: Political and Analytical Challenges*, ed. Kurt Richard Luther and Ferdinand Müller-Rommel (Oxford: Oxford University Press, 2002), 143–167.

108. Narud and Valen, *Demokrati og ansvar*, 140ff.

109. Hilmar Rommetvedt, "Partiavstand og partikoalisjoner." Report 246/91, Rogaland Research and PhD dissertation, University of Bergen, Stavanger, 1991; Rommetvedt, "Norway: Resources Count, But Votes Decide?," 750.

110. Compare Herbert Kitschelt, *The Transformation of European Social Democracy* (Cambridge: Cambridge University Press, 1994).

111. Lawson, "When Parties Dedemocratize," 358–360.

112. See Ola Listhaug, "Oil Dissatisfaction and Political Trust in Norway: A Resource Curse," *West European Politics* 28 (2005): 834–851; Narud and Valen, *Demokrati og ansvar*, chapter 12.

113. Kaare Strøm, "Parliamentary Democracy and Delegation," in *Delegation and Accountability in Parliamentary Democracies*, ed. Kaare Strøm, Wolfgang C. Müller, and Torbjörn Bergman (Oxford: Oxford University Press, 2006), 55.

114. Ibid., 62.

115. Ibid., 64ff.

116. Richard S. Katz, "Party Government and Its Alternatives," in *Party Governments: European and American Experiences*, ed. Rudolph W. Wildenmann and Richard S. Katz (Berlin: de Greuyter, 1987), 4.

117. The Norwegian Study of Power and Democracy argues that both judicialization—in terms of increased judicial independence and review—and Europeanization—that is, the effects of Norwegian membership in European Economic Area—have significantly weakened the parliamentary model by constraining the authority of the Storting. Such external constraints on parliamentary deliberations are partly a result of political decisions, but may in turn have weakened the power of parties in general (Østerud and Selle, "Power and Democracy in Norway"). Here, however, we shall concentrate on parties' specific contributions through their institutional design of the various branches of government and their own organizational outlook and behavior.

118. In 2005, more than 50% of Norwegian voters reported to have at least had a look at party manifestos before the general election, but the reliability of these figures is questionable: see Narud and Valen, *Demokrati og ansvar*, 137.

119. Elin H. Allern and Jo Saglie, "Between Electioneering and 'Politics as Usual': The Involvement of Interests Groups in Norwegian Electoral Politics," in *Non-Party Actors in Electoral Politics: The Role of Interest Groups and Independent Citizens in Contemporary Election Campaigns*, ed. David Farrell and Rüdiger Schmitt-Beck (Baden-Baden: Nomos, 2008), 86ff.

120. Helge Østby, "Media in Politics: Channels, Arenas, Actors, Themes," in *Challenges to Political Parties: The Case of Norway*, ed. Kaare Strøm and Lars Svåsand (Ann Arbor: University of Michigan Press, 1997), 220–221.

121. Strömback and Aalberg show, by comparing election news coverage of leading Swedish and Norwegian newspapers in 2002–2005, that Norwegian parties tended to frame their articles in terms of "game" (as opposed to "issue") more frequently than Swedish newspapers: 66% of the articles studied from Norway were framed in this way. See Jesper Strömbäck and Toril Aalberg, "Election News Coverage in Democratic Corporatist Countries. A Comparative Study of Sweden and Norway," *Scandinavian Political Studies* 31 (2008): 91–106.

122. Allern, "Fra politikermakt til journalistmakt"; Bernt Aardal, Anne Krogstad, and Hanne Marthe Narud, "Valgkamp på norsk," in *I valgkampens hete*, ed. Bernt Aardal, Anne Krogstad, and Hanne Marthe Narud (Oslo:

Universitetsforlaget, 2004), 387ff; Kjersti Thorbjørnsrud, "Inne eller ute? Casting av politikere til valgdebatt," *Tidsskrift for samfunnsforskning* 49 (2008): 481–516.

123. Hanne Marthe Narud, "Hvem skal styre landet?," in *Velgere i villrede . . . En analyse av stortingsvalget 2001*, ed. Bernt Aardal (Oslo: N. W. Damm & Sønn, 2003), 191.

124. Hanne Marthe Narud, "Fra mindretallsregjering til flertallsregjering," in *Norske velgere. En studie av stortingsvalget 2005*, ed. Aardal, 265.

125. Narud, "Hvem skal styre landet?," 192–93; see also Strøm, Narud, and Valen, "A More Fragile Chain of Governance in Norway," 799.

126. Valen, Narud, and Skare, "Norway: Party Dominance and Decentralized Decision-Making," 211.

127. Hanne Marthe Narud, "Norway: Professionalization—Party-oriented and Constituency-based," in *The Political Class in Advanced Democracies*, ed. Jürgen Zeiß and Jens Borchert (Oxford: Oxford University Press, 2003).

128. See, for example, Alan Ware, *The Logic of Party Democracy* (London: Macmillan, 1979), 78.

129. Narud and Strøm, "Norway: An Unconstrained Polity."

130. See also Rommetvedt, "Partiavstand og partikoalisjoner," 312; Kaare Strom, *Minority Government and Majority Rule* (Cambridge: Cambridge University Press, 1990), 51.

131. Strøm and Narud, "Norway: An Unconstrained Polity," 527ff.

132. Rommetvedt, *The Rise of the Norwegian Parliament*; Narud and Strøm, "Norway: An Unconstrained Polity."

133. Knut Heidar, "Parliamentary Party Groups" and Torben K. Jensen "Party Cohesion," both in *Beyond Westminster and the Congress: The Nordic Experience*, ed. Peter Esaiasson and Knut Heidar (Columbus: Ohio State University Press, 2000), 204 and 232–235.

134. Strøm, Narud, and Valen, "A More Fragile Chain of Governance in Norway," 797.

135. Thomas Poguntke and Paul Webb, ed., *The Presidentialization of Politics: A Comparative Study of Modern Democracies* (Oxford: Oxford University Press, 2007).

136. Hilmar Rommetvedt, *The Rise of the Norwegian Parliament* (London: Frank Cass, 2003).

137. Strøm, Narud, and Valen, "A More Fragile Chain of Governance in Norway."

138. Narud and Strøm, "Norway: An Unconstrained Polity."

139. See Elin H. Allern and Nicholas Aylott, "Overcoming the Fear of Commitment? Pre-electoral Coalitions in Norway and Sweden," *Acta Politica* 44 (2009): 259–285. This development might of course have balanced the relationship again, but it remains to be seen whether majority coalitions are the only exception that proves the rule.

140. Tom Christensen and Per Lægreid, *Reformer og lederskap: Omstilling i den utøvende makt* (Oslo: Universitetsforlaget, 2002).

141. Rune J. Sørensen, "Et folkestyre i fremgang: Demokratisk kontroll med brannalarmer og autopiloter," *Nytt Norsk Tidsskrift* 22 (2005): 258–270.

142. This chapter benefited from comments by participants in a seminar at the Institute for Social Research in Oslo the autumn of 2008. I am also grateful for comments from those attending the workshop Voters, Parties and Political Institutions at the Norwegian Political Science Association's annual conference in

Hønefoss, April 7–9, 2009. Thanks are also due to Hanne Marthe Narud and Lars Svåsand for useful remarks. I accept full responsibility for the contents of this chapter.

CHAPTER 8, POLITICAL PARTIES AND DEMOCRACY: THE POLISH CASE

1. Samuel P. Huntington, *Trzecia fala demokratyzacji* [*The Third Wave Democratization in the Late Twentieth Century*] (Warszawa: Wydawnictwo Naukowe PWN, 1995).

2. Joachim Lelewel, *Wybór pism historycznych* [*Selected Historical Writings*] (Wrocław: Ossolineum, 1949), 271.

3. Adam Zamoyski, *The Polish Way: A Thousand-Year History of the Poles and Their Culture* (London: John Murray Publishers, 1987), 206–258.

4. These acts were the first electoral statutes passed by the parliament and senate of independent Poland of November 28, 1918, the Little Constitution (Mała Konstytucja) of February 20, 1919, the March Constitution (Konstytucja marcowa) of March 17, 1921, and the April Constitution (Konstytucja kwietniowa) of April 23, 1935. Of these four acts it was the electoral statute and the March Constitution that were of particular importance for the development of democracy.

5. *Encyklopedia Powszechna Gutenberga*, Vol. XIII (Encyklopedia Powszechna Gutenberga), 187.

6. *Encyklopedia Powszechna* PWN 1975, Vol. 3:736. Andrzej Garlicki, *Przewrót majowy* [*May Coup d'état*] (Warsaw: Czytelnik, 1987), 385–388.

7. Andrzej Burda, *Konstytucja marcowa. Dokumenty naszej tradycji. 1921* [*The March Constitution. Documents of Our Tradition. 1921*] (Lublin: Wydawnictwo Lubelskie, 1983), 59.

8. Andrzej Garlicki, *Od Brześcia do maja* [*From Brest to May*] (Warsaw: Czytelnik, 1986), 5.

9. The president had the right to issue decrees by law, to veto acts of parliament, and was also endowed with so-called prerogatives (e.g., the right to dissolve the Sejm and the senate ahead of time, nominate the prime minister, the supreme head, and the general inspector of the armed forces and to appoint one-third of all senators). Furthermore, he was not held accountable to the nation, but only before "God and History" (*Encyklopedia Powszechna Gutenberga*, Vol. XXI: 250; Tadeusz Łepkowski, ed., *Słownik historii Polski* [*Dictionary of the History of Poland*] [Warsaw: Wiedza Powszechna, 1969], 153.)

10. Andrzej Werblan, *Stalinizm w Polsce* [*Stalinism in Poland*] (Warszawa: Wydawnictwo FAKT, 1991); Paul Brooker, *Twentieth-Century Dictatorships. The Ideological One-Party States* (New York: New York University Press, 1995).

11. Konstytucja Polskiej Rzeczypospolitej Ludowej z 22 lipca 1952 [Constitution of the Polish People's Republic of 22nd July 1952] (Warszawa: Książka i Wiedza, 1983:8)

12. Carl J. Friedrich and Z. B. Brzeziński, *Totalitarian Dictatorship and Autocracy* (Cambridge: Harvard University Press, 1956), 3–13.

13. As noted in Juan Linz, "Totalitarian and Authoritarian Regimes," in *Handbook of Political Science* 3 (New York: Addison Wesley, 1975), chapters II and IV.

14. Andrzej Paczkowski, *Droga do 'mniejszego zła'. Strategia i taktyka obozu władzy—lipiec 1980-styczeń 1982* [*The Way to the 'Smaller Evil'. Strategy and Tactics*

of the Ruling Camp—from July 1980 to January 1982] (Kraków: Wydawnictwo Literackie, 2001); Feliks Prusak, ed., *Stan wojenny w Polsce. Refleksje prawno-polityczne* [*Martial Law in Poland. Legal and Political Reflections*] (Warsaw: Książka i Wiedza, 1982).

15. According to the Extraordinary Parliamentary Committee for the Inspection of the Ministry of Internal Affairs (MSW) Activities, established in autumn of 1989, of the 122 unexplained deaths of opposition activists, 88 were directly linked to the activities of MSW officials. According to estimates made by the Institute for National Remembrance (IPN) in 2006 in the first year of martial law 9,736 people were interned.

16. *Wielka Encyklopedia* PWN, Vol. 21, 2004: 559.

17. Andrej Graczow, *Gorbachev* (Warsaw: Wydawnictwo ISKRY, 2003), 151–188.

18. Walter D. Connor and P. Płoszajski, eds., *Escape from Socialism. The Polish Route* (Warsaw: IFiS Publishers, 1992).

19. Jerzy J. Wiatr, *Wybory parlamentrane 19 września 1993 r. Przyczyny i następstwa* [*Parliamentarian Election of September 1993. Causes and Consequences*] (Warsaw: Instytut Socjologii Uniwesytetu Warszawskiego, 1993); Jerzy J. Wiatr, *Krótki Sejm* [*Short Seym*] (Warsaw: Oficyna Wydawnicza BGW, 1993); Jerzy J. Wiatr, *Zmierzch systemu* [*Declining Days of the System*] (Warsaw: Fundacja Kelles Krauza, 1991); Edmund Wnuk-Lipiński, *Socjologia życia publicznego* [*Sociology of Public Life*] (Warsaw: Wydawnictwo Naukowe SCHOLAR, 2005).

20. Other important clauses: The system of government in Poland is "based on the separation of and balance between the legislative, executive and judicial powers" (Chapter I, Article 10(1)). The economic system is based on all forms of private ownership and freedom of economic activity (Chapter I, Article 20). The constitution guarantees equal rights to all churches and religious organizations and obligates the public authorities to "be impartial in matters of personal conviction, whether religious or philosophical," and to ensure "their freedom of expression in public life." By guaranteeing these collective entities and religious organizations common respect, autonomy, and independence, this basic act calls on them at the same time to cooperate "for the individual and the common good." The Constitution specifies that the relations between the Republic of Poland and the Roman Catholic Church "shall be determined by international treaty concluded with the Holy See, and by statute" (Chapter I, Article 25(1–5)). The freedoms, rights, and obligations of persons and citizens are specified in Chapter II of the Constitution. These stem from the "inherent and inalienable dignity of the person," which is also inviolable and for this reason "respect and protection thereof shall be the obligation of public authorities." This respect in turn is regarded as the "source of human freedom and rights," including equality (irrespective of sex, race, ethnic origin, and religious belief), freedom of speech, and communicating with others.

21. Kay Lawson, *The Human Polity. A Comparative Introduction to Political Science* (Boston: Houghton Mifflin, 1993), 586.

22. Peter Mair, *Party System Change. Approaches and Interpretation* (Oxford: Clarendon Press, 1998); Seymour M. Lipset and S. Rokkan, *Party Systems and Voter Alignments: Cross-National Perspectives* (New York: Free Press, 1967).

23. While acknowledging that in many cases the division between certain types of modern political parties and nongovernmental organizations (NGOs) is becoming vague, in this chapter I take it as a given that at least in the

foreseeable future, NGOs will not be an alternative for parties in the creation of democracy.

24. For this reason it was also the case that paramilitary organizations came into being, or even military-independence organizations; Andrzej Burda, *Konstytucja marcowa. Dokumenty naszej tradycji. 1921* [*The March Constitution. Documents of Our Tradition. 1921*] (Lublin: Wydawnictwo Lubelskie, 1983), 41.

25. Following internal divisions, 10 years later two parties emerged from the PSL: PSL-Lewica and PSL-"Piast." Two years later in the area of the former kingdom of Poland, PSL "Wyzwolenie." Its program presumed that in the future the revived Poland would be a democratic state, with nationalized basic natural resources, radical agricultural reforms, and, among other things, obligatory education to all.

26. In 1934, part of the SN became the politically radical Union of Young Nationalists (Związek Młodych Narodowców). Further division among the "young ones" shortly led to the emergence of the fascist-like National-Radical Camp (Obóz Narodowo-Radykalny [ONR]).

27. That is, decrees, the elections statute of 1918, the Little Constitution of 1919, followed by Article 108 of the March Constitution and acts relating to the Constitution.

28. Led by Wincenty Witos, a very important peasant statesman of those years.

29. Jerzy Tomaszewski, *Rzeczypospolita wielu narodów* [*The Republic of Many Nations*] (Warsaw: Czytelnik, 1985).

30. This was also brought about by the partition period when the church performed in public life some functions of the nonexisting state, maintained historical awareness, and retained the continuity of symbolic culture. In those years being Polish simply meant being Catholic.

31. Ryszard Bender, "Kościół katolicki w Polsce odrodzonej wobec problemów narodowych i społecznych 1918–1939" [Catholic Church Approaches to National and Social Problems of Re-born Poland, 1918–1939], in *Życie polityczne w Polsce 1918–1933* [*Political Life in Poland 1918–1939*], ed. J. Żarnowski (Kraków: Ossolineum, 1985), 335–341.

32. The Sejm of the third term of office (1928–1930) contained nine parties bearing their own name and having 281 mandates at their disposal. The situation was much the same in the Sejm of the fourth term of office (1930–1935). Although by this time the BBWR already held a majority, the Sejm was still represented by a center–left coalition of five parties and five other parties.

33. The new constitution came into force on April 23, 1935, and the new electoral regulations on July 8, 1935.

34. The right to participate in the electoral assemblies was also given to delegations of groups of citizens, providing that each of them held a list (certified by a notary) of at least 500 citizens supporting them.

35. According to the census of 1921, 33.1 percent of inhabitants in Poland above the age of 10 were illiterate; in 1931 this value was still high and stood at 23.1 percent. Mały Rocznik, *Statystyczny Rzeczypospolitej Polskiej* [*Small Statistical Yearbook of the Polish Republic*] (Warsaw: Główny Urząd Statystczny, 1939), 28–29.

36. Admittedly amended in 1947 by the so-called Little Constitution and acts referring to civic rights and duties, but still in keeping to some of the standards of democracy.

37. Jerzy J. Wiatr, *Socjologia polityki* [*Political Sociology*] (Warsaw: Wydaw-nictwo Naukowe SCHOLAR, 1999), 276.

38. These were the PAX Association (Stowarzyszenie PAX), already in exis-tence since the autumn of 1945, the Social Association of Polish Catholics (Spo-eczne Towarzystwo Polskich Katolików [ChSS]), which emerged following the political climate brought about by the "Polish October" of 1956, the Catholic In-telligentsia Club (Klub Inteligencji Katolickiej [KIK]), and the Polish Catholic-Social Union (Polski Związek Katolicko-Społeczny [PZKS]), registered as late as 1981.

39. PZPR, *Zjazdy, posiedzenia plenarne KC, władze naczelne* [*PUWP. Congresses, Central Committee Sessions, Members of CC*] (Warsaw: Centaralne Archiwum KC PZPR, 1983); Norbert Kołomejczyk, *Polska Zjednoczona Partia Robotnicza 1948–1986* [*The Polish United Workers' Party 1948–1986*] (Warsaw: Książka i Wiedza, 1988). Hieronim Kubiak, "Political Parties and NGOs: Competitors for Power or Two Faces of an Emerging Democracy?," in *Between Animosity and Util-ity. Political Parties and their Matrix*, ed. H. Kubiak and J. J. Wiatr (Warsaw: Wydawnictwo Naukowe Scholar, 2000), 47–66.

40. In existence since 1945; following the 1947 elections and the departure from Poland of Stanisław Mikołajczyk the leadership of the party was taken over by the PSL-left faction, in existence since 1946.

41. *Rocznik Statystyczny 1962* [Statistical Yearbook of 1962] (Warszawa: Główny Urząd Statystyczny, 1962: 27)

42. In 1947 it changed its name to the PAX Association and five years later attained the formal status of association.

43. Apart from having groupings in many cities, PAX also engaged in its own profitable enterprises and publishing activities.

44. The ChSS, much the same as PAX, engaged in economic and publishing activities. Immediately after this creation, the ChSS had three members in the Sejm.

45. Including Tadeusz Mazowiecki, the first noncommunist prime minister of Poland. The beginning of systemic changes symbolized by the 1989 year come from this social milieu.

46. Formally, this was a social movement concentrating political parties, trade unions, associations, and social and youth organizations. The front had regional, district, and urban branches, and its formal purpose was to represent all citizens of the Polish People's Republic.

47. In 1952–1989 (i.e., from the first to the ninth terms of office of the Sejm) the algorithm applied by PZPR gave about 55% of all mandates to the PZPR, 25.5% to the ZSL, 8.5% to the SD, and approximatly 10.5% to nonparty mem-bers. Hieronim Kubiak, "Formowanie się systemu partyjnego we współczesnej Polsce" ["Formation of the Political Party System in Modern Poland"], in *Oblicza społeczeństwa* [*Faces of Society*], ed. K. Gorlach and Z. Seręga (Kraków: Uniwersy-tet Jagielloński, 1996), 205.

48. *The Constitution of the Republic of Poland* (Warsaw: Sejm Publishing Office, 1997).

49. For example, the Democratic Left Alliance, which, starting from 1991, con-stituted an electoral coalition for eight years comprising the Socjaldemokracja Rzeczypospolitej Polskiej (SdPR), the Polish Republic's Social Democrats, which emerged following the dissolution of the PZPR, 7 other parties, 10 trade unions,

a handful of associations of veterans, and around 10 other associations and organizations (a uniform party with the same name emerged from this coalition as late as 1999). Kubiak, "Political Parties and NGOs," 53.

50. Frances Millard, "Poland," in *Political Parties of Eastern Europe, Russia and the Successor States*, ed. B. Szajkowski (Essex: Longman Information and Reference, 1994), 338.

51. Indicating the degree of deviation of actual distribution of gross domestic product from perfectly equal distribution, when 0 indicates absolute equality of distribution for all households, and 1, total concentration of the product in only one of them. As a comparison, in other countries the value of the Gini index in 2005 was: United States, 0.41, Germany, 0.28, Sweden and Belgium, 0.25. Marcin Mazurek, "O miarach nierówności w dochodach" ["About Measures of Income Inequality"] (2008), originally available at: http://www.nbportal.pl/pl/commonPages, no longer available.

52. It stems from the Human Development Index in 2005 that "the HDI for Poland is 0.870, which gives the country a rank of 37th out of 177 countries with data." The values of three variables constituting the index placed Poland among the analyzed countries as follows: 46 for life expectancy at birth, 38, education level (measured by adult literacy and enrollment at the primary, secondary, and tertiary level), and 48, gross domestic product per capita. *Human Development Report 2007–2008* (New York: UNDP), 133–153.

53. Janusz Czapiński and T. Panek, *Diagnoza społeczna 2007. Warunki i jakość życia Polaków* [*Social Diagosis 2007. Conditions and Quality of Life in Poland*] (Warsaw: Rada Monitoringu Społecznego, 2007); Małgorzata Głowacka-Grajper and E. Nowicka, eds., *Jak się dzielimy i co nas łączy?* [*How Are We Divided and What Unites Us?*] (Kraków: Zakład Wydawniczy NOMOS, 2007).

54. Peter M. Senge et al., eds., *The Fifth Discipline Fieldbook*, Polish edition (Warsaw: Wolters Kluwer Polska, 2008), 165–170.

55. Maria Jarosz, ed., *Poska, ale jaka?* [*Poland, but What Kind of Poland?*] (Warsaw: Oficyna Naukowa, 2005).

56. These parties were: Socjaldemokracja Polska (Social Democracy of Poland [SdPL]), Unia Pracy (Union of Labour [UP]), and Partia Demokratyczna—demokraci.pl (Democratic Party—democrats.pl [PD]). The coalition dissolved itself in the spring of 2008.

57. Mainly depending on the course of events that may or may not be favorable for the parent party.

58. Hieronim Kubiak, "Genius Loci and Voting Behaviour," *Polish Sociological Review* 4 (1998): 357–370; Jacek Raciborski, *Polskie wybory. Zachowania wyborcze społeczeństwa polskiego w latach 1989–1995* [*Polish Elections. Electoral Behavior of Polish Society in 1989–1995*] (Warsaw: Wydawnictwo Naukowe SCHOLAR, 1997); Antoni Dudek, *Pierwsze lata III Rzeczypospolitej 1989–1995* [*The First Years of the Third Republic, 1989–1995*] (Kraków: Wydawnictwo GEO, 1997), 184–185, 291; Mikołaj Cześniak, *Partycypacja wyborcza w Polsce. Perspektywa porównawcza* [*Electoral Participation in Poland. A Comparative Perspective*] (Warsaw: Wydawnictwo Naukowe SCHOLAR, 2007).

59. *PBS DGA*, in *Platforma silna PiSem* [*Law and Justice Rejection Reinforces the Civic Platform*] "Gazeta Wyborcza," *Wojciech Szacki* (July 24, 2008), 3.

60. Still incapable of finding its place under the new system or because of its age and low human capital it has no chance of attaining this; it inhabits rural

areas and small towns, regions that were once dominated by the State Agricultural Farms (PGR); it also occupies the south-east areas of Poland from which for many years people emigrated in search for a better life and to which few immigrated; it is dominated by the tradition of religious folk. It is younger, better educated, more mobile, and not afraid of unemployment; it inhabits the large cities and belongs to the "Church of choice." Irena Borowik and W. Zdaniewicz, eds., *Od kościoła ludu do kościoła wyboru* [*From the Church of People to the Church of Choice*] (Kraków: Zakład Wydawniczy "NOMOS," 1996).

61. Florian Znaniecki, *Socjologia wychowania, tom I* [*Sociology of Education,* vol. I] (Poznań: Komisja Pedagogiczna MWRiOP, 1928), 235.

62. *Informator o organizacjach pozarządowych w Polsce* [*Guidebook on Nongovernmental Organizations in Poland*] VII–XIX (Warszawa: Fundusz Współpracy, 1995).

63. Jakub Wygnański, ed., *Trzeci sektor dla zaawansowanych. Współczesne teorie trzeciego sektora. Wybór tekstów* [*The Third Sector for Advanced. Modern Theories of the Third Sector. Collection of Essays*] (Warsaw: Stowarzyszenie Klon/Jawor, 2006).

64. Ewa Siedlecka, "Gdzie społeczeństwo obywatelskie?" ["Where Is the Civic Society?"] *Gazeta Wyborcza* (August 4, 2008), 6.

65. Alexander Zinoviev, *Homo Sovieticus* (London: Polonia Book Found, 1984); Józef Tischner, *Etyka solidarności oraz Homo sovieticus* [*Solidarity Ethics and Homo Sovieticus*] (Kraków: Znak, 1992).

66. Piotr Sztompka, "The Theory of Social Becoming: An Outline of the Concept," *Polish Sociological Bulletin* 4 (1991): 271.

67. Michael Kennedy, "Transformation of Normative Foundations and Empirical Sociology: Class, Stratification, and Democracy in Poland," in *Escape from Socialism. The Polish Route*, ed. W. D. Connor and P. Płoszajski (Warsaw: IFiS Publishers, 1992), 301–302.

68. Mario Vargas Llosa, "Run Away from the Captivity of Race, Nation, Fanaticism," *Gazeta Wyborcza* (December 28–29, 1996), 13.

69. Jean Baechler, *Democracy: An Analytical Survey* (Paris: UNESCO Publishing, 1995), 65.

70. Hieronim Kubiak, "Democracy and the Individual Will," in *Democracy: Its Principles and Achievement*, ed. C. Bassiouni (Geneva: Inter-Parliamentary Union, 1998), 57.

CHAPTER 9, THE RELATIONSHIP BETWEEN PARTIES AND DEMOCRACY IN HUNGARY

1. On the political history of Hungary see Attila Ágh, *Politics of Central Europe* (London: Sage, 1998); Attila Ágh, *Emerging Democracies in East Central Europe and the Balkans* (Cheltenham: Edward Elgar, 1998). The founding congress of MSZP has been described by Patrick O'Neil, *Revolution from Within: The Hungarian Socialist Workers' Party and the Collapse of Communism* (Cheltenham: Edward Elgar, 1998). There has been a danger of overgeneralizing about the former ruling parties and or "postcommunist" countries. See J. H. Wilhelem, "The Failure of the American Sovietological Profession," *Europe-Asia Studies* 55 (2003), 59–74. The emergence of MSZP is indeed an exceptional case. See Attila Ágh, "Social Democratic Parties in East-Central Europe: The Party and Civil Society

Relationship," in *Social Democracy in Europe*, ed. Pascal Delwit (Brussels: Université Libre de Bruxelles, 2005), see its standard support in Table 9.3.

2. There is a huge literature in Hungary on parties. This chapter does not aim at reviewing this literature, and I refer here only to some relevant books and papers on the Hungarian parties and party systems. See Róbert Angelusz and Róbert Tardos, eds., *Törések, hálók, hidak: Választói magatartás és politikai tagozódás Magyarországon* [*Cleavages, Nets, Bridges: Voter Behavior and Political Structure in Hungary*] (Budapest: Hungarian Center for Democracy Studies Foundation, 2005); Zsolt Enyedi, "The Role of Agency in Cleavage Formation," *European Journal of Political Research* 44 (2005): 697–720; Zsolt Enyedi, "A befagyott felszín és ami alatta van. A 2006-os választás és a magyar pártrendszer" ["The Frozen Surface and What Lies Behind It. The 2006 Elections and the Hungarian Party System"], in *Parlamenti választás 2006* [*Parliamentary elections in 2006*], ed. Gergely Karácsony (Budapest: Hungarian Center for Democracy Studies Foundation, 2006), 205–228; Gergely Karácsony, "A történelem fogságában. Generciók, életutak és politikai preferenciák Magyarországon" ["Captured by the History: Generations, Ways of Life and Political Preferences in Hungary"], in *Törések, hálók, hidak*, ed. Angelusz and Tardos; Herbert Kitschelt et al., *Post-Communist Party Systems* (Cambridge: Cambridge University Press, 1999), 161–206; Attila Ágh and Judit Kis-Varga, eds., *New Perspectives for the EU Team Presidencies: New Members, New Candidates and New Neighbours* (Budapest: Together for Europe Research Center at the Hungarian Academy of Sciences, 2008); Attila Horváth, "Stabilization and Concentration in the Party Systems of the Visegrád Countries," in *New Perspectives for the EU Team Presidencies*, ed. Ágh and Kis-Varga; Renata Uitz, "Hungary," in *Populist politics and Liberal Democracy in Central and Eastern Europe*, ed. Grigorij Meseznikov, Olga Gyárfásová, and Daniel Smilov (Bratislava: Institute for Public Affairs, 2008), 251–302. I focus here on the specificity of the Hungarian parties and the Hungarian party system, although it shares many common features with the East-Central European (ECE) countries (Poland, Czech Republic, Slovakia, and Slovenia).

3. I have recently analyzed the ECE parties and party systems in detail and I have pointed out their common features in terms of anticipative and adaptive Europeanization in Attila Ágh "Democratization and Europeanization of the East-Central European countries," in *New Perspectives for the EU Team Presidencies*, ed. Ágh and Kis-Varga, 11–74. On the ECE parties see Jack Bielesiak, "Party Competition in Emerging Democracies: Representation and Effectiveness in Post-communism and Beyond," *Democratization* 12 (2005): 331–356; Ingrid van Biezen, *Political Parties in New Democracies* (Houndmills: Palgrave Macmillan, 2003); Jack Bielesiak, "On the Theory and Practice of Party Formation and Adaptation in New Democracies," *European Journal of Political Research* 44 (2005): 147–174; András Bozóki and John Ishiyama, eds., *The Communist Successor Parties of Central and Eastern Europe* (New York: M. E. Sharpe, 2002); John Ishiyama and Andras Bozóki, "Adaptation and Change: Characterizing the Survival Strategies of the Communist Successor Parties," *Journal of Communist Studies and Transition Politics* 17 (2001), 32–51; Wolfgang Ismayr, ed., *Die politischen Systeme Osteuropas* (Wiesbaden: VS Verlag für Sozialwissenschaften, 2006); Kitschelt et al., *Post-Communist Party Systems*; Petr Kopecky and Maria Spirova, "Parliamentary Opposition in New Democracies," *Journal of Legislative Studies* 14 (2008),

133–159; Tomas Kostelecky, *Political Parties after Communism: Developments in East-Central Europe* (Baltimore: Johns Hopkins University Press, 2002); Paul Lewis, *Political Parties in Post-Communist Eastern Europe* (London: Routledge, 2000); Paul Lewis, ed., *Party Development and Democratic Change in Post-Communist Europe: The First Decade* (London: Frank Cass, 2001); Paul Lewis and Zdenka Mansfeldová, eds., *The European Union and Party Politics in Central and Eastern Europe* (New York: Palgrave Macmillan, 2006); O'Neil, *Revolution from Within*; Thomas Poguntke et al., "The Europeanization of National Party Organizations: A Conceptual Analysis," *European Journal of Political Research* 46 (2007), 741–743; Stephen White, Judy Batt, and Paul Lewis, eds., *Developments in Central and East European Politics* 4 (New York: Palgrave Macmillan, 2007). Democratization as a domestic process and Europeanization as a structural adaptation have been analyzed by Aurel Croissant and Wolfgang Merkel, *Democratization* 11 (2004) and Geoffrey Pridham, "The EU's Political Conditionality and Post-Accession Tendencies," *Journal of Common Market Studies* 46 (2008), 1–23, respectively.

4. On the connections between the start of the accession negotiations and early consolidation see Geoffrey Pridham and Attila Ágh, eds., *Democratic Transition and Consolidation in East-Central Europe* (Manchester: Manchester University Press, 2001).

5. The electoral participation in the June 2004 European Parliament election was 28 percent in the new member states compared to 47 percent in the old member states, namely, 27.9, 21.2, 38.5, and 20.0 in the Czech Republic, Poland, Hungary, and Slovakia, respectively. It is interesting to note in this respect that the ECE states have developed quite different traditions of electoral participation. It has been the lowest in Poland, usually around 45 to 50 percent and the highest in Hungary, around 65 to 70 percent. On the low electoral participation combined with other forms of protest see Patrick Bernhagen and Michael Marsh, "Voting and Protesting: Explaining Citizen Participation in Old and New European Democracies," *Democratization* 14 (2007): 44–72.

6. MSZP has a tradition of participatory democracy, since it was organized in October 1989 under popular pressure. The party statute has a loose party democracy as a permanently "discussing" and "congressing" party. For instance, MSZP organized 10 party congresses in the 2002–2006 parliamentary cycle. In August 2004, there was a "popular uprising" against the MSZP party leadership and its official candidate for the post of prime minister was voted down. An "opposition candidate" emerged with wide popular support and received more than two-thirds of the vote in an extraordinary party congress. This opposition candidate, Ferenc Gyurcsány, became the prime minister in September 2004. The term cartel party was introduced by Richard Katz and Peter Mair, "Changing Models of Party Organization and Party Democracy: The Emergence of the Cartel Party," *Party Politics* 1 (1995), 5–28. On the weakness of organizational linkages of parties with society see Karácsony, "A történelem fogságában."

7. The relationship between the declining industrial society and the emerging populism has been described by Alexandra Cole, "Old Right or New Right? The Ideological Positioning of Parties of the Far Right," *European Journal of Political Research* 44 (2005): 203–230, that leads to an ambiguity in the parties' situation Hans Becker and René Cuperus, "The Party Paradox: Political Parties between Irrelevance and Omnipotence," 2004, available at: www.fes.de/europolity

8. These tendencies have recently been analyzed in all ECE countries by Horváth, "Party Systems of the Visegrád Countries," so I have taken the following data from his paper that have summarized the Hungarian research efforts in this respect.

9. Fidesz has changed its name several times accordingly but kept the "Fidesz" brand name. Fidesz as an acronym meant originally "Alliance of Young Democrats" but later Civic Party was added. Since 2003 its full name is Fidesz-Civic Alliance.

10. Many Hungarian analysts have concluded that there has been some kind of "freezing" in the Hungarian party system, see the recent overview of literature in Horváth, "Party Systems of the Visegrád Countries," and Uitz, "Hungary." According to the Eurobarometer 68 (2007), the trust in the Hungarian parties was just 8 percent. The Hungarian party system is strong and weak, stable and fragile, at the same time.

11. According to Freedom House Report (2008) on Hungary: "The main political parties are the MSZP and the conservative Fidesz, which has moved in an increasingly nationalist direction . . . the opposition leader, Fidesz's Viktor Orban, stressed "populist themes." Available at: www.freedomhouse.org. See also Jeanette Goehring, ed., *Nations in Transit 2007* (New York: Freedom House), 773.

12. On the decisive impact of the Western values on the Hungarian society in empirical analyses see Fritz Plasser, Peter Ulram, and Harald Waldrauch, *Democratic Consolidation in East-Central Europe* (Basingstoke: Macmillan, 1998) and Peter Ulram and Fritz Plasser, "Mainly Sunny with Scattered Clouds: Political Culture in East-Central Europe," in *Democratic Transition and Consolidation in East-Central Europe*, ed. Pridham and Ágh, 115–137. This has also been confirmed by the series of Eurobarometer surveys. About transnational elite socialization, see Geoffrey Pridham, *Designing Democracy: EU Enlargement and Regime Change in Post-Communist Europe* (New York: Palgrave Macmillan, 2005).

13. The dominant view on the limited impact was represented by Simon Hix, Amie Kreppel, and Abdul Noury, "The Party System in the European Parliament: Collusive or Competitive?" *Journal of Common Market Studies* 1 (2003), 309–332, and Robert Ladrech "National Political Parties and European Governance" *West European Politics* 30 (2007), 945–960, who pointed out later that the impact of the EU was felt in many fields.

14. There have been many smaller parties in Hungary beyond the five parliamentary parties, for example, for the Nation-centric Left there is a small Hungarian Communist Party (earlier Workers Party). SZDSZ is basically left-liberal but strongly pro-European, while FKGP and KDNP as intraparty units in Fidesz are certainly markedly nation-centric right, the main line of Fidesz. But some parts of Fidesz are pro-European or at least they have played this role in the controversial mixture of the Fidesz EU policies. The box of nation-centric right is very crowded with many smaller organizations, the most important one being Jobbik ("Better"—it also refers to the "Right") that runs the Magyar Gárda (Hungarian Guard) the neo-Nazi paramilitary organization. The only current Europeanized right party is MDF, and is the smallest party in the parliament in a bitter fight with Fidesz.

15. I do not accept the view that "European integration did not become a primary point of reference for party differentiation" (Heather Grabbe, *The EU's Transformative Power: Europeanization through Conditionality in Central and Eastern Europe* [New York: Palgrave Macmillan, 2006], 109), since behind the national consensus on seeking EU membership there have been two opposing EU models. The parties on the right in ECE have followed the nation-centric EU model since 1998, and the parties on the left advocated a much more "federalist" EU model. Certainly, in the Hungarian case the Hungarian Socialist Party has played the role of a reform party and Fidesz the role of an antireform party.

16. See the analysis of Uitz, "Hungary," 39.

17. See Ivan Berend, "Social Shock in Transforming Central and Eastern Europe," *Communist and Post-Communist Studies* 40 (2007): 269–280.

18. The same happened after the 2006 elections. As Renata Uitz notes, the parliamentary elections followed an unusually divisive electoral campaign with thus-far unprecedented political mobilization facilitated by Fidesz. Following its defeat in the most acrimonious parliamentary elections of 2006, Fidesz retained all opportunities to engage in politics outside the constitutional framework. As the senior opposition party it uses prominent occasions to refuse to participate in institutionalized political procedures (e.g., parliamentary work) and challenges government actions and policies by reaching directly to the people through symbolic acts and referendum initiatives (Uitz, "Hungary," 40).

19. On the recent crisis: "Fidesz tried to oust the Gyurcsány government by mobilizing a protest movement. . . . Orbán's aggressive mobilization campaigns encourage right-wing extremists and hooligans to stir up violent protests against the government in Budapest. . . . However, FIDESZ leader Orbán repeatedly demonstrated his disrespect for democratic institutions and conventions by resorting to extraparliamentary strategies and means of opposition." Bertelsmann Stiftung, ed., *Bertelsmann Transformation Index 2007* (Gütersloh: Verlag Bertelsmann Stiftung, 2008), 8, available at: www.bertelsmann-stiftung.de

20. Renata Uitz has recently given a general evaluation of the Fidesz activity as follows: The party that has consistently relied on populist rhetoric since its successes as a conservative catchall party is Fidesz. Becoming increasingly leader centered and clearly capitalizing on the charisma of its leader, Viktor Orbán, Fidesz succeeded in polarizing the political sphere in an "us against them" fashion, constantly questioning the legitimacy of the transition elites and constitutional arrangements resulting from the transition compromises (Uitz, "Hungary," 40).

21. The ratings of politicians in the public opinion surveys have radically declined in the past two to three years from the level of the 70 percent support for the most liked politicians to the level of 40 percent for the best liked. On the impact of the EU entry on the Hungarian party system see Attila Ágh, "East-Central Europe: Parties in Crisis and the External and Internal Europeanization of the Party System," in *Globalising Democracy: Party Politics in Emerging Democracies*, ed. Peter Burnell (London: Routledge, 2006), 88–103 and on the Hungarian pessimism see Eurobarometer 69 (2008).

22. About the political purges in the Hungarian public administration, see Jan-Hinrik Meyer-Sahling, "The Changing Colours of the Post-Communist State: The Politicization of the Senior Civil Service in Hungary," *European Journal of Political Research* 47 (2008), 1–33.

CHAPTER 10, THE CZECH PARTY SYSTEM AND DEMOCRACY: A QUEST FOR STABILITY AND FUNCTIONALITY

1. See Arend Lijphart, ed., *Parliamentary versus Presidential Government* (Oxford: Oxford University Press, 1992).

2. See Arend Lijphart, *Patterns of Democracy* (New Haven, Conn.: Yale University Press, 1999); Miroslav Novák, "Démocratie(s) et efficience(s). Y a-t-il un choix constitutionnel supérieur à tous les autres?," *Revue internationale de politique comparée* 3 (1996), 689–712.

3. Giovanni Sartori and Giacomo Sani believe that the main variable (not just for a party system) is polarization—the ideological distance between the relevant parties. See Sani and Sartori, "Polarization, Fragmentation and Competition in Western Democracies," in *Western European Party Systems: Continuity and Change*, ed. Hans Daalder and Peter Mair (Beverly Hills, Calif.: Sage, 1982), 307–340.

4. On the emergence of the Czech party system I have written inter alia an English chapter in a collection of essays (Miroslav Novák, "The Czech Party System," in *Czech Republic—The First Elections in the New Republic, 1992–1996, Analyses, Documents and Data, Czech Republic—1992 and 1996*, ed. Zdenka Mansfeldová [Berlin: Edition Sigma, 2003, 29–57]) and a book in French, Miroslav Novák, *Une transition démocratique exemplaire? L'émergence d'un système de partis dans les pays tchèques* (Prague: Editions du CEFRES, 1997). The latter publication represents a continuation of my first book in French (Miroslav Novák, *Du Printemps de Prague au Printemps de Moscou. Les formes de l'opposition en Union soviétique et en Tchécoslovaquie de janvier 1968 à janvier 1990* (Genève: Georg, 1990). I compare the genesis of the Czech party system with the Polish and Hungarian; also in French, Miroslav Novák, "Les systèmes de partis en République tchèque, en Pologne et en Hongrie," in *Partis politiques et démocratie en Europe centrale et orientale*, ed. Jean-Michel De Waele (Bruxelles: Editions universitaires de Bruxelles, 2002); Miroslav Novák, "Les systèmes de partis en Europe du Centre-Est entre stabilisation et désintégration: République tchèque, Pologne et Hongrie," *Revue d'études politiques et constitutionnelles est-européennes* 3 (2008). Central European party systems (including Czech) are treated particularly in the work of the Belgian political scientist Jean-Michel De Waele, *L'émergence des partis politiques en Europe centrale* (Bruxelles: Editions universitaires de Bruxelles, 1999); Jean-Michel De Waele. "Consolidation démocratique, partis et clivages en Europe centrale et orientale," in *Partis politiques et démocratie en Europe centrale et orientale*, ed. De Waele.

5. See Scott Mainwaring and Timothy Scully, *Building Democratic Institutions: Party Systems in Latin America* (Stanford, Calif.: Stanford University Press, 1995) and Scott Mainwaring, "Party Systems in the Third Wave," *Journal of Democracy* 9 (1998), 67–81.

6. Angelo Panebianco, *Political Parties: Organization and Power* (Cambridge: Cambridge University Press, 1988).

7. Novák, "Les systèmes de partis en Europe du Centre-Est entre stabilisation et désintégration."

8. In this section I briefly sum up the results of my earlier publications. See Miroslav Novák, "La différenciation politique du Forum civique en Tchécoslovaquie," in *Die Schweiz und das demokratische Erwachen Osteuropas/La Suisse face à la renaissance démocratique en Europe de l'Est*, ed. Rolland Ruffieux (Schloss

Lenzburg: Schriftenreihe des Forum Helveticum, 42–57), and Novák, *Une transition démocratique exemplaire? L'émergence d'un système de partis dans les pays tchèques.*

9. Among others, 8 federal ministers and 10 ministers of the Czech government, including its prime minister, Petr Pithart, took part.

10. In my book (Novák, *Une transition démocratique exemplaire? L'émergence d'un système de partis dans les pays tchèques*), I tried to describe it on the basis of a systematic monitoring of the announcements of its representatives in their party daily *Lidová demokracie.*

11. Wilhelm Röpke, one of the liberal economists and philosophers who most inspired the postwar "economic miracle," made use of the term "the third way." (See namely Wilhelm Röpke, *Die Gesellschaftskrisis der Gegenwart* (Erlenbach-Zürich: Eugen Rentsch Verlag, 1943).

12. See Miroslav Novák, "Transition to Democracy—the Czech Way: The Czech Republic in Comparative Perspective of Political Transition of the former Communist Countries of Central Europe," in *Political Changes in the Czech Republic and Taiwan: Comparison,* ed. Bořivoj Hnízdo (Prague: Institute of Political Science, Faculty of Social Sciences, Charles University, 2002, 3–14, first printing December 2001). On the transition of Central and East European countries see Klaus von Beyme "Osteuropaforschung nach dem Systemwechsel. Der Paradigmawandel der 'Transitologie'," *Osteuropa* 49 (1999) and Juan J. Linz and Alfred C. Stepan, *Problems of Democratic Transition and Consolidation* (Baltimore: Johns Hopkins University Press, 1996).

13. Jerzy J. Wiatr, *Four Essays on East European Democratic Transformation* (Warsaw: Scholar Agency, 1992), 47–48. These distinctions resemble those made by Guy Hermet, "La démocratie à l'amiable: de l'Espagne à la Pologne," *Commentaire* 13 (1990), 279–286 (Hermet speaks of "transition cogérée" and "transition octroyée"); and Samuel P. Huntington, *The Third Wave: Democratization in the Late Twentieth Century* (Norman: University of Oklahoma Press, 1991) (for Huntington, the terms are transplacement and transformation).

14. Some Western political scientists who are not very familiar with the conditions in Central and Eastern European countries, such as Philippe C. Schmitter (Terry Lynn Karl and Philippe C Schmitter, "Modes of Transition in Latin America, Southern and Eastern Europe", *International Social Science Journal* 128, 1991) or Samuel P. Huntington (Huntington, *The Third Wave*), have been misled by the similarity of the external form of the Roundtables in Poland and Czechoslovakia, and so classified the two countries in the same category of transition to democracy. Those political scientists who have a better knowledge of Central European countries (e.g., Jean-Michel De Waele, Jacques Rupnik /*L' Autre Europe—Crise et fin du communisme,* Paris: Odile Jacob, 1990 or Jerzy Wiatr), have avoided this mistake.

15. Communists came in second in the first and second free legislative elections under the Czecho-Slovak Federation (1990, 1992) and third in the elections to the Chamber of Deputies of the new Czech state in 1996, 1998, 2002, and 2006.

16. From this point of view the crucial year was 1993, when the communist congress led to the division of communists into three separate organizations: a dogmatic core (KSČM) and two small reformist groups (SDL and Left Bloc) that

had no real chance of reaching the 5 percent threshold necessary to enter parliament. The small postcommunist parties disappeared from political life (some of their supporters joined the ČSSD). Attempts to democratize the KSČM disappeared from its agenda for the foreseeable future.

17. Daniel-Louis Seiler, *Le cas des partis politiques dans les nouvelles démocraties de l'Est européen* (Lausanne: Université de Lausanne, 1991); Jean Charlot and Monique Charlot, "Les groupes politiques dans leur environnement," in *Traité de science politique* 3, ed. Madeleine Grawitz and Jean Leca (Paris: Presses universitaires de France, 1985), 449.

18. On the relevance of the division of the political scene into left and right even today, see the important book, Norberto Bobbio, *Left and Right* (Cambridge: Polity Press, 1996).

19. On the Czech level, there were regionalists demanding autonomy for Moravia. On the federal level there were Slovak separatists (SNS), and in Slovakia itself there were Hungarian minority parties. On the other hand, we can say that on the federal level the dispute between the Czech centralists (particularly in the ODA and the ODS) and Slovak supporters of a confederation (particularly in the Movement for a Democratic Slovakia [HZDS]) was more important.

20. Miroslav Novák, "La réforme économique dans la recomposition des forces politiques en Tchécoslovaquie," *Cahiers du CEFRES* 3 (1994), 111–140.

21. Szonja Szelényi et al., "Interests and Symbols in Post-Communist Political Culture: The Case of Hungary," *American Sociological Review* 61 (1996), 466–477.

22. Petr Matějů and Blanka Řeháková, "Obrat doleva nebo proměna vzorců volebního chování sociálních tříd?," *Sociální trendy* 2 (1997): 15. The later political development in the former GDR, of course, differed from that in the Czech and Slovak Federal Republic, since the GDR was integrated into a reunified Germany.

23. See Klára Vlachová and Petr Matějů, "Krystalizace politických postojů a politického spektra v České republice," *Sociologický časopis* 34 (1998): 145–170.

24. Ibid. According to the most recent surveys on the left–right opinion line (based on attitudes and values), there has been a visible shift from the left to the center since 1996, and as far as subjective self-placement on the left–right scale is concerned, between 1998 and 1999 for the first time a shift from the right to the center was observed.

25. Ibid.

26. Sani and Sartori, "Polarization, Fragmentation and Competition in Western Democracies."

27. The term "hegemonic party" is employed in the sense introduced by G. Sartori. See Giovanni Sartori, "The Typology of Party System: Proposals for Improvement," in *Mass Politics: Studies in Political Sociology*, ed. Erik Allardt and Stein Rokkan (New York: Free Press), 322–352; Giovanni Sartori, *Parties and Party Systems. A Framework for Analysis* (New York: Cambridge University Press) following Jerzy J. Wiatr, "One Party-System: The Concept and Issue for Comparative Studies," in *Cleavages, Ideologies, and Party Systems*, ed. Erik Allardt (Helsinki: Academic Bookstore), 21–55.

28. Lukáš Linek and Štěpán Pecháček, "K důvodům nízkého počtu členů českých politických stran," in *Participace a zájmové organizace v České republice*, ed. Zdenka Mansfeldová and Aleš Kroupa (Praha: Slon, 2005), 61.

29. At its national conference at the beginning of 2002, the KDU-ČSL branded the ODA plan for repayment of its debt as untrustworthy, with the result that of the original Coalition of Four, only the "coalition" of the KDU-ČSL and US-DEU subsequently remained, and ran on a joint ticket in the elections to the Chamber of Deputies in 2002.

30. The right-wing ODS represented most of the former supporters of OF, and its chairman, Václav Klaus, had actually been elected chairman of OF in 1990. Conversely, the OH, whose members and sympathizers had occupied a great majority of the decision-making posts in the first legislative term (1990–1992) and consisted for the most part of supporters of the moderate left (although they most often called themselves liberals, as did the subsequent chairman of the Social Democratic Party, Miloš Zeman), failed to obtain seats in the second free parliamentary elections in 1992. Understandably, during the term 1990–1992, major shifts took place in legislative bodies (the two chambers of the Federal Parliament and the single chamber of the Czech National Council), particularly among the deputies originally elected on the ticket of the victorious OF.

31. Karel Vodička, "Koaliční ujednání: rozdělíme stát! Volby '92 a jejich důsledky pro československou státnost," in *Rozloučení s Československem*, ed. Reidiger Kipke and Karel Vodička (Prague: Český spisovatel, 1993), 89.

32. The Czech National Council, which proclaimed itself the Chamber of Deputies of the new state, while both federal chambers ceased to exist after the dissolution of the Czecho-Slovak Federation. The second chamber of the new state, the Senate, with considerably fewer powers than the Chamber of Deputies, remained vacant during the whole legislative term. The first elections to the Senate did not take place until the autumn of 1996, several months after the subsequent elections to the Chamber of Deputies.

33. To measure the size of parties when we are considering their parliamentary rather than electoral power, it is naturally better to use the percentage of parliamentary seats rather than the percentage of votes.

34. Georges Lavau, "Partis et systèmes politiques: interactions et fonctions," in *Canadian Journal of Political Science/Revue canadienne de science politique* 2 (1969), 18–44.

35. Jean Charlot, *Les Partis Politiques* (Paris: A. Colin, 1971), 218, Otto Kirchheimer, The Transformation of the Western European Party Systems, in *Political Parties and Political Development*, ed. Joseph La Palombara and Myron Weiner (Princeton: Princeton University Press, 1966).

36. Maurice Duverger, *Les Partis Politiques* (Paris: A. Colin, 10th. ed. 1981, 1st. ed. 1951).

37. Klaus was reelected president of the Czech Republic in 2008.

38. Not to be confused with the earlier pseudo-coalition of the same name. KSČM leaders actually criticized the Left Bloc for illegitimately using the label.

39. For web-pages of this research agency see http://www.scac.cz/).

40. Gordon Smith, "In Search of Small Parties: Problems of Definition, Classification and Significance," in *Small Parties in Western Europe. Comparative and National Perspectives*, ed. Ferdinand Müller-Rommel and Geoffrey Pridham (London: Sage, 1991).

41. At the end of 1997, the party underwent a difficult inner crisis brought on by various financial scandals. Most of the party's leaders deserted it. It virtually disintegrated in 1998. It did not participate in the 1998 parliamentary election

and it has survived only in the Senate. As I mentioned above, its involvement in the Coalition of Four did not last long.

42. Duverger, *Les Partis Politiques*; Richard S. Katz and Peter Mair, "Changing Models of Party Organization and Party Democracy: The Emergency of the Cartel Party," *Party Politics* 1 (1995), 5–28. In 1998, this place was occupied more or less by the new party, Freedom Union, formed at the beginning of that year as a result of a crisis in the ODS (most of its founders were former ministers or deputies of the ODS, led by the former interior minister Jan Ruml, together with some people not previously engaged in political life).

43. Duverger, *Les Partis Politiques*, 394.

44. Mainwaring and Scully, *Building Democratic Institutions*.

45. Sartori, *Parties and Party Systems*.

46. Miroslav Novák, "Malá politologická úvaha o vládní stabilitě," in *Parlamentní zpravodaj* 2 (1996): 296–297.

47. By this I do not mean to say that we should abolish the 5 percent threshold, a move considered by the Social Democratic Prime Minister Vladimír Špidla (2002–2004). That would be like trying to douse a fire with gasoline.

48. In between the KDS ceased to exist by merging with the ODS.

49. Novák, "Malá politologická úvaha o vládní stabilitě."

50. In January 2000, the ČSSD and the ODS agreed on the following compromise: They suggested an increase in the number of constituencies from 8 to 35 and a change in the method of calculating mandates from that of Hagenbach-Bischoff quota to the modified D'Hondt divisor (where the first divisor is 1.42 instead of 1.0, used in the standard D'Hondt divisor).

51. Miroslav Novák, "Types of Government and Their Formation in the Czech Republic in Comparative Perspective," in *Electoral Laws and Party Systems: The Czech Experience*, ed. Miroslav Novák and Tomáš Lebeda with Rein Taagepera (Dobrá Voda: Aleš Čeněk, 2005), 9–43 and Miroslav Novák, "The Relevance of Small Parties: From a General Framework to the Czech 'Opposition Agreement'," *Czech Sociological Review* 36 (2000), 27–47.

52. For their results and corresponding indices see Novák and Lebeda with Taagepera, *Electoral Laws and Party Systems*.

53. Lukáš Linek and Ladislav Mrklas, *Volby do Poslanecké sněmovny 2002* (Prague: Sociologický ústav AV ČR, 2003), 240.

54. This is, however, a controversial question because it is not clear whether we should count the KDU-ČSL and US-DEU coalition as a single entity. I am inclined to think that we are dealing with two formations, not one. If we considered the coalition as two subjects, a slight increase in the index of the effective number of parliamentary parties would result (from 3.71 for 1998 to 3.81 in 2002).

55. In the 2002 elections to the Chamber of Deputies, 12.53 percent of votes were lost, while in 1998 the figure was only 11.32 percent and in 1996 11.16 percent. In the 2006 elections, the number dropped to 5.97 percent.

56. See my postscript to the Czech translation of Giovanni Sartori, *Comparative Constitutional Engineering* (London: Macmillan, 1994). Czech translation: Giovanni Sartori, *Srovnávací ústavní inženýrství* (Prague: Sociologické nakl. SLON, 2001), 212–214.

57. We can in any case ask whether it would not be useful to see these two types of party system (polarized and moderate pluralism) as *ideal types* in the

Weberian sense to which concrete party systems more or less approximate but do not necessarily fully embody. The problem of the Czech Republic, however, is in my view different. Unlike many Western European democracies, where there has usually been a process of increasing party fragmentation in recent decades, a shift toward extreme multipartyism (which is unpleasant, but in no way dramatic), the Czech party scene is no longer so fragmented and is moving away from polarized pluralism. Strong polarization is unfortunately more dangerous for the smooth functioning of democracy than is high fragmentation.

58. Herbert Kitschelt defines a structured party system as one in which the structuring of the party system by program predominates over relationships to a charismatic leader and clientele networks. Herbert Kitchelt, "Party Systems in East Central Europe: Consolidation or Fluidity," paper presented at the American Political Science Association annual meeting, Durham, N.C., March 24–27, 1994. Angelo Panebianco, *Political Parties*, sees the institutionalization of parties in terms of organizational consolidation and professionalization. We reach a less unambiguous conclusion if we use the definition of institutionalization presented by Scott Mainwaring (see Mainwaring and Scully, *Building Democratic Institutions*, and Mainwaring, "Party Systems in the Third Wave"). According to his criteria, the Czech party system would be institutionalized only in the sense that the parties here are organizationally fully developed and have social bases; but on the other hand, models of interaction between the parties have not yet been established, and elections and parties are far from universally regarded as legitimate political institutions (seen in various attempts to create "nonpolitical politics").

59. Gordon Smith, *Politics in Western Europe* (Aldershot: Gower, 1983), 81–83.

60. Jan-Erik Lane and Svante O. Ersson, *European Politics: An Introduction* (London: Sage, 1996), 123.

61. Jean Blondel, "Party Systems and Pattern of Government in Western Democracies," in *Canadian Journal of Political Science/Revue canadienne de science politique* 1 (1968), 180–203.

62. This is pointed out by Karl Popper, who argues that the day of elections is not the day that legitimizes a new government, but the day on which the previous government is judged, the day on which the government must "give an account" of its activities. The negative power to unseat an existing government is much more important than the positive power to install a government or its chairman, which by comparison is only an "unimportant correlative." Karl R. Popper, "Popper on Democracy: The Open Society and Its Enemies Revisited," *The Economist* (April 23, 1998). Democratic regimes are not "governments of the people" but "courts of the people." From this position Popper criticized the German system of two-and-a-half parties, in which a small third party had disproportionate weight. See Popper, "Popper on Democracy" and Miroslav Novák, "Popper contre Schumpeter: une autre théorie non classique de la démocratie," in *Mélanges en l'honneur de Slobodan Milacic. Démocratie et liberté: tension, dialogue, confrontation*, ed. Philippe Claret et al. (Bruxelles: Bruylant, 2007), 915–927.

63. As I remarked in an earlier work (Novák "Types of Government and Their Formation in the Czech Republic in Comparative Perspective"), scholars who write about the influence of electoral systems upon party systems usually only take into account its effect on each election separately. They therefore ignore the

fact that an electoral system with majoritarian effects also has long-term repercussions: It helps in the achievement of the desirable bipolarity, and when this has been achieved, it helps to keep it in place.

64. Composed of parties that are not too distant from each other in terms of ideology and program.

65. The Green Party in the Czech Republic succeeded in overcoming the 5 percent threshold (and gaining several seats in the Chamber of Deputies) for the first time in the 2006 elections. Keep in mind that for the time being, the Green Party refuses to join a coalition with the social democrats (especially after the ČSSD leader and former prime minister Jiří Paroubek announced his intention to create a minority government supported by the communists). Still, it remains to be seen whether the Green Party will become a permanent feature of the Czech party system.

66. Petr Fiala and Vít Hloušek, "Stranický systém České republiky," in *Středoevropské systémy politických stran*, ed. Petr Fiala et al. (Brno: Mezinárodní politologický ústav, 2003), 49.

67. It has been correctly pointed out by Juan J. Linz and Alfred Stepan, for example, that even between consolidated democracies there can be a significant difference in quality. See Linz and Stepan, *Problems of Democratic Transition and Consolidation*, 137.

68. See Novák, "Démocratie(s) et efficience(s)"; Miroslav Novák, "Is There One Best 'Model of Democracy'? Efficiency and Representativeness: 'Theoretical Revolution' or Democratic Dilemma?" *Czech Sociological Review* 5 (1997), 131–157; Miroslav Novák, "Is There an Optimal Model for Democracy?," in *The Challenges on Theories of Democracy*, ed. Stein U. Larsen (Boulder, Colo.: Social Sciences Monographs/New York: Columbia University Press, 2000), 370–394; Miroslav Novák, "Les concepts utilisés dans le modèle consensuel de la démocratie: entre Sartori et Lijphart," in *Penser la politique comparée. Un état de savoirs théoriques et méthodologiques* (Paris, Editions Karthala, 2004), 143–159. See also Sartori, *Comparative Constitutional Engineering*, 71–72; Rudi B. Andeweg, "Lijphart versus Lijphart: The Cons of Consensus Democracy in Homogenous Societies," *Acta Politica* 36 (2001); Liam Anderson, "The Implications of Institutional Design for Macroeconomic Performance: Reassessing the Claims of Consensus Democracy," *Comparative Political Studies* 34 (2001). "British democracy is no worse than Continental democracy. It would appear that British democracy could become increasingly attractive in Europe, where old cleavages are losing their relevance. When the electorate is volatile and the party system highly fractionalized, then perhaps WM [Westminster model] does stabilize the situation. Why use CM [Consensus model] when there is not a so-called divided society?" Jan-Erik Lane and Svante O. Ersson, *The New Institutional Politics: Performance and Outcomes* (London: Routledge, 2000), 223–224.

Contributors

GENERAL EDITOR

KAY LAWSON is Professor Emerita of political science at San Francisco State University. She was a visiting professor at the University of Paris, Sorbonne, 1992–2000, and coeditor of the *International Political Science Review*, 2000–2009. She is general editor of two series: "Political Parties in Context" (Praeger) and "Perspectives in Comparative Politics" (Palgrave). She is the author of numerous books and articles on political parties including *The Comparative Study of Political Parties* (1976) and editor of many others including *Political Parties and Linkage* (1980), *When Parties Fail* (1988), and *When Parties Prosper* (2007), the last two with Peter Merkl. Her textbook, *The Human Polity: A Comparative Introduction to Political Science*, is now in its fifth edition. In 2003 she received the Samuel J. Eldersfeld Career Achievement award of the section on Political Organizations and Parties of the American Political Science Association.

VOLUME I: THE AMERICAS

JAMES BICKERTON is professor of political science at Saint Francis Xavier University in Nova Scotia, Canada. Recent publications include coeditorship of *Canadian Politics*, 5th ed. (2009), coauthorship of "Regions" in Danielle Caramani, ed., *Comparative Politics* (2008), and *Freedom, Equality, Community: The Political Philosophy of Six Influential*

Canadians (2006). His research interests include federalism, nationalism, and regionalism, as well as Canadian party and electoral politics.

DIANA DWYRE is professor of political science at California State University, Chico. She is coauthor with Victoria Farrar-Myers of *Legislative Labyrinth: Congress and Campaign Finance Reform* (2001) and *Limits and Loopholes: The Quest for Money, Free Speech and Fair Elections* (2008), as well as author of many journal articles and book chapters on political parties and political finance. She was the William Steiger American Political Science Association Congressional Fellow in 1998 and the Australian National University Fulbright Distinguished Chair in American Political Science in 2009–2010.

ALFREDO JOIGNANT is professor and researcher of the Instituto de Políticas Públicas Expansiva UDP, Diego Portales University in Chile, and past president of the Chilean Political Science Association (1998–2000). He is the author of several articles on political parties, political competence, and political socialization in the *Revue française de science politique*. His work currently focuses on the political sociology of elites and the politics of memory.

JORGE LANZARO is professor at the Instituto de Ciencia Política, Universidad de la República (Uruguay), of which he was founder and director. Among his latest publications: "A Social Democratic Government in Latin America," in Steven Levitsky and Kenneth Roberts, eds., *Latin America's Left Turn* (Cambridge University Press, forthcoming); "Uruguayan Parties: Transition within Transition," in Kay Lawson and Peter Merkl, eds., *When Political Parties Prosper*; "La 'tercera ola' de las izquierdas en América Latina," in *Las izquierdas latinoamericanas* (Madrid: Pablo Iglesias); and *Tipos de Presidencialismo y Coaliciones Políticas en América Latina* (Buenos Aires: Clacso).

FERNANDO MAYORGA is professor and director of CESU-UMSS, Saint Simon University in Cochabamba, Bolivia. He is the author of *Encrucijadas. Essays about Democracy and State Reform in Bolivia* (Gente Común 2007) and *The Antiglobalization Movement in Bolivia* (Plural/ UNRISD 2008) as well as multiple book chapters and articles about neo-populism, parties, and political discourse.

ANA MARÍA MUSTAPIC is an associate professor in the Department of Political Science and International Studies of the Torcuato Di Tella University in Buenos Aires. Her primary areas of research include Congress, political parties, and electoral systems. She has served as a consultant for the OAS, the UNDP, and the IDB on political reform. She is currently finishing a book on the micro foundations of party politics in Argentina.

JAIRO NICOLAU is professor in the Department of Political Science, Instituto Universitário de Pesquisas do Rio de Janeiro (IUPERJ), Brazil. He is author of *História do Voto no Brasil* (2002) and *Sistemas Eleitorais* (2004), and multiple book chapters and articles on political parties, electoral systems, and elections.

ESPERANZA PALMA is professor in the Department of Social Sciences, Universidad Autónoma Metropolitana-Cuajimalpa, in Mexico City. She is the author of *Las bases políticas de la alternancia en México: un estudio del PAN y el PRD durante la democratización* (México, UAM-A 2004) and author of multiple book chapters and articles on political parties during transitional processes in Latin America, particularly in Mexico, the so-called crisis of parties, and the perspectives of consolidation of the leftist parties in Mexico.

MARTIN TANAKA is Peruvian and took his PhD in political science from FLACSO Mexico. He is currently a senior researcher at the Institute of Peruvian Studies (IEP) and professor at the Catholic University of Peru. He is the author of numerous books, book chapters, and articles on political parties, democracy, and social movements, in Peru and in Latin America; published by the IEP, Cambridge and Stanford University Presses, Brookings Institution Press, and the University of London, among many others.

VOLUME II: EUROPE

ATTILA ÁGH is a professor of political science at the Budapest Corvinus University and director of the research center Together for Europe at the Hungarian Academy of Sciences. He has published books in the United Kingdom on the democratization of the east-central European region and has recently edited a series of books in English on the new member states of the European Union, focusing on governments, parties, and organized interests.

ELIN HAUGSGJERD ALLERN is postdoctoral fellow of political science at the University of Oslo, Norway. Her research interests include party organizational change, the relationship between parties and interest groups, and multilevel government and political parties. Her work has appeared in several edited volumes and journals, including *West European Politics* and *European Journal of Political Research*, as well as her book, *Political Parties and Interest Groups in Norway* (ECPR Press 2010).

JØRGEN ELKLIT is professor of political science at Aarhus University in Denmark. His main professional interests are local and national politics and elections in Denmark and elections and democratization in new democracies. His latest book is *Nye kommunalvalg? Kontinuitet og forandring ved valget i 2005* (New local elections? Continuity and change in the 2005 elections) (2007, coedited with Roger Buch).

CHRISTIAN ELMELUND-PRÆSTEKÆR is an assistant professor at the Department of Political Science, University of Southern Denmark. His most recent book is on negative campaigning in Danish elections (*Kammertoner og Unoder i valgkamp*, University Press of Southern Denmark 2009). He has published several articles on political communication, negative campaigning, agenda-setting, and party organization.

JUERGEN FALTER is professor of political science at the University of Mainz (Germany) and was president of the German Association of Political Science (2000–2003). He has published about 25 books and monographs, and over 200 articles on voting behavior, the Nazi electorate, political extremism, political attitudes, and methodological problems of the social sciences.

PIERO IGNAZI is professor of comparative politics at the faculty of political science of the University of Bologna, Bologna, Italy. His recent publications include *Political Parties and Political Systems: The Concept of Linkage Revisited* (Praeger 2005, coedited with A. Rommele and D. Farrell), *Extreme Right Parties in Western Europe* (Oxford University Press 2006*), and Partiti politici in Italia* (Il Mulino 2008).

ULRIK KJAER is professor of political science, University of Southern Denmark. His most recent book is on local political leadership (*Lokalt politisk lederskab*, with Rikke Berg, University Press of Southern Denmark 2007). He has published several articles and book chapters on political recruitment, elections, parliamentarians, local governments, and local party systems.

HIERONIM KUBIAK is professor of sociology at the Jagiellonian University and Andrzej Frycz Modrzewski Cracow University, Poland. Among his recent publications are: *Democracy and the Individual Will* (1997); *Parties, Party Systems and Cleavages in Poland: 1918–1989* (1999); *Reformers in PUWP* (2000); *Poland's Democratic Left Alliance: Beyond Post-communist Succession* (2007); and *On the Threshold of the Post-Westphalia Era. A Theory of Nation* (2007).

LAURA MORALES is a research fellow at the Institute for Social Change of the University of Manchester. Her interests lie in the areas of political behavior, social capital, and political parties. She is the author of *Joining Political Organisations* (ECPR Press 2009) and of many book chapters and articles, among which is "European Integration and Spanish Parties: Elite Empowerment amidst Limited Adaptation" (with L. Ramiro), in Thomas Poguntke et al., eds., *The Europeanization of National Political Parties: Power and Organizational Adaptation* (London: Routledge 2007).

MIROSLAV NOVAK is the first professor of political science at the Charles University and rector of the CEVRO Institute, both in Prague. He has published regularly in French and in Czech, including *Systemy politickych stran* (Political Party Systems, 1997). He is—among other appointments—a member of the editorial boards of *La Revue internationale de politique compare, La Revue d'etudes politiques et constitutionelles est-europeennes,* and *l'Annuaire francais des relations internationals.*

LUIS RAMIRO is associate professor of political science at the University of Murcia, Spain. He is the author of many book chapters and articles on political parties, including "Euroscepticism and Political Parties in Spain" (with I. Llamazares and M. Gmez-Reino), in P. Taggart and A. Szcerbiak, eds., *Opposing Europe? The Comparative Party Politics of Euroscepticism* (Oxford University Press 2008) and "European Integration and Spanish Parties: Elite Empowerment amidst Limited Adaptation" (with L. Morales), in T. Poguntke et al., eds., *The Europeanization of National Political Parties: Power and Organizational Adaptation* (Routledge 2007).

NICOLAS SAUGER is senior research fellow at Sciences Po (Paris) and associate professor at the Ecole Polytechnique, France. He has coedited the special issue "France's Fifth Republic at Fifty" of *West European Politics* 32(2) (2009) and several book chapters on political parties, institutions, and methodological issues related to survey research.

PAUL WEBB is professor of politics at the University of Sussex. His research interests focus on representative democracy, particularly party and electoral politics. He is author or editor of numerous publications, including *The Modern British Party System* (Sage 2000), *Political Parties in Advanced Industrial Societies* (Oxford University Press 2002, with David Farrell and Ian Holliday), and *Party Politics in New Democracies* (Oxford University Press 2005, with Stephen White). He is currently coeditor of the journal *Party Politics.*

VOLUME III: POST-SOVIET AND ASIAN POLITICAL PARTIES

Post-Soviet

IGOR BOTAN is the executive director of the Association for Participatory Democracy, an independent center of analysis and consultation on the decision-making, political, electoral, and socioeconomic processes in the Republic of Moldova. He is the author of many articles on electoral and party system development in Moldova and is also the political analyst for Moldovan issues at Radio Free Europe/Romanian Service and at the Intelligence Unit of *The Economist*.

ANATOLY KULIK is senior research fellow in political science at the Russian Academy of Sciences and lecturer at State University—Higher School of Economics (Moscow). He writes widely on comparative party politics, political party development in post-Soviet Russia, and e-governance. Among his recent publications are: "Russian 'Mnogopartijnost' in the Light of Political Competition," in *Political Competition and Parties in Post-Soviet States*, edited by E. Meleshkina et al. (2009); "Russian Party System after Electoral Cycle 2007–2008: The End of the History?," in *The New Political Cycle: Agenda for Russia*, edited by O. Maliniva et al. (2008); and "To Prosper in Russia: Parties Deep in the Shadow of the President," in *When Parties Prosper: The Use of Electoral Success*, edited by Kay Lawson and Peter Merkl (2007).

ANDREY A. MELESHEVYCH is professor and dean of the School of Law, National University of Kyiv-Mohyla Academy in Ukraine. He is the author of *Party Systems in Post-Soviet Countries: A Comparative Study of Political Institutionalization in the Baltic States, Russia, and Ukraine* (2007) and multiple book chapters and articles on political parties, electoral law, and institution building in transitional countries.

GEORGE TARKHAN-MOURAVI is codirector of the Institute for Policy Studies (IPS) in Tbilisi, Georgia, and chairman of the board of directors, PASOS association of Eastern European think tanks based in Prague, Czech Republic. He has authored a number of publications on political developments and regional security in the Caucasus and the Black Sea region, interethnic relations, forced migration, human development, and democratic transition in Georgia.

Asia

BAOGANG HE received his MA from the People's University of China, Beijing, and PhD from ANU, Australia. He is chair in international studies at the School of Politics and International Studies, Deakin University, Melbourne, Australia, and author of four books, three edited books, and numerous refereed articles. His current research interests include deliberative democracy, Chinese democratization, and Chinese politics.

EDMUND TERENCE GOMEZ is an associate professor of political economy at the Faculty of Economics and Administration, University of Malaya, and recently (2005–2008) served as research coordinator at the United Nations Research Institute for Social Development (UNRISD) in Geneva. His many books include *Malaysia's Political Economy: Politics, Patronage and Profits* (1997), *The State of Malaysia: Ethnicity, Equity and Reform* (2004), *Politics in Malaysia: The Malay Dimension* (2007), and *The State, Development and Identity in Multi-ethnic Countries: Ethnicity, Equity and the Nation* (2008).

M. V. RAJEEV GOWDA is professor of economics and social sciences at the Indian Institute of Management Bangalore. He coedited *Judgments, Decisions, and Public Policy* (2002). He is also active in Indian politics. He has authored book chapters and articles on Indian political parties and also on e-democracy.

TAKASHI INOGUCHI is president of the University of Niigata Prefecture, professor emeritus of University of Tokyo, executive editor of the Japanese *Journal of Political Science*, and director of the AsiaBarometer project. He has published 80 books and numerous journal articles on Japan and international affairs. His current interests include political party systems, political cultures, and cross-national comparisons of norms and values through surveys. He is the coeditor of *Globalization, the State and Public Opinion* (with Ian Marsh, 2008) and "Demographic Change and Asian Dynamics: Social and Political Implications," *Asian Economic Policy Review* (June 2009).

HOON JAUNG is professor of political science at Chung-Ang University in Seoul, Korea. He is the author of *President Roh Moo Hyun and New Politics in South Korea* (2003) and numerous articles on party politics and democratization issues of Korea. He was Reagan-Fascell Fellow at the National Endowment for Democracy (Washington, D.C.) in 2005 and now serves as editor-in-chief for *Korean Legislative Studies*.

ESWARAN SRIDHARAN is the academic director of the University of Pennsylvania Institute for the Advanced Study of India (UPIASI), New Delhi. His research interests are in comparative party systems and coalition politics, political economy of development, and international relations of South Asia. He has written or edited five books, published over 40 journal articles and book chapters, and is the editor of *India Review* (Routledge).

VOLUME IV: AFRICA AND OCEANIA

Africa

ADEKUNLE AMUWO is professor of politics at the Howard College Campus, University of KwaZulu-Natal, Durban, and has recently completed a term as executive secretary of the African Association of Political Science (2004–2009). He is a widely published pan-African scholar and activist. Two recent works are *Constructing the Democratic Developmental State in Africa: A Case Study of Nigeria, 1960–2007* (2008) and a coedited book on *Civil Society, Governance and Regional Integration in Africa* (2009).

NICOLA DE JAGER holds a DPhil in political science from the University of Pretoria and is a lecturer at the political science department of the University of Stellenbosch in South Africa. She has published in peer-reviewed research publications and has consulted locally and internationally on issues of democratization, dominant party systems, political society, and civil society with a specific focus on South African and African politics.

LEAH KIMATHI holds a BED (Hons) from Moi University and an MA in history specializing in international relations from Kenyatta University. She also holds a fellowship in international philanthropy from Johns Hopkins University. A recipient of the Claude Ake Memorial Award in 2004, she has been involved in several research works in the area of the African state and has published in the same. She is programs coordinator with Africa Peace Point, a Pan-African conflict resolution organization, and a part-time lecturer at the Catholic University of Eastern Africa in Nairobi. She is currently a conflict mediator and researcher.

WILLIAM A. LINDEKE now serves as the senior research associate for democracy and governance at the Institute for Public Policy Research (IPPR) in Windhoek, Namibia. He was professor of political science at the University of Massachusetts Lowell (retired) and professor of political studies at the University of Namibia. He has authored or coauthored several book chapters and articles on Namibian politics and on SADC issues. He is co-national investigator for Round Four of the Afrobarometer in Namibia.

ANDRÉ DU PISANI is professor of political studies and former dean of faculty at the University of Namibia (UNAM) and is the director in Namibia of the Southern African Defence and Security Management Network (SADSEM). He is the author, editor, or coeditor of several books and numerous articles on Namibian politics and security issues in the SADC region.

LUC SINDJOUN is professor and head of the political science department at University of Yaoundé II (Cameroon). He is the author of several books, chapters, and articles on comparative politics, African politics, and international relations.

HERMAN TOUO is a lecturer at the University of Ngaoundéré, Cameroon. His PhD dissertation was titled "Les dynamiques d'ancrages du pluralisme partisan au Cameroun (1990–2006): l'economie des rapports entre pouvoir et opposition." He is also interested in youth movements, especially the impact of youth mobilization on democratic governance in Cameroon. He participated as 2002–2003 fellow on Understanding Exclusion, Creating Value: African Youth in a Global Age, a project initiated by the Africa Program of the Social Science Research Council (SSRC).

Oceania

ALUMITA L. DURUTALO is a lecturer in the Division of Politics and International Affairs at the University of the South Pacific, Fiji Islands. She obtained her PhD from the Australian National University in Canberra and specializes in party and electoral politics and customary and modern political leadership in the Pacific. Her numerous journal articles and book chapters include "Fiji: Party Politics in the Post-Independent Period" (Roland Rich et al., eds.).

RAYMOND MILLER is an associate professor and chair of the Department of Politics at the University of Auckland, where he specializes in political parties, representation, electoral systems and elections, and leadership. He has collaborated on a number of election studies, including *Proportional Representation on Trial* (2002) and *Voters' Veto* (2004). Recent publications include *Party Politics in New Zealand* (2005), *New Zealand Government and Politics* (2006), and *Political Leadership in New Zealand* (2006).

GORDON LEUA NANAU is a researcher at the Solomon Islands College of Higher Education (SICHE). In 2009 he completed his PhD at the School of International Development, University of East Anglia, U.K., with a doctoral dissertation on insecure globalization in the South Pacific. His research interests are in the areas of rural development, decentralization, conflicts and peace making, globalization, and international development. His chapter on "Intervention and Nation-Building in Solomon Islands: Local Perspectives" appeared in *Interventionism and State-building in the Pacific: The Legitimacy of "Cooperative Intervention"* (eds. Greg Fry and Tarcisius Tara Kabutaulaka, Manchester University Press, 2008).

MARIAN SIMMS is professor of political studies and Head of Social Sciences at Deakin University in Melbourne, Australia. She has published numerous articles and books including "Australian and New Zealand Politics: Separate Paths but Path Dependent," *The Round Table*, 2006, and *From the Hustings to Harbour Views; Electoral Administration in New South Wales, 1856–2006* (University of NSW Press, 2006). Her next book, *Kevin07: The 2007 Australian Election*, is in press.

ISALEI SIOA is a senior lecturer in history and head of the social sciences department at the National University of Samoa. She has made contributions to the following books, *Lagaga: A Short History of Western Samoa, Tamaitai Samoa (Women of Samoa: Their Stories),* and has published articles in the *Journal of Arts Faculty*, National University of Samoa.

VOLUME V: THE ARAB WORLD

Arab World

MOHAMED OULD MOHAMED ABDERRAHMANE MOINE is a Professor of Diplomacy in the Ecole nationale d'administration of Nouakchott University in Mauritania. From 1992 to 2008, he occupied diplomatic and governmental positions in Belgium, Canada, and South Africa. He is the author of numerous articles on the subjects of human rights protection, international relations, and democratization.

MOKHTAR BENABDALLAOUI is professor of philosophy and head of the Department of Philosophy at Hassan II University, Casablanca, and director of the Center for Studies and Research in the Humanities.

SAAD EDDIN IBRAHIM is professor of sociology at the American University in Cairo, founding chairman of the Ibn Khaldun Center for Development Studies and founder of the Arab Organization for Human Rights. He is widely known for his work on electoral fraud in Egyptian elections, work that led to his arrest and conviction and a global outpouring of support from scholars, human rights organizations, and political leaders. Recently convicted a third time, he is now in exile. During 2008–2009 he served as professor of political sociology at Indiana University and as the Shawwaf Chair Professor at the Center of Middle East Studies at Harvard University. His numerous awards and publications are listed at http://www.eicds.org.

SALAHEDDINE JOURCHI is a journalist and the vice president of the Tunisian Human Rights League in Tunis.

ABDERRAZAK MAKRI is a medical doctor and holds an M.A. in Islamic law and a post-graduate degree in Management Sciences. He is a founding member of the Movement Society of Peace (MSP) in Algeria and is currently the vice-president of the Movement and an elected member of the Parliament in Algeria. Dr. Makri is the author of several publications, including *Islam and Democracy, Towards an Effective Citizenship*, which was developed by the Center for the Study of Islam and Democracy (CSID) and Street Law, Inc., and has been used as a training manual for NGO leaders and Imams throughout the Arab world.

ANTOINE NASRI MESSARRA is professor of political science at Lebanese University and Saint Joseph University, Beirut. He is president of the Lebanese Political Science Association and program coordinator of the Lebanese Foundation for Permanent Civil Peace.

EMAD EL-DIN SHAHIN is the Henry Luce Professor of Religion, Conflict and Peacebuilding at the University of Notre Dame. He was an associate professor of political science at the American University in Cairo and visiting associate professor of the Department of Government, Harvard University, while writing for this study. His recent works include *Political Ascent: Contemporary Islamic Movements in North Africa* (1997); coeditorship of *Struggling over Democracy in the Middle East and North Africa* (2009); and coauthorship of *Islam and Democracy* (2005, in Arabic).

Neighboring States

YUNUS EMRE is a Ph.D. candidate at Bogazici University, Istanbul, and a graduate assistant at Istanbul Kultur University. His research interests are European and Turkish politics, the economic and social history of modern Turkey, and 20th-century historiography.

YAEL YISHAI is Professor Emerita of political science at the University of Haifa, Israel. She is the author of several books including *Land of Paradoxes. Interest Politics in Israel* (SUNY, 1991) and multiple articles and book chapters on interest groups, civil society, and political parties in Israel. Her current research interests are in the processes leading to "antipolitics" and its outcomes.

Index

Figures indicated by *f*. Tables indicated by *t*.